HANDBOOKS

D0188276

DALLAS & FORT WORTH

JONANNA WIDNER

Contents

Maps

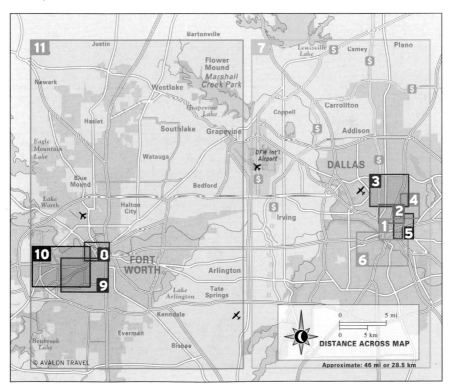

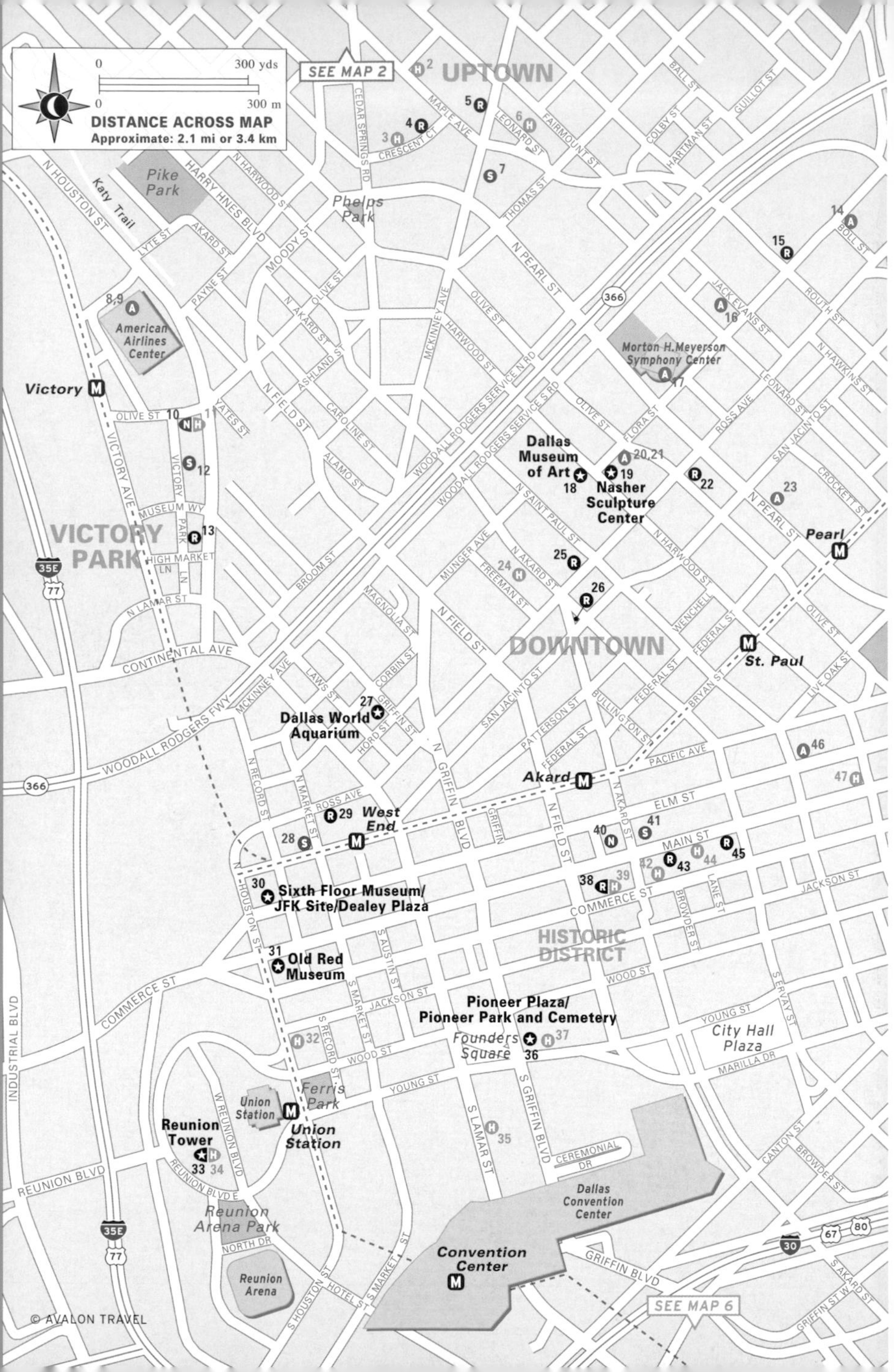

MAP 1

0   300 yds
0   300 m

DISTANCE ACROSS MAP
Approximate: 2.1 mi or 3.4 km

SEE MAP 2

UPTOWN

Pike Park

Phelps Park

Harry Hines Blvd

Katy Trail

N Houston St

Cedar Springs Rd

Harwood St

Crescent Ct

Maple Ave

N Leonard St

Fairmount St

Colby St

Hartman St

Guillot St

Ball St

Thomas Ave

N Pearl St

14

15

American Airlines Center

Victory M

Olive St

Yates St

Payne St

Moody St

Olive St

N Field St

Ashland St

Alamo St

Caroline St

N Akard St

N St Paul St

Woodall Rodgers Service Rd

Olive St

Flora St

Ross Ave

366

Jack Evans St

16

N Hawkins St

Morton H. Meyerson Symphony Center

17

Dallas Museum of Art
18

Nasher Sculpture Center
19

20, 21

22

23

Pearl M

San Jacinto St

N Pearl St

Crockett St

12

VICTORY PARK

35E
77

Museum Wy

Victory Park

High Market Ln

N Lamar St

Broom St

Magnolia St

Munger Ave

N Akard St

Freeman St

N St Paul St

N Harwood St

24

25

26

DOWNTOWN

Wenches

Bryan St

Live Oaks St

St. Paul M

Continental Ave

McKinney Ave

Corbin St

N Field St

Laws St

San Jacinto St

Federal St

Patterson St

Billington St

Federal St

Pacific Ave

46

27

Dallas World Aquarium

N Record St

N Market St

Ross Ave

Akard M

Elm St

Main St

47

Woodall Rodgers Fwy

366

29 **West End**

28

M

40

41

Griffin Blvd

Main St

N Field St

43

44

45

30 **Sixth Floor Museum/ JFK Site/Dealey Plaza**

S Market St

S Austin St

Griffin St

38

39

Commerce St

42

Lane St

Jackson St

HISTORIC DISTRICT

31 **Old Red Museum**

Commerce St

S Market St

S Record St

Jackson St

Wood St

Pioneer Plaza/ Pioneer Park and Cemetery

Young St

City Hall Plaza

Industrial Blvd

32

S Record St

Wood St

Young St

Founders Square 36

37

Marilla Dr

Ferris Park

Union Station

M **Union Station**

35

S Lamar St

S Griffin Blvd

Ceremonial Dr

Canton St

Browder St

Reunion Tower

33 34

W Reunion Blvd

Reunion Blvd

S Houston St

Dallas Convention Center

Young St

30

67   80

Reunion Arena Park

35E
77

Reunion Blvd

North Dr

S Market St

Hotel St

Convention Center M

Griffin Blvd

Lamar St

Griffin St

SEE MAP 6

Reunion Arena

© AVALON TRAVEL

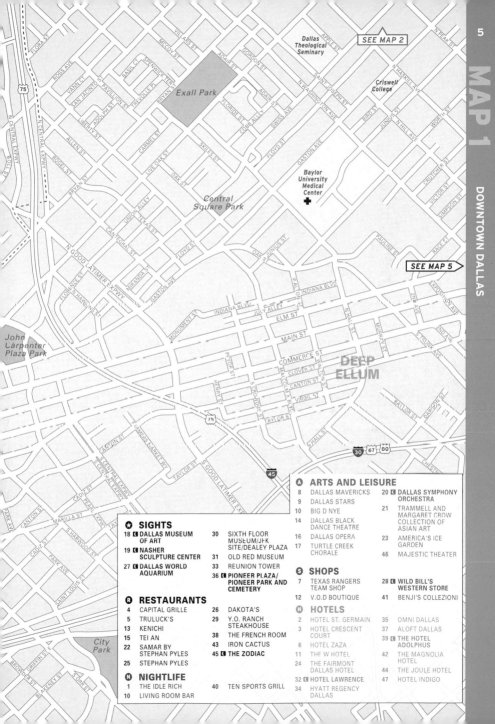

⊕ SIGHTS

18 **€ DALLAS MUSEUM OF ART**	30 SIXTH FLOOR MUSEUM/JFK SITE/DEALEY PLAZA
19 **€ NASHER SCULPTURE CENTER**	31 OLD RED MUSEUM
27 **€ DALLAS WORLD AQUARIUM**	33 REUNION TOWER
	36 **€ PIONEER PLAZA/ PIONEER PARK AND CEMETERY**

® RESTAURANTS

4 CAPITAL GRILLE	26 DAKOTA'S
5 TRULUCK'S	29 Y.O. RANCH STEAKHOUSE
13 KENICHI	38 THE FRENCH ROOM
15 TEI AN	43 IRON CACTUS
22 SAMAR BY STEPHAN PYLES	45 **€ THE ZODIAC**
25 STEPHAN PYLES	

Ⓝ NIGHTLIFE

1 THE IDLE RICH	40 TEN SPORTS GRILL
10 LIVING ROOM BAR	

Ⓐ ARTS AND LEISURE

8 DALLAS MAVERICKS	20 **€ DALLAS SYMPHONY ORCHESTRA**
9 DALLAS STARS	21 TRAMMELL AND MARGARET CROW COLLECTION OF ASIAN ART
14 BIG D NYE	
14 DALLAS BLACK DANCE THEATRE	
16 DALLAS OPERA	23 AMERICA'S ICE GARDEN
17 TURTLE CREEK CHORALE	46 MAJESTIC THEATER

Ⓢ SHOPS

7 TEXAS RANGERS TEAM SHOP	28 **€ WILD BILL'S WESTERN STORE**
12 V.O.D BOUTIQUE	41 BENJI'S COLLEZIONI

Ⓗ HOTELS

2 HOTEL ST. GERMAIN	35 OMNI DALLAS
3 HOTEL CRESCENT COURT	37 ALOFT DALLAS
6 HOTEL ZAZA	39 **€ THE HOTEL ADOLPHUS**
11 THE W HOTEL	42 THE MAGNOLIA HOTEL
24 THE FAIRMONT DALLAS HOTEL	44 THE JOULE HOTEL
32 **€ HOTEL LAWRENCE**	47 HOTEL INDIGO
34 HYATT REGENCY DALLAS	

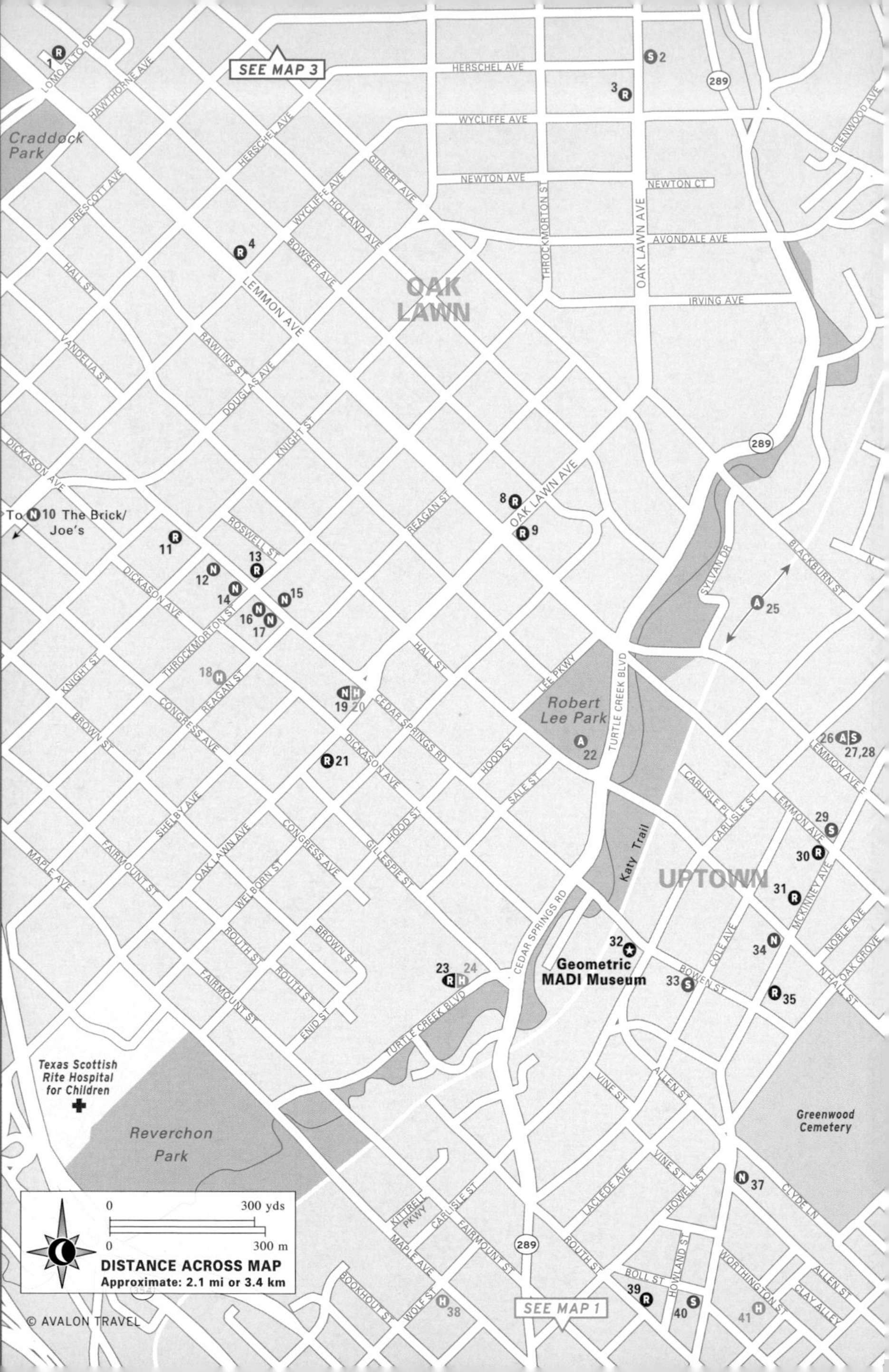

MAP 2

Craddock Park

SEE MAP 3

HERSCHEL AVE

289

S 2

3 R

WYCLIFFE AVE

NEWTON AVE

NEWTON CT

OAK LAWN

AVONDALE AVE

IRVING AVE

289

LONG ALGO DR

HAWTHORNE AVE

R

PRESCOTT AVE

HERSCHEL AVE

GILBERT AVE

WYCLIFFE AVE

HOLLAND AVE

HALL ST

R 4

BOWSER AVE

LEMMON AVE

ANGELIA ST

RAWLINS ST

DOUGLAS AVE

KNIGHT ST

REAGAN ST

OAK LAWN AVE

THROCKMORTON ST

OAK LAWN AVE

GREENWOOD AVE

BLACKBURN ST

DICKASON AVE

To N 10 The Brick/
Joe's

11 R

ROSWELL ST

8 R

9 R

SAYLAND DR

13 R

A 25

12 N

14 N

16 N N 17

N 15

KNIGHT ST

DICKASON AVE

THROCKMORTON ST

HALL ST

BROWN ST

18 R

REAGAN ST

19 N M 20

CEDAR SPRINGS RD

LEE PKWY

Robert Lee Park

TURTLE CREEK BLVD

26 A S

27,28

LEMMON AVE

CONGRESS AVE

R 21

DICKASON AVE

HOOD ST

22 A

Katy Trail

CARLISLE ST

CARLISLE ST

LEMMON AVE

29 R

SHELBY AVE

HOOD ST

SALE ST

GILLESPIE ST

30 R

31 N

MCKINNEY AVE

MAPLE AVE

OAK LAWN AVE

WELBORN ST

BROWN ST

CONGRESS AVE

COLE AVE

NOBLE AVE

UPTOWN

34 N

32 ☆

Geometric
MADI Museum

BODEEN ST

33 S

35 R

TURTLE CREEK BLVD

23 24
R H

ROUTH ST

ROUTH ST

FAIRMOUNT ST

VINE ST

ALLEN ST

NOB HILL OAK GROVE

Texas Scottish
Rite Hospital
for Children

Reverchon
Park

CEDAR SPRINGS RD

VINE ST

Greenwood
Cemetery

LACLEDE AVE

HOWELL ST

37 N

CLYDE LN

ALLEN ST

0   300 yds
0   300 m

DISTANCE ACROSS MAP
Approximate: 2.1 mi or 3.4 km

ALLTREE PKWY

CARLISLE ST

FAIRMOUNT ST

MAPLE AVE

289

ROUTH ST

BOLL ST

HOLLAND AVE

39 R

40 S

WORTHINGTON ST

CLAY ALLEY

BOOKHOUT ST

NOBLE ST

H 38

SEE MAP 1

41

© AVALON TRAVEL

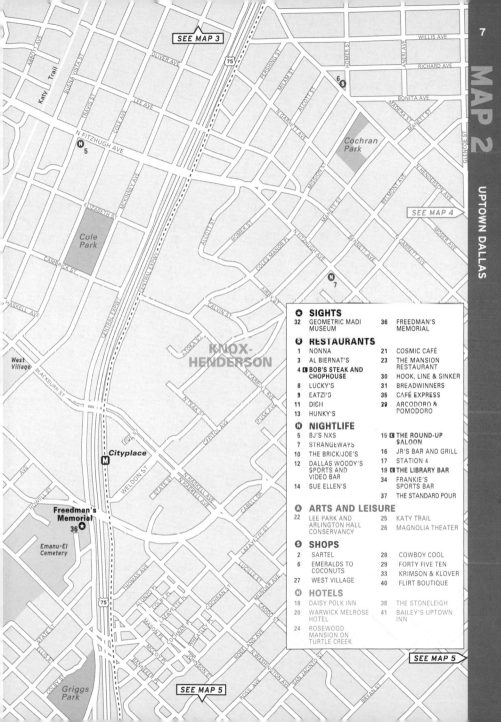

SEE MAP 3

75

Katy Trail

Cochran Park

SEE MAP 4

Cole Park

West Village

KNOX-HENDERSON

Cityplace

Freedman's Memorial
36

Emanu-El Cemetery

Griggs Park

SEE MAP 5

SEE MAP 5

◎ SIGHTS

| 32 | GEOMETRIC MADI MUSEUM | 36 | FREEDMAN'S MEMORIAL |

◎ RESTAURANTS

1	NONNA	21	COSMIC CAFÉ
3	AL BIERNAT'S	23	THE MANSION RESTAURANT
4 ◐	BOB'S STEAK AND CHOPHOUSE	30	HOOK, LINE & SINKER
8	LUCKY'S	31	BREADWINNERS
9	EATZI'S	35	CAFÉ EXPRESS
11	DISH	39	ARCODORO & POMODORO
13	HUNKY'S		

◎ NIGHTLIFE

5	BJ'S NXS	15 ◐	THE ROUND-UP SALOON
7	STRANGEWAYS	16	JR'S BAR AND GRILL
10	THE BRICK/JOE'S	17	STATION 4
12	DALLAS WOODY'S SPORTS AND VIDEO BAR	19 ◐	THE LIBRARY BAR
		34	FRANKIE'S SPORTS BAR
14	SUE ELLEN'S	37	THE STANDARD POUR

◎ ARTS AND LEISURE

| 22 | LEE PARK AND ARLINGTON HALL CONSERVANCY | 25 | KATY TRAIL |
| | | 26 | MAGNOLIA THEATER |

◎ SHOPS

2	SARTEL	28	COWBOY COOL
6	EMERALDS TO COCONUTS	29	FORTY FIVE TEN
27	WEST VILLAGE	33	KRIMSON & KLOVER
		40	FLIRT BOUTIQUE

◎ HOTELS

18	DAISY POLK INN	38	THE STONELEIGH
20	WARWICK MELROSE HOTEL	41	BAILEY'S UPTOWN INN
24	ROSEWOOD MANSION ON TURTLE CREEK		

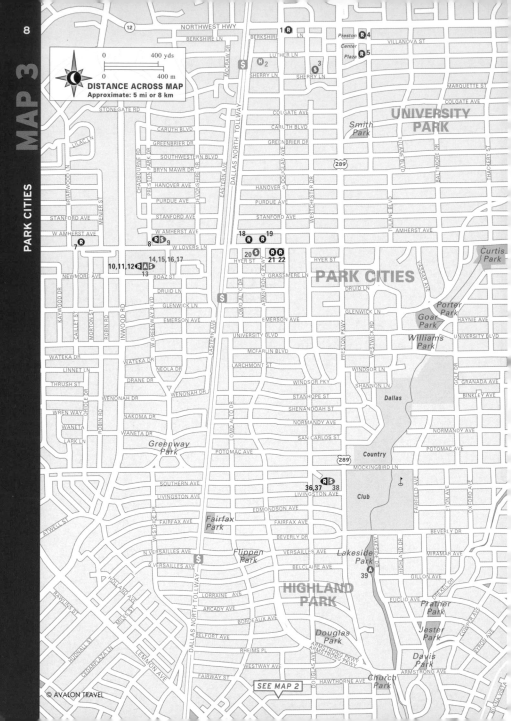

MAP 3

DISTANCE ACROSS MAP
Approximate: 5 mi or 8 km

0   400 yds
0   400 m

UNIVERSITY PARK

PARK CITIES

HIGHLAND PARK

SEE MAP 2

© AVALON TRAVEL

⊙ SIGHTS
32 SOUTHERN METHODIST UNIVERSITY

⊗ RESTAURANTS
1	SOUTH PAW'S GRILL	22	YUMMY DONUTS
4	SPRINKLES CUPCAKES	23	DUPRE'S SHORT STOP
5	THE CULTURED CUP	24	BUBBA'S
7	NEIGHBORHOOD SERVICES	25	AUSTINUTS
8	DUNSTON'S	28	PEGGY SUE BBQ
10	RISE NO. 1	29	GOFF'S HAMBURGERS
11	BIJOUX	36	CAFÉ PACIFIC
12	CAFÉ ISTANBUL	37	MI COCINA
18	MANGO THAI	40	CAFÉ MADRID
19	KATHLEEN'S SKY DINER	41	LITTLE KATANA
21	DRIP	45	FADI'S
		46	HIBISCUS

⊗ NIGHTLIFE
35 ACROSS THE STREET BAR

⊗ ARTS AND LEISURE
13	INWOOD THEATER	39	LAKESIDE PARK

⊗ SHOPS
3	CLOTHES CIRCUIT	27	ALLIE-COOSH
6	NORTHPARK CENTER	30	CULLWELL & SON
9	ST. BERNARD SPORTS	33	LUKE'S LOCKER
14	COLLECTOR'S COVEY	34	CD SOURCE
15	HAUTE BABY	38	HIGHLAND PARK VILLAGE
16	RAGAN BURNS	42	FROGGIE'S 5&10
17	RICH HIPPIE	43	CARLA MARTINENGO BOUTIQUE
20	MINE	44	NEST
26	SNIDER PLAZA		

⊗ HOTELS
2	HILTON DALLAS PARK CITIES	31	HOTEL LUMEN

SEE MAP 4 ▸

MAP 4

GREENVILLE

® RESTAURANTS
4	CAMPISI'S	13	NANDINA
5	CAFÉ IZMIR	20	LA CALLE DOCE
6	AW SHUCKS	21	GOLD RUSH CAFÉ
9	THE GRAPE	22	LAKEWOOD LANDING
11	THE LIBERTINE	26	THE COCK AND BULL

ℕ NIGHTLIFE
7	THE GRANADA THEATER	18	BARCADIA
12	ZUBAR	19	SHIPS
14	BILLIARD BAR	23	COSMO'S RESTAURANT AND BAR
15	THE CAVERN		
17	SLIP INN	27	BALCONY CLUB

Ⓐ ARTS AND LEISURE
3	ANGELIKA FILM CENTER	24	SWISS AVENUE HOME TOURS

Ⓢ SHOPS
2	MOCKINGBIRD STATION	10	GREENVILLE AVENUE
8	HD'S CLOTHING COMPANY	16	GOOD RECORDS
		25	CURIOSITIES

Ⓗ HOTELS
1	HOTEL PALOMAR

DISTANCE ACROSS MAP
Approximate: 1.2 mi or 1.9 km

0   300 yds
0   300 m

© AVALON TRAVEL

SEE MAP 3
SEE MAP 2
SEE MAP 5

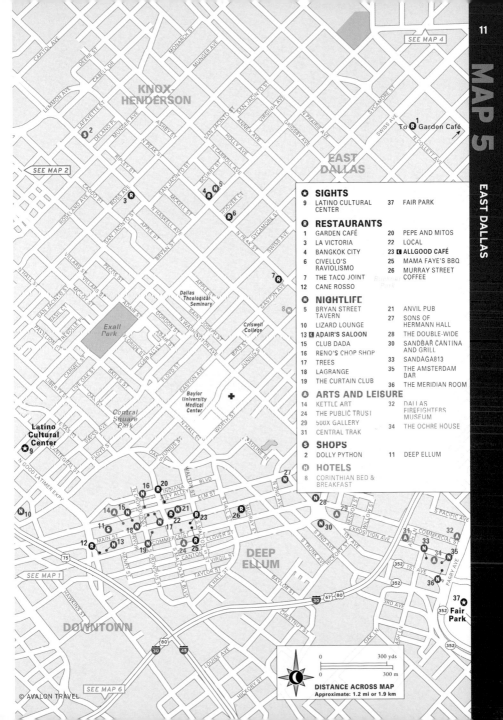

SEE MAP 4

KNOX-HENDERSON

EAST DALLAS

SEE MAP 2

To Garden Café

⊗ SIGHTS

9 LATINO CULTURAL CENTER

37 FAIR PARK

⊕ RESTAURANTS

1 GARDEN CAFÉ
3 LA VICTORIA
4 BANGKOK CITY
6 CIVELLO'S RAVIOLISMO
7 THE TACO JOINT
12 CANE ROSSO

20 PEPE AND MITOS
22 LOCAL
23 ◖ ALLGOOD CAFÉ
25 MAMA FAYE'S BBQ
26 MURRAY STREET COFFEE

⊕ NIGHTLIFE

5 BRYAN STREET TAVERN
10 LIZARD LOUNGE
13 ◖ ADAIR'S SALOON
15 CLUB DADA
16 RENO'S CHOP SHOP
17 TREES
18 LAGRANGE
19 THE CURTAIN CLUB

21 ANVIL PUB
27 SONS OF HERMANN HALL
28 THE DOUBLE-WIDE
30 SANDBAR CANTINA AND GRILL
33 SANDAGA813
35 THE AMSTERDAM BAR
36 THE MERIDIAN ROOM

⊕ ARTS AND LEISURE

14 KETTLE ART
24 THE PUBLIC TRUST
29 500X GALLERY
31 CENTRAL TRAK

32 DALLAS FIREFIGHTERS MUSEUM
34 THE OCHRE HOUSE

⊕ SHOPS

2 DOLLY PYTHON   11 DEEP ELLUM

⊕ HOTELS

8 CORINTHIAN BED & BREAKFAST

Dallas Theological Seminary

Criswell College

Exall Park

Baylor University Medical Center

Central Square Park

Latino Cultural Center 9

DEEP ELLUM

S PACIFIC AVE

SEE MAP 1

DOWNTOWN

Fair Park 37

SEE MAP 6

DISTANCE ACROSS MAP
Approximate: 1.2 mi or 1.9 km

0   300 yds
0   300 m

© AVALON TRAVEL

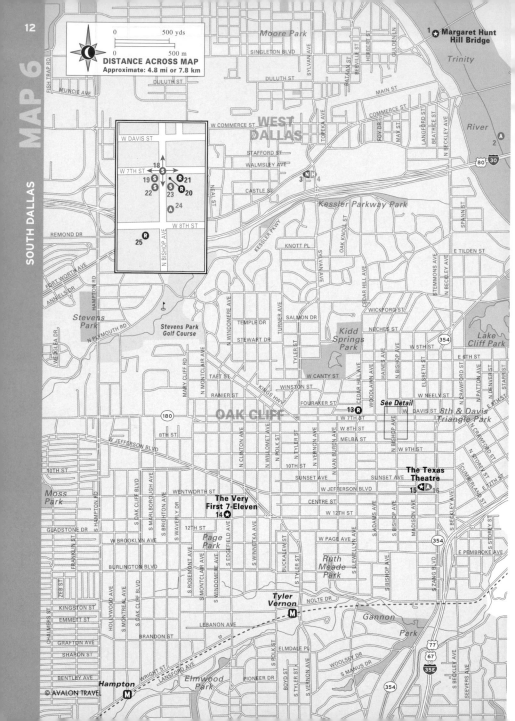

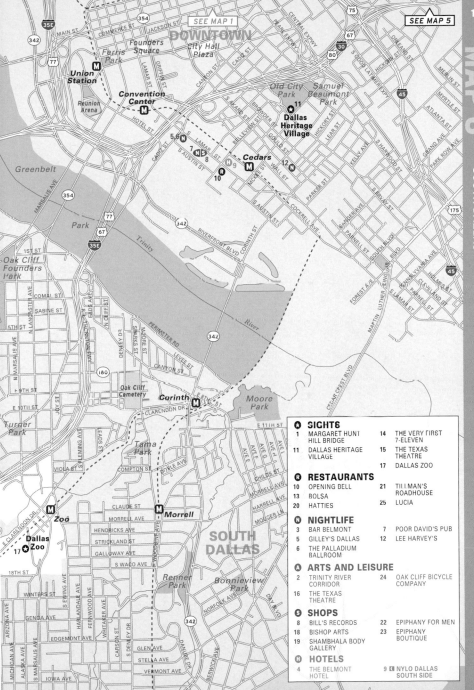

SEE MAP 1

DOWNTOWN

SEE MAP 5

A SIGHTS

1	MARGARET HUNT HILL BRIDGE	14	THE VERY FIRST 7-ELEVEN
11	DALLAS HERITAGE VILLAGE	15	THE TEXAS THEATRE
		17	DALLAS ZOO

R RESTAURANTS

10	OPENING BELL	21	TILLMAN'S ROADHOUSE
13	BOLSA	25	LUCIA
20	HATTIES		

N NIGHTLIFE

3	BAR BELMONT	7	POOR DAVID'S PUB
5	GILLEY'S DALLAS	12	LEE HARVEY'S
6	THE PALLADIUM BALLROOM		

A ARTS AND LEISURE

| 2 | TRINITY RIVER CORRIDOR | 24 | OAK CLIFF BICYCLE COMPANY |
| 16 | THE TEXAS THEATRE | | |

S SHOPS

8	BILL'S RECORDS	22	EPIPHANY FOR MEN
18	BISHOP ARTS	23	EPIPHANY BOUTIQUE
19	SHAMBHALA BODY GALLERY		

H HOTELS

| 4 | THE BELMONT HOTEL | 9 | NYLO DALLAS SOUTH SIDE |

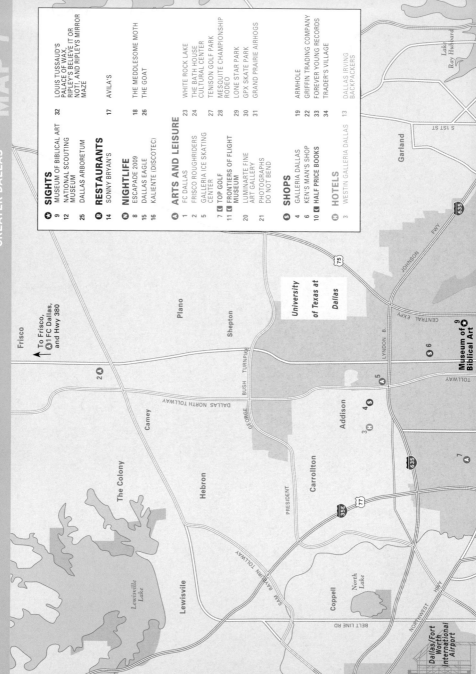

SIGHTS
- 9 MUSEUM OF BIBLICAL ART
- 12 NATIONAL SCOUTING MUSEUM
- 25 DALLAS ARBORETUM
- 32 LOUIS TUSSAUD'S PALACE OF WAX, RIPLEY'S BELIEVE IT OR NOT!, AND RIPLEY'S MIRROR MAZE

RESTAURANTS
- 14 SONNY BRYAN'S
- 17 AVILA'S

NIGHTLIFE
- 8 ESCAPADE 2009
- 15 DALLAS EAGLE
- 16 KALIENTE (DISCOTEC)
- 18 THE MEDDLESOME MOTH
- 26 THE GOAT

ARTS AND LEISURE
- 1 FC DALLAS
- 2 FRISCO ROUGHRIDERS
- 5 GALLERIA ICE SKATING CENTER
- 7 TOP GOLF
- 11 FRONTIERS OF FLIGHT MUSEUM
- 20 LUMINARTE FINE ART GALLERY
- 21 PHOTOGRAPHS DO NOT BEND
- 23 WHITE ROCK LAKE
- 24 THE BATH HOUSE CULTURAL CENTER
- 27 TENISON GOLF PARK
- 28 MESQUITE CHAMPIONSHIP RODEO
- 29 LONE STAR PARK
- 30 GPX SKATE PARK
- 31 GRAND PRAIRIE AIRHOGS

SHOPS
- 4 GALLERIA DALLAS
- 6 KEN'S MAN'S SHOP
- 10 HALF PRICE BOOKS
- 19 ARMHOLE
- 22 GRIFFIN TRADING COMPANY
- 33 FOREVER YOUNG RECORDS
- 34 TRADER'S VILLAGE

HOTELS
- 3 WESTIN GALLERIA DALLAS
- 13 DALLAS IRVING BACKPACKERS

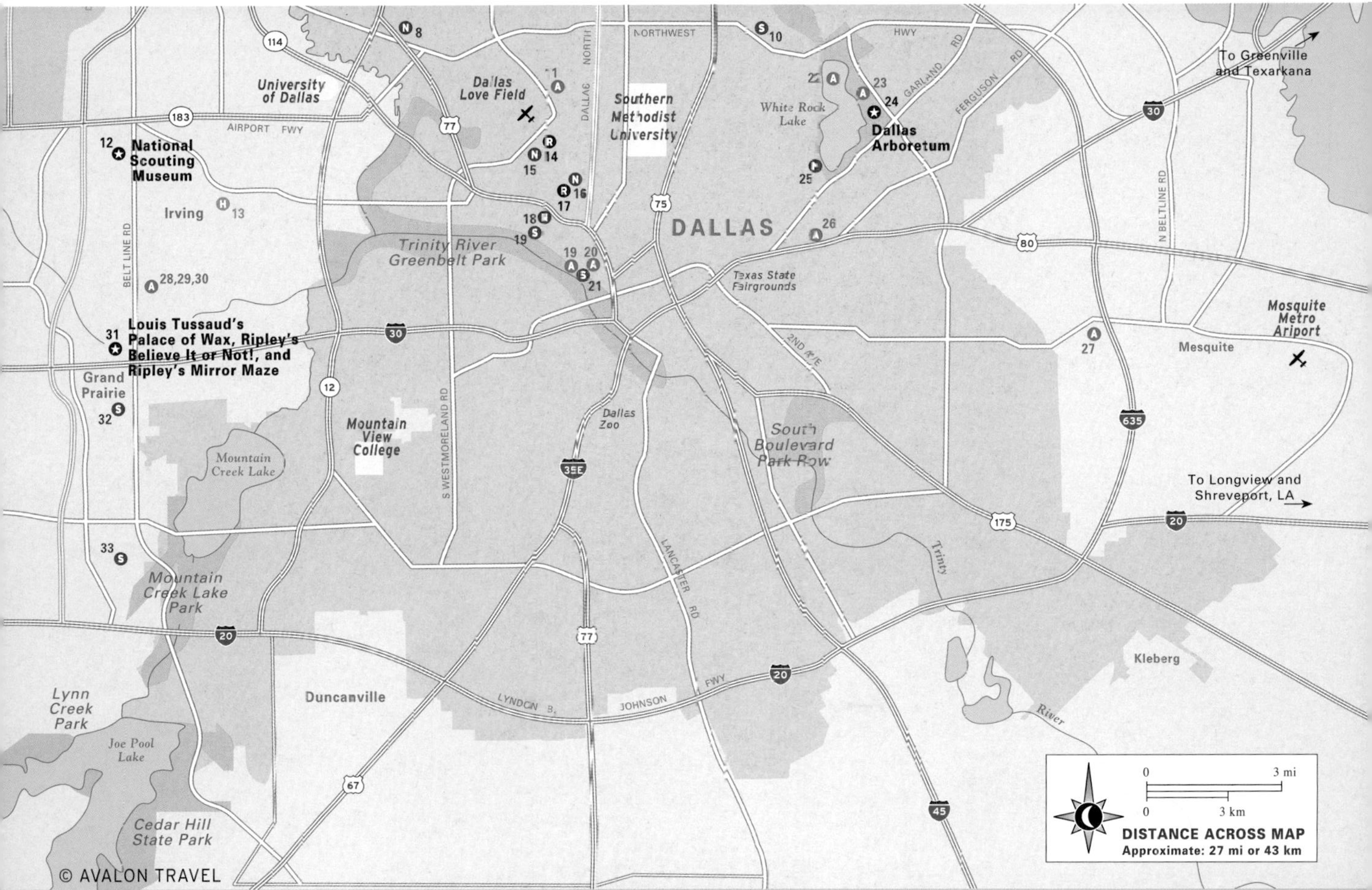

MAP 7

DISTANCE ACROSS MAP
Approximate: 27 mi or 43 km

3 mi

3 km

0

0

Mosquite
Metro
Airport

Mesquite

To Greenville
and Texarkana

To Longview and
Shreveport, LA

N BELTLINE RD

30

635

27

80

175

Kleberg

River

45

Trinty

FERGUSON RD

GARLAND RD

HWY

23

24

Dallas
Arboretum

25

26

22

White Rock
Lake

10

South
Boulevard
Park Row

2ND AVE

20

DALLAS

Texas State
Fairgrounds

NORTHWEST

Southern
Methodist
University

75

LANCASTER RD

FWY

JOHNSON

DALLAS NORTH

Dallas
Love Field

7

13

14

15

16

17

18

19

19 20

6

21

Dallas
Zoo

35E

77

LYNDON B.

8

77

Trinity River
Greenbelt Park

S WESTMORELAND RD

University
of Dallas

114

AIRPORT FWY

30

Mountain
View
College

Duncanville

67

12

National
Scouting
Museum

12

13

Irving

28,29,30

Louis Tussaud's
Palace of Wax, Ripley's
Believe It-or-Not!, and
Ripley's Mirror Maze

31

Mountain
Creek Lake

Mountain
Creek Lake
Park

20

Cedar Hill
State Park

183

BELT LINE RD

Grand
Prairie

32

33

Joe Pool
Lake

Lynn
Creek
Park

© AVALON TRAVEL

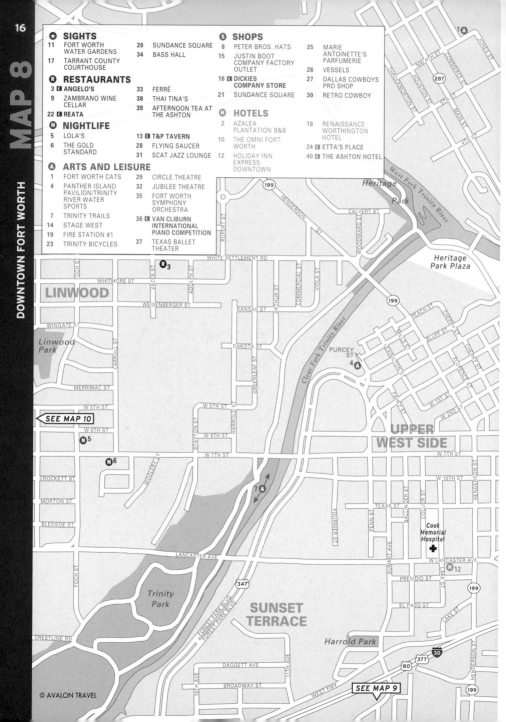

✪ **SIGHTS**
11 FORT WORTH WATER GARDENS
17 TARRANT COUNTY COURTHOUSE
20 SUNDANCE SQUARE
34 BASS HALL

Ⓡ **RESTAURANTS**
3 Ⓒ ANGELO'S
9 ZAMBRANO WINE CELLAR
22 Ⓒ REATA
33 FERRÉ
38 THAI TINA'S
39 AFTERNOON TEA AT THE ASHTON

Ⓝ **NIGHTLIFE**
5 LOLA'S
6 THE GOLD STANDARD
13 Ⓒ T&P TAVERN
28 FLYING SAUCER
31 SCAT JAZZ LOUNGE

Ⓐ **ARTS AND LEISURE**
1 FORT WORTH CATS
4 PANTHER ISLAND PAVILION/TRINITY RIVER WATER SPORTS
7 TRINITY TRAILS
14 STAGE WEST
19 FIRE STATION #1
23 TRINITY BICYCLES
29 CIRCLE THEATRE
32 JUBILEE THEATRE
35 FORT WORTH SYMPHONY ORCHESTRA
36 Ⓒ VAN CLIBURN INTERNATIONAL PIANO COMPETITION
37 TEXAS BALLET THEATER

Ⓢ **SHOPS**
8 PETER BROS. HATS
15 JUSTIN BOOT COMPANY FACTORY OUTLET
16 Ⓒ DICKIES COMPANY STORE
21 SUNDANCE SQUARE
25 MARIE ANTOINETTE'S PARFUMERIE
26 VESSELS
27 DALLAS COWBOYS PRO SHOP
30 RETRO COWBOY

Ⓗ **HOTELS**
2 AZALEA PLANTATION B&B
10 THE OMNI FORT WORTH
12 HOLIDAY INN EXPRESS DOWNTOWN
18 RENAISSANCE WORTHINGTON HOTEL
24 Ⓒ ETTA'S PLACE
40 Ⓒ THE ASHTON HOTEL

© AVALON TRAVEL

Arnold Park

GARVEY ST

ROCK ISLAND/ SAMUELS AVE

Pioneers Rest Cemetery

GOUNAH ST

West Fork Trinity River

Greenway Park

To 2 Azalea Plantation B&B

35W

287

121 377

BELKNAP ST

Tarrant County Courthouse
✪ 17

287

347

W WEATHERFORD ST

TAYLOR ST

THROCKMORTON ST

HOUSTON ST

E 1ST ST

287

18 Ⓗ

19 Ⓐ

COOK ST

W 2ND ST

E 2ND ST

Sundance Square

20 21
Ⓐ Ⓢ 22 Ⓡ

25 Ⓢ
27 Ⓢ

26 Ⓢ

28 Ⓝ

Ⓐ Ⓗ 24

287

Heritage Park

DOWNTOWN

See Detail

W 3RD ST 23

E 3RD ST

COMMERCE ST

CALHOUN ST

W 4TH ST

30 Ⓢ
29 Ⓐ

33 Ⓡ

Ⓝ 31

32 Ⓐ

34 Ⓐ 35,36,37

MAIN ST

F 4TH ST

Bass Hall

W 5TH ST

39 Ⓡ 40
Ⓗ

38 Ⓡ

Harmon Field Park

287

W 6TH ST

347

287

9 Ⓡ

Ⓡ

Burk Burnett Park

287

287

11TH ST

13TH ST

35W

377

BUTLER

TEXAS ST

10 Ⓗ

Fort Worth Amtrak Station

Fort Worth Water Gardens
✪ 11

19TH ST

18TH ST

80 30

W 13TH ST

180

W LANCASTER AVE

180

180

13 Ⓝ

DALLAS ALLEY

PRESIDIO ST

CEDAR ST

287

80 377 30

INDUSTRIAL AVE

35W

NEAR EAST SIDE

W VICKERY BLVD

14 Ⓐ

15 Ⓢ

16 Ⓢ

JARVIS ST

DAGGETT AVE

DAGGETT AVE

BROADWAY AVE

0		300 yds
0		300 m

DISTANCE ACROSS MAP
Approximate: 2.5 mi or 4.1 km

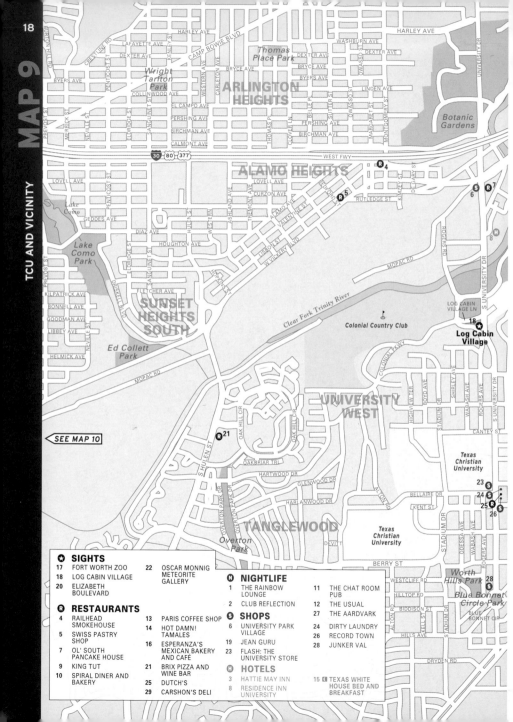

☼ SIGHTS

17	FORT WORTH ZOO
18	LOG CABIN VILLAGE
20	ELIZABETH BOULEVARD
22	OSCAR MONNIG METEORITE GALLERY

® RESTAURANTS

4	RAILHEAD SMOKEHOUSE
5	SWISS PASTRY SHOP
7	OL' SOUTH PANCAKE HOUSE
9	KING TUT
10	SPIRAL DINER AND BAKERY
13	PARIS COFFEE SHOP
14	HOT DAMN! TAMALES
16	ESPERANZA'S MEXICAN BAKERY AND CAFÉ
21	BRIX PIZZA AND WINE BAR
25	DUTCH'S
29	CARSHON'S DELI

ℕ NIGHTLIFE

1	THE RAINBOW LOUNGE
2	CLUB REFLECTION
11	THE CHAT ROOM PUB
12	THE USUAL
27	THE AARDVARK

Ⓢ SHOPS

6	UNIVERSITY PARK VILLAGE
19	JEAN GURU
23	FLASH: THE UNIVERSITY STORE
24	DIRTY LAUNDRY
26	RECORD TOWN
28	JUNKER VAL

Ⓗ HOTELS

3	HATTIE MAY INN
8	RESIDENCE INN UNIVERSITY
15 ◖	TEXAS WHITE HOUSE BED AND BREAKFAST

◄ SEE MAP 10

© AVALON TRAVEL

☼ SIGHTS

12 ⓒ MODERN ART MUSEUM OF FORT WORTH
13 ⓒ THE KIMBELL ART MUSEUM
15 AMON CARTER MUSEUM
16 WILL ROGERS MEMORIAL CENTER
19 FORT WORTH MUSEUM OF SCIENCE AND HISTORY
21 ⓒ THE NATIONAL COWGIRL MUSEUM AND HALL OF FAME
22 FORT WORTH BOTANIC GARDENS

ⓡ RESTAURANTS

1 LAMBERT'S
3 SAINT-EMILION
5 J&J OYSTER BAR
7 FRED'S TEXAS CAFE
23 MONTGOMERY ST. CAFE
24 CURLY'S CUSTARD
28 THE ORIGINAL MEXICAN EATS CAFE
31 ⓒ KINCAID'S
33 ⓒ ROY POPE GROCERY
34 SZECHUAN
35 MAMA'S PIZZA
36 DREW'S PLACE
37 GALLIGASKIN'S SUBMARINE SANDWICH
38 FORTUNA ITALIAN RESTAURANT
40 ITALIAN INN RIDGLEA
41 EL FENIX
43 JAPANESE PALACE
44 EDELWEISS

ⓝ NIGHTLIFE

11 THE POUR HOUSE
14 CAPITAL BAR

ⓐ ARTS AND LEISURE

2 LEONARD'S MUSEUM
10 BACKWOODS
18 CASA MAÑANA
20 ⓒ FORT WORTH STOCK SHOW AND RODEO
39 FOREST PARK

ⓢ SHOPS

4 NAMASTE
6 CAMP BOWIE
8 7TH STREET AND FOCH STREET
9 BESS & EVIE'S
17 CATTLE BARN FLEA MARKET
25 A. HOOPER'S & CO.
26 SOBO FASHION LOUNGE
27 ⓒ J. SAUNDERS
29 MISS MOLLY'S TOY & CANDY SHOP
30 SPOILED PINK
32 PS THE LETTER
42 WESTERN WEAR EXCHANGE

0   500 yds
0   500 m
DISTANCE ACROSS MAP
Approximate: 5.3 mi or 8.6 km

To Decatur and
Wichita Falls

To Denton

Flower
Mound

Marshall
Creek Park

Grapevine
Lake

Grapevine
Lake

Dallas/Fort Worth
International Airport

INTERNATIONAL PKWY

360

AIRPORT FWY

121

Trinity River

West Fork

NORTHWEST PKWY

GRAPEVINE HWY

Bedford

Grapevine

DAVIS BLVD

Watauga

North
Richland Hills

820

12

121

DENTON HWY

WATAUGA RD

NORTHEAST LOOP

Halton
City

28TH ST

Fort Worth
Meacham
Int'l Airport

11

1709

NORTH FWY

287

BLUE MOUND RD

Bureau of Printing
and Engraving
6

7

Fort Worth

Blue
Mound

N SAGINAW BLVD

NORTHWEST LOOP

820

SEE
DETAIL

Lake
Worth

Lake
Worth

Eagle
Mountain
Lake

Newark

2

5

9

10

SIGHTS

6	BUREAU OF PRINTING AND ENGRAVING
22	SIX FLAGS HURRICANE HARBOR
28	SIX FLAGS OVER TEXAS
50	TEXAS COWBOY HALL OF FAME
51	FORT WORTH STOCKYARDS NATIONAL HISTORIC DISTRICT

RESTAURANTS

13	GEORGE'S SPECIALTY FOODS
14	PEROTTI'S PIZZA
21	PICCOLO MONDO
29	CRAWDADDY'S SHACK
30	CHOP HOUSE BURGERS
31	TASTE OF EUROPE
43	CATTLEMEN'S STEAKHOUSE
53	SARSAPARILLA SALOON
54	LONESOME DOVE
55	JOE T. GARCIA'S

NIGHTLIFE

37	BILLY BOB'S TEXAS
39	THE THIRSTY ARMADILLO
40	LONGHORN SALOON
44	BOOGER RED'S
47	WHITE ELEPHANT SALOON

ARTS AND LEISURE

1	TEXAS MOTOR SPEEDWAY (NASCAR)
2	THE GOLF CLUB AT THE RESORT
3	GRAPEVINE OPRY
5	EAGLE MOUNTAIN LAKE
7	THE GOLF CLUB AT FOSSIL CREEK
8	TEXAS BRAHMAS
9	FORT WORTH NATURE CENTER AND REFUGE
10	HIP POCKET THEATRE
11	BURGER'S LAKE
12	IRON HORSE GOLF COURSE
15	BENBROOK STABLES
16	LAKE BENBROOK
18	GATEWAY PARK
19	RIVER LEGACY PARK
20	ARLINGTON MUSEUM OF ART
23	TOP O' HILL TERRACE
25	DALLAS COWBOYS
26	INTERNATIONAL BOWLING MUSEUM AND HALL OF FAME
27	TEXAS RANGERS
32	LAKE ARLINGTON
34	TIERRA VERDE GOLF CLUB AT THE RESERVE
35	COWTOWN SPEEDWAY
49	STOCKYARDS STABLES

Eagle
Mountain
Lake

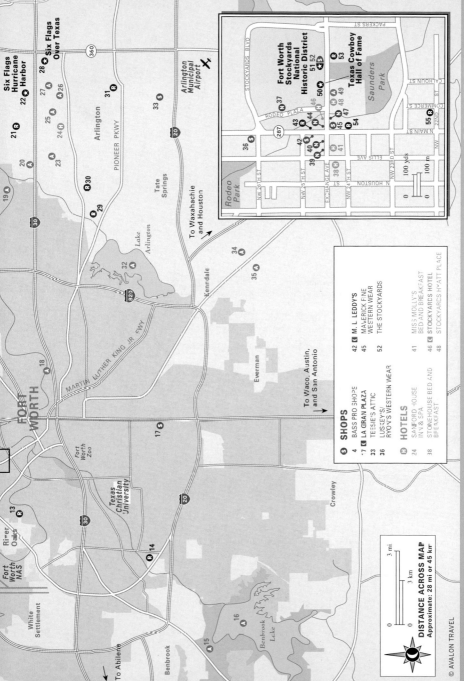

Six Flags Hurricane Harbor
Six Flags Over Texas

Arlington
Arlington Municipal Airport
PIONEER PKWY
Tate Springs

To Waxahachie and Houston

Lake Arlington

Kennedale

Everman

To Waco, Austin, and San Antonio

Crowley

MARTIN LUTHER KING JR FWY

FORT WORTH

Fort Worth Zoo

Fort Worth NAS

River Oaks

Texas Christian University

White Settlement

Benbrook

Benbrook Lake

To Abilene

Fort Worth Stockyards National Historic District

Texas Cowboy Hall of Fame

Saunders Park

Rodeo Park

PACKERS ST
STOCKYARDS BLVD
RODEO PLAZA
CALHOUN ST
COMMERCE ST
N MAIN ST
ELLIS AVE
N HOUSTON
EXCHANGE AVE
NW 26TH ST
NW 25TH ST
NW 24TH ST
NW 23RD ST
NW 22ND ST

100 yds
100 m

SHOPS
4   BASS PRO SHOPS
7   LA GRAN PLAZA
33 TEESIE'S ATTIC
36 LUSKEYS/
    RYON'S WESTERN WEAR
42 M. L. LEDDY'S
45 MAVERICK FINE
    WESTERN WEAR
52 THE STOCKYARDS

HOTELS
24 SANFORD HOUSE
    INN & SPA
38 STONEHOUSE BED AND
    BREAKFAST
41 MISS MOLLY'S
    BED AND BREAKFAST
46 STOCKYARDS HOTEL
48 STOCKYARDS HYATT PLACE

DISTANCE ACROSS MAP
Approximate: 28 mi or 45 km

0   3 mi
0   3 km

© AVALON TRAVEL

Discover
Dallas & Fort Worth

Recently, the folks at NASA released a satellite photo of Dallas-Fort Worth. From outer space, DFW looks like a colossal nebula. From ground level, that's what DFW is, too: Grandly sprawling but anchored by distinct communities, DFW is made up of several individual stars that shine brightly on their own; yet, taken as a whole, they form one giant light. Considering the grandness of the region and the variety of what it has to offer, such a metaphor is essential. How else can one describe a place large enough to make room for its cowpoke tradition *and* its globalist future?

In Dallas, for example, you'll find honky-tonks right next door to alternative music venues. Just to the west, denizens of Fort Worth might dine on a humble chicken-fried steak in the old Stockyards, then hustle downtown afterward to see the opera at the resplendent Bass Hall. You want rodeos? We've got them. You want shopping worthy of Rodeo Drive? We've got that, too.

Both towns overflow with variety, and such symbiotic fusing of disparate cultures is what sets DFW apart. What this means for a visitor is being ready for tradition and surprise—you'd better bring your blue jeans *and* your little black dress. No matter where you choose to wear them, you'll find things in DFW are bright indeed.

Planning Your Trip

▶ WHERE TO GO

Downtown Dallas

Downtown Dallas

Anchored by a cluster of skyscrapers, the central part of Dallas is where you'll find all the perks of the big city, along with a number of historical sights. Downtown Dallas also encompasses the Arts District, home of world-class visual and performing arts, alongside the more laid-back, historic West End.

Uptown Dallas

The denizens of Uptown tend to fall into three categories: gay, upwardly mobile, or some combination of the two. This is a part of town where you're most likely to find the trendiest food, clothes, drinks, and entertainment. Some of it is quite charming, especially the older high- and mid-rise apartments you'll find flanking lush Turtle Creek and the bars and clubs that make up the "gayborhood" off Oak Lawn Avenue. Other parts are a bit plastic, though with all the amenities

and the high concentration of fancy joints, it's hard to complain.

Park Cities

Butting up against the busy concrete bustle of Uptown and the vibrant Oak Lawn party scene, Park Cities is an opulent oasis of giant houses, Lexus SUVs, and exclusive shopping centers (and the home of former president George W. Bush). This is the best place to go if you need the latest Chanel bag or a unique (and probably expensive) gift.

Greenville

Lower Greenville Avenue is the central artery that connects the patchwork of neighborhoods and aesthetics that make up this area. On the southeastern end of the street, you'll find the outer edges of Lakewood, which is populated by an improbable combination of yuppies and hipsters, lured by beautiful older houses and bungalows. They are also lured by their proximity to the heart of Lower Greenville, long a raucous, popular destination for nightlife, dining, and shopping, although lately it's suffered a downturn.

East Dallas

East Dallas has almost always been the bastion of Dallas's funky, edgy population. Shaded by tons of old oak trees, the neighborhoods here are charming and old-school, though there are definitely some rough edges. Deep Ellum—long the epicenter of Dallas's music scene—is perhaps the most well-known neighborhood here, with its low-slung redbrick clubs, restaurants, and shops, but hipster Expo Park and the more family-oriented Lakewood have plenty of shopping, food, and entertainment to offer.

South Dallas

Long a troubled, blighted area, South Dallas has experienced quite a renaissance lately. Fine-dining establishments now stand where crumbling warehouses once did, and a number of old hotels and structures have been rehabbed into new, hip watering holes and down-home restaurants, with stunning views of the downtown skyline and the surrounding refurbished homes. The Bishop Arts area is particularly hopping, especially on weekend nights when young revelers, queer folks, and hip families stroll the streets and peer into the cute, unique boutiques before grabbing dinner.

Greater Dallas

Irving, Grand Prairie, Plano, Frisco—the greater Dallas area contains many a suburb and "mid-city," as the towns between Fort Worth and Dallas are known. Usually rivals, citizens of both Dallas and Fort Worth used to agree on one thing: their mutual disdain for the greater Dallas area and its "boring" suburban feel. Nowadays, however, as these small cities continue to grow and make a name for themselves, city dwellers actually view them as sports, food, recreation, and shopping destinations.

Downtown Fort Worth

It's almost hard to swallow, but downtown Fort Worth just might be giving the

Downtown Fort Worth

Bass Hall at Sundance Square, Fort Worth

Stockyards district a run for its money when it comes to attracting revelers, at least on weekends, when the streets come alive with partiers, shoppers, diners, and music lovers. The center of all the activity is about 20 square blocks of renovated, refurbished, and renewed city center called Sundance Square.

TCU and Vicinity

The acres upon hilly acres upon which stately Texas Christian University now sits were once the hinterland. Now, they're prime real estate, just down the road from the Cultural District and minutes from downtown. Yet, thanks to the university, the area has its own distinct personality: The crisp, green lawns of the school, the lights of a new football stadium, and a good concentration of clubs, bars, and hangouts lend the neighborhood a perpetually collegiate air.

West Side Fort Worth

In many ways, Western Fort Worth is the heart of the city. Many year-round activities and festivals take place in this section of town, and this is the part where culture reigns supreme, be it in the form of world-renowned museums or a wide variety of food and shopping. Most recently, the area around Foch Street and West 7th Avenue has erupted with life; where there once sat rapidly design 1970s buildings, old leathercraft warehouses, and boring offices, now you'll find bars, restaurants, and boutiques.

Greater Fort Worth

No other part of town reflects Fort Worth's history more genuinely than in the North Side Forth Worth area, which embraces the Fort Worth Stockyards National Historic District. The Stockyards continue to maintain old traditions with wooden sidewalks, brick streets, and a daily, real-live cattle drive that attracts tourists and locals alike. Glen Rose and Grapevine are beautiful, full of nature, country air, and fun activities. Arlington is the ultimate mid-city, made up of mostly concrete and gargantuan-scale tourist attractions, which happen to be some of the best in the world, including the Dallas Cowboys Stadium.

the Dallas Arboretum on a foggy morning

► WHEN TO GO

North Texas is at its best during autumn. This time of year, the prairie's ample, mature oak, maple, and pecan trees blaze with color, and the smell of burning mesquite logs fills the air as the weather gets colder. Fall also marks the beginning of football season. It may sound silly to the uninitiated, but the sport lends the air an extra crackle as high school, college, and pro teams kick off their seasons. The weather is generally crisp but comfortable. Spring is also a lovely time here. Moderate temperatures and the hint of summer in the air encourage outdoor activities and several open-air festivals. Many visitors love the mild winters, but the leafless trees and dead grass come off as somewhat stark. Most of all, however, make all attempts to avoid the scorching heat of summer if you can.

autumn in Dallas

Explore Dallas & Fort Worth

▶ THE TWO-DAY BEST OF DALLAS AND FORT WORTH

Day 1: Dallas

▶ Start your day off with a genuine down-home breakfast at the AllGood Café in the heart of historic Deep Ellum (you're going to need some energy for the activities ahead, so consider the chicken-fried steak and egg breakfast).

▶ Head down to the official Dallas Visitors Information Center at the Old Red Museum and grab some maps and tourist information, then pop upstairs to orient yourself with a tour of the museum's History of Dallas County exhibit. The folks at the museum are extremely knowledgeable and friendly—this is the place to stock up on Dallas details before heading out. This is also a good spot to ask directions to get to your next stop, the Arts District (it's also downtown, but a bit of a walk, so consider taking a Dallas Area Rapid Transit train).

▶ The Arts District will present you with several stellar choices. You probably won't be able to hit them all, so a good two-for-one option would be to see the Dallas Museum of Art and the Nasher Sculpture Center, which are adjacent to each other. While you can pay separately to enter either, combination tickets are available at discount prices at both the DMA and Nasher box offices. Another good choice is the Trammell and Margaret Crow Collection of Asian Art, which is free.

▶ You'll be tempted to stay in the Arts District for the remainder of the afternoon, and if that's your choice, grab a quick bite from one of the many food trucks lolling about, or for a big midday splurge, try Stephan Pyles—a popular spot just down the street.

▶ Should you choose to move on, a true Dallas experience awaits: Lunch at The Zodiac restaurant in the Neiman Marcus flagship store at the corner of Main and

the Nasher Sculpture Center

TEN WAYS TO ESCAPE THE TEXAS SUN

the air-conditioned Galleria Dallas

- Head to one of the best malls in America, the **Galleria Dallas,** and hit up the indoor ice skating rink.

- Take a dip in the pool at **QuikTrip Park,** home of Independent Baseball's pro team the **Grand Prairie AirHogs.** Just behind the outfield, the pool allows you to see the action and stay cool.

- Get soaked at **Six Flags Hurricane Harbor**—one of the biggest water parks in the country. Or check out the indoor water park at **Great Wolf Lodge.**

- North Texas is full of lakes, and recreation at them ranges from skinny-dipping to Jet Skiing. One of the biggest is **Lake Texoma,** about an hour-and-half drive north of the Metroplex.

- Catching a flick at one of the many movie taverns in the area is a great way to soak up a few hours of air-conditioning—and a pitcher or two of beer. Try one of Fort Worth's several **Movie Tavern** locations or Dallas's **Angelika Film Center, The Inwood Theatre,** or **The**

Texas Theatre (yes, that's the one of Lee Harvey Oswald fame). In addition, both Dallas and Fort Worth boast dark, state-of-the-art **IMAX theaters.** Dallas's can be found at the **Museum of Science and Nature** in Fair Park; Fort Worth's is in the **Natural History Museum.**

- The rooftop pool at the **Joule Hotel** is cool in all senses of the word. Its eye-catching design makes it the hippest soak in town.

- While the outdoor habitats may not escape the sun, the indoor penguin exhibit at the **Fort Worth Zoo** provides a fun educational respite that kids and adults both enjoy.

- Three words: **Joe T.'s margarita.**

- Rent a kayak or canoe from storied Fort Worth outdoor outfitter **Backwoods** and cruise around the West Fork or Clear Fork of the Trinity River. A bigger challenge: standup paddleboards (and lessons), available for rental from **Aloha Paddleboards.**

Ervay Streets. Make sure you work up an appetite by perusing the legendary racks of couture beforehand.

► If your legs are up for more exploring, Dealey Plaza and the Sixth Floor Museum—the site of the John F. Kennedy assassination—are just a few blocks away.

► A 15-minute car ride from downtown, the Bishop Arts District is a low-key way to top off your day. Stroll along the picturesque, historic block until you reach Tillman's Roadhouse, where a blood orange margarita awaits. If you like a gussied-up roadhouse atmosphere, stick around for dinner. If not, Bishop Arts presents tons of dining options.

Day 2: Fort Worth

► First, you must indulge in Paris Coffee Shop's Texas-size breakfast. Then, get thee straight to the Modern Art Museum of Fort Worth, and give thyself plenty of time to appreciate this amazing building and its world-class collection of post–World War II paintings, sculpture, video, and mixed media works.

► The next stop is that other world-famous museum, The Kimbell Art Museum, whose Louis Kahn–designed walls just happen also to house one of the best museum restaurants in the country. Take a break and eat here, or send someone in your party up the street to pick up some Kincaid's burgers for a picnic on the lovely grassy park next to the Kimbell's reflecting pool.

► Then it's off for an afternoon of Old West history in the Stockyards. Make sure you get there in time for the Fort Worth Herd cattle drive, after which you can stroll the wooden sidewalks and see the sights.

► Shop for souvenirs, boots, hats, and belt buckles at places like M. L. Leddy's. Next, shake the dust off your boots and hunker

down over a cold one at the White Elephant Saloon or Booger Red's before moving on to check out the Exchange building, where ranchers once haggled over the price of steer.

► Hit up Cattlemen's Steakhouse for a big slab of Texas beef—don't worry, you'll dance it off at Billy Bob's Texas, the world's biggest honky-tonk, just down the road.

► If boot scooting isn't your thing, head downtown and grab a drink or dinner on the rooftop at one of Fort Worth's most popular restaurants, the always-buzzing Reata, which overlooks Sundance Square.

► From there, choose from any number of entertainment options, from the casual and understated (a brew or two at the Flying Saucer) to the swank (jazz and cocktails at Scat Jazz Lounge) to the fancy (a performance at Bass Hall).

Billy Bob's Texas

Peppering your visit with some local treasures is the best way to experience true richness of the area.

SIGHTS AND RECREATION
You know how in most cities, the locals don't really go to their own art museums unless they're showing around an out-of-towner? Well, Fort Worthers soak up music, great food, and art (of course) at the **Modern Art Museum of Fort Worth** (aka **The Modern**) *a lot.*

Cowboys, socialites, and regular ol' folks comingle at the annual **Fort Worth Stock Show and Rodeo,** one of the area's best tradition.

Fort Worth's pride as the host of the storied **Van Cliburn International Piano Competition** lands beyond the upper end of the scale.

The DFW GLBT community turns out for its annual Pride celebration in droves, of course, but everyone knows the real party's at the **Cedar Springs Halloween Parade,** when tens of thousands of costumed souls take to the streets of the "gayborhood."

The **Fort Worth Cats** baseball team has a long history—and with seats as cheap as four bucks, you can be a part of it too.

FOOD
Locals know that **The AllGood Café**'s chicken-fried steak is the platonic ideal of that particular dish, enhanced by the AllGood's cute, Texas-centric decor.

Kathleen's Sky Diner, known for its inventive take on upscale diner cuisine, is a Lovers Lane favorite, especially on Sunday nights, when entrées are half off.

Mama Faye's BBQ will stay on your mind months after your visit. Your mouth will still water at the thought of their brisket.

The garlicky crust and perfect sauce at **Mama's Pizza** has brought Fort Worth diners back since 1968 (it now offers

franchises, so stick to the original West Side location).

Once a local secret, **Fuel City Tacos** have been touted by the likes of CNN and other national media. That doesn't keep hungry Dallasites from going back.

Tim Love's Love Shack provides the very Fort Worthian experience of eating a greasy, yet gourmet, burger smack in the middle of the Stockyards.

NIGHTLIFE
The fantastically high ceilings and art deco environs of **The T&P Tavern,** housed in a former train station, provide an impressive yet casual spot in which to quaff local beers.

Looking to embarrass yourself in front of strangers and friends? Karaoke at the friendly dive bar **The Goat** is the perfect place to do so.

More mellow than most of the other entertainment districts in the area, the **Bishop Arts** neighborhood is all redbrick charm, good food, and grown-up bars.

The Granada Theater remains a reliable go-to for an eclectic lineup of live music, ranging from big local bands to national faves.

Fuel City Tacos

SIGHTS

Even though together they form an anchor for the cultural world of the South and Southwest—and, in some ways, for much of the country—Dallas and Fort Worth maintain very separate identities. Dallas, for instance, has catapulted itself into the world-class tier with dazzling speed, after years of being construed as "not quite there," and now the downtown Arts District, home to the Dallas Museum of Art, the Morton H. Meyerson Symphony Center, the Trammell and Margaret Crow Collection of Asian Art, and the 10-acre AT&T Performing Arts Center, has evolved into a cultural powerhouse. Fort Worth, meantime, has built up a world-class reputation in a quieter way. On one end of Fort Worth's cultural spectrum is the international cachet of the Kimbell Art Museum; the other is manned by cowboys and rodeo queens.

There's history here, too, in both towns. The area's rich and sometimes strange past is reflected in its refurbished art deco buildings, Fort Worth's storied Stockyards, humble gravestones, and soaring towers. Sadly, much of that history centers on the somber Dallas block where President John F. Kennedy was shot and killed. But happier sights abound, too—such as Reunion Tower, one of downtown Dallas's most famous landmarks.

Whether you want lofty views or a piece of down-home history, DFW boasts many locations to seek out and enjoy. The sights you see during your visit will demonstrate a unique type of Texas spirit: entrepreneurial, generous, sometimes failing, sometimes peculiar, but always striving for the best, and always proud.

© BRANDON SEIDEL/123RF.COM

HIGHLIGHTS

LOOK FOR (TO FIND RECOMMENDED SIGHTS.

© CLAY COLEMAN/DALLAS CVB

the bronze cattle at Pioneer Plaza, by sculptor Robert Summers of Glen Rose, Texas

(**Best Free Excursion:** The **Dallas Museum of Art** is worth the price of admission, but if you're on a budget, check it out Thursday 5–9 P.M., when it's free to enter (page 35).

(**Best Way to Wear Your Kids Out:** It's a touch pricey, but the **Dallas World Aquarium** will thrill the young 'uns with its amazing indoor jungle habitat. By the end of the tour even moms and pops will be tuckered out (page 36).

(**Best Contemplation Spot:** Turrell's skyscape at the **Nasher Sculpture Center** fosters a quiet, meditative feel. It's blissfully quiet as multicolored pastel lights slowly brighten and fade like the sun (page 36).

(**Best Use of Fake Livestock:** The dozens of bronze cattle that make up the herd at Dallas's **Pioneer Plaza** may not be historically accurate (there was never a lot of cattle driving through Dallas), but they sum up the cowboy spirit of North Texas (page 37).

(**Best Place to Catch Your Breath: The Kimbell Art Museum** is known as much for its architecture as for the art inside. The north-

ern exterior features a portico and reflecting pool that open out onto a grassy area flanked by holly trees. On a sunny day, the effect is wondrous (page 57).

(**Best Museum:** For the **Modern Art Museum of Fort Worth,** Japanese architect Tadeo Ando designed a contemporary cathedral to house one of the best collections of post-World War II art in the world. Don't even think about skipping it (page 58).

(**Best Gift Shop: The National Cowgirl Museum and Hall of Fame**'s first-floor shop is filled with kitschy items like "Bronco Babes" lunch boxes, boot-leather purses, and retro belt buckles. Just don't spend all your time there— you'll want to peruse the museum's many interactive exhibits that celebrate the lives of feisty Western women (page 58).

(**Best Use of Real Livestock:** Get a taste of the Old West by checking out the Fort Worth Herd and the world's only twice-daily cattle drive, in the **Fort Worth Stockyards National Historic District** (page 59).

Downtown Dallas

Map 1

◖ DALLAS MUSEUM OF ART

1717 N. Harwood, 214/922-1803,
www.dallasmuseumofart.org
HOURS: Fri.-Wed. 11 A.M.-5 P.M., Thurs. 11 A.M.-9 P.M.,
third Fri. of every month, 11 A.M.-midnight
COST: $10 adult, $7 senior and military, $5 student,
free children under 11

The Dallas Museum of Art was founded in 1903, and it has taken about 100 years for it to pull itself out of its status as a second-tier art institution and into world-class territory. The museum's first giant leap occurred in 1984 when it finally found a permanent home on Harwood Street, where it has anchored the Arts District ever since. The 2005 acquisition of major contemporary works from three prominent collectors cemented the transition to the top tier, as have fantastic choices when it comes to traveling exhibits.

The aforementioned 2005 procurement of 800 works (along with rights to future acquisitions) bolstered a decent permanent collection, which is divided along both temporal and geographic lines. Art from Europe includes all the notable names—Picasso, Monet, Matisse, Degas, etc.—while the American collection features Andrew and N. C Wyeth, Sargent, Hopper, and O'Keeffe, among others. The countries overlap in the contemporary collection's works from Jasper Johns, Donald Judd, Matthew Barney, and an increasingly significant collection of German artist Sigmar Polke.

Two collections stand out as unique. First, the varied pieces of ancient indigenous and traditional art that comprise the Art of the Americas are stunningly comprehensive. The second, the Wendy & Emery Reves Collection, is notable more for its peculiarity. The

IF YOU RENOVATE IT, THEY WILL COME

The architecture of downtown Dallas has never exactly wowed. In the modern era, the general philosophy among those who have erected new buildings has been, "Get some glass and some steel. Now go up." And sadly, this town exhibits few qualms about tearing down the more interesting edifices. (Example: The amazing, mid-century **Dallas Statler Hilton**, where Tina Turner snuck away from her then-husband Ike in 1976, teetered on the edge of extinction until 2011, when a developer purchased it and promised to return it to its old glory.)

But there are still some gems to be seen. A few years ago, developers gobbled up several notable buildings in various states of disrepair, gussied them up, and converted them into fashionable mixed-use retail/residential lofts. The buildings now hum with activity and life, and their unique architectural features make for a fun subject of study on a quick lunch break or a leisurely walk. Here are four within a few blocks of each other to get you started:

Built in 1916 as a terminal for several local railways, the nine-story **Interurban Building**'s architectural details evoke the Chicago School.

In the early 2000s, renovators began restoring the lobby of the 100-year-old **Dallas Power and Light** building. Removal of seven layers of drywall revealed long-forgotten walls of onyx-colored marble, now the gleaming signature of the cavernous lobby. Further work inside and outside restored this prime example of gorgeous, gleaming art deco to its original glory.

Built in 1913 at the behest of beer baron Adolphus Busch as a companion to his hotel across the street, the **Kirby Building** is a stately nod to old-school Gothicism, right down (or up) to the rooftop gargoyles that guard the "Old Girl," as the building is known.

The mid-century **Republic Center** is actually two buildings: a 50-story former office and a 32-story building capped by a 150-foot spire. Both buildings are covered in a unique facade made of interlocking aluminum plates. It definitely stands out.

collection is presented in a separate upstairs gallery that re-creates the living room of the Reves' good friend Coco Chanel, complete with priceless paintings by Toulouse-Lautrec, Cézanne, and Monet, among many other masterworks.

The museum houses two restaurants: the upscale Seventeen-Seventeen and the more casual Atrium Café. Different types of tours are available, including recorded or docent-led, for groups of any size. The GTE Collections Information Center, where visitors can download and print out information on the museum's works, is also a handy way to get to know the collection.

DALLAS WORLD AQUARIUM

1801 N. Griffin St., 214/720-2224, www.dwazoo.com
HOURS: Daily 9 A.M.–5 P.M.
COST: $20.95 adult, $16.95 senior, $12.95 youth, free under 2

"Aquarium" might not be quite accurate: A multistory venue densely packed with flora and fauna, the main space at the Dallas World Aquarium is more like a mini-ecosystem, and it provides one of the most vivid and intimate zoological experiences available. At roughly $20 per adult, this sucker had better deliver, and it does: Visitors wend their way through a verdant multilevel exhibit, gazing up as exotic birds whiz by the 30-foot waterfall, then gasping at eye-level amazements like crocodiles, stingrays, and tree sloths. The habitat provides up-close encounters with creatures large (panthers) and small (spiders, snakes, and lizards) and splinters off into side rooms, with individual aquariums devoted to different reef ecosystems from throughout the world. The reefs are a treat, full of colorful, exotic fish and strange sea creatures, but they are only a warm-up for the pièce de résistance: a 22,000-gallon overhead tank filled with sharks, manatees, and other creatures of the deep.

NASHER SCULPTURE CENTER

2001 Flora St., 214/242-5100,
www.nashersculpturecenter.org
HOURS: Tues.-Sun. 11 A.M.–5 P.M.
COST: $10 adult, $7 senior and military, $5

Nasher Sculpture Center

© TIM HURSLEY/COURTESY NASHER SCULPTURE CENTER

student, free under 12, free first Sat. of each month, 10 A.M.–5 P.M.; free students and teachers Thurs., 5 P.M.–9 P.M.; joint ticket with Dallas Museum of Art $16 adult, $12 senior, $8 student

Intended not just as a museum but as an artistic oasis amid the hustle and bustle of downtown, the Nasher Sculpture Center was designed by Renzo Piano as an open, airy, inviting space. With its five parallel stone walls and unique "roofless" design that allows indirect light to filter in from above, the building itself could be considered a sculpture. Piano collaborated with landscape architect Peter Walker to create a seamless transition from the airy inner space to the verdant outdoor area, the museum's centerpiece. Unfortunately, while the building and grounds themselves are striking, both the temporary exhibits and permanent collection often lean toward the stale, despite being peppered with de Koonings, Picassos, and Rodins. Some of the enormous outdoor sculpture collection feel dated, too, but it's definitely worth the price of admission to take a soothing stroll among the giant works, topped off by a bit of contemplation at the James Turrell skyspace.

A good way to check out the Nasher is to buy the Dallas Museum of Art/Nasher combination ticket, which offers a discounted price, or to attend the lovely Saturday Night in the City events, during which the museum stays open past dark and holds a party favored by the well-heeled and artsy alike.

OLD RED MUSEUM

100 S. Houston St., 214/745-1100, www.oldred.org
HOURS: Daily 9 A.M.–5 P.M.
COST: $8 adult, $6 senior, $5 child

Long lying comatose and forgotten at the western base of downtown, Old Red finally started getting some attention a few years back and has been refurbished to its Romanesque Revival glory. Outside, the blazing red-colored limestone and signature turrets make this former Dallas County Courthouse immediately recognizable. Inside, a dramatic staircase leads to the second floor, which houses a museum recounting the history of Dallas County. Old Red also serves as home base for the Dallas Visitors

The Old Red Museum is housed in the former Dallas County Courthouse.

© CLAY COLEMAN/DALLAS CVB

Information Center, where you'll find maps, brochures, pamphlets, and a friendly staff ready to help you make the best of your trip.

◖ PIONEER PLAZA/ PIONEER PARK AND CEMETERY

1428 Young St., www.dallasparks.org
HOURS: Daily 24 hours

The dramatically defining feature of this park consists of 49 bronze cattle, each weighing well over half a ton, herded by three bronze cowboys on horseback. The four-acre park in which sculptor and native Texan Robert Summers crafted this extraordinary sculpture (installed in stages between 1993 and 2008) sits smack in the middle of the asphalt-encrusted environs surrounding the Dallas Convention Center, and the juxtaposition of rugged cowboy drama and modern concrete jungle proves striking. (Be forewarned: Tourists often are tempted to ignore the signs reminding them not to sit on the cattle; the Texas sun heats those bronze statues as hot as a skillet, so those who disobey are karmically rewarded with a set of scalded inner thighs. They would be well advised to cool off in the man-made waterfall and stream that also make up part of the park.)

The cattle drive understandably overshadows the second feature of interest here, but the adjacent Pioneer Cemetery commands attention on its own. The shade of the tree-lined graveyard provides a welcome respite after the sun-drenched plaza, and visitors strolling through the spot will find graves and memorials of many of Dallas's founding families, plus heroes from the Texas Revolution. The Confederate Memorial, a 60-foot obelisk bedecked with all sorts of ornate words and imagery, lords over the southeast corner of the site.

REUNION TOWER

300 W. Reunion Blvd., 214/741-5560, www.reuniontower.com

HOURS: Sun.-Thurs. 10 A.M.-10 P.M., Fri.-Sat. 9 A.M.-6 P.M.

COST: $2 adult, $1 child

Reunion Tower

Sometimes not-so-endearingly called "the Dallas phallus," this recognizable piece of the Dallas skyline has been taking locals and visitors alike to new heights since 1978. Standing around 560 feet high, the tower doesn't consist of much: Three concrete shafts hold elevators that ferry visitors to the top of the tower (a fourth is for mechanical storage), which is a ball-shaped giant geodesic dome ensconced in a network of flashing lights.

The ball holds three levels. The revolving restaurant Antares once comprised the entire second floor, but a two-year renovation has combined it with the third-floor lounge; now, the new restaurant, called Fifty-Six, is helmed by none other than Wolfgang Puck. The first floor consists of an observation deck that provides the city's best views of Dallas, Fort Worth, and the surrounding environs.

SIXTH FLOOR MUSEUM/ JFK SITE/DEALEY PLAZA

411 Elm St., 214/747-6660, www.jfk.org

HOURS: Tues.-Sun. 10 A.M.-6 P.M., Mon. noon-6 P.M.

COST: $13.50 adult, $12.50 youth, $7 senior, free under 5

It's often a startling moment for visitors when they first encounter the nexus of Houston and Elm Streets, the location where President John F. Kennedy was shot to death on November 22, 1963. Suddenly, the black-and-white images familiar to so many of us change to color, and the Abraham Zapruder film comes to life. The sadly well-known panorama is all there: the grassy knoll, the triple underpass, and, of course, the Texas School Book Depository, from which the shots that killed Kennedy were fired by depository employee Lee Harvey Oswald (at least, according to some witnesses and the Warren Commission).

The Texas School Book Depository actually sits in the middle of what was, pre-1963, already a historic site. Named after *Dallas Morning News* founder George Dealey, the parklike area commemorated both its namesake and the city's founder, John Neely Bryan, who had established his pioneer outpost on

© NATALIA BRATSLAVSKY/123RF.COM

I. M. PEI'S GIANT "OOPS": DALLAS CITY HALL

© CLAY COLEMAN / DALLAS CVB

Dallas City Hall

World-renowned architect I.M. Pei has designed several lauded buildings in Dallas: His **Fountain Place skyscraper** (1445 Ross Ave.), for instance, is a modern, eye-bending, downtown beauty that soars to the sky amid an oasis of frothy fountains. His **Meyerson Symphony Center** (2301 Flora St.) wonderfully fuses geometric shapes, with curves and right angles somehow nestling together in beautiful symmetry. The three triangles that form his **Energy Plaza skyscraper** (1601 Bryan St.) pose a striking figure in the middle of downtown.

But his **Dallas City Hall** design at 1500 Marilla St.? Ugh. Clearly, it is an ambitious design: The base of the wedge-shaped building—planned and built in the '70s—is much thinner than its top. The downtown-facing facade juts out sharply at 34 degrees, top-down, in an intimidating way over the "buffer zone" that separates the building from the closest street. The design was meant to be democratic and accessible, but, frankly, it's weird and also a pain in the

butt (if you park on the street, it takes forever to walk across the buffer zone to actually reach the front doors). It's a menacing effect, futuristic and secretive—no wonder it was used in movie *RoboCop* and in the TV show *Lois and Clark* (both times as headquarters for monolithic supercorporations). The *Dallas Morning News* City Hall blog called the building "a big doorstop balanced precariously on its tip," and commenters agreed with the disparagement, saying it looked more like "a manure spreader" or even "a punishment to all the senses."

The sad thing is, in theory, Pei's idea was a good one. The angled design helps keep the blazing Texas sun out of the windows, and the dramatic top-heavy sight line instills a sense of awe—how are the higher floors supported?

But even the $70 million it took to build the thing couldn't save it. Which, of course, is all the more reason to go see it: How often do you get to see a mistake on such a scale? It may be a failure, but true to Texas form, at least it's a gargantuan one.

TAKE A TOUR

The nonprofit **Dallas Historical Society's** (3939 Grand Ave., 214/421-7500, www.dallash-istory.org, call for schedule and a availability) tours are an excellent resource for discovering the city's overt charm as well as its hidden secrets. The knowledgeable and friendly Dallas-philes who lead the tours prove better ambassadors than the Chamber of Commerce, especially when it comes to the more eclectic aspects of Dallas's past.

The DHS's wide variety of tour offerings reflects that eclecticism. While the group offers a number of comprehensive tours that provide a historical overview, the best ones are more focused on specific aspects or themes of Dallas history, small windows of time, or singular events that helped define the larger picture of the city's past. Some suggestions:

The Extreme Dallas Tour gets to the nitty-gritty, underground details of Dallas's past. The tour visits things like the Pennsylvania Railroad engine that led the Robert F. Kennedy funeral procession in 1968, which is housed here, plus numerous other little secrets like the United States' art deco monument. Music fans should check out the **Deep Ellum**

Walking Tour, during which visitors stroll the very red brick roads that scores of jazz and blues legends like Blind Lemon Jefferson and Robert Johnson traveled. Tour guide Marc Traynor knows his stuff, and he points out old speakeasies amid new clubs, and hidden points of origin of today's bohemian Deep Ellum.

Alternative history buffs will be especially interested in the **Historic Oak Cliff Tour.** Separated from much of Dallas by the Trinity River and, for many years, along racial lines, Oak Cliff has always enjoyed its own flavor, much of it thanks to its distinct racial and cultural mix. Its contributions to Dallas's past are just as varied: Bonnie and Clyde once ran here, near where Lee Harvey Oswald lived and hid after allegedly shooting the president, down the road from the site of where the 7-Eleven empire was born.

Speaking of Oswald, perhaps the most popular tour, **Retracing the Steps of Lee Harvey Oswald,** is a chilling excursion that follows Oswald's route the day of the Kennedy assassination, including the Texas Theatre, as well as stops at his boardinghouse and other points of interest.

the spot in 1841. The area's open-air Bryan Colonnade (upon which Zapruder stood to film the motorcade) was built, along with other additions, as part of a Works Progress Administration (WPA) project during Franklin D. Roosevelt's presidency.

For decades after the assassination, Dealey Plaza and the Texas School Book Depository saw very little in the way of official commemoration of such a world-changing event. The primary source of information about the assassination, in fact, was the handful of conspiracy theorists who gathered there daily and who still mill about near the grassy knoll today. Some of these are charlatans, hoping to hawk a few brochures, books, or videotapes. Others are genuinely passionate and knowledgeable about the subject. Still others, like Robert Groden—who is responsible for painting the white "Xs"

that mark the exact spot on Elm Street where the assassin's bullets found their mark—are a little of both.

When the School Book Depository company moved out of the building in 1970, Dallas didn't quite know what to do with the place. Many Dallasites called for the building's destruction, citing it as a painful reminder. That same year, the city took a huge step toward officially recognizing the assassination by unveiling the Philip Johnson–designed Kennedy Memorial. Consisting of 50-foot-high marble slabs that partially enclose a contemplation area, the structure is meant, according to the architect, "not as a memorial to the pain and sorrow of death," but as "a permanent tribute to the joy and excitement of one man's life."

The depository changed hands for several

years, almost succumbing to an arsonist's fire in 1972, until Dallas County acquired the building in 1977. The Dallas County Commission used the bottom five floors as office space; the sixth and seventh floors remained empty.

Finally, in 1989, the Sixth Floor Museum opened, and Dallas began to come to terms with its place in a dark day in history. The museum does an excellent job of easing visitors toward a rather macabre ending—the sniper's nest, re-created with boxes positioned as they were on the day of the assassination. Much of the exhibit places Kennedy's presidency in social, cultural, and historical context before moving on to interactive stations featuring video of his speeches and footage of his entire visit to Texas. There are plenty of displays dedicated to the assassination as well, including the built-to-scale diorama of Dealey Plaza used by the FBI, journal pages from witnesses and doctors at Parkland Hospital, and a timeline of the actions of Lee Harvey Oswald, among hundreds of fascinating pieces. As a whole, the museum is good for those who remember as well as those who are too young to have experienced that time in history.

Uptown Dallas   Map 2

FREEDMAN'S MEMORIAL
Lemmon Ave. and Central Expy., 214/670-3284

It's kind of a mixed bag at the Freedman's Memorial. On one hand, the memorial's grand granite arches with poems etched into the entryway provide a touching tribute to the slaves and former slaves who were buried in the cemetery nearby. On the other hand, knowing that many of those graves were disinterred and moved during a rash of development during the 1960s doesn't exactly stir the soul. Still, the $2 million work is a beautiful, if belated, acknowledgement.

GEOMETRIC MADI MUSEUM
3109 Carlisle St., 214/855-7802,
www.geometricmadimuseum.org
HOURS: Sat.-Wed. 11 A.M.-5 P.M., Thurs. 11 A.M.-7 P.M.,
Sun. 1-5 P.M.
COST: Free

Begun in the 1940s as an artistic reaction against the Juan Perón dictatorship in Argentina, the MADI movement (no one really knows what the initials stand for) is a visual style marked by extreme color and a focus on the interplay of geometric forms. When well-known Dallas arts patrons Bill and Dorothy Masterson were first introduced to the style, they fell in love with it, to the extent that Masterson decreed that the new digs of his law firm would be encased in a MADI-style building. Masterson commissioned MADI artist and architect Volf Roitman to recast a stuffy old 1970s edifice as a MADI building—replete with huge, bright geometric pieces covering the exterior—which Masterson's Kilgore Law Center now calls home.

While legal eagles come and go, visitors can

the exterior of the Geometric MADI Museum

COURTESY OF THE MADI MUSEUM

REMEMBERING JFK

Large Xs mark the spot where John F. Kennedy was shot.

Dallas is famous for a lot of things; sadly, one of them involves a terrible chapter in our country's history. The assassination of President John F. Kennedy occurred at 12:30 P.M., Friday, November 22, 1963 on the north side of Elm Street in downtown Dallas. The city has never forgotten it.

The city also has had a tough time reconciling its relationship with the historic tragedy. For many years, Dallas collectively *tried* to forget, even coming close to tearing down the Texas School Book Depository building, from which Kennedy's alleged assassin Lee Harvey Oswald fired his shots.

Fortunately, the Depository still stands. The building is a scar on the city—Elm Street is still highly trafficked, and it's an eerie feeling to drive past it on the way to work or for an evening on the town. But imagine if it weren't there, if it had been destroyed and replaced by a skyscraper or a strip mall. Would that have changed something in our collective national

memory? Would it have caused it to fade in a different way? Would it have altered how we see the assassination?

Fortunately, we don't have to answer those questions, as not only does the Depository remain, its infamous Sixth Floor has been transformed into an excellent museum. In fact, while much of the Dallas landscape has changed, plenty of sites relating to the Kennedy assassination are still there. Here are some of the main ones.

THE SIXTH FLOOR MUSEUM

The Sixth Floor Museum is pricey, but well worth it. The self-guided tour begins with an extensive exhibit that puts Kennedy's presidency into social, historical, and political context—especially helpful for the younger folks who were not alive to experience it themselves. The comprehensive set of artifacts and displays set the stage for understanding the significance of what happened on November 22. The tour then moves on to a timeline of Kennedy's Dallas-Fort Worth visit, complete with detailed notes, photos, videos, and imagery. Finally, the assassination is covered, in bleak detail. There's no original evidence shown here, which is probably for the best, but a centerpiece is the actual, to-scale FBI model of Dealey Plaza designed for the Warren Commission. The most chilling display of all comes at the end of the tour; there, you'll find the "sniper's nest," recreated with book boxes to look just as it did the day Oswald supposedly fired out of it.

DEALEY PLAZA

Completed as a WPA project in 1940, Dealey Plaza is named for George Dealey, an early civic leader in Dallas and former publisher of the *Dallas Morning News*. Visitors with even the most casual knowledge of the Kennedy assassination recognize the plaza, and today it teems with tourists and history buffs exploring its many notable sites, including:

The Base of the Depository Building: If you prefer not to pay the fee to get upstairs, or would like to supplement your museum experience, exploring Dealey Plaza is a fascinating way to spend anywhere from 30 minutes to a couple of hours. The truly adventurous should start with a chat with any number of the conspiracy theorists who mill about at the base of the Depository building. These people may be considered crazy by some and truth-seekers by others, but no matter what your personal theories about the JFK assassination are, they provide a never-ending flow of fodder. Some prove to truly be wackos, while others actually are bona fide amateur historians. Take note: They also usually want money, so if you end up talking for a while, you might want to throw a buck or two in a donations jar or buying a pamphlet—it's all part of the experience.

The North Pergola/Grassy Knoll: Dealey Plaza is flanked by two pergolas—dramatic colonnades—that many people mistakenly think are Kennedy memorials. They are actually monuments to figures of Dallas history and predate the assassination. The pergola on the north side of Elm Street (the side by the Depository) is a memorial to Dallas founder John Neely Bryan. This is where Abraham Zapruder famously stood with his 8mm camera filming the motorcade and capturing the assassination on film. The North Pergola sits on the grassy knoll, from which many witnesses claim to have heard gunshots.

Wooden Fence/North Tower: At the top of the slope of the grassy knoll you'll find a wooden fence, the area where some witnesses claim they saw a puff of smoke shortly after the shots. The fence that currently stands is not the original—it long ago fell into disrepair and was replaced—but visitors can access both sides of it. If you walk around the back of the fence, you will be near the railroad tower commonly called the "North Tower." A few witnesses also claimed to see mysterious men—including the famous "hobos"—milling around the fence and the North Tower that day.

Xs: Two large white Xs are taped to the pavement in the middle of Elm Street. Both mark the approximate spots where the two bullets that struck Kennedy hit. While many people think the Xs are official markers, they are actually placed there by amateur historians. While it's extremely morbid to contemplate, the Xs actually help bring the assassination into full perspective. When viewed from both the Sixth Floor and

then the Grassy Knoll, for instance, it's easy to see how much more difficult Oswald's shot was than one would be from behind the fence.

Also rather morbidly, many visitors dodge cars and stand on the Xs to have their pictures taken. If you attempt this, here's a word of warning: Elm Street is still in use and heavily trafficked—such activity is not recommended.

John F. Kennedy Memorial: The smooth white walls of Philip Johnson's 30-foot concrete cenotaph meld seamlessly with Dealey Plaza's concrete pergolas, but still manages to stand out as the more streamlined, somber piece. The cenotaph consists of four walls, with airy entryways and no roof. The inside, meant by Johnson to be a place of contemplation amid the bustle of downtown, centers on a single slab of marble bearing only three words: John Fitzgerald Kennedy. The monument can be found about two blocks east of where Kennedy was shot.

The Sixth Floor Museum

© JFK MUSEUM/VISITDALLAS.COM

enter the first floor museum at their leisure, and meandering about striking, colorful works is a treat, especially for lovers of art, architecture, and design. With its surfeit of colors and playful forms, this is a great place to introduce kids to art. The museum offers both a permanent and rotating collection, along with occasional lectures and events.

Park Cities   Map 3

SOUTHERN METHODIST UNIVERSITY
6425 Boaz Ln., 214/628-2000, www.smu.edu

Officially chartered in 1911 (classes began in 1915), Southern Methodist University has grown into a focal point of higher education in the Southwest. The university's popularity and prowess are demonstrated by its billion-dollar-plus endowment, beautiful campus of green lawns, Ivy League–style buildings, and old-growth trees, as well as its consistent graduating of professionally degreed students. It's also the home to the George W. Bush Presidential Library (which has met with some opposition from Dallas's less conservative population).

SMU has much to offer visitors. The university calendar is overflowing with lecture series, symposia, concerts, and exhibits. Many of the events are free or low-cost and/or open to the public. Athletic events are some of the most popular pastimes. Ever since enduring the severe death penalty punishment in 1987 due to serious recruiting violations in 1985, the Mustangs football team has been subpar, though in late years it has bounced back, and hopes have risen for the future with the 2007 hiring of respected coach June Jones. Before games, many fans choose to tailgate or picnic along Bishop Boulevard before moving to Gerald J. Ford Stadium. The soccer team is also popular, having dominated its competition in recent years. SMU is a member of the NCAA's Division I Conference USA.

Another popular campus destination is the Meadows Museum, home of one of the world's largest collections of Spanish art. The neo-Palladian space provides a spectacular area in which to view the works from the 10th to 20th centuries, including Picassos, Goyas, Riberas, and El Grecos, among many others.

East Dallas   Map 5

FAIR PARK
1121 1st Ave., 214/426-3400, www.fairpark.org

Fair Park contains a city's worth of sports and entertainment facilities, historical sights, museums, and architectural delights, all rolled into one 277-acre complex. Built in 1936 for the Texas State Centennial (celebrating 100 years of liberty from Mexico), the Fair Park grounds and buildings are bedecked in amazing art deco style, with WPA-era murals, grand esplanades, and dramatic detailing. Aside from the delights they house, the buildings themselves are considered important historic works.

A favorite edifice is the Hall of State, a grand beaux arts structure with an entrance guarded by *The Tejas Warrior,* an 11-foot-tall gilded statue of a Native American brandishing a bow at the sky. The exterior of the building is inscribed with the names of 59 Texas luminaries of the past. Inside you'll find the "Hall of Heroes," with its six statues of Texas's most revered historical figures. The building now provides a home to the Dallas Historical Society as well as the G. B. Dealey Library and its three million historic documents.

Other highlights include the African American Museum, the Women's Museum, and the Science Place (a great choice for kids). A Fair Park Pass, available on the Fair Park website, gets you entry to these three and the Hall of State, plus four other museums on the grounds: the Age of Steam Railroad Museum,

© DALLAS CVB

Big Tex, a 52-foot talking cowboy, lords over the Texas State Fair at Fair Park

Texas Discovery Gardens, Dallas Aquarium, and Museum of Natural History.

Every fall the grounds are home to the Texas State Fair, the largest of its kind in the country, attended by millions of visitors. It can seem odd to witness flip-flop-clad families scarfing down corn dogs and fried Nutter Butters in the shadow of the grand facades and statues that

adorn the Hall of State, but then, Dallas has always prided itself on contradiction—that's part of the fun.

Let's not forget the famous Cotton Bowl, recently renovated and expanded to 80,000 seats, which looms at the northern half of the park complex. Until 2008, the State Fair festivities involved the Red River Shootout, the annual football game between the University of Oklahoma and the University of Texas. That game moved to the new Dallas Cowboys stadium in Arlington, but the Cotton Bowl still hosts the annual State Fair Classic between Grambling State and Prairie View A&M. Frankly, the football teams usually aren't very good—but fans still pack the stadium for the spectacular battle of the bands at halftime.

LATINO CULTURAL CENTER
2600 Live Oak St., 214/671-0045,
www.dallasculture.org/latinoCulturalCenter
HOURS: Tues.-Sat. 10 A.M.-5 P.M.
COST: Free
Mexican architect Ricardo Legorreta crafted this stunning faux-adobe building that opened in 2003. The exterior performs a miracle: The shadow play created by Legorreta's angled walls intermingles with the building's sharp edges and even sharper colors, transforming the industrial blight of Live Oak Street into a bit of visual magical realism. The center itself is a focal point of Latino art, music, literary events, dance, and education.

South Dallas   Map 6

DALLAS HERITAGE VILLAGE
1515 S. Harwood St., 214/421-5141,
www.dallasheritagevillage.org
HOURS: Tues.-Sat. 10 A.M.-4 P.M., Sun. noon-4 P.M.
COST: $9 adult, $5 child, $7 senior
This living history village consists of 21 different buildings, constructed in different parts of Texas between 1840 and 1910, which were disassembled and reconstructed on the site of Dallas's oldest park (called, logically enough, Old City Park). Scattered across the village's

13 acres, refurbished buildings like the Worth Hotel, Dog Trot House, and the Main Street Saloon provide a Victorian backdrop for all sorts of historical demonstrations, reenactments, and entertainment. Perhaps the most popular stop is the Millermore House, a Greek Revival mansion that shows how the well-to-do kicked it mid-1800s style (antique lovers and fans of very busy carpet will love it). Beyond that, expect guides and actors clad in period attire depicting how life was for Texans of old.

© JONANNA WIDNER

The Dallas Heritage Village living history museum is a popular stop.

It's easy to spend an entire day here, especially with kids.

An added anachronistic bonus: The proximity of the Cedars Food Park, where a number of food truck proprietors have circled their wagons. The juxtaposition of a modern food truck plaza next to a living museum dedicated to life a century ago may seem odd, but, hey, it beats eating hardtack coated in buffalo tallow.

DALLAS ZOO

650 S. R. L. Thornton Fwy., 695/554-7500, www.dallaszoo.com

HOURS: Daily 9 A.M.–5 P.M.

COST: $12 adult, $9 youth and senior, free under 2

Even though it covers a potentially daunting 95 acres of land, the Dallas Zoo's organized layout makes for a fun, easy, educational foray. The zoo is basically divided into two parts: the Wilds of Africa and ZooNorth. A stroll along the nature path at the Wilds of Africa takes visitors through river, desert, forest, mountain, brush, and woodland habitats filled with chimps, gorillas, crocs, and other African species. One mildly annoying feature, though, is that many of the other Wilds of Africa animals are only visible from the Monorail Safari.

ZooNorth is a great place to take kids, especially considering the highly interactive Lacerte Family Children's Zoo, where the little ones can clamber through a giant bird's nest or an oversize "spiderweb."

It should be noted that despite its acreage, the zoo can come off as very small and disappointing as far as the number and variety of animals. The past several years have seen a revived effort to improve the grounds and facilities, including an initiative to recycle animal waste into power for the site. Still, even attempts to improve the zoo have sparked controversy, most recently when Jenny the Elephant was forced into smaller quarters while waiting for the expansion of the elephant habitat.

MARGARET HUNT HILL BRIDGE

Connects Singleton Blvd. to Woodall Rogers Freeway

Did Dallas really need this 1,200-foot bridge, which cost $120 million to build and took five years to be finished? Probably not in any practical sense, but the power of this bridge goes beyond just getting people from Woodall Rogers Freeway to West Dallas. World-class cities need world-class landmarks, and boy, does this one work. Designed by famous Spanish architect Santiago Calatrava and named for a beloved Dallas philanthropist, the bridge features a dramatic, 400-foot spiraling arch that can be seen for miles around, providing a transcendent element to the skyline (you may recognize it from the opening credits of the 2012 version of the TV show *Dallas*). It takes a second or two for the bridge's ingenious design to really sink in, but once your eyes adjust, the cables flit and twist like a double-helixed Mobius strip, while the arch itself moves in and out of different visual fields.

TEXAS THEATRE

231 W. Jefferson Blvd., 214/948-1546, www.thetexastheatre.com

HOURS: Daily starting at 5 P.M.

COST: $8-10

Dallas has a conflicted relationship with the residuals from the Kennedy assassination. On one hand is the impulse to preserve the important historical structures associated with that fateful day. On the other, who wants to maintain and preserve painful reminders?

Such was the quandary faced when it came to one of the most iconic and recognizable buildings associated with the Kennedy murder: the Texas Theatre, where Oswald sat in the fifth seat from the aisle, in the third-to-last row, watching *War Is Hell* as the Dallas Police Department closed in.

When it opened in 1931 as part of Howard Hughes's national chain, the theater was one of the fanciest and most technologically advanced in the country, and it was inaugurated with great fanfare as the anchor of the Jefferson Boulevard district. The place flourished, and even after the infamous November day in 1963, the theater continued to beckon patrons with its air-conditioning and signature sign that spelled out T-E-X-A-S in huge vertical neon letters.

Slowly, however, upkeep lessened along with attendance, and the interior grew shabby as fewer and fewer patrons showed up. The beautiful details and paintings were lathed over, and the Jefferson area suffered from a rough reputation, keeping moviegoers away. In 1989, the theater closed.

In the ensuing years, the historic spot narrowly escaped several dates with a wrecking ball, until it was finally rescued by a collaboration between the Dallas Summer Musicals group and the city in 2001. Since then, the venue has undergone well more than a million dollars in renovation and restoration.

The theater's latest incarnation stands as a testament to tenacity. Now run by a group of film lovers, the theater thrives as an art house cinema and venue for music and other entertainment, proving that while Dallas will never fully embrace its Kennedy history, at least the Texas Theatre stands of a reminder of the possibility of some redemption.

THE VERY FIRST 7-ELEVEN

Corner of Edgefield Ave. and W. 12th St.

Dallas has long been populated with entrepreneurs, and when Joe Thompson took his shot in 1927, it paid off. Thompson started as a worker in an Oak Cliff icehouse called Southland Ice Company when he realized that, given the restricted hours and far-flung locations of local grocery stores, there was a killing to be made selling "convenience items" like eggs, milk, and bread along with ice. Soon, Thompson was moving more sundries than ice, and he eventually bought Southland and set up shop. The original site remained a 7-Eleven until 1995; today, the old icehouse holds different occupants, but it's still the birthplace of an American institution.

OSWALD SITES

Many of the sites associated with Lee Harvey Oswald can be found in Oak Cliff. A primarily residential area on the south side of Dallas, Oak Cliff is where Lee Harvey Oswald lived around the time of the assassination. Oak Cliff is also the area where Oswald allegedly killed Dallas Police Officer J.D. Tippit and where Oswald was arrested at the Texas Theatre. Today, much of Oak Cliff struggles with poverty and crime, although that has improved somewhat in recent years. The Bishop Arts District (near most of the Oak Cliff Oswald sites) neighborhood, for instance, has undergone a notable revitalization, although these changes have been criticized by some as gentrification.

- **Oswald Family Residence:** From the street, it's tough to see the backyard of the Oswald Residence (212 W. Neely St.), where the well-known photos of Oswald holding his Carcano rifle were taken (of course, according to many, the photos were faked). Oswald's address was actually the top floor, 214 W. Neely. Nowadays the house is definitely the worse for wear, but it's still clearly recognizable.

- **Oswald's Residence, 1963:** In November 1963, Oswald was living at a rooming house at 1026 N. Beckley Avenue, just south of Zang Boulevard.

The house still stands in good condition today, and it's easy to drive by and see it (just don't knock on the door).

- **Site of Tippit Murder:** Less than a mile southeast of the Beckley house you'll find this nondescript residential intersection (Corner of E.10th St. and Patton Ave.), where Oswald (or, again according to some theorists, someone else) shot and killed Dallas Police Officer J.D. Tippit somewhere between 1 and 1:15 P.M. the afternoon of the assassination. Tippit had been driving east down East 10th when he pulled over to talk to Oswald, according to witnesses, about 100 feet past the intersection with Patton Avenue. When he got out of the car to speak further, Oswald shot him.

- **Hardy Shoe Store/Texas Theatre:** After Tippit's shooting, Oswald slipped into the Hardy Shoe Store (213 W. Jefferson Ave.), where a clerk named Johnny Brewer noticed him acting peculiar. Oswald then popped back out and made the short walk down the street to the Texas Theatre (231 W. Jefferson Ave.). He entered without paying for his ticket, and shortly afterward Brewer alerted the ticket taker to call the police. Oswald was arrested after a scuffle. The seat he was sitting in at the Texas

Greater Dallas   Map 7

DALLAS ARBORETUM
8525 Garland Rd., 214/515-6500,
www.dallasarboretum.org
HOURS: Daily 9 A.M.–5 P.M.
COST: $15 adult, $9 youth, $11 senior ($6 every Tues.), free under 3

A peaceful oasis on the edge of White Rock Lake, the Arboretum covers 66 acres of real estate with endless swaths of flowers, trees, and other lush botanical delights. Each of the 12 different gardens has its own personality, sometimes wowing visitors with blazing colors, other times soothing with pastoral charm. The pecan grove provides a relaxing, tree-shaded picnic area, and kids will enjoy Toad Corners, with its oversize toad statues that squirt water. An afternoon stroll through the grounds proves a relaxing antidote to the glare and grime of the city, and makes downtown feel miles away, when really it's just down the road. On-site parking is $5 ($10 for valet), though there is off-site parking with a shuttle available during peak times.

Theatre now bears his name in gold leaf.

- **Oswald Murder Site:** The basement where Jack Ruby shot Lee Harvey Oswald still exists underneath the building that once served as Dallas City Hall (2001 Commerce St., now the City Municipal Building). By all accounts, the site looks pretty much the same, with the addition of a second pair of glass doors, but it's tough to get down there without getting kicked out or possibly arrested, so don't try it. Similarly, the public is not allowed access to the fifth floor, where Oswald was being held before the attempt, thwarted by Ruby, to transfer him to the city jail. Still, the beautiful beaux arts structure is worth seeing, and a quick walk-by is worth it.

- **Former Site of the Carousel Club:** Owned and operated by Jack Ruby, this semi-seedy burlesque bar, the Carousel Club (1312 Commerce St.), was long ago replaced by a modern office building across the street from both the Adolphus and Magnolia hotels. Still, if you walk by the site, it's eerie to notice just how close it is to other important sites like the old City Hall, where Ruby shot Oswald, and Dealey Plaza itself.

- **Campisi's Egyptian Lounge:** While Campisi's (5610 E. Mockingbird Ln.) by

now has grown into a citywide chain, its flagship still oozes history and dark ambience. The Campisi's chain was begun by Carlo Campisi and his sons Joseph and Sam, who back in the day were well-known mob figures in Dallas. According to the House Committee on Assassinations, this is where Jack Ruby ate a steak dinner the night before Kennedy's death. It is still open, still family owned, and still easily identified by its mod "Egyptian Lounge" neon sign—although the place is 100 percent Italian, Joe Campisi kept the sign after he bought the place. You might recognize the current proprietor Carlo "Corky" Campisi and his daughters from the E! network's reality show *Wildest Party Parents.*

- **Oswald's Grave:** Oswald is buried at Rose Hill Cemetery (7301 F. Lancaster Ave., Fort Worth) underneath a simple marker that reads simply "Oswald." Don't ask cemetery employees where the grave is—their policy is to not reveal its location. In a weird twist, a comedian named Nick Beef purchased the plot next to Oswald so that he would be remembered as...the person buried next to Lee Harvey Oswald. The ploy worked, so now cemetery employees refuse to give directions to the grave of Nick Beef as well.

LOUIS TUSSAUD'S PALACE OF WAX, RIPLEY'S BELIEVE IT OR NOT!, AND RIPLEY'S MIRROR MAZE

601 E. Palace Pkwy., Grand Prairie, 972/263-2391, www.ripleys.com/grandprairie

HOURS: Mon.-Fri. 10 A.M.-5 P.M., Sat.-Sun. 10 A.M.-6 P.M.

COST: For one site: $16.99 adult, $8.99 youth; for two sites: $19.99 adult, $10.99 youth; for all three sites: $25.99 adult, $15.99 youth

A seven-foot Leaning Tower of Pisa and the life of Jesus depicted in wax are just a couple of the sometimes goofy, sometimes amazing sights at these two attractions under one roof. While it's a touch pricey, both of these spots keep the kids happy and the parents amused.

If you only have time for one, choose the Palace of Wax; the Ripley's "odditorium" section relies a bit heavily on photos and two-dimensional displays. The recent addition of the **Ripley's Mirror Maze** supplies additional zing, but it's considered a third attraction and costs extra—believe it or not.

MUSEUM OF BIBLICAL ART

7500 Park Ln., 214/368-4622, www.biblicalarts.org

HOURS: Tues.-Wed., Fri.-Sat. 10 A.M.-5 P.M., Thurs. 10 A.M.-9 P.M., Sun., 1-5 P.M.

COST: $12 adult, $1 seniors and students, students free Thurs. 5-9 P.M.

Devastated by a 2005 fire that destroyed its

building and almost all of its 2,500 pieces of art, the Museum of Biblical Art has been resurrected in 30,000 square feet of stunning new space. Regardless of religious opinion, everyone from the nonbeliever to the devout can agree that the scope, scale, and quality of the works here are something to behold with reverence. Enhanced via hundreds of loaned pieces from other museums as well as private collectors, the exhibit ranges from drawings to sculptures, rare Bibles to massive paintings, as well as items such as the breathtaking solid gold casting of Michelangelo's *Madonna* (the only one in the world). A surprisingly high-echelon list tops the artists represented here: Marc Chagall, Andy Warhol, and John Singer Sargent are but a few of the recognizable names you'll find as you wander the spacious 11 galleries' worth of art. There's a lot here—from the Golden Ziggurat that evokes ancient stepped pyramids to the outdoor sculptures of the Via Dolorosa to the Jewish Ceremonial Art Gallery—so you might want to set aside a couple hours to view it all.

NATIONAL SCOUTING MUSEUM

1329 W. Walnut Hill Ln., Irving, 800/303-3047, www.bsamuseum.org

HOURS: Tues.-Sat. 10 A.M.-5 P.M., Mon. 10 A.M.-7 P.M., Sun. 1 P.M.-5 P.M.

COST: $8 adult, $6 youth or senior, free under 4, $5 scouts

Scouting may be an old tradition, but this museum focusing on the history of the Boy Scouts of America is state-of-the-art. Next door to the Boy Scouts of America's national headquarters in Irving, the site uses every inch of its 50,000 square feet, much of it dedicated to interactive displays and historic campsite dioramas. A shooting range, kayaking zone, derby car race-track, and many other blockbuster activities keep the place well out of the dry, boring museum category. In addition, the museum tells the story of Boy Scouting by way of a robotic Lord Robert S. S. Baden-Powell, the founder of the Scouts, and 500,000 artifacts, including the very first Eagle Scout badge (it's too fragile to be shown consistently—call ahead to see if it's on display). If you and the kids aren't too exhausted, check out the art collection, which boasts the largest number of Norman Rockwell paintings under one roof, on your way out.

Downtown Fort Worth   Map 8

BASS HALL

525 Commerce St., 817/212-4280, www.basshall.com

This 10-story, 2,200 seat performance center, designed by David Schwarz and funded entirely by private contributions, stands as the ostentatious crown jewel of downtown's revitalization. Built in 1998, the hall is guarded by two 50-foot limestone angels, trumpets lifted, as if heralding a new age of Fort Worth culture. In the entranceway, Jimmy Choos click alongside cowboy boots on the cut marble floors that lie underneath the lofty domed ceiling's trompe l'oeil clouds. The performance hall itself follows a horseshoe shape that provides excellent sight lines and even better acoustics, especially important, as it is now the permanent home of the Fort Worth Symphony Orchestra, the Van Cliburn International Piano Competition, the Texas Ballet Theater, and the Fort Worth Opera. The latter may have garnered Bass Hall's first major accolade—in 1998, *Travel + Leisure* magazine deemed it one of the top ten opera houses in the world.

FORT WORTH WATER GARDENS

1502 Commerce St.

Architect Philip Johnson designed this downtown site, consisting of three unique water sculptures, as an oasis in the middle of the city's concrete and skyscrapers. The three pieces are vastly different. The first is a meditation pool, a plane of water as flat as glass that drops off over a 90-degree edge onto a sunken walkway. A more dynamic second pool is made of several

COURTESY OF FORT WORTH CVB

Bass Hall houses many of Fort Worth's performing arts offerings.

BUTCH AND SUNDANCE

While neighboring Dallas boasts an outlaw history with Bonnie and Clyde, Fort Worth brags of its own infamous pair. At the turn of the 20th century, Robert LeRoy Parker, aka **Butch Cassidy,** and Harry Longabaugh, aka the **Sundance Kid,** tore through the West with the Wild Bunch on a killing and robbing spree made famous by the semi-fictional film *Butch Cassidy and the Sundance Kid.* While the pair moved about constantly, they spent a good amount of time in Fort Worth, especially in the gangsters' paradise known as Hell's Half Acre.

Filled with gambling, violence, drinking, and prostitution, Hell's Half Acre might well have boasted the most debauched behavior per square foot of any place west of the Mississippi. Butch and Sundance fit right in. While there, they and few others from the Wild Bunch gussied themselves up and popped into John Swartz's photography studio to get their portrait taken. The photo of the "Fort Worth Five," as they became known, ended up as one of the most recognizable relics of the Wild West.

It also got them into trouble. Some folks claim that the gang, feeling their oats, mailed the portrait to one of the banks they had robbed, which then turned it over to the Pinkerton Detective Agency. Others claim a passing lawman recognized the crooks' picture in Swartz's window. Either way, the photo made its way into Pinkerton hands, and it was used to track down the Wild Bunch, one by one. Pinkerton agents even distributed hundreds of copies in South America, where Butch and Sundance had fled. Sure enough, the two men were found in Bolivia and killed by law enforcement.

Hell's Half Acre eventually succumbed to the progress of law and order, too, and many skyscrapers that house downtown Fort Worth's respected, international businesses sit atop the site of the boisterous old district. The gangsters have even grown respectable—when city fathers revitalized and refurbished downtown, they decided to name its central area, full of family-friendly shops and restaurants, Sundance Square.

small, spraying fountains, while the most popular is the "active pool," in which water falls down four terraced walls into a central square pool (you may recognize it from the 1976 film *Logan's Run*). The effect is both hypnotic and dramatic.

SUNDANCE SQUARE

Between 1st and 5th Sts., from Throckmorton St. to Jones St., www.sundancesquare.com

Named after legendary gangster the Sundance Kid, Sundance Square is 20 square blocks of the revamped downtown Fort Worth, replete with shopping, festivals, bars, restaurants, and sightseeing. The square is a tourist haven, though locals also flock to it for its family-friendly activities and its fun, safe nightlife.

But it wasn't always that way. As a major stop on the Chisholm Trail, Fort Worth in the late 1800s endured its fair share of scallywags and debauched behavior, the most depraved of which occurred in the downtown red-light district known as Hell's Half Acre, right around where Sundance Square sits today. This is where the Sundance Kid, Butch Cassidy, and others of their ilk came to gamble, fight and, er, indulge in other carnal delights.

After years of gunfights, gambling, and political stalling (after all, there's profit in sin), the town powers finally got fed up and began to crack down on the rowdy neighborhood. The area eventually cleaned up, and as time went on, the old bordellos and saloons were replaced by skyscrapers and hotels. By modern times, Hell's Half Acre had grown into a downright respectable downtown.

And it was boring. At least until the Bass family got their hands on it. About a hundred years after the Half-Acre's heyday, one of Fort Worth's richest oil dynasties, the Basses, spearheaded a huge effort to reimagine downtown into a viable entertainment district, a tourist draw, and a moneymaker. The Basses and the city worked together to refurbish the old art deco and turn-of-the-20th-century-style buildings and lured businesses, retail, and entertainment venues back downtown. They designated wide swaths of free parking and

Sundance Square

© KENNY BRAUN/TRAVELTEX.COM

THE TALE OF THE TIN CAN TOWER

There are many different advantages to the location of North Texas, but avoiding tornadoes isn't one of them. DFW sits in the thick of a wide swath of the Midwest known as **Tornado Alley,** and twisters here are more common in the spring than ticks on a hound dog.

Tornadoes often hit rural areas and, somewhat less commonly, suburban areas, but rarely do they hit downtowns. Yet that's just what happened on March 28, 2000, when an F3 tornado ripped through the skyscrapers of downtown Fort Worth.

Two people were killed by the storm, scores more injured, and a four-mile track of damage included 15 destroyed buildings, 17 damaged skyscrapers, and between $450 and 500 million dollars in damage. One of the worst hit buildings was the iconic 37-story Bank One Tower that overlooks Sundance Square. The building, one of the trademark silhouettes of the skyline, sustained extraordinary damage—

most of the windows were shattered, and that, combined with the interior damage, led most to conclude that rebuilding would be too dangerous and expensive. The fifth tallest building in downtown Fort Worth, the tower was slated to be torn down.

But, miraculously, after sitting for about a year covered in plywood and metal—hence its adopted nickname: The Tin Can Tower—the building got a reprieve. Local developer TLC Realty purchased the building and completely restructured it, adding an octagonal facade and an even an extra 34 feet on the top floor. TLC then converted the interior into condos, with a few retail spots on the ground floor, and renamed the property simply, "The Tower." Today, with downtown hopping, The Tower stands at full capacity. The Tower also now measures as the fourth tallest tower in downtown (thanks to that extra 34 feet).

created a security bike patrol with a visible presence.

Today, what was once known as Hell's Half Acre is now a civic centerpiece. Simply walking around staring at renovated buildings like the Worthington National Bank makes for a lovely, and cheap, pastime there. The WNB was built in 1914 and, even though it's a working bank, the building feels more like a meticulously crafted museum re-creation, with iron bars guarding the teller windows, authentic fixtures and decor, and custom-cut marble floors glossed to a high sheen. Other architectural highlights include the Knights of Pythias Hall, a red sandstone edifice replete with turrets and a giant knight, and the Jett Building, on the side of which you'll find Richard Haas's three-story-high mural depicting cowpokes driving cattle on the Chisholm Trail. The open expanse abutting Haas's piece often serves as the epicenter of year-round cultural and civic festivals and events, including everything from huge music fests to open-air movie screenings.

In addition to citywide celebrations,

shopping, nightlife, and architecture, there's also culture. There's probably no better place for the Sid Richardson Museum, for instance, than such a historic locale. This Western art museum commissioned by a the legendary local oilman often falls under the radar in comparison to the Cultural Districts behemoths, but 50,000 visitors a year still come to the modest Sundance Square building that houses works by Remington, Russell, and others.

TARRANT COUNTY COURTHOUSE
100 W. Weatherford St., 817/884-1111

Surrounded by gleaming high-rises, the dramatic Tarrant County Courthouse still commands attention. You might recognize the pink granite structure, built in an opulent American beaux arts style and topped with its signature clock tower, from the TV show *Walker, Texas Ranger.* Construction began on the courthouse in 1893 and didn't end until 1895, at a cost of more than $400,000, thanks in part to the fees of the Kansas City firm who designed it, Gunn and Curtis Architects, and the expense of importing the granite from Austin. The townsfolk, disgusted at what they deemed an unnecessary extravagance, responded by ousting the entire Tarrant County Commissioners'

Court, but nowadays, the building stands as a testament to the vision of Fort Worth's early citizens. Tours aren't given on a regular basis, but can be requested.

TCU and Vicinity   Map 9

ELIZABETH BOULEVARD
Elizabeth Blvd. between 8th and College Aves.

Much like Swiss Avenue in Dallas, Elizabeth Boulevard is rich in history and architectural eye candy. The street, intentionally developed by John C. Ryan as a residential area for the town's oil gentry and professionals, saw its first house built in 1911. Ryan envisioned the neighborhood as an exclusive enclave to rival "Quality Hill," and even had ornate stone entry gates built to mark the area's specialness. From there, house after house followed, each employing its own variation on any number of revival themes: Mission, Mediterranean, Georgian, classical, and others, and some of them bordering on palatial. Smaller touches, such as tiled curb signs and streetlights, add to the rarified atmosphere here, and make a drive or walk down the street a pleasant diversion.

FORT WORTH ZOO
1989 Colonial Pkwy., 817/759-7555,
www.fortworthzoo.org
HOURS: Late Oct.-late Feb. daily 10 A.M.-4 P.M., late Feb.-late Mar. daily 10 A.M.-5 P.M., late Mar.-late Oct. Mon.-Fri. 10 A.M.-5 P.M., Sat.-Sun. 10 A.M.-6 P.M.
COST: $12 adult, $9 youth, $7 senior, free under 2

Well-funded and well-visited, the Fort Worth Zoo practically bursts with animals and activities. Founded in 1909, the zoo fell on hard times in the early 1990s as upkeep faltered and attendance dropped. Soon after, the nonprofit Fort Worth Zoological Society took over fundraising and management, and the zoo rapidly improved. Since then, almost every section has seen expansion and restructuring, resulting in what amounts to an entirely new zoo—one of the best in the country.

The only downside: There are several days' worth of premium exhibits—15 in all—so

choices have to be made. If you only have a day or two, here are some suggestions:

Asian Falls: Carved out of an existing hillside, this is one of the zoo's most popular sites. Visitors make their way down a windy path that includes aboveground boardwalks from which to ogle elephants, rhinos, sun bears, and various hoof stock animals, many of whom cool themselves in the waterfall-fed pools. Dramatic enough, but the real highlight is a pair of rare Malayan tigers, not to mention their feline counterparts across the ravine—a pair of gorgeous white tigers.

Cheetos Cheetahs: The good thing about the Zoological Society is its ability to raise funds from large companies; the flip side is that some of the zoo's most refined and exciting exhibits are plastered with reminders of the corporate side of things, like Frito-Lay's Cheetos. But even the biggest corporate intrusions are quickly forgotten at this exhibit. The area is divided into three separate sections accommodating three different species. The first is a grassy forest clearing, home to African bongos, which are large antelope with dramatic spiraled antlers. The second is also a grassy plain dotted with hills and stands of trees, under which the zoo's group of cheetahs often lounge. The third is the warthog yard, where the hogs are often found cooling off in their mud pool.

Australian Outback/Great Barrier Reef: Sadly, the koala that's been on loan from the San Diego Zoo has been returned, but this exhibit still has plenty of wow factor, most notably the 10,000-gallon aquarium full of colorful fish, coral, and sharks. The reef conjoins with the larger Australian Outback area, home to a number of kangaroos and wallabies.

African Savannah: Giraffes, rhinos, and ostriches compete for attention as visitors

SIGHTS

navigate the overhead boardwalks and ground-level sidewalks.

Komodo Dragons: They don't do much but loll in the sun, but these seven-foot reptiles are still somehow fascinating, as exemplified by the crowds they draw.

Texas Wild!: While it may not have the international appeal of some of the more exotic exhibits, the Texas Wild! habitat is a must-see for anyone interested in the land, flora, and fauna of the Lone Star State. With its size and scope, Texas Wild! could well be a theme park unto itself, as visitors tour around the "habitats" of the state: the Texas Hill Country, High Plains and Prairies, Pineywoods and Swamps, Gulf Coast, Brush Country, and Mountains and Desert sections are filled with animals native to their respective areas. Expect to see armadillos, rattlesnakes, alligators, and big cats, among many other species.

LOG CABIN VILLAGE
2100 Log Cabin Village Ln., 817/392-5881, www.logcabinvillage.org
HOURS: Tues.-Fri. 9 A.M.-4 P.M., Sat.-Sun. 1-5 P.M.
COST: $5 adult, $4.50 youth and senior, free under 3
Tucked away among the trees in verdant Forest Park, Log Cabin Village is a highly interactive living history museum. Visitors can tour the 11 historic log structures, which were relocated from other parts of the state (many of them saved from destruction) and restored to their original look. Each structure embodies a different aspect of 19th-century life. You'll find a one-room schoolhouse, water-powered gristmill, smokehouse, blacksmith shop, herb garden, and humble abodes. Along the way, authentically clad historical interpreters reenact prairie life with demonstrations of candle-making, weaving, and spinning.

Local parents love the village because children's prices are inexpensive and a visit will definitely kill an afternoon. For large groups, a number of different tours and family programs are available, as well as summer camps and adult classes—check the website for details.

OSCAR MONNIG METEORITE GALLERY
2950 W. Bowie St., 817/257-6277, www.monnigmuseum.org
HOURS: Mon.-Fri. 1-4 P.M., Sat. 9 A.M. 4 P.M.
COST: Free
This world-class facility on the campus of Texas Christian University appeals to the science nerd in everyone. Those in the astronomy know laud Oscar Monnig as one of the greatest meteorite collectors and scientists to ever live. His collection, donated to TCU between 1978 and 1986, is considered one of the best ever cataloged.

West Side Fort Worth   Map 10

AMON CARTER MUSEUM
3501 Camp Bowie Blvd., 817/738-1933, www.cartermuseum.org
HOURS: Tues.-Wed. and Fri.-Sat. 10 A.M.-5 P.M., Thurs. 10 A.M.-8 P.M., Sun. noon-5 P.M.
COST: Free
Fort Worth's celebrated oilman and philanthropist Amon G. Carter intended the museum that bears his name to house his 400-piece collection of Western art. He never counted on the vision and foresight of those who took care of his art after he was gone. Carter's collection contained some very important 400 pieces, to be sure, many of them bearing the name Remington or Russell, but the museum's first director, Mitchell A. Wilder, drummed up a vision to surpass even that of his former boss. Carter had envisioned a vibrant museum devoted to Western art, but Wilder interpreted "Western" quite liberally, expanding the collection in unexpected directions. After he took the reins, one of the world's most important and comprehensive collections of American art was born.

The building itself, designed by Philip Johnson, sits quietly atop a museum district hill and admission is free (both the location and cost as per Carter's wishes). Paintings,

COURTESY OF FORT WORTH CVB

Thanks to its founder (and namesake), the Amon Carter Museum is free.

sculpture, and works on paper by 19th- and 20th-century artists as varied as Alexander Calder, Thomas Eakins, and Alfred Stieglitz are housed here next to 21st century video and photographic works from some of today's most well-known artists. The museum also owns more than 30,000 photographic prints and is considered one of the most important photography repositories in the country—more than 4,000 square feet of the museum is dedicated to photographic exhibits alone.

FORT WORTH BOTANIC GARDENS

3220 Botanic Garden Blvd., 817/871-7686, www.fwbg.org
HOURS: Garden Center: Mon.-Fri. 8 A.M.-10 P.M., Sat. 8 A.M.-7 P.M., Sun. 1-7 P.M. (Daylight Savings Time), Mon.-Fri. 8 A.M.-10 P.M., Sat. 8 A.M.-5 P.M., Sun. 1-5 P.M. (Standard Time); Conservatory: Mon.-Sat. 10 A.M.-6 P.M., Sun. 1-6 P.M. (Daylight Savings Time), Mon.-Sat. 10 A.M.-4 P.M., Sun. 1-4 P.M. (Standard Time); Japanese Garden: daily 9 A.M.-7 P.M. (Daylight Savings Time), daily 10 A.M.-2:30 P.M. (Standard Time)
COST: Conservatory: $1 adult and youth, $0.50 senior

and children, free under 4; Japanese Garden: Mon.-Fri. $3 adult, $2 youth, $2.50 senior, free under 4, Sat.-Sun. and holidays $3.50 adult, $1 youth, $3 senior, free under 4

"Lush" doesn't even begin to describe this venue. With three different areas—the Garden Center, Japanese Garden, and Conservatory—and more than 2,500 species of flowers and plants, the Botanic Gardens overflow with color and life. Even though families flock to the verdant surroundings and special musical programs here, almost every path, nook, or corner provides a serenity to go along with the scenery. Favorites among the many gardens include the classic Rose Garden and the seven-acre Japanese Garden, with several picturesque wooden bridges crisscrossing koi ponds and creeks. Docent-guided tours are available.

FORT WORTH MUSEUM OF SCIENCE AND HISTORY

1501 Montgomery St., 817/255-9300, www.fwmuseum.org
HOURS: Mon.-Sat. 10 A.M.-5 P.M., Sun. noon-5 P.M.

COURTESY OF FORT WORTH CVB

The Kimbell Art Museum features an impressive art collection in a world-class building.

COST: $16 general adult, $12 youth and senior, free under 1

This kid-friendly institution has undergone a massive renovation, to mixed effect: Gone are the kitschy exhibits featuring antique dentist tools and ancient cave dwellers performing surgery. In their place has sprung a more contemporary approach, with dozens of interactive stations where young 'uns can get their hands dirty and learn at the same time. The centerpiece of the museum is the IMAX theater (the first of its kind in Texas) and the newly refurbished, state-of-the-art Noble Planetarium. Call for times and prices for both, as they are subject to change.

◖ THE KIMBELL ART MUSEUM
3333 Camp Bowie Blvd., 817/332-8451, www.kimbellart.org
HOURS: Tues.-Thurs. and Sat. 10 A.M.-5 P.M., Fri. noon-8 P.M., Sun. noon-5 P.M.
COST: Free

The Kimbell may not be the largest museum in the world, but the quality of its collection wows art newbies and experts alike. A small but impressive array of classic European works by the masters such as Picasso, Caravaggio, El Greco, Rembrandt, Monet, and other greats takes precedence here. The quality over quantity philosophy applies to the rest of the collection, too, including a significant batch of antiquities as well as Asian, Pre-Columbian, African, and Oceanic art.

The building in which these pieces are displayed, however, might be the Kimbell's most famously lauded work of all. Designed by Louis Kahn, the building is immediately recognizable for its series of repeated barrel vaults which give the edifice a classical yet completely contemporary feel. The genius of the structure, its coherence, symmetry, and timelessness, simply cannot be overstated. Inside, the elegant design provides a seamless viewing experience. Four piers support the vaults at either end, eliminating obtrusive obstructions in the exhibition area, and as the sun diffuses through the endless skylights, the aura is one of reverence.

Admission is always free, but the museum

often charges for special exhibitions, which are half price all day on Tuesday and after 5 P.M. on Friday.

◖ MODERN ART MUSEUM OF FORT WORTH

3200 Darnell St., 817/738-9215, www.themodern.org
HOURS: Tues.-Sat. 10 A.M.-5 P.M.
COST: $10 adult and youth, $4 students and seniors; free under 12, free first Sun. of every month

Thanks mainly to the world-class Kimbell Art Museum, Fort Worth has always enjoyed an international reputation when it comes to art. With the Modern Art Museum of Fort Worth, that rep has skyrocketed. The Modern's permanent collection of top-tier sculpture, paintings, photography, drawings, and mixed media work from the world's greatest artists will wow all comers. There are thousands of works by post–World War II artists like Andy Warhol, Willem de Kooning, Agnes Martin, Yves Klein, Cy Twombly, and Cindy Sherman—to name but a very few—in the permanent collection, but the museum fears neither risk nor wide range, especially when it comes to touring shows.

Then there's the building itself, such a perfect balance between aesthetic comfort and artistic setting that it transforms The Modern from a top museum to a house of visual worship. Designed by Japanese architect Tadeo Ando, the museum is guarded at the door by a massive Richard Serra sculpture that hints at the scale of the delights within. Inside, the cool, dark concrete walls, the smooth-surfaced reflecting pool, and the breeze circulating throughout the high-ceilinged pavilions are soothing and beautiful, but their main purpose is to give the art ample room, without drowning it out. That they do.

The Modern offers tons of educational opportunities and civic events in the form of classes, lectures, tours, a film series called Magnolia at the Modern, and other functions. Especially popular are the First Fridays series, which attracts visitors with evening happy hours and docent-led tours, and the excellent alternative music lineups provided by Spune productions. Call or check the website for details.

◖ THE NATIONAL COWGIRL MUSEUM AND HALL OF FAME

1720 Gendy St., 817/336-4475, www.cowgirl.net
HOURS: Daily 10 A.M.-5 P.M.
COST: $5, free under 2

This fun museum, one of the newest additions to the Cultural District, is as refreshing and spunky as the women it celebrates. Housed in a nouveau art deco building that complements its big brother, the Will Rogers complex, the Cowgirl Museum is much more modern on the inside than you'd think. The three-tiered exhibit space kicks off with cool, glass-based murals that move as you do, a harbinger of the interactive concentration of the whole place. The museum's thousands of artifacts, photos, videos, and films paint a vivid picture of the strength, character, and general giddyup of lady ropers, cowhands, barrel racers, and their chaps-wearing ilk. Mind you, the celebration here doesn't center solely on ladies who were handy with a lariat: The focus expands, rightly, to feisty Western notables as disparate as Patsy Cline, Lady Bird Johnson, and Georgia O'Keeffe.

WILL ROGERS MEMORIAL CENTER

3401 W. Lancaster Ave., 214/392-7469

Smack-dab in the middle of the Cultural District, the 85-acre grounds of this center include a 2,900-seat auditorium, an impressive network of stock and equestrian grounds, and an 8,000-seat coliseum, the first of its kind in the world. Though the complex's trademark piece, the Landmark Pioneer Tower, is highly visible from the outside, its ornate art deco design only hints at the treats indoors: cowboy murals, terrazzo tile, and ornamental adornments embellish much of the interior. The center is used year-round for cultural and sporting events, but is perhaps best known for hosting the Southwestern Exposition and Livestock Show, attended by 800,000 people every year. Overall, the Will Rogers park sees around two million visitors a year—and most folks assume Rogers would've liked every single one.

Greater Fort Worth
Map 11

BUREAU OF PRINTING AND ENGRAVING

9000 Blue Mound Road, 817/231-4000,
www.moneyfactory.gov

HOURS: Aug.-May Mon.-Fri. 8:30 A.M.-3:30 P.M., June and July Mon.-Fri. 8:30 A.M.-5:30 P.M.

COST: Free

One of only two facilities that print U.S. currency (the other is in Washington, DC), the Bureau is a fun, educational excursion that, ironically, won't cost you any money. A tour winds through displays and exhibits that cover the history of U.S. currency and its production process, but the best part is the elevated walkway above the production floor, from which visitors eyeball how money is made, literally. A few things to keep in mind: First, it's advisable to arrive at least 30 minutes before your tour is scheduled to begin, as there's a bit of security rigmarole to navigate beforehand. Second, the 45-minute tours fill up on a first-come, first-served basis for walk-up visitors and begin every

half-hour. Those who have to wait can check out the Visitor Center's informational film, displays, and gift shop, so the wait isn't too boring. The final tour begins at 2 P.M., except in June and July, when the final tour begins at 4 P.M.

FORT WORTH STOCKYARDS NATIONAL HISTORIC DISTRICT

131 E. Exchange Blvd., 817/336-4373,
www.fortworthstockyards.org

HOURS: Mon.-Fri. 11:30 A.M. and 4 P.M.

COST: Free

Fort Worth has not forgotten its history—it's alive and well and can be enjoyed by all at the Stockyards. The Fort Worth Stockyards National Historic District is the actual hub of livestock commerce that gave Fort Worth its fame on the Chisholm Trail. The original buildings, live music, and cowboys, all of which are still there, make this a part of town that you don't want to miss. In fact, every day,

© KENNY BRAUN/TRAVELTEX.COM

Fort Worth Stockyards National Historic District

history appears in the cobblestone streets of the Stockyards in the form of 15 braying longhorns and their drovers—the Fort Worth Herd. Cowboys decked out in authentic period gear guide the cattle along Exchange Boulevard, just like they did in the old days, as the great beasts groan and mew, kicking up dust—an impressive sight.

SIX FLAGS HURRICANE HARBOR

1800 E. Lamar Blvd., Arlington, 817/640-8900, www.sixflags.com/hurricaneHarborTexas

HOURS: Vary

COST: Varies

Texas summers can be, well, brutal, and a good way to beat the heat is to hit up Hurricane Harbor water park. The park opened in the 1990s, and ever since then has been added rides and attractions of increasingly thrilling proportions, culminating in 2009's **Mega Wedgie,** in which thrill-seekers drop four stories down a giant slide, only to be propelled back up another slide, then back down. A longtime favorite is **Der Stuka,** with its 72-foot free-fall drop.

If that's not quite your speed, more mellow rides are available, including ones for very young children. Overpriced theme park food abounds here, of course. No coolers are allowed, so expect to shell out some cash. Similarly, entry fees are expensive—check the website for special deals, discounts, and passes. Prices and times vary seasonally and even day-to-day, so call or check the website for details.

SIX FLAGS OVER TEXAS

2201 Road to Six Flags, Arlington, 817/640-8900, www.sixflags.com/overTexas

HOURS: Vary

COST: Varies

As the original birthplace of the theme park chain that bears its name, the Six Flags in Arlington holds a special place in the hearts of roller-coaster lovers. Of course, nowadays, much of the park is taken up with corporate-themed screamers like Warner Bros.' Mr. Freeze and Superman coasters—which will do their job to set your heart pounding—but nostalgists will still find plenty of thrills in the Shock Wave (one of the first roller coasters to have two upside-down loops, and to go backwards), and the Judge Roy Scream, one of the last all-wood coasters in the country, which loops and lopes over eight acres of lakes. Prices and times vary seasonally and even day-to-day, so call or check the website for details.

TEXAS COWBOY HALL OF FAME

128 E. Exchange Ave., Historic Barn A, 817/626-7131, www.texascowboyhalloffame.org

HOURS: Mon.-Thurs. 10 A.M.-6 P.M., Fri.-Sat. 10 A.M.-7 P.M., Sun. 11 A.M.-5 P.M.

COST: $5 adult, $4 student and senior, $3 youth

If you're looking for a place that hammers home Texas's ranch 'n' range heritage, you've moseyed into the right place. It's easy to fall into stereotypical cowboy parlance upon entering: The place is housed, after all, in a mule barn that was built in 1888, burned down after a stray railway spark lit a fire, and then rebuilt in 1912 as the first "fireproof" barn. Exhibits cover several aspects of Texas history, including the Chisholm Trail; horse bits and wagons; and heroes of the Texas Republic, along with an interactive exploratorium for kids. While true cowboys like bootmaker John Justin and 17-time rodeo champion J. J. Hampton receive special emphasis, "cowboy" is interpreted loosely here, incorporating "the Texas men and women who have excelled in the sport and business of rodeo and the western lifestyle." That latter part explains inductees like Nolan Ryan and Tommy Lee Jones, but who can argue with their leathery cachet? It's all part of the fun.

RESTAURANTS

For years Dallas-Fort Worth dining has been all about the dichotomy of big and small. Some folks call the former "power dining"—we want the most illustrious chefs and the largest scoop of caviar. Venerable restaurants have long swept us off our feet with classic fare.

But slowly, DFW has begun to rediscover its neighborhoods, and in doing so, it has begun to embrace inventive menus filled with local, organic ingredients. The result has been scores of new hyper-local hangouts, each buzzing with friends and neighbors sharing small plates and big steaks.

As you might imagine, steak houses here are about as ubiquitous as Starbucks—with the surplus of fine options for fillets, sirloins, and T-bones in such abundance that meat eaters will practically be slobbering on the sidewalk.

Meanwhile, if you prefer your meat hickory-smoked and slathered in sauce, there's always that other famous Texas cuisine: barbecue. No trip to DFW is complete without sampling what local restaurant critic Dotty Griffith calls "the most American food." For all the lovely upscale dining to be had, a $6 barbecue brisket sandwich really can't be beat.

The other low-budget, high-cal cuisine for which DFW is known is Tex-Mex. For folks who grew up on this hybrid of American and south-of-the-border tastes, the gooey cheeses, fried tortillas, and chili con carne sauces are second nature. Most Tex-Mex is affordable, even when coupled with a traditional margarita, but it has slowly made its way into middle and upper levels of cuisine.

© MARCOS ORTEGA

RESTAURANTS

HIGHLIGHTS

LOOK FOR ◖ TO FIND RECOMMENDED RESTAURANTS.

COURTESY OF REATA

Reata

◖ **Best Retro Experience:** Even though the zodiac-themed wallpaper and *Mad Men* aesthetic have long been replaced by bright colors and sleek tables, **The Zodiac** still evokes an era when there were ladies who lunched, and when they lunched, they wore hats (page 63).

◖ **Best Steak:** Most high-end steakhouses don't provide TVs tuned to ESPN, but this is Dallas, remember? Settle into a cozy leather booth, order one of the best steaks in a town full of them, and bask in the boys' club atmosphere of **Bob's Steak and Chophouse** (page 70).

◖ **Best Soufflés:** Either in savory or sweet form, the soufflés at **Rise No. 1** will have you rethinking the egg (page 72).

◖ **Best Down-Home Cookin':** Expect long lines at **Bubba's,** a neighborhood institution, especially after church on Sunday, when you can only pray they don't run out of fried chicken (page 73).

◖ **Best Chicken-Fried Steak:** Flavorful, fried in a light, crisp batter, and never greasy, the chicken-fried steak at the **AllGood Café,** a funky Deep Ellum cornerstone, comes in Frisbee-size servings; it makes a great leftover breakfast the next day (page 79).

◖ **Best People-Watching:** Before the tornado that blasted it from the top floor of the Bank One Tower, Fort Worth institution **Reata** really had a view. No matter: Its new location on the admittedly lower rooftop of the former Caravan of Dreams provides a bird's-eye view of the goings-on at Sundance Square (page 81).

◖ **Best Barbecue:** It's a tie: You'll smell like smoke for days after gorging on **Angelo's** tender brisket, fall-off-the-bone ribs (page 82). Then again, the **Railhead Smokehouse**'s woodsmoke sauce can't be beat (page 83).

◖ **Best Breakfast:** The chile-slathered Tex-Mex breakfasts at **Esperanza's Mexican Bakery and Café** prove there is a deity of some sort running things. How else to explain the heavenly *migas* (page 85)?

◖ **Best Burger:** Nobody really knows the secret behind **Kincaid's** hamburgers, but considering the constant stream of patrons who frequent the venerable Camp Bowie spot, it doesn't matter (page 86).

◖ **Best Grocery Store:** Westsiders have loved the epicurean, locally owned **Roy Pope Grocery** since 1943 (page 86).

◖ **Best Use of An Exotic Animal:** **Lonesome Dove** proprietor Tim Love's effusive creativity is no more apparent than in his varied use of kangaroo meat (page 89).

PRICE KEY

💲 Most entrées less than $10

💲💲 Most entrées $10-20

💲💲💲 Most entrées more than $20

With its fearless melding of flavors and aesthetics, Tex-Mex might just be the most democratic of foods, and that's the beauty of it: There are no boundaries here. From power dining to organic salads, from top chefs to taco carts, DFW leaves no palate disappointed.

Downtown Dallas   Map 1

AMERICAN
CAPITAL GRILLE 💲💲💲
500 Crescent Ct., #135, 214/303-0500, www.thecapitalgrille.com
HOURS: Mon.-Thurs. 11 A.M.-2:30 P.M. and 5-10 P.M., Fri. 11 A.M.-2:30 P.M. and 5-11 P.M., Sat. 5-11 P.M., Sun. 5-10 P.M.
Nouveau-foodies and vegetarians need not bother entering the Capital Grille, the expertly run, classic high-end grill housed in one of Dallas's fanciest hotels. Steak lovers and those who long for the days of three-martini lunches, however, will feel right at home amid the glossy mahogany, the booths of stitched buttery leather, and the gleaming brass railings. An exercise in refined simplicity, the menu here represents a similar perfection of timeless aesthetic. The culinary centerpiece is definitely steak—dry-aged cuts, many of them accented only by au jus—along with seafood offerings and rich side dishes like béchamel creamed spinach. And you can expect four-star service, from the valet to the sommelier.

STEPHAN PYLES 💲💲💲
1807 Ross Ave., 214/580-7000, www.stephanpyles.com
HOURS: Mon.-Wed. 11:30 A.M.-2 P.M. and 6-10:30 P.M., Thurs.-Fri. 11:30 A.M.-2 P.M. and 6-11 P.M., Sat. 6-11 P.M.
As one of the godfathers of upscale Southwestern cuisine, Stephan Pyles already enjoyed a fabled reputation as an innovator; with the 2006 opening of his eponymous restaurant smack in the middle of the Arts District, he cemented his legacy. Pyles has created a menu that builds on his history of infusing American fine dining with Latin traditions and flavors, and the results have enticed the crème fraîche of Dallas's social crop. The menu (executed by executive chef Tim Byres) includes Pyles's famous giant Cowboy Ribeye, but it's the ample variations on ceviche that have pulled in scores of usually meat-hungry Texans every night. Other seafood is also co piously—and inventively—represented on the menu, along with creative spins on everything from gazpacho to poached pear. The decor is just as singular, its interwoven copper bands, updated Southwestern landscape photography, and antler sculptures reflective of what Pyles calls "New Millennium Southwestern cuisine."

◖ THE ZODIAC 💲💲💲
Neiman Marcus, 1618 Main St., Sixth Floor, 214/573-5000, www.neimanmarcus.com
HOURS: Mon.-Sat. 11 A.M.-3:30 P.M.
Zodiac is a celebrated bastion of almost-lost elegance. While groovy zodiac-sign wallpaper once adorned the walls, the room now indulges in a more understated (and slightly more generic) modern sleekness, but the menu is much the same as it was back when socialite shoppers and oil barons made this *the* place to lunch. When you eat here, tradition suggests ordering the renowned Mandarin Orange Soufflé, preceded by popovers slathered with strawberry butter, but much of the menu (which still bears the touch of legendary chef Helen Corbitt) makes for a classic and luscious meal. Be aware that The Zodiac doesn't accept Visa or MasterCard.

ASIAN
KENICHI 💲💲💲
2400 Victory Park Ln., 214/871-8883, www.kenichirestaurants.com

RESTAURANTS

HOURS: Sun.-Thurs. 5:30-10 P.M., Fri.-Sat. 5:30-11 P.M.

It's a bit pricey at this upscale spot for sushi and Asian fusion dishes, but the food isn't the only draw here: you're paying for the hip decor and modern sensibility. Young Dallas flocks to Kenichi (one of a chain of locations in upscale areas like Aspen and Kona) for elegantly presented sushi and inventive cocktails. Small plates and entrees draw on influences broader than Japan and feature ingredients and techniques from Asia and beyond. The "hot rock" appetizer features seafood, veggies, or meat seared on a rock heated to 1,000 degrees.

TEI AN $$

1722 Routh St., 214/220-2828, www.tei-an.com

HOURS: Sun., Tues.-Thurs., 11:30 A.M.-2 P.M. and 6-10:30 P.M., Fri. 11:30 A.M.-2 P.M. and 5:30-10:30 P.M., Sat. 6-10:30 P.M.

Firm and toothsome house-made soba is the dish that brings the cravings at this upscale Japanese restaurant in the Arts District. Get the cooling zaru soba for a classic dish that showcases the terrific buckwheat noodles, or have a gussied-up version like the tea-infused green soba topped with tender, deeply flavored chashu pork. Chef/owner Teiichi Sakura creates authentic Japanese flavors in a serene space with a rooftop patio perfect for date night. Looking for something to go along with your soba? Don't miss the white seaweed salad or the pristine sashimi. One of Dallas's best sake selections, too.

FRENCH
THE FRENCH ROOM $$$

1321 Commerce St., 214/742-8200, www.hoteladolphus.com/adolphus_dining.aspx

HOURS: Tues.-Sat. 6-9:30 P.M.

The French Room is the gastronomic equivalent of *The Queen Mary* in its heyday—opulent, palatial, and ornate, but with the goods to back it up. Just entering the room is akin to traveling back to the high court of Versailles: The floor is a fine, green marble, the ceilings painted with chunky cherubs, the walls literally gilded. The food might as well be gilded, too, as rich and finely wrought as it is. élan. If you splurge on

just one restaurant in Dallas, it should be this one. Jackets required.

MEDITERRANEAN
SAMAR BY STEPHAN PYLES $$$

2100 Ross Ave., 214/922-9922, www.samarrestaurant.com

HOURS: Mon.-Thurs. 11 A.M.-2 P.M. and 5-10 P.M., Fri. 11 A.M.-2 P.M. and 5-11 P.M., Sat. 5-11 P.M.

Small plates that draw on the complexly flavored and exotically spiced dishes of India, Spain, and the Mediterranean: If the menu at Samar sounds ambitious, maybe that's because Samar (full name, Samar by Stephan Pyles) is the brainchild of the chef who almost single-handedly created Southwestern cuisine. Samar threads its culinary way through these diverse countries, offering dynamic dishes like squash blossoms stuffed with haloumi and sensitively spiced Indian favorites from the tandoor oven. Dishes from the Spanish page of the menu include both the familiar (sautéed padron peppers) and the exotic (foams and colloids inspired by Spain's legendary El Bulli). In the unlikely event you aren't transported by the food, the evening-at-the-casbah decor and outdoor hookah lounge will most certainly put you in a global mood.

SEAFOOD
TRULUCK'S $$$

2401 McKinney Ave., 214/220-2401, www.trulucks.com

HOURS: Sun.-Thurs. 11 A.M.-2 P.M. and 5-10 P.M., Fri. 11 A.M.-2 P.M. and 5-11 P.M., Sat. 5-11 P.M.

Even amid the glitz and glam of McKinney Avenue, the bright green and blue light trimming the Truluck's building is hard to miss, not so much for the sizzle of the neon light, but for the constant stream of Uptowners entering and exiting. There's a reason they're there: If you're craving crab legs in landlocked Dallas, Truluck's should be your number one choice. Inside, the well-lit, art deco interior is swank but welcoming, as is the service. It's a bit overpriced, but since Truluck's almost always delivers a fine specimen from the ocean deep (thanks to their own fisheries in Florida and on the Isle of Capri), consider it a consistency tax.

THE BEST TACO YOU'LL EVER EAT AT A TRUCK STOP

Fuel City is open 24 hours, and there is always a line.

Fuel City is the type of place street food obsessives dream about. Only, technically, **Fuel City** (801 S. Riverfront Blvd., Dallas 75207, 214/426-0011) is not on the street—it's a gigantic truck stop/gas station, lording over an unholy chunk of real estate at the nexus of what used to be called Industrial Boulevard (the name says it all) and I-35.

It's not the most picturesque locale, but the atmosphere actually provides part of the fun. The parking lot is a scene in itself, as a constant stream of lowriders and big rigs navigate around the pavement. Behind the building is a small grassy plot, home to a few longhorn cattle, and a swimming pool, home to several bikini-clad young women hired to hang out there. Seriously.

Once you're inside, however, you've reached taco nirvana. The taqueria is open 24 hours a day. Expect a line no matter what the clock says (word of great tacos travels fast in these parts). Two things are essential when you order: First, choose the moist, thick corn tortillas over flour, and second, try the picadillo, named the best

taco in Texas by venerable *Texas Monthly* magazine. You'll never encounter a more perfect mixture of flavors: spicy, chile laced ground beef, soft potato chunks, and onions. The pastor taco comes in a very close second, with asada-style marinated beef, onion, cilantro, and a hell of a kick to it on the back end. The tacos all come with two types of salsa—tomatillo and red—about which there is much debate: Some say there's already such a perfect blend of flavors, the sauces are unnecessary. Others claim they'll send your palate into spasms of joy.

A stop at the *elotes* (a cup filled with roasted corn, sour cream, butter, lemon pepper, and cayenne pepper) cart on your way out might seem indulgent, but this is Fuel City, so go for it!

The food at Fuel City is cash-only, but you won't need that much (the tacos top out at about $1.25 each), and don't forget to grab yourself a beer from the swimming-pool-size ice cooler or one of the many Mexican sodas available—either is a perfect chaser for the spicy meat and salsas.

COURTESY DAVE HENSLEY

RESTAURANTS

STEAK HOUSE

DAKOTA'S ❸❸❸
600 N. Akard St., 214/740-4001,
www.dakotasrestaurant.com
HOURS: Mon.-Thurs. 11 A.M.-2:30 P.M. and 5:30-10 P.M.,
Fri. 11 A.M.-2:30 P.M. and 5:30-10:30 P.M.,
Sat. 5:30-10:30 P.M.

There's more than just aesthetics behind Dakota's sunken garden-patio dining area, found at the crowded nexus of skyscrapers known as One Arts Plaza. Seems the property now occupied by the classy eatery was once owned by the First Baptist Church, which contractually forbade future owners from selling alcohol "on the grounds." Dakota's proprietors circumvented the obligation through a little creative excavating, building *below* the grounds. A happy side result was Dakota's intimate, unique outdoor area, complete with ivy-laden walls, a lush fountain, and, of course, some of the best steaks around.

Y.O. RANCH STEAKHOUSE ❸❸❸
702 Ross Ave., 214/744-3287,
www.yoranchsteakhouse.com
HOURS: Mon.-Thurs. 11 A.M.-10 P.M., Fri. 11 A.M.-11 P.M.,
Sat. noon-11 P.M., Sun. noon-10 P.M.

One of the few non-chain restaurants in the touristy West End, the Y.O. Ranch Steakhouse leans heavily on cowboy cachet—as the stuffed animal heads and yee-haw decor proves. Expect the usual Texas attention to beef, along with wild game surprises like the signature buffalo filet mignon.

TEX-MEX

IRON CACTUS ❸❸
1520 Main St., 214/749-4766,
www.ironcactus.com/dallas.asp
HOURS: Sun.-Wed. 11 A.M.-11 P.M., Thurs. 11 A.M.-midnight, Fri.-Sat. 11 A.M.-2 A.M.

The food at the Iron Cactus is fair-to-middling, but the view and the tequila can't be beat. Seriously, there's nothing more heavenly than grabbing a balcony table here at sunset—so much the better if the sun goes down around happy hour, when you should indulge in Dallas's most popular cocktail, the margarita. The concoctions here range from traditional to inventive, and all are made with fresh-squeezed lime juice and top-notch choices from the extensive tequila menu. If you prefer cutting straight to the source, try a flight of

---

TEX-MEX IS BETTER THAN SEX

For the uninitiated—or for those who like to eat, you know, healthy—a rundown of the cornerstones of Tex-Mex is perplexing: Processed cheese? Lard-laden refried beans? Vats of sour cream? What exactly is it about the combination of these ingredients that beckons to Texans so strongly? What makes Tex-Mex so special?

It can't be explained. You'll just know it when you taste it. Here are some suggested spots to begin your Tex-Mex education:

A little less junky than many of its ilk, **Manny's Uptown Tex-Mex Restaurant** (3521 Oak Grove Ave., 214/252-1616) is a good place to start. This place is well-pedigreed (it's owned by a member of the Mi Cocina family), and it's found in a cute frame house, tucked away from the hustle and bustle of Uptown. Inside, there's plenty of hustle and bustle, however, as the menu's specialty offerings like a luscious, spicy sunset dip (chile con queso with hot peppers) and unique takes on old faves keep the crowds coming consistently.

For a more straightforward approach, check out **Herrera's Café** (4001 Maple Ave., 214/528-9644), a family-owned BYOB place whose long menu can prove intimidating to the uninitiated. Stick to the basics until you get used to it. Try one of the many combination plates available, and make sure to include at least one beef enchilada. Also make sure you don't fill up too much on the hot, hot salsa, fresh chips, and corn tortillas with butter before your meal arrives!

Good tortillas are key to good Tex-Mex, and at **El Ranchito** (610 W. Jefferson Blvd., 75208, 214/946-4238) they're made fresh on the festive, faux-authentic premises. From this base are built the cornerstones of the cuisine: crisp bean chalupas, peppery fajitas, and dense, classic enchiladas.

tequila, with three half-ounce samplers of your choice. Of course, with all of this booze, it's best to eat something. Choose carefully from this hit-or-miss menu: Try the much-improved ceviche, or the ever-popular chile con queso—it's hard to mess up cheese.

Uptown Dallas Map 2

AMERICAN

AL BIERNAT'S ❸❸❸

4217 Oak Lawn Ave., 214/219-2201,
www.albiernats.com
HOURS: Mon.-Fri. 11:30 A.M.-2:30 P.M. and 5:30-10 P.M.,
Sat. 5:30-11 P.M., Sun. 11 A.M.-2:30 P.M. and 5:30-9 P.M.

You know you're in a upscale restaurant when the chef uses expensive ingredients to sauce other even more expensive ingredients. At Al Biernat's—a classic steak house that draws athletes, politicians, and other Dallas elites—a dish called "Air, Land, and Sea" features quail, buffalo, and prawns sauced with foie gras. Yes, it's as expensive as you imagine, but the steaks and chops are exquisite—Waygu filet mignon, Niman Ranch wet-aged fillet and porterhouse steaks for two, specialty-producer pork and lamb. Attentive, professional service; white tablecloths; and private club-style decor complete the monied atmosphere.

BREADWINNERS ❸❸

3301 McKinney Ave., 214/754-4940,
www.breadwinnerscafe.com
HOURS: Mon. 8 A.M.-4 P.M., Tues.-Thurs. 8 A.M.-4 P.M.
and 5-10 P.M., Fri.-Sat. 8 A.M.-4 P.M. and 5-11 P.M.,
Sun. 9 A.M.-3 P.M. and 6-5 P.M.

First, a word of warning: If you're hitting up this charming brick-and-ivy spot for a weekend breakfast, you'll be hard-pressed to score a table in less than an hour. But if you're a fan of thick slabs of caramel-infused French toast or giant, savory crepes, it's worth the wait. For those in need of a bit of the hair of the dog, you can't beat the refreshing frozen peach Bellini, which serves to mitigate the pain of waiting. Breadwinners also serves up hearty lunch salads and an upscale dinner menu.

CAFÉ EXPRESS ❸

3230 McKinney Ave., 214/999-9444,
www.cafe-express.com
HOURS: Daily 11 A.M.-11 P.M.

Although it's a chain, Café Express is a handy spot for a quick, inexpensive lunch or dinner. The wide-ranging menu of soups, pastas, salads, and sandwiches is tailor-made for groups with disparate tastes or for those days when you just can't decide what you want. There's not really a bad choice here, but it's essential to pair your meal with the house-made limeade. There is a second location at 5307 Mockingbird Lane (214/841-9444).

DISH ❸❸

4123 Cedar Springs Rd., 214/522-3474,
www.dish-dallas.com
HOURS: Sun. 11 A.M.-2:30 P.M. and 5-10 P.M.,
Tues.-Thurs. 5-10 P.M., Fri.-Sat. 5-11 P.M.

Whether you hanker for DJ beats or well-grilled meats, at Dish you can satisfy many desires at once. Dish features a slate of well-prepared comfort foods that make good use of seasonal ingredients. Graze your way through the menu of shareable small plates (don't miss the popular flatbreads) while sipping on innovative cocktails made from fresh juices and interesting herbs, all served in a clean, modern atmosphere that exudes cool. Pull out your finest feather boa for Dish's once-a-month "drag brunch."

EATZI'S ❸

3500 Oak Lawn Ave., 214/525-1515,
www.eatzis.com
HOURS: Daily 7 A.M.-10 P.M.

The epicurean groceries available are a delight, but they still play second fiddle to Eatzi's ample to-go offerings. The square footage of this place barely holds its huge deli (packed with things like Kobe meat loaf and crab cakes, as well as simpler fare), plus the grill, the salad bar, the sandwich bar, the pasta bar, and the pre-packed

RESTAURANTS

items, all of which supply restaurant-quality food to take back to your office, apartment, or hotel room. The convenience comes at a bit of a markup, but there are still deals to be had: The rotisserie chicken dinner, which comes with sides and corn bread, is a succulent steal, and every night around 9 P.M., patrons crowd like vultures around the pre-packed station, waiting for the evening "red dot" clear-out specials.

HUNKY'S ❶

4000 Cedar Springs Rd., 214/522-1212,
www.hunkys.com

HOURS: Sun.-Thurs. 11 A.M.-10 P.M., Fri.-Sat. noon-11 P.M.

In Dallas, you don't crave just a burger—you crave a Hunky's. This 1950s diner-themed institution has held down its spot at the epicenter of gay Dallas long enough to be considered an institution. The made-to-order burgers, perfectly fried tater tots and onion rings, and handmade shakes are so beloved, you'll need good luck to find a table during lunch hour.

THE MANSION RESTAURANT ❶❶❶

2821 Turtle Creek Blvd., 214/443-4747

HOURS: Mon.-Thurs. 6:30-10:30 A.M., 11:30 A.M.-2 P.M., and 6-10 P.M.; Fri. 6:30-10:30 A.M., 11:30 A.M.-2 P.M., and 6-11 P.M.; Sat. 7-10:30 A.M., 11:30 A.M.-2 P.M., and 6-11 P.M.; Sun. 7-10:30 A.M., 11:30 A.M.-2 P.M., and 6-10 P.M.

Ripples of fear surged through town in 2006 when The Mansion first began a belated retooling. After all, this may be the most storied, most respected restaurant in all of Dallas's history. It's here that so many heads of state have dined, where famed chef Dean Fearing perfected his tortilla soup, where power dining established its first Dallas foothold 28 years ago. The fear proved unfounded. The Mansion has not suffered a foolish attempt to keep up with trends; rather, it has been renovated, reenergized, and reinvigorated.

The feeling of exclusive luxury begins before you even step inside. While many four-star hotels feel the need to flash their opulence, The Mansion is tucked away in the lush Turtle Creek greenbelt. This place indeed served as the palatial estate of a cotton magnate, and the detailed touches still make it feel like home.

COURTESY OF ARCODORO & POMODORO

Arcodoro & Pomodoro

ITALIAN

ARCODORO & POMODORO ❶❶

2708 Routh St., 214/871-1924, www.arcodoro.com

HOURS: Mon.-Wed. 11 A.M.-3 P.M. and 5-10 P.M., Thurs.-Fri. 11 A.M.-3 P.M. and 5-11 P.M., Sat. 5-11 P.M.

Two Sardinian brothers own this spot—half hip café, half refined for the stuffier set—and they've done their island proud, serving up toothsome versions of authentic Italian dishes, much of it based on homemade pastas, but also with a tasty nod to the seafood perfected in their homeland.

NONNA ❶❶❶

4115 Lomo Alto Dr., 214/521-1800,
www.nonnadallas.com

HOURS: Fri. 11:30 A.M.-2 P.M., Mon.-Sat. 5:30 P.M.-close

The buzz around chef/owner Julian Barsotti's Nonna began well before the bistro's late-2007 opening, and with good reason. Although the service is spotty, this is food with a good deal of thought behind it, well-considered and stunningly executed. The menu (comprised of sustainable ingredients) changes nightly, but expect handmade pastas, handmade sausages, delicate

RESTAURANTS

Nepalese pizza crusts and wonderful seafood, all in an elegant, minimalist atmosphere.

MEDITERRANEAN
COSMIC CAFÉ $$
2912 Oak Lawn Ave., 214/521-6157,
www.cosmiccafedallas.com
HOURS: Mon.-Thurs. 11 A.M.-10:30 P.M.,
Fri.-Sat. 11 A.M.-11 P.M., Sun. noon-10 P.M.

Cosmic Café's elaborate, colorful building certainly stands out from the glitz, glam, and commerce of Uptown, as does the delicious vegetarian food and Zen-infused atmosphere. The interior dining area of this casual café is a bohemian oasis, though the tasty, thoughtful menu, influenced by Mediterranean and Indian cuisine, appeals to all walks of life. The samosas, dahl, and chutneys are to die for. This is the perfect spot for a healthy lunch, but be prepared to succumb to the slower pace of the place.

SEAFOOD
HOOK, LINE & SINKER $$
3103 Lemmon Ave., 214/965-0707
HOURS: Sun.-Thurs. 11 A.M.-10 P.M., Fri.-Sat. 11 A.M.-11 P.M.

How this bustling faux fish shack—replete with rusty boat gear, paddles, and other briny accoutrements—pulls off the miracle of serving deep-fried catfish that's almost greaseless is anybody's guess, but why question a good thing? Not that the menu is particularly light, what with ample cornmeal-fried delights like shrimp, hush puppies, and taters, or other goodies like oysters and gumbo. Thankfully, though the food may stretch your waistband, it won't stretch your budget.

SOUTHERN
LUCKY'S $
3531 Oak Lawn Ave., 214/522-3500,
www.luckysdallas.com
HOURS: Daily 7 A.M.-11 P.M.

The breakfast scene at Lucky's, the welcoming corner diner in the midst of the gay-friendly Oak Lawn area, is as buzzing and social as a night out at the clubs down the street. The food is straightforward diner here—giant, gooey omelets, steak and eggs, large strips of bacon—but the crowd is definitely not straight, and the menu is all-encompassing. Despite the happy clatter around them, the staff remains friendly and

RESTAURANTS

© JONANNA WIDNER

Have a hearty breakfast at Lucky's.

efficient, and the kitchen is quick and handy with a griddle.

STEAK HOUSE

🄲 BOB'S STEAK AND CHOPHOUSE $$$
4300 Lemmon Ave., 214/528-9446, www.bobs-steakandchop.com
HOURS: Mon.-Thurs. 5-10 P.M., Fri.-Sat. 5-11 P.M.

The nondescript windowless, low-lying building that houses Bob's Lemmon Avenue location is plunked on the very corner where the street starts getting, shall we say, sketchy. But the constant line of cars and ever-hustling valets tell the story of just how different it must be inside. Pass through these famous doors, and there's an entirely different world—a man's world, really, with large leather booths flanked by dark walls and horse racing memorabilia. The stiff drinks and TVs (hey, this is Dallas, where watching sports is essential, even when you're fine-dining) only bolster the boys' club effect. It's actually the perfect environment for cutting into the most celebrated steak in town, and you might even spot a celeb or two while you're doing it (if you consider Tony Romo a celebrity).

Park Cities
Map 3

AMERICAN

AUSTINUTS $
6915 Hillcrest Ave., 512/323-6887, www.austinuts.com
HOURS: Mon.-Sat. 10 A.M.-6 P.M.

This Dallas satellite of Austin's favorite nut house is a godsend when you're looking for gift baskets, gourmet snacks, or just a tasty treat. Austinuts specializes in perfectly roasted and flavored nuts and fancy-pants chocolates, often presented in Texas kitchen-chic packaging. While the products are a bit pricey, they are stunningly good (and fresh!).

DUPRE'S SHORT STOP $
6920 Snider Plaza, 214/360-0311
HOURS: Mon.-Fri. 8 A.M.-6 P.M., Sat. 9:30 A.M.-2:30 P.M.

If you need a quick meal on the go, Dupre's is a great alternative to fast food. Tucked away in the swank Highland Park Village shopping center, this mostly takeout spot offers sandwiches, salads, soups, oven-ready meals, and even breakfast. Parking can be a bit of a hassle, but it's well worth it to avoid the high cost of many of the local restaurants, or if you just want a quiet evening meal without having to cook or order in.

GOFF'S HAMBURGERS $
6401 Hillcrest Ave., 214/520-9133, www.goffshamburger.com
HOURS: Daily 11 A.M.-9 P.M.

Goff's is a Dallas institution, though it has moved from its longtime location on Lovers Lane and changed owners (the legendary former proprietor had a habit of peppering his patrons with insults before serving them their food). The patties are your general, well-seasoned beef variety, but it's Goff's hickory sauce, secret-recipe relish, and shredded cheddar that make burgers so transcendent. The menu also includes hot dogs and a few other grill items, but most folks stick with the burgers—and wisely so.

HIBISCUS $$$
2927 N. Henderson Ave., 214/827-2927, www.hibiscusdallas.com
HOURS: Mon.-Sat. 5-11 P.M.

Hibiscus has managed to quietly coerce the chophouse into the 21st century (a tough thing to do in Dallas). The traditional low lighting, leather furniture, and manly touches remain—and a steak, of course, is still a steak—so Hibiscus finds its niche with its chic Uptown vibe. This could be annoying or appealing, depending on your mind-set, but the stunningly good steaks and sides eventually win everybody over.

KATHLEEN'S SKY DINER $$
4424 Lovers Ln., 214/691-2355
HOURS: Mon.-Thurs. 7 A.M.-10 P.M., Fri. 7 A.M.-11 P.M., Sat.-Sun. 8 A.M.-10 P.M.

Formerly known as Kathleen's Art Café, Kathleen's Sky Diner switched from a folk-artsy aesthetic to more of a concept café revolving around a travel theme. No matter what the motif, the spot is an excellent choice for a long lunch filled with updated comfort food, like the scrumptious meat-loaf sandwich, or slightly more refined fare, such as bite-size ravioli with fresh tomato and basil sauce. Beware: Kathleen's is known for great food but occasionally rude service.

NEIGHBORHOOD SERVICES ❸❸❸
5027 W. Lovers Ln., 214/350-5027,
www.neighborhoodservicesdallas.com
HOURS: Mon.-Thurs. 5-10 P.M., Fri.-Sat. 5-11 P.M.

Just because the name sounds like it should be offering sliding-scale mental health counseling, don't assume you can't get a great meal at Neighborhood Services. High-end American comfort food is chef/owner Nick Badovinus's passion, and Neighborhood Services delivers. The chuck-and-brisket cheeseburger is a towering ode to the pleasures of saturated fat—it's consistently rated one of the best upscale burgers in town. You can't go wrong with the nightly special, which ranges from rabbit to chicken potpie. It's all served in an atmosphere that dovetails perfectly with the food: comfy but polished. One caveat: Neighborhood Services does not provide the service of reservations—at peak times, be prepared for a wait, though you can call ahead to put your name on the list.

SOUTH PAW'S GRILL ❸
6009 Berkshire Ln., 214/987-0351,
www.southpawsgrill.com
HOURS: Mon.-Fri. 7 A.M.-8 P.M., Sat. 9 A.M.-4 P.M.

South Paw's (the name refers to owner Reza Anvarian, who is a lefty amateur boxer) is proof that healthy food can be yummy. The food here comes courtesy of Luigi Troncoso, who once helmed the kitchen at the fine-dining establishment Trece, and though the fare here is much simpler and way less expensive, Troncoso's influence guarantees health food that transcends the usual pile of wilted alfalfa spouts on a plate. There's even an element of heartiness, as in the rotisserie chicken and tabbouleh sandwich. Of

course, you've gotta try a smoothie—lightly sweetened with agave or honey, coupled with your choice of six different types of milk.

ASIAN
LITTLE KATANA ❸❸
4527 Travis St., 214/443-9600, www.littlekatana.com
HOURS: Mon.-Fri. 11 A.M.-2:30 P.M., Sat. 11:30 A.M.-11 P.M., Sun. 5 P.M.-10 P.M.

Hip, hot, and heavy on the Uptown vibe, Little Katana's exposed brick walls and dark intimacy provide a good-looking framework for an exquisite meal. The inventive Japanese and Asian fusion dishes jazz up the mind and the palate, while the rich sushi creations defy the minimalism usually associated with the cuisine—with fabulous results.

MANGO THAI ❸❸
4448 Lovers Ln., 214/265-9996,
www.mangodallas.com
HOURS: Daily 11 A.M.-10 P.M.

D Magazine calls it "pop Asian," and the *Dallas Morning News* calls it "new Asian," but really, Mango Thai is just straight-up good. Located in the older shopping strip on Lovers Lane (beware—parking is a beast here), Mango fills the need for all things curry, spicy, and noodle-y in Park Cities. The service is straightforward and friendly, and the decor is casual but well thought-out with orange and blue walls and a modern feel.

BARBECUE
PEGGY SUE BBQ ❸
6600 Snider Plaza, 214/987-9188,
www.peggysuebbq.com
HOURS: Sun.-Thurs. 11 A.M.-9 P.M., Fri.-Sat. 11 A.M.-10 P.M.

The charming little hole-in-the-wall that houses Peggy Sue BBQ has barbecue in its brick and mortar. Before Peggy Sue opened in 1989, the spot was Peggy's Beef Bar, and before that, it was Howard and Peggy's. Peggy Sue has done its predecessors proud, maintaining a 1950s-type atmosphere and succulent, smoked meats (the ribs are especially tasty, pre-rubbed before they're smoked), along with fresh, perfectly steamed veggies.

RESTAURANTS

COFFEE AND TEA
THE CULTURED CUP ⑤
8312 Preston Center Plaza Dr., 972/960-1521 or
888/VIP-TEAS, www.theculturedcup.com
HOURS: By appointment

Once you enter The Cultured Cup, you'll never want to leave. The atmosphere is warm and comfortable, but updated, neither prim nor precious. Similarly, the customer service is friendly, helpful, and generous—upon arriving, you are usually offered a tea sampling of your choice and a plate of tea chocolates. Besides a huge selection of loose teas, the Cup also sells tins, gorgeous china teacups and sets, coffee accoutrements, and many other fun gifts and home items for every budget.

DRIP ⑤
4343 Lovers Ln., 214/599-7800,
www.dripcoffeeco.com
HOURS: Mon.-Fri. 6:30 A.M.-6 P.M., Sat. 7 A.M.-6 P.M.,
Sun. 8 A.M.-6 P.M.

For too long, Park Cities dwellers were held in the grip of bad coffee, with few options when it came to a true, casual coffee shop. Drip changed all that. This casual yet modern place roasts its beans right on the spot, and you can taste the freshness in every latte. A small selection of other beverages and snacks is available, too.

FRENCH
BIJOUX ⑤⑤⑤
5450 W. Lovers Ln., #225, 214/350-6100,
www.bijouxrestaurant.com
HOURS: Mon.-Fri. 11-2 P.M., Mon.-Sat. 5:30--close

A gorgeous gem of a restaurant, Bijoux is opulent and expensive—and totally worth it. The food is slightly updated classic French—think cheese courses, coddled egg with caviar, arugula, foie gras, scallops, truffles—and is available in three- and five-course prix fixe menus, or in a whopping nine-course tasting menu. The service is impeccable; the wine menu features perfect pairings ranging from $34 to more than $600 a bottle. Sure, you might have to check your bank balance before you go, but

with food, drink, and atmosphere this good, it's a satisfying splurge.

⚔ RISE NO. 1 ⑤⑤⑤
5360 W. Lovers Ln., 214/366-9900,
www.risesouffle.com
HOURS: Tues.-Thurs. 11 A.M.-10 P.M., Fri.-Sat.
11 A.M.-11 P.M., Sun. 11 A.M.-9 P.M.

Never heard of a soufflé house? Rise No. 1 is an excellent introduction to the eggy French specialty. The menu here, of course, is mainly soufflés, from the traditional ham and cheese to an indulgent Maine lobster filling to sweet dessert offerings like chocolate, ginger, and raspberry. The wine menu is extensive and available in very affordable flights—ask your server for help, as the service is friendly and well-versed in French food and drink.

MEDITERRANEAN AND MIDDLE EASTERN
CAFÉ ISTANBUL ⑤⑤
5450 W. Lovers Ln., 214/902-0919,
www.cafe-istanbul.net
HOURS: Daily 11 A.M.-11 P.M.

The only establishment in the DFW area serving solely Turkish cuisine, Café Istanbul could easily rest on its laurels, but it doesn't. Chef Erol Girgin serves a creative, savory menu of Turkish classics as well as updated—and slightly upscale—versions of traditional foods like hummus, kebabs, and lesser-known exotic delights.

FADI'S ⑤⑤
3001 Knox St., 214/528-1800, www.fadiscuisine.com
HOURS: Mon.-Thurs. 11 A.M.-9 P.M., Fri.-Sat.
11 A.M.-10 P.M., Sun. 11 A.M.-8:30 P.M.

The storefronts on this side of town have a certain duality: If they face Knox Street, they are cute and boutique-y; if they face the highway, they invariably are in a strip mall. Fadi's falls into the latter category, which is just fine, because this awesome Mediterranean diner isn't about artifice, it's about hummus. And baba ghanoush. And just about every Middle Eastern dish you could think of, amazingly prepared and served cafeteria-style. Quick, convenient, and better than many four-star joints around.

PASTRIES

SPRINKLES CUPCAKES $

4020 Villanova St., 214/369-0004,
www.sprinklescupcakes.com
HOURS: Mon.-Sat. 9 A.M.-9 P.M., Sun. 10 A.M.-8 P.M.

Okay, Sprinkles Cupcakes is a chain. But if there were ever a nonlocal place to recommend, this is it. Sprinkles crafts the Platonic ideal of cupcakes, moist and lip-smackingly good, in a variety of inventive flavors, along with new twists on the classics. The place is almost always crowded, so you might want to preorder so you can jump to the shorter to-go line. Or just pop in and grab one to munch on while you window-shop along the Plaza at Preston Center.

YUMMY DONUTS $

4355 Lovers Ln., 214/520-7680
HOURS: Wed.-Mon. 6 A.M.-noon

Chic, sleek, and with a twist of humor, Yummy Donuts is a great place to grab something to go, but an even better place to sit down and linger. Why not, since the place has Wi-Fi, piping hot coffee, and, of course, doughnuts? The menu offers the classics like glazed, but you can also find seasonally themed doughnuts and mega-indulgent varieties like Moon Pie. For those with less of a sweet tooth, there's a good mix of breakfast sandwiches to keep you full all morning.

SEAFOOD

CAFÉ PACIFIC $$$

24 Highland Park Village, 214/526-1170,
www.cafepacific.com
HOURS: Mon.-Sat. 9 A.M.-10 P.M., Sun. 9 A.M.-2:30 P.M.

Café Pacific is what you'd expect from a Highland Park seafood eatery: upscale dining with upscale prices. The fresh, cleanly prepared seafood is worth a dent to your credit card, though, as one bite of the lobster, shrimp, and scallop ceviche will prove. Decor-wise, it's all "brass, glass, and class," as one local paper

puts it, but at its heart, Café Pacific is a neighborhood place, dressed up but friendly.

SOUTHERN

🍴 BUBBA'S $

6617 Hillcrest Ave., 214/373-6527,
www.bubbascatering.org
HOURS: Daily 6:30 A.M.-10 P.M.

If you're seeking full-on Southern-fried vittles, Bubba's is the perfect destination. This is a place that's not afraid of a deep fryer, and puts it to best use making legendary fried chicken (Bubba's and its sister restaurant, Babe's, were named by *Southern Living* magazine as among the best places in the South for fried chicken). Tasty rolls, biscuit-centered breakfasts, and cobblers are popular, too. If you go during peak times, especially Sunday, expect to wait for a table or in the serpentine drive-through line, but it's well worth it.

STEAK HOUSE

DUNSTON'S $$

5423 Lovers Ln., 214/352-8320,
www.dunstonssteakhouse.com
HOURS: Mon.-Thurs. 11 A.M.-10 P.M., Fri. 11 A.M.-11 P.M., Sat. 5-11 P.M., Sun. 5-10 P.M.

Wood-paneled walls, old-school steak-house art, busy carpet—Dunston's has been around since 1969, and it shows. The place is a true throwback, with wonderfully unironic atmosphere and patrons who have been regulars for 30 years. Sadly, the quality of the food has suffered with the times, but Dunston's is a must-see for an example of a real Texas open-grill steak-house atmosphere. We suggest you grab a drink there.

TEX-MEX

MI COCINA $$

77 Highland Park Village, 214/521-6426,
www.mcrowd.com
HOURS: Sun.-Thurs. 11 A.M.-10 P.M., Fri.-Sat. 11 A.M.-11 P.M.

There is great debate among Dallas denizens as to whether Highland Park's Mi Cocina—or "Mico," as it is often called—is the real deal or just a "scene." If you like Tex-Mex, you'll most

RESTAURANTS

likely love Mico's *queso,* crispy shrimp tacos, and strong tropical-themed cocktails. Some purists, however, don't dig the "upscaling" of Tex-Mex, and the Highland Park Mico's chi-chi digs and beautiful people are considered by some to be heretical treatment of the cuisine. Either way, you've gotta check out the Highland Park location (there are many across town), as it's one of the most Dallas-y experiences you'll have—eating tacos across the street from Jimmy Choo.

WINE BAR AND TAPAS
CAFÉ MADRID $$
5401 Travis St., 214/528-1731,
www.cafemadrid-dallas.com

HOURS: Mon.-Thurs. 5-11 P.M., Fri.-Sat. 11:30 A.M.-midnight

Anyone can throw together a table full of small plates, but the folks at Café Madrid know the ins and outs of true tapas. This place can't be beat for saffron-infused, authentic ambience (right down to the occasionally indifferent waitstaff, à la Europe, which is one of the few drawbacks here). On busy nights, friends gather at tables crowded with traditional Spanish fare (a shockingly good blood sausage, well-considered cheeses, perfect tortilla Española), along with a few curveballs (the goat cheese balls fried in honey, for instance). Skip the wine list and order a few pitchers of the balanced, boozy sangria, which pairs well with everything.

Greenville   Map 4

AMERICAN
LAKEWOOD LANDING $
5818 Live Oak St., 214/823-2410,
www.lakewood-landing.com
HOURS: Daily 3 P.M.-2 A.M.

The sign outside the Lakewood Landing advertises it as "an upscale dive," and that sums up the place nicely. This is a spot that doesn't take itself too seriously—despite the smattering of hipsters, you get the feeling the wood paneling covering the walls is not meant ironically. The Landing does, however, take its juicy, high-piled, nicely priced hamburgers seriously, and you should, too. If you stray from the burger, the remainder of the menu is simple bar food, but it's, well, *really good* bar food. Thankfully, Dallas recently passed a smoking ordinance, so the cloud of smoke that once obscured the heat of the tasty jalapeño poppers and the freshly fried chips and salsa is gone for good.

ASIAN
NANDINA $$
5631 Alta Ave., 214/826-6300,
www.nandinarestaurant.com
HOURS: Daily 5 P.M.-3 A.M.

Billing itself as an "Asian tapas" restaurant, Nandina sometimes tries to be too much at once, but the menu's wide variety ultimately pleases. Tucked away on a side street off Greenville Avenue, the place offers a cool, dark respite from the revelry going on a block away. Whether you'd like a full, lingering dinner of cocktails and unusual sushi, genuine dishes like 1,000-year egg, or a solution to your 3 A.M. drunken noodle craving, Nandina will have you covered. And they deliver.

ITALIAN
CAMPISI'S $$
5610 E. Mockingbird Ln., 214/827-0355,
www.campisis.us
HOURS: Sun.-Fri. 11 A.M.-10 P.M., Sat. 11 A.M.-11 P.M.

By now Campisi's has a few locations scattered about the Dallas area, but the original location on Mockingbird Lane is really the only choice. That's not only because this Campisi's has provided toothsome ravioli, lasagna, and pizza for decades; it's also because of the joint's history. Back in the day, Joe Campisi was rumored to be a major mafia crime boss, supposedly involved in the assassination of President John F. Kennedy. In fact, Jack Ruby—the man who shot Kennedy's assassin, Lee Harvey Oswald—ate a steak dinner here the night before Kennedy was killed. From the weird, inexplicable "Egyptian Lounge" sign outside to the dark interior, remnants of Campisi's mystery still infuse a dining experience there. Of course, some of the panache was lessened by the recent reality show *Wildest Party Parents,* which featured Joe's son Corky and his daughter Amber Campisi, fresh off a *Playboy* shoot.

MEDITERRANEAN AND MIDDLE EASTERN

CAFÉ IZMIR ❸❸

3711 Greenville Ave., 214/826-7788, www.cafeizmir.com

HOURS: Sun.-Mon. 5:30-9:30 P.M., Tues. and Fri.-Sat. 5:30-11:30 P.M., Wed.-Thurs. 5:30-10:30 P.M.

It's a shame the intimacy of Café Izmir discourages large groups, because the Middle Eastern tapas at this popular Greenville Avenue spot are perfect for sharing among a big bunch of friends—even more so on half-price "Tapas Tuesday," which also features great wine specials. Make sure to order an extra plate of Izmir's creamy hummus because you won't want to share, no matter how many people are at your table. Of course, thanks to Izmir's next-door casual deli, you can always take some home with you.

PUB FOOD

THE COCK AND BULL ❸❸

6330 Gaston Ave., 214/841-9111, www.cockandbulldallas.com

HOURS: Mon.-Fri. 3 P.M.-2 A.M., Sat.-Sun. noon-2 A.M.

It's probably not easy to provide a genuine English pub atmosphere, but The Cock and Bull rises to the occasion handily, with cozy if somewhat shabby—and dark—environs and a fine bar menu, including reliable blue plate specials on Sunday. For $6, the latter is more than just meat loaf; think instead grilled fish, pork chops, and hanger steak. Well, sometimes there's meat loaf, too. Just check the specials board to find out.

© JONANNA WIDNER

The Cock and Bull serves up budget-friendly English pub food.

THE LIBERTINE ❸❸

2101 Greenville Ave., 214/824-7900, www.libertinebar.com

HOURS: Mon.-Thur. 4 P.M.-2 A.M. Fri.-Sun. 11 A.M.-2 A.M., Sat. noon-2 A.M.

A fine selection of beers, a casual atmosphere, and elevated pub grub make the Libertine a favorite destination for Lower Greenville denizens. The quasi-English decor, replete with brass bar and big comfy booths, belies both the beer and food menus, in a good way. The requisite nods to shepherd's pie and fish-and-chips are replaced, for instance, by a varied and inspired menu that's not too complicated, but definitely not simplistic. The popular steak sandwiches and portobello fries taste even better on Sundays, when the menu is half-price.

RESTAURANTS

RESTAURANTS

SEAFOOD

AW SHUCKS $
3601 Greenville Ave., 214/821-9449,
www.awshucksdallas.com
HOURS: Sun.-Thurs. 11 A.M.-10 P.M.,
Fri.-Sat. 11 A.M.-11:30 P.M.
If you want something fried and cheap, hit up this quirky joint that has held down the same spot on Greenville Avenue for well more than two decades. Despite its bivalve-oriented name, the oysters at Aw Shucks are best avoided, but the fried-to-order shrimp and catfish will leaved you stuffed. Extra points for location (just across the street from the Granada Theater), atmosphere (simple wooden tables adorned only with condiments and a roll of paper towels), and convenience (payment is on the honor system, so there's no messing with the check).

LA CALLE DOCE $$
1925 Skillman St., 214/824-9900,
www.lacalledoce-dallas.com
HOURS: Mon.-Thurs. 11 A.M.-10 P.M.,
Fri.-Sat. 11 A.M.-11 P.M., Sun. 11 A.M.-9 P.M.
Even though it occupies a nondescript storefront in a landlocked city, La Calle Doce's clean, white walls and seafood-heavy menu evoke a breezy Acapulco café. Fish is king here, be it in fillet, cocktail, or ceviche form. La Calle Doce caters to locals and is friendly to families—though many a happy hour margarita has been swilled here, no doubt.

SOUTHERN

GOLD RUSH CAFÉ $
1913 Skillman St., 214/823-6923
HOURS: Mon.-Sat. 7 A.M.-5 P.M.
If you're on the go or looking for hearty, simple, and cheap, the Gold Rush is the perfect little greasy spoon diner for breakfast or lunch. The eggy breakfast items are generously portioned, especially the taco meat omelet, but the tastiest treat is the hand-battered chicken-fried steak. Try it in sandwich form. You'd never know it from the fake brick decor and simple wooden tables, but this place has a storied past as a haven for hungover Dallas musicians and their aficionados.

WINE BAR AND TAPAS

THE GRAPE $$$
2808 Greenville Ave., 214/828-1981,
www.thegraperestaurant.com
HOURS: Mon.-Thurs. 5:30 P.M.-10 P.M.,
Fri.-Sat. 5:30 P.M.-10:30 P.M., Sun. 10:30 A.M.-2 P.M. and 5:30 P.M.-10 P.M.
This down-the-block bistro has been around for almost 40 years and has maintained many of its original traditions, like the chalkboard menu, the much-lauded mushroom soup, and the dimly lit, tiny dining area. The Grape was Dallas's first wine bar, a fact reflected by the ample wine list and Euro-feel, but the food never comes second best in chef/owner Brian Luscher's kitchen. Luscher's brunches are especially celebrated, having won several mentions in national and local publications and "Best Brunch" awards in the local papers.

East Dallas

Map 5

AMERICAN

GARDEN CAFÉ ⑤

5310 Junius St., 214/887-8330, www.gardencafe.net

HOURS: Tues.-Fri. 8 A.M.-2 P.M., Sat.-Sun. 9 A.M.-3 P.M.

With its hippie-dippy charm and funky feel, the Garden Café is like a little piece of Austin in the midst of the Big D. The key to this little neighborhood spot is its adjacent namesake greenery, from which veggies, herbs, and greens are plucked fresh to order for patrons' omelets, salads, and sandwiches. Seating is available in the garden, and it's fun to lounge over a sunny lunch or all-day breakfast and watch the goings-on of this eclectic neighborhood street.

LOCAL ⑤⑤⑤

2936 Elm St., 214/752-7500, www.localdallas.com

HOURS: Tues.-Sat. 5:30-10 P.M.

While some upscale joints justify their higher prices with dishes so "innovative" they challenge our very notion of what food is, at Tracy Miller's Local, the emphasis is on food that is artful, delicious, and real. High quality ingredients at the peak of their freshness make straightforward dishes like grilled grass-fed beef tenderloin (served with panko-crusted tater tots), deep-fried green beans, and tangelo-soy glazed salmon more than the sum of their parts. Miller's ingredients range throughout the country—Hudson Valley foie gras, Maine lobster—lending even more authenticity to her inspired American cuisine. You'll rub shoulders with Dallas's beautiful people in a space as intimate as it is minimalist. It's a respite from the lively Deep Ellum neighborhood where it's situated, but the tiny number of tables means that reservations are a must.

ASIAN

BANGKOK CITY ⑤⑤

4301 Bryan St., Ste. 101, 214/824-6200, www.bangkokcityrestaurant.com

HOURS: Mon.-Sun. 11 A.M.-10 P.M.

Not to be confused with the lesser establishment on Greenville Avenue that shares a similar name, the East Dallas Bangkok City has maintained consistency and quality since 1992. The exterior promises a dive, but the interior is all clean lines, California hues, and crisp service. The menu won't win any awards for originality, but it doesn't need to, as it's executed with a practiced precision and quality. The sticky rice is the perfect sticky; the crispy duck is enhanced by a balanced brown sauce, not drowning in it; and the curries pack a toothsome combo of heft and heat.

BARBECUE

MAMA FAYE'S BBQ ⑤

2933 Commerce St., 217/741-3144, www.mamafayesbbq.com

HOURS: Daily 10 A.M.-8:30 P.M.

You gotta love a barbecue joint that categorizes a smoked turkey leg as an "Odds and Ends" item on their menu, as if the club-sized hunk of smoky, tender meat were merely a toss-off. Such is the luxury of Mama Faye's, where the extensive menu offers up an embarrassment of riches, including really tender baby back ribs that slide off the bone and spicy sausage. Southern staples like turnip greens, yams, and black-eyed peas liven up the more common offerings like potato salad and pintos. Dishes are available in combo form—a meat and two or three sides—or the meat is available by the pound. If a pound of brisket seems like a lot, that's because it is, so if you choose that route, make sure you leave room for a slice of sweet potato pie. A small caveat: The character of this sparse-but-clean spot grows on you slowly (especially due to the BBQ-praising mural on the wall), but the service, which ranges from casual to slow-as-a-Southern-drawl may not.

COFFEE SHOP

MURRAY STREET COFFEE ⑤

103 Murray St., 214/655-2808, www.murraystreetcoffee.com

HOURS: Mon.-Fri. 7 A.M.-7 P.M., Sat. 8 A.M.-6 P.M.

Murray Street Coffee is hip and sleek, but still

RESTAURANTS

comfortable. Head upstairs in this airy bi-level space and sip a giant latte or nosh on a bagel topped with farmers market arugula and to-matoes as you listen to one of the Wednesday night DJs. Or pop in on a Saturday morning for a mimosa and chat with owners Liz and Doug Davis, who combine a sharp eye for design, a good ear for music, and a penchant for hiring some of the friendliest baristas around.

ITALIAN

CANE ROSSO ❸❸

2612 Commerce St., 214/741-1188, www.ilcanerosso.com

HOURS: Mon. 6 P.M.-10 P.M., Tues.-Thurs. 11 A.M.-3 P.M. and 5-10 P.M., Fri.-Sat. 11 A.M.-3 P.M. and 5 P.M.-11 P.M.

Cane Rosso opened in 2011, and in less time than it takes to slice a salami, the Italian joint landed on top ten and critic's favorite lists all over the area. No wonder: Founder and owner Jay Jerrier's enthusiasm for creating the best piz-zas borders on obsessive, and patrons happily reap the benefits as they savor the pies' tooth-some crusts, perfectly bubbly on the outside and billowy on the inside. Developing the per-fect pie has been a labor of love: A former "dis-gruntled corporate drone," as he puts it, Jerrier trained under the Associazione Verace Pizza Neapoletana, imported a handmade wood-burning oven from Italy, and constantly culls authentic ingredients from far-flung places (ex-cept the sausage, which comes from Jimmy's Food Store up the street).

CIVELLO'S RAVIOLISMO ❸❸

1318 N. Peak St., 214/827-2989, www.civellosraviolismo.com

HOURS: Mon.-Fri. 9 A.M.-3 P.M., Sat. 10 A.M.-2 P.M.

This family-owned and operated takeout spot is a delight on otherwise bleak Peak Street. Chena and Phil Civello have supplied local eateries (such as the famous Campisi's) with superlative ravioli for years, and theirs is a con-venient spot to grab a quick, easy, and yummy dinner. An 18-pack of ravioli will only set you back $4–6. Selection varies daily and is always freshly made with everything from traditional beef/ricotta to the more inventive, like locally raised buffalo. Civello's also provides other pasta dishes and salads to go.

MEXICAN

LA VICTORIA ❸

1605 N. Haskell Ave., 214/827-0101

HOURS: Mon.-Sun. 7 A.M.-2 P.M.

If you happen to come across this humble little spot—one of Dallas's most popular for break-fast burritos—on a Saturday, a long line of the hungry and hungover might await you, but whether you're shaking off the vestiges of last night's rum and Cokes or dead sober, noth-ing quite hits the spot like one of La Victoria's giant burritos stuffed with goodies—eggs, cho-rizo, roasted poblanos, beans, potatoes—all for $2.25. Extras like cheese, sour cream, avocado, and the like will run you a quarter apiece, so feel free to spend your dough on beer the night before.

PEPE AND MITOS ❸❸

2911 Elm St., 214/741-1901, www.pepeandmitos.com

HOURS: Mon.-Tues. 11 A.M.-3 P.M., Wed.-Thurs. 11 A.M.-10 P.M., Fri.-Sat. 11 A.M.-11 P.M.

Bright, differently hued pastel painted walls greet visitors to this Deep Ellum favorite, which leans a little more toward the Mex side of Tex-Mex. Skip the botanas appetizer, which features the type of fried apps you can find anywhere in town, and opt instead for the tacos norteños: homemade flour tortillas wrapped around pep-pers, chiles, and skirt steak sautéed in a unique wine sauce that imparts a distinctive savory tartness. Less commonly ordered but a must-have is the albondigas soup, which consists of meat patties cooked in a zingy, cumin-based broth. Of course, more people may begin or-dering the soup ever since it was featured on *Diners, Drive-Ins, and Dives,* wherein host Guy Fieri took one slurp and proclaimed it "gang-ster." Service is spotty but friendly, and worth indulging.

THE TACO JOINT ❸

911 N. Peak St., 214/826-8226, www.thetacojoint.com

HOURS: Mon.-Fri. 6:30 A.M.-2 P.M., Sat. 8 A.M.-2 P.M.

Seems Austin's obsession with breakfast tacos

finally made its way north up I-35 and planted its first flag in East Dallas. The Taco Joint's breakfast fare—made sans lard and trans fats—has rapidly become a citywide favorite. Although the lunch menu is nothing to sneeze at, it's the breakfast combos of tortillas, eggs, black beans, cheese, and chorizo that lure scores of families in the mornings and hungover hipsters just before noon (on weekdays, breakfast ends at 11:45 A.M.; on Saturday, it's served all day). In fact, you might try going at an off time; otherwise, be prepared for the ravenous crowds elbowing for position at the salsa bar.

© JONANNA WIDNER

RESTAURANTS

The AllGood Café's chicken-fried steak breakfast has cured many a hangover.

SOUTHERN

◖ ALLGOOD CAFÉ $$

2934 Main St., 214/742-5362, www.allgoodcafe.com
HOURS: Tues.-Sat. 9 A.M.–9 P.M., Sun.-Mon. 9 A.M.–2 P.M.

It doesn't get much more homey than the AllGood, a Deep Ellum stalwart owned by Texas music lover Mike Snider, who has covered the walls in cool old posters and flyers. Snider has been serving up some of the best country-style veggies, eggs, and chicken-fried steak since Deep Ellum was just a sparkle in some developer's eye, and he has speckled his grits-'n'-griddle menu with fresh, local ingredients and a few surprises. On most nights

the place transforms into a primarily alt-country venue, so it's not uncommon to catch a show there at night, then shuffle over the next morning for a late and hearty breakfast.

South Dallas

Map 6

AMERICAN

BOLSA $$

614 W. Davis St., 214/367-9367, www.bolsadallas.com
HOURS: Mon.-Thurs. and Sun. 11 A.M.–10 P.M., Fri.-Sat. 11 A.M.–11 P.M.

While much of Dallas's dining tradition tends toward see-and-be-seen and large-scale finery, Bolsa occupies a comfortable neighborhood niche, and the neighbors have taken quite kindly to it. The café, which doubles as an epicurean grocery, is located in a former auto repair garage and the chatty buzz of the nighttime crowd gives the impression of familiar comfort. Ditto the food: Chef Graham Dodds

clearly recognizes the connections between the Mediterranean culinary aesthetic and Texas's ample supply of fresh organic ingredients, and walks the walk. "No freezer, no fryer" is Bolsa's motto.

So, for Dodds, fresh means *fresh*, a concept that turns simple into sumptuous. The popular bruschetta, for instance, intermingles inventive toppings like figs and honey, or salmon and crème fraîche, all of which stand out with the extra zing of the newly procured. Pizzas are popular here, too, for similar reasons, with the unique flatbread base deftly holding local cheeses, veggies, and meats.

DEEP-FRIED!

Of all the colloquial culinary oddities you can find in Texas, the **deep-fried food competition** at the **Texas State Fair** might just take the cake—as long as the cake has been dipped in batter, submerged in eight inches of cooking oil, and then covered with ice cream and chocolate.

Though the State Fair begins in late September and only lasts until the end of October, the competition actually starts a few weeks before that, when dozens of food vendors unveil the artery-clogging concoctions they've been cooking up for an entire year, pitting them against each other for the Big Tex Awards. For the public, the competition is a lighthearted affair, but for the most part, it's serious business: The winners enjoy a huge amount of publicity, which drives customers to their booths by the thousands. Hence, the escalating creativity. Past win-

ners have created fried banana pudding, fried Nutter Butters, and fried peanut butter and jelly sandwiches. By current standards, these actually seem pretty pedestrian, because in recent years, contestants have cranked it up a notch, producing things like fried Coca-Cola (a three-year winner), chicken-fried bacon, and something called the Donkey Tail, which involves a hot dog split down the middle, filled with cheese, wrapped in a tortilla, deep-fried, and then covered in chili.

If all of this sounds decadent, well...it is. And if it sounds disgusting, well...some of it is. But for the most part, the indulgent treats usually range from pretty good to downright mind-blowing, and the fun of eating them in the shadow of a massive Ferris wheel makes them taste all the much better.

HATTIES $$

418 N. Bishop Ave., 214/942-7400, www.hatties.net
HOURS: Mon. 11:30 A.M.-2:30 P.M., Tues.-Sat. 11:30 A.M.-2:30 P.M. and from 5:30 P.M., Sun. 11 A.M.-2:30 P.M. and from 5:30 P.M.

Housed smack in middle of the charming storefronts that make up the core of the Bishop Arts District, Hatties pours on the upscale Southern charm. The bistro specializes in grown-up comfort food in a refined but comfy atmosphere (which tends to get a bit loud, especially on weekends). Make sure to order the four-cheddar mac 'n' cheese.

LUCIA $$$

408 West 8th St., 214/948-4998,
http://luciadallas.com
HOURS: Tues.-Sat. 5:30-10 P.M.

With its rustic pressed-tin ceiling, mismatched chairs, and homey decor, tiny Lucia may be the funkiest restaurant you've ever had to make reservations a month in advance to get into. Worth the wait? Only if your taste buds desire to be seduced by compelling house-cured salumi, airy foie gras stuffed into prunes, and tender house-made pastas covered in voluptuously flavored

ragus. The menu changes often, but the cozy atmosphere, the warm service, and the luxurious Italian food endure.

TILLMAN'S ROADHOUSE $$

324 W. 7th St., 214/942-0988,
www.tillmansroadhouse.com
HOURS: Tues.-Thurs. 11:30 A.M.-2 P.M. and 5:30-9 P.M., Fri. 11:30 A.M.-2 P.M. and 5:30-11 P.M., Sat. 11 A.M.-3 P.M. and 5:30-11 P.M., Sun. 10 P.M.-2 P.M.

You won't find any stray tobacco juice on the knotted wood floor of this particular roadhouse; considering proprietor Sara Tillman's fancy take on classic Texas aesthetic (culinary and otherwise), you're more likely to encounter a spot of stray truffle oil. Surrounded by repurposed barn wood and distressed leather, the crowd at Tillman's is as happily raucous as any roadside tavern ruffians, but it's telling that the social lubricant here is blood orange margaritas, often found astride a bowl of venison Frito pie or a plate of chicken-fried hanger steak.

Ah, yes, that chicken-fried steak. Amazingly crisp, not lying flat across the plate like most, but piled gloriously high and enmeshed in a mountain of whipped garlic potatoes, this is the kind of meal you dream about on cold winter days. And that savory combo of comfort and cuisine forms the crux of Tillman's appeal.

COFFEE SHOP
OPENING BELL ❸
1409 S. Lamar St., #12, 214/565-0383, www.openingbellcoffee.com

HOURS: Mon.-Thurs. 7 A.M.-10 P.M., Fri. 7 A.M.-midnight, Sat. 9 A.M.- midnight, Sun.9:30 A.M.-2 P.M.

Despite its slightly cloying Wall Street theme, Opening Bell is a welcoming, hang-out-all-day kind of spot, tucked into an intimate corner of the gargantuan South Side on Lamar building (a former Sears & Roebuck distribution warehouse, now refurbished into a mixed-use development). Bypass the meager food offerings and grab a comfy couch and a latte as you catch one of the many local musical acts that perform here amid the concrete walls and exposed ductwork.

Greater Dallas — Map 7

BARBECUE
SONNY BRYAN'S ❸
2202 Inwood Rd., 214/357-7120, www.sonnybryans.com

HOURS: Mon.-Sun. 10 A.M.-9 P.M.

No trip to Dallas would be complete without a trip to the original Sonny Bryan's, which opened in 1910. And no trip to Sonny Bryan's would be complete without loosening a notch on your belt buckle to make room for chopped beef sandwiches and fat, juicy sausages, all dripping with Sonny's signature smoky sauce. Settling into one of the school desks they've utilized as seating here for decades might feel weird at first, but once the first piece of heavenly meat hits your taste buds, you'll forget where you are anyway.

TEX-MEX
AVILA'S ❸❸
4714 Maple Ave., 214/520-2700, www.avilasrestaurant.com

HOURS: Mon.-Thurs. 11 A.M.-9 P.M., Fri.-Sat. 10 A.M.-8 P.M.

The parking sucks, the location might be called "light industrial," and the decor won't win any awards, but none of the dozens of people who call this place their lunchtime home care. Avila's is Tex-Mex in all its gooey glory. It's impossible to go wrong ordering any of the enchilada platters, sided by smoky refried beans and Spanish rice, but the special board is really where it's at, especially when the brisket burrito makes an appearance.

Downtown Fort Worth — Map 8

AMERICAN
AFTERNOON TEA AT
THE ASHTON ❸❸❸
610 Main St. (in the Ashton Hotel), 817/332-0100, www.theashtonhotel.com

HOURS: Thurs.-Sat. 2-4 P.M.

Dressing up is part of the fun at the Ashton Hotel's afternoon tea, served in the 610 Grille. The lush fabrics and burnished woods of the Grille make for an elegant setting for the tea service. Traditional tea accompaniments such as finger sandwiches, house-made scones, and petit fours will make you feel like you've stepped into another time and place, as does the historic luxury of the Ashton overall. Reservations are required 24 hours in advance.

◖ REATA ❸❸❸
310 Houston St., 817/336-1009, www.reata.net

HOURS: Daily 11 A.M.-2:30 P.M. and 5-10:30 P.M.

Reata was originally located atop a skyscraper—until a tornado blew through and swept it away in March 2000. But like a phoenix rising from the ashes—or at least from the

RESTAURANTS

COURTESY OF REATA

Reata

debris—this Cowtown favorite has been reborn in Sundance Square. With a rooftop patio and tables that offer plenty of privacy, Reata is rightly celebrated as one of Fort Worth's most romantic fine-dining spots. The Southwestern menu matches the decor and offers a slate of updated regional favorites from the South and the West—grits and chicken-fried steak both appear on the menu—alongside with traditional Mexican dishes.

ASIAN
THAI TINA'S ⑤⑤
600 Commerce St., 817/332-0088
HOURS: Sun.-Thurs. 11 A.M.-9 P.M., Fri.-Sat. 11 A.M.-10 P.M.
Who knew the hot spot in Tex-Mex and steak-obsessed Cowtown would be a tiny hole-in-the-wall Thai joint? A former semisecret, Thai Tina's used to look like a bunker, and a move to new downtown digs has merely enhanced its colorful world of zingy duck dishes, sweet-sour sauces, and pad thai up the yin-yang. The entrée offerings here are plentiful; in fact, you might find yourself overwhelmed. Thai

Tina's classic choices—a pad thai, say, or crab Rangoon—are transcendent, but don't fear experimenting (especially with the duck!).

BARBECUE
❮ ANGELO'S ⑤
2533 White Settlement Rd., 817/332-0357, www.angelosbbq.com
HOURS: Mon.-Sat. 11 A.M.-10 P.M.
At Angelo's, the pit produces some of the best barbecue in Texas. The brisket is moist and tender while the meat falls from the rib bones—but give the sides a pass. Although the sawdust on the floor may be long gone, the atmosphere at Fort Worth's most historical place to worship at the altar of 'cue is still profoundly unpretentious—plasticware and Styrofoam plates and a space that looks less like a restaurant and more like a warehouse. But the legion of regulars wouldn't have it any other way.

ITALIAN
FERRÉ ⑤⑤⑤
215 E. 4th St., 817/332-0033, www.ferrerestaurant.com

HOURS: Mon.-Thurs. 4-10 P.M., Fri.-Sat. 4-11 P.M.

With an interior that is sleek and stylish, Ferré feels more Big Apple than Cowtown. The flavors of Tuscany are what you'll find here: An open-fire grill gives the steaks and other meats a smoky edge. A stone-fired pizza oven guarantees the pizzas come out shatteringly crisp. House-made pastas show off the kitchen's commitment to freshness and intriguing mixes of ingredients (like the sweet potato gnocchi with applewood bacon). The location, near Sundance Square and across the street from Bass Hall, makes it a good spot for pre-performance dining.

WINE BAR AND TAPAS
ZAMBRANO WINE CELLAR ❸❺
910 Houston St., 817/850-9463,
www.zambranowines.com

HOURS: Mon.-Fri. 4:30-11 P.M. (kitchen closes at 9 P.M.), Sat. 5:30 P.M.-1 A.M. (kitchen closes at 10:30 P.M.)

With more than 300 wines available (50 by the glass), you probably won't make it all the way through Zambrano Wine Cellar's extensive wine list—but you'll probably have fun trying. Zambrano's menu is tailored to enhance the wine drinking experience and features house-made pizzas, sophisticated cured meats, and a couple of different entrées each night. The knowledgeable staff can help steer you toward a bottle that fits your taste and pocketbook, whether you're a seasoned wine drinker or a raw newbie. While the bar is open late, the kitchen closes most evenings around 9 P.M.

TCU and Vicinity

Map 9

AMERICAN
CARSHON'S DELI ❸
3133 Cleburne Rd., 817/923-1907,
www.carshonsdeli.com
HOURS: Mon.-Sat. 9 A.M.-3 P.M. (dining room closes at 2:30 P.M.)

Yes, there are Jews in cowboy country, and 80 years ago, one of them went and started a deli. Although the bare-bones atmosphere at Carshon's is nothing to *kvell* about, the pastrami, corned beef, and other deli meats are as authentic a deli experience as you'll find in the area. For the most authentic New York–style deli experience, try the chopped liver, though the Reuben is the most popular item on the menu. Come hungry—portions are big. Open for breakfast and lunch only.

DUTCH'S ❸
3009 S. University Dr., 817/927-5522,
www.dutchshamburgers.com
HOURS: Sun.-Wed. 11 A.M.-10 P.M., Thurs.-Sat. 11 A.M.-11 P.M.

Texas chef Grady Spears's burger joint draws 'em in with grilled all-natural beef burgers in a range of sizes and toppings. The mini sliders, with grilled onions and cheddar cheese, are great for soaking up some of the fruits of Dutch's better-than-average beer list. Non-beef-eaters have choices here, too, including a flavorful grilled chicken sandwich festooned with green chiles. Lots of chrome and steel give this spot in a historic building near TCU a nice retro feeling.

◖ RAILHEAD SMOKEHOUSE ❸
2900 Montgomery St., 817/738-9808,
www.railheadonline.com
HOURS: Mon.-Sat. 11 A.M.-9 P.M.

You'd think that the Railhead Smokehouse, with its authentic Texas barbecue, would be found amid the cowpokes and boot-scooters of the Stockyards, but this joint sits quietly in a nondescript building smack in the middle of a parking lot, near the cosmopolitan Museum District. Inside, however, it's a genuine Texas smokehouse, with brisk but friendly service, simple wooden tables, neon beer signs, dark plank walls, and mesquite-tinged air. For less than $10, you can choose from a variety of traditional barbecue favorites: moist, smoky

PICNIC TIME

Fort Worth's many excellent restaurants, laid-back attitude, and less congested urban space make it perfect for picnicking. Here are some suggestions for melding the town's best food with its most picturesque spots:

Grab a fabulous sandwich from the **Carshon's Deli** and head to the Cultural District, where the grassy park behind the Kimbell Art Museum makes for a lovely place to idle.

There may be no more romantic spot in town than the Botanic Gardens. Pack up some gourmet to go from **Bistro Louise** and indulge amid the petals of the Rose Garden.

Spiral Diner creates some of the most imaginative and tasty vegan vittles around. Couple your bean burger and fresh coconut limeade with a sunny **Forest Park** excursion.

brisket, its edges crusted with caramelized bits of the Railhead's heavenly, balanced sauce; chopped beef sandwiches falling apart under the weight of their own juices; red-hot ribs battling plump sausages for space next to a pile of mustard-y potato salad. All of it goes great with a cantaloupe-size beer goblet full of icy Lone Star beer.

SPIRAL DINER AND BAKERY ❸

1314 W. Magnolia Ave., 817/332-8834, www.spiraldiner.com
HOURS: Tues.-Sat. 11 A.M.-10 P.M., Sun. 11 A.M.-5 P.M.

Cowtown can be hard on a vegetarian—let alone a vegan. But the Spiral Diner is a happy exception to that rule. Voted 2007's Best Restaurant of the Year by *Veg News* magazine, Spiral Diner features vegan-ized versions of Southwestern favorites like biscuits and gravy, *migas,* taco salads, and two different kinds of burgers, all made with as many organic ingredients as feasible. Although service can be spotty, an extensive beer list is the icing on the vegan cupcake—speaking of which, leave room for some of Spiral's luscious baked goods or house-made vegan ice cream.

BREAKFAST

OL' SOUTH PANCAKE HOUSE ❸

1509 South University Dr., 817/336-0311
HOURS: Daily 24 hrs.

Every great city has a great breakfast place, and in Fort Worth, it's the straightforward, diner-y Ol' South Pancake House. Since it's open 24 hours, sooner or later you'll see every demographic saunter in: late-night party people in the wee hours, working men and women during the week, families and couples on the weekends. The German pancakes, as big as your head and sweet-tart with lemon juice and powdered sugar, are what the cognoscenti are eating here. Forget about IHOP.

COFFEE SHOP

PARIS COFFEE SHOP ❸

700 W. Magnolia Ave., 817/335-2041,
http://pariscoffeeshop.net
HOURS: Mon.-Fri. 6 A.M.-2:30 P.M., Sat. 6-11 A.M.

Don't come to the Paris Coffee Shop expecting croissants and café au lait. Instead, you'll find hearty Texas-style breakfasts like biscuits and gravy and country ham, along with fluffy pancakes and golden waffles. Weekends bring both out-the-door lines and red-eye gravy. At lunchtime, the menu switches to classic diner fare. With an atmosphere as welcoming and old-fashioned as the 80-year-old Paris Coffee Shop's, bet on the pies—which are to a Texan what a fine croissant is to a Parisian—to be spectacular.

ITALIAN

BRIX PIZZA AND WINE BAR ❸❸

2747 S. Hulen St., 817/924-2749, www.brixpizzeria.com
HOURS: Mon.-Sat. 11 A.M.-10 P.M., Sun. 4-10 P.M.

The new pizzeria on the block, Brix gets its pedigree from owner Daniele Puelo, who really knows his stuff. The pizzas here are Neapolitan style—light, crisp, and perfectly fired in the wood oven, with simple but tasty toppings. For those not craving a pie, the menu features a healthy slate of appetizers and main dishes, many of which take advantage of the wood-fire oven.

MEDITERRANEAN AND MIDDLE EASTERN

KING TUT ❸

1512 W. Magnolia Ave., 817/335-3051, www.kingtutegyptian.com

HOURS: Mon.-Sat. 11 A.M.-2:30 P.M. and 5:30-9 P.M., Sun. noon-6 P.M.

If you're looking for good Middle Eastern food in Fort Worth, King Tut, a hole-in-the-wall Egyptian restaurant on funky Magnolia Avenue, fills the bill nicely. Regulars rave about the hummus, baba ghanoush, and falafel (though less so about the service, which can be a bit slow when the restaurant is busy). To cap off your meal, enjoy an authentic Turkish coffee with one of King Tut's traditional Middle Eastern desserts, rich and sweet with honey.

PASTRIES

SWISS PASTRY SHOP ❸

3936 W. Vickery Blvd., 817/732-5661, www.swisspastryonline.com

HOURS: Tues.-Fri. 6:30 A.M.-5:30 P.M., Sat. 7 A.M.-4 P.M.

If the only thing the Swiss Pastry Shop sold was its renowned Black Forest cake—layers of meringue, whipped cream, and shaved chocolate—people would still flock to this simply decorated, old-fashioned bakery. But the Swiss Pastry Shop also has a full roster of superb pies, cookies, and cakes, all at reasonable prices. The shop puts out a good lunch, too: sausages, soups, and sandwiches. If you're not getting it to go, head here when you have time to dawdle; service can be slow.

TEX-MEX

❰ ESPERANZA'S MEXICAN BAKERY AND CAFÉ ❸

1601 Park Place Ave., 817/923-1961, www.joets.com

HOURS: Mon.-Thurs. 6 A.M.-9 P.M., Fri.-Sat. 6:30 A.M.-10 P.M., Sun. 6:30 A.M.-5 P.M.

The little sister to the much-beloved Joe T. Garcia's is the best non-kept secret in the world of Fort Worth breakfast. You know you're in for a treat when a bank of colorful barrels of horchata divides up the dining area, and this charming yet no-nonsense café delivers on the promise of its atmosphere. Those hoping for queso-covered Tex-Mex will be disappointed here, but others will be over the moon for the chorizo, homemade corn tortillas, and intense portions. Signature dishes include the *migas* (scrambled eggs combined with green chile and topped with shredded chicken). The huevos rancheros benefit from a zingy red sauce, and almost all the dishes come with generously ladled sides like rice and traditional refried beans. Be prepared to walk out with leftovers.

HOT DAMN! TAMALES ❸

713 W. Magnolia Ave., 817/926-9909, www.hotdamntamales.com

HOURS: Sat.-Sun. 11 A.M.-3 P.M.

Purists may scoff, but the lard-free tacos at Hot Damn! are fluffy and moist and come in intriguing varieties, including ancho pork and beef and jalapeño, as well as several vegan- and vegetarian-friendly varieties like fresh corn and poblano as well as wild mushroom and Texas goat cheese. (Don't forget to save room for chocolate, cherry, and roasted pecan tamales for dessert, by the way.) Hot Damn! is mostly a mail order and takeout operation, but a tiny four-table restaurant serves up tamale plates and other Mexican favorites. If you find the dining area occupied, do yourself a favor: Pick up a couple dozen tamales and take them home.

RESTAURANTS

West Side Fort Worth — Map 10

AMERICAN

CURLY'S CUSTARD $
4017 Camp Bowie Blvd., 817/763-8700,
www.curleysfrozencustard.com
HOURS: Sun.-Thurs. 11 A.M.-9 P.M., Fri.-Sat. 11 A.M.-10 P.M.

Don't call it ice cream. Paradoxically richer and yet lighter than ice cream, frozen custard is softly served, and at Curly's you can have your vanilla or chocolate flavor custard "concrete" style, with your choice of a rainbow of candy and fruit toppings whipped in. On nice days, enjoy your custard outside in Curly's grassy, parklike yard. Curly's also serves a mean Frito pie.

FRED'S TEXAS CAFÉ $
915 Currie St., 817/332-0083, www.fredstexascafe.com
HOURS: Daily 10 A.M.-midnight

A classic roadhouse respite in the midst of the hubbub of the West 7th/Foch Street. Fred's Texas Café is a great place to grab a beer and a stellar burger while relaxing in kitschy gold booths or listening to live music on the spacious patio. The food is better than you'd ever expect in the midst of such a dive-y atmosphere. "Outlaw Chef" Terry Chandler's most famous creation may be the fiery Diablo Burger, but the half-pound Fredburger is nothing to sneeze at. Not into burgers? Fred's also features steaks, Tex-Mex favorites, and some of the best quail dishes(!) in the region.

GALLIGASKIN'S SUBMARINE SANDWICH $
5817 Camp Bowie Blvd., 817/714-0383,
www.eatgalligaskins.com
HOURS: Mon.-Sat. 7 A.M.-9 P.M.

Conditioned as we are to chain sub sandwich shops that boast of their healthiness, it's easy to forget the joys of a real overstuffed made-to-order sub sandwich. Galligaskin's features a slate of more than 20 hot and cold subs, from egg salad to—yes—chicken-fried steak. The Fort Worth cognoscenti like the cheesesteak and the meaty Italian cold-cut varieties. And forget a bag of chips as an accompaniment—Galligaskin's features hand-cut fries as well as other deep-fried treats (try the mushrooms, with a side of ranch dressing, for extra trashy goodness).

KINCAID'S $
4901 Camp Bowie Blvd., 817/732-2881,
www.kincaidshamburgers.com
HOURS: Mon.-Sat. 11 A.M.-8 P.M., Sun. 11 A.M.-3 P.M.

Sure, you can have a thick, juicy, char-grilled hamburger almost anywhere (okay, maybe not), but you can't beat the original location of Kincaid's for a truly unique experience. Rub shoulders with what feels like all of Fort Worth as you chow down on Kincaid's oozingly flavorful burgers at the long, stand-up counters that run the length of this former grocery store, "where friends meet to eat." The mid-century grocery store trappings remain intact, making for a charmingly retro atmosphere. Spend your extra calories on the onion rings instead of the fries, and you might as well throw in a house-made shake while you're at it—not that the best burger in town needs any accompaniment.

MONTGOMERY ST. CAFÉ $
2000 Montgomery St., 817/733-8033,
www.themontgomerystcafe.com
HOURS: Mon.-Sat. 6 A.M.-2 P.M.

Old-fashioned service, a bottomless cup of coffee, and nearly unbelievably inexpensive prices—what more can you ask from a 60-year-old breakfast/lunch place? Delicious food? Montgomery St. has that, too. Go for the regional specials, like biscuits and gravy and grits to accompany your eggs and juicy thick-sliced ham. Atmosphere is early oilcloth, but with the friendly service and low prices, nobody really cares.

ROY POPE GROCERY $
2300 Merrick St., 817/732-2863,
www.roypopegrocery.com
HOURS: Mon.-Sat. 8 A.M.-7 P.M.

Even in a town that takes its time shedding the past, Roy Pope Grocery is a throwback. This neat neighborhood epicurean grocery, which has been around since 1943, is known for its excellent meat selection, not to mention hard-to-find foodstuffs and gourmet cheeses and deli items. Premade to-go and daily hot meals round out the offerings. Things get really old-school, however, when it comes to service: The grocery still delivers groceries, in cardboard boxes, to your door.

ASIAN
JAPANESE PALACE ❸❸❸
8445 Camp Bowie W., 817/244-0144,
www.japanesepalace.net
HOURS: Sun.-Thurs. 5-10 P.M.,
Fri.-Sat. 5 P.M.-midnight

The serene pond that greets you on your arrival to Japanese Palace is just one indicator that you're in for an exotic experience. Be prepared for a wait, but you'll enjoy spending that time in the bizarre lounge, where pictures of nude women and other kitschy decor abound. In the restaurant itself, you can choose from traditional Japanese floor seating or chairs around a big hibachi grill, where the chefs do performance cooking. The Japanese Palace also offers some of the better sushi in town—you can often circumvent the wait by requesting a seat at the sushi bar.

SZECHUAN ❸❸
5712 Locke Ave., 817/738-7300
HOURS: Sun.-Thurs. 11 A.M.-9:30 P.M.,
Fri.-Sat. 11 A.M.-10:30 P.M.

With a huge menu encompassing more than 150 items, ordering at Szechuan can be a daunting experience. But relax—you almost can't go wrong with any of the Chinese dishes here, especially the "Chef's Suggestions" at the front of the menu. This is a good choice for vegetarians and health-conscious diners; Szechuan offers several meatless dishes and a large selection of entrées cooked without oil. Lunch specials are a bargain.

FRENCH
SAINT-EMILION ❸❸❸
3617 W. 7th St., 817/737-2781,
www.saint-emilionrestaurant.com
HOURS: Tues.-Thurs. 5:30-9 P.M., Fri.-Sat. 6-9 P.M.

There's French, and then there's *French*— and Saint-Emilion definitely qualifies as the italicized version. This Fort Worth mainstay sticks closely to the überclassic French fare; think sweetbreads, fois gras, and things tartare, all worked with a Gallic magic. For years, Valentine's dates, prom couples, and anniversary celebrators have flocked to the intimate digs and prix fixe goodies here, and both the atmosphere and cuisine have been honed to perfection.

GERMAN
EDELWEISS ❸❸
3801 Southwest Blvd., 817/738-5934,
www.edelweissrestaurant.com
HOURS: Thurs. 5-10 P.M., Fri. 5-11 P.M., Sat. 4-11 P.M.,
Sun. noon-9 P.M.

Sometimes you want to go to a dark, quiet place and have a nice conversation. That's not when you should go to Edelweiss. Instead, head there when you're in the mood for a raucous evening of chicken dancing; listening to traditional German music (sometimes on an authentic alpenhorn); drinking a wide variety of hard-to-find German beers; and consuming massive plates of schnitzel, wurst, spaetzle, and other hearty Bavarian dishes. While the food may be uneven sometimes, Edelweiss owner Bernd Schnerzinger makes sure everyone has fun.

ITALIAN
FORTUNA ITALIAN RESTAURANT ❸
5837 Camp Bowie Blvd., 817/737-4469
HOURS: Mon.-Thurs. 11 A.M.-10 P.M., Fri.-Sat. 11 A.M.-11 P.M.

A solid menu of basic Italian entrées, along with pizza and pastas, is what you'll find at this family-owned restaurant. The prices are good for the quality, and the extensive menu means you will probably find exactly what you're craving.

RESTAURANTS

RESTAURANTS

ITALIAN INN RIDGLEA ❸❸
6323 Camp Bowie Blvd., 817/737-0123,
www.theitalianinn.com
HOURS: Sun.-Thurs. 5-10 P.M., Fri.-Sat. 5-11 P.M.

Romance is what you'll find at the Italian Inn. Sit in a closed-door private booth and canoodle with your honey, or choose a table where you can take in the sights and sounds of the singing waitstaff. Either way, the atmosphere at this below-street-level spot is dark and cavernous. The food is definitely as old-fashioned as the romance: Veal marsala, eggplant Parmesan, and big plates of pasta are what you'll find here. The graffiti on the walls of the booths from previous lovers' visits inspires some, but isn't everyone's cup of tea.

MAMA'S PIZZA ❸
5800 Camp Bowie Blvd., 817/731-6262,
www.mamaspizzas.net
HOURS: Mon.-Thurs. 11 A.M.-10 P.M., Fri.-Sat. 11 A.M.-11 P.M.

Mama's sat in a warehouse-type building on Camp Bowie for many years before finally moving to a much more inviting locale just up the road. The wooden booths and bustling atmosphere are a great improvement, but the pizza has never needed an upgrade, thanks to the just-the-right-thickness crust that's brushed with garlic butter and a slightly sweet sauce that gives the pies here their unique taste.

SEAFOOD
J&J OYSTER BAR ❸
612 University Dr., 817/335-2756,
www.jjbluesbar.com
HOURS: Sun.-Thurs. 11 A.M.-10 P.M., Fri.-Sat. 11 A.M.-11 P.M.

Friendly and just slightly dive-y, J&J is the place to go when you want a plate of briny, sparkling oysters and a cold schooner of beer. To follow that up, order the grilled snapper or something from J&J's slate of Southern favorites, like a fried oyster po'boy (with addictive hand-cut fries), a mound of boiled crawfish, or a bowl of gumbo. Hit the popular patio to cool off with a pitcher of beer on a hot day, and you won't be sorry.

LAMBERT'S ❸❸❸
2731 White Settlement Rd., 817/882-1161,
www.lambertsfortworth.com
HOURS: Mon.-Thurs. 5-10 P.M., Fri.-Sat. 5-11 P.M., Sun. 11 A.M.-3 P.M.

As straightforward as its motto—"Steaks. Seafood. Whiskey."—Lambert's menu features natural beef steaks along with decadent family-style side dishes like the justly celebrated cauliflower gratin. The live oak grill and smoker lead to succulent creations like smoked prime rib and brown sugar–crusted rib eye. The atmosphere is dark and comfortable but modern, with witty nods to Cowtown culture like a rack of saddles suspended from the ceiling and trophy heads mounted behind the bar.

SOUTHERN
DREW'S PLACE ❸
5701 Curzon Ave., 817/735-4408,
www.drewssoulfood.com
HOURS: Tues.-Thurs. 10:30 A.M.-7 P.M., Fri. 10:30 A.M.-8 P.M., Sat. 10:30 A.M.-6 P.M., Sun. 11 A.M.-4 P.M.

The smothered pork chops at Drew's Place have been known to make grown men weep. This family-owned home-cooking lunch spot in the Como section of Fort Worth features great soul food at amazingly low prices. Entrées like catfish, buffalo wings, and chicken-fried steak all come with two sides (make sure one of them is the collard greens). There's not much atmosphere here, but with a plate of soul food goodness and a big glass of sweet tea in front of you, you won't much care.

TEX-MEX
EL FENIX ❸❸
6391 Camp Bowie Blvd., 817/732-5584,
www.elfenix.com
HOURS: Daily 11 A.M.-10 P.M.

Although it's no longer family-owned, the 90-year-old El Fenix chain of Mexican restaurants still serves up solid Mexican comfort food. There is universal acclaim for their chips and salsa, perfect accompaniments to El Fenix's slate of potent margaritas, including one blended with a swirl of sangria, for those who can't decide between the two. Enchiladas are a specialty here; order them by themselves or as an element on one of El Fenix's many combination plates while you bask in the cheesy matador atmosphere. Olé!

THE ORIGINAL MEXICAN EATS CAFÉ ⑤
4713 Camp Bowie Blvd., 817/738-6226
HOURS: Daily 11 A.M.-9 P.M.
Tex-Mex, old-school style, is what you'll find at

The Original Mexican Eats Café, Fort Worth's oldest Latino-owned restaurant. The prices are reasonable, and the portions of enchiladas, nachos, fajitas, and other Mexican favorites are large. The refried beans here are particularly good, rich, and creamy. "Bare bones" is the best way to describe the atmosphere, which looks as if it hasn't changed since Franklin D. Roosevelt dined here during his presidency.

Greater Fort Worth   Map 11

RESTAURANTS

AMERICAN
CHOP HOUSE BURGERS ⑤
1700 W. Park Row, #116, Arlington, 817/459-3700,
www.chophouseburgers.com
HOURS: Mon.-Sat. 11 A.M.-9 P.M.
There is a place for clean, minimalist cuisine in this world. But that place is not in a burger joint. When you want a burger, less is not more. More is more. And that's where Arlington's Chop House Burgers comes in. Not content to make his burgers out of plain ol' hamburger meat, Chop House's Kenny Mills fashions his patties from a heady mixture of slow-roasted beef brisket and ground beef for a messy, meaty burger you won't soon forget. Not baroque enough for you? Get the "cheeseburger," a chargrilled burger served on a bun made from two grilled cheese sandwiches. With an ambience as cheesy as the smoked cheddar on their burgers, the Chop House is the perfect place to indulge an artery-hardening craving.

CRAWDADDY'S SHACK ⑤
4101 W. Green Oaks Blvd., Arlington, 817/692-7460,
www.whosyourcrawdaddy1.com
HOURS: Mon.-Thurs., 10:30 A.M.-9 P.M.,
Fri.-Sat., 10:30 A.M.-10 P.M.
New Orleans natives homesick for the flavors of their fatherland can get an authentic taste of Louisiana at Arlington's Crawdaddy's Shack. If it's famous in the Big Easy, it's on the menu here: jambalaya, gumbo, red beans and rice, a nice boudin, and even alligator sauce piquant. But the deep fryer is where Crawdaddy's Shack shines. Most of the creatures of the Gulf are

found here, covered in a tasty batter and fried to crisp perfection. In spite of the sea-centered vittles and friendly, zippy service, the vibe here is less crazy crab shack and more family fun, with kids chomping popcorn shrimp as older folk nurse their BYOB beverages.

🄲 LONESOME DOVE ⑤⑤⑤
2406 N. Main St., 817/740-8810,
www.lonesomedovebistro.com
HOURS: Tues.-Sat. 11:30 A.M.-2:30 P.M.,
Mon.-Thurs. 5-10 P.M., Fri.-Sat. 5 P.M.-11 P.M.
Generally, it's wise to steer clear of restaurants named after popular movies, but with Lonesome Dove, it's safe to make an exception. Chef Tim Love has created an adventurous bistro menu that both celebrates and updates Western flavors. It's located in the Stockyards historical district, but that doesn't mean the food is limited to steak. You're as likely to order quail, elk, or boar here—all exquisitely prepared—as you are beef. But while the menu is modern, the decor is pure Old West, with a tin ceiling, a long wooden bar, and chefs in cowboy hats visible in the open kitchen.

SARSAPARILLA SALOON ⑤
140 E. Exchange Ave., 817/625-1822,
www.oldetymemercantile.com
HOURS: Mon.-Fri. 10 A.M.-6 P.M., Sat. 10 A.M.-7 P.M.,
Sun. noon-6 P.M.
Located in the Stockyards, the Sarsaparilla Saloon fits right into its Old West surroundings. It's an offshoot of the Old Tyme Mercantile, purveyors of 19th-century

reproduction cowboy duds, and the Sarsaparilla is itself a re-creation of an old-fashioned saloon. The simple menu features just a few fresh-made sandwiches. The real draw here is dessert: shakes, malts, and sundaes, of course, but also decadent choices like pecan pie and cheesecake.

ITALIAN

PEROTTI'S PIZZA ⑤

6136 Southwest Blvd., 871/377-2202,
www.perrottispizza.net

HOURS: Mon.-Wed. 10 A.M.-10 P.M., Thurs. 10 A.M.-11 P.M., Fri.-Sat. 10 A.M.-midnight, Sun. 11 A.M.-10 P.M.

When you can't decide between pizza and "grinders" (East Coast lingo for sub sandwiches), Perotti's has got you covered. The secret to this family-owned spot's delicious pizza? Freshly house-made crust—garlicky, thick, and deep-dished to perfection. Grinders come in hot and cold varieties, but the meatball sandwich is king here. There's a slate of pastas, too.

PICCOLO MONDO ⑤⑤⑤

829 Lamar Blvd. E., Arlington, 817/265-9174,
www.piccolomondo.com

HOURS: Mon.-Thurs. 11:30 A.M.-2:15 P.M. and 5:30-10 P.M., Fri. 11:30 A.M.-2:15 P.M. and 5:30-11 P.M., Sat. 5:30-11 P.M., Sun. 5-10 P.M.

Piccolo Mondo has never let its strip mall locale hinder it. In fact, considering that much of Arlington is asphalt and concrete, the location is rather suitable in some sense. It doesn't match, however, the elegance of the surroundings and deliciousness of the Italian fare that lies within. Expect straightforward, classic Italian pastas with a touch of seafood here. No trendy molecular cooking or overwrought descriptions to throw you for a loop—just excellent service, friendly atmosphere, and well-executed food. A couple quick caveats: Piccolo Mondo is one of the most popular places in town, so be prepared for a lively buzz. And the restaurant features piano entertainment during peak times, seven days a week, so if that sort of thing annoys you, best to avoid it.

Piccolo Mondo

COURTESY OF PICCOLO MONDO

MEDITERRANEAN

GEORGE'S SPECIALTY FOODS ⑤

4424 White Settlement Rd., 817/737-0414
HOURS: Tues.-Sat. 9:30 A.M.-5 P.M.

This Greek grocery and café has sat quietly on a nondescript stretch of White Settlement Road for decades, silently beckoning to lovers of dolma, baklava, and gyros (they're the best in town). While there are a few tables at this unassuming spot, it serves takeout clientele admirably, along with epicureans in search of olive oils, olives, and other imported goodies.

RUSSIAN

TASTE OF EUROPE ⑤⑤

1901 W. Pioneer Pkwy., Arlington, 817/275-5530,
www.tasteofeuropetx.com

HOURS: Tues.-Sat. noon-9 P.M., Sun. noon-5 P.M.

Slightly resembling a concrete bunker and set amidst a spate of car dealerships and stereo stores, A Taste of Europe is not the kind of place that turns heads. But the earthy,

RESTAURANTS

authentic Russian food here—rich, tender pierogies, stuffed cabbage with meat or rice and vegetables, a pickle-y chilled beet borscht (perfect for a hot summer day), and lacy potato pancakes—belie the boring digs. Proprietor Mikhail Frumkin doesn't waste an inch of space of this when it comes to his entrepreneurial gumption: The restaurant doubles as a retail venue offering handmade Russian treasures, with nesting dolls alongside Communist-era memorabilia and a nice selection of imported groceries.

STEAK HOUSE

CATTLEMEN'S STEAKHOUSE ❸❸❸

2458 N. Main St., 817/624-3945, www.cattlemenssteakhouse.com
HOURS: Mon.-Thurs. 11 A.M.-10:30 P.M., Fri.-Sat. 11 A.M.-11 P.M., Sun. noon-9 P.M.

When viewing all those longhorns on the hoof at the Stockyards gives you a deep hankering for a thick steak (but no desire to bust your wallet paying for it), swing the family on into Cattlemen's Steakhouse, a Fort Worth institution for more than half a century. There are more than a dozen different steaks on the menu (ranging from porterhouse to chicken-fried) to slake your thirst for red meat. There's even a six-ounce hunk of steak on the children's menu (after all, you gotta teach 'em young). Kids and adults alike will dig the atmosphere of unpretentious Old West kitsch, too.

TEX-MEX

JOE T. GARCIA'S ❸❸

2201 N. Commerce St., 817/626-4356, www.joets.com
HOURS: Mon.-Thurs. 11 A.M.-2:30 P.M. and 5-10 P.M., Fri.-Sat. 11 A.M.-11 P.M., Sun. 11 A.M.-10 P.M., no credit cards accepted

Back in the day, the only way to access the dining area at Joe T. Garcia's was to walk though the kitchen. Now occupying a full city block, Joe T's is more like a Mexican restaurant theme park than an actual Mexican restaurant. Strolling mariachis, opulent decor, a poolside outdoor seating area, and seating for 1,000 make it a sure bet that a meal here will be memorable. The menu is not the draw—dinner offerings are limited to fajitas or enchiladas. Well, actually, maybe it's the *lack* of menu that's the draw: Joe T's has been famous for doing a few things but doing them amazingly well. Plus, you'll need to eat after indulging in the strong margaritas.

RESTAURANTS

NIGHTLIFE

Considering Texas's brassy reputation, is it any wonder this is a population that likes to go out? When it comes to hanging out at clubs, bars, lounges, discos, sports bars, or any other gathering spot, you can count on DFW denizens of all stripes to be there en masse. Night owls here don't wait for the weekend—there are simply too many places to go.

A good place to start is with a band—the DFW area has a long, intimate relationship with live music. Many Dallasites, for instance, are lured out into the night by the long row of live music venues that make up Lower Greenville Avenue, while Fort Worthers indulge in the town's long legacy of small, intimate stages and unexpected venues like the Modern and even grocery stores.

Twists on the usual bar games are popular, too: Trivia nights abound, as do karaoke nights (even some with live backing bands), Golden Tee tournaments, and retro video games. Even a version of Texas's extensive underground poker scene has wriggled its way aboveground: The cards fly once or twice a week at poker night at many different places (not for cash, of course—winners get gift certificates or other prizes).

A few things to remember: In Dallas, parking will most likely be a hassle no matter where you go, so bring extra cash for valet service or be prepared to walk. Fort Worth's parking situation is much easier to contend with, especially in the free lots and garages that surround Sundance Square. Second,

© NIKKI GREER/DALLAS CVB

though a few after-hours dance clubs speckle the scene, state law dictates that alcohol-serving establishments must close no later than 2 A.M., and most close a few minutes before that. Finally, smokers should be aware that Dallas adheres to a strict smoking ban.

HIGHLIGHTS

LOOK FOR 🌙 TO FIND RECOMMENDED NIGHTLIFE.

© JOHANNA WIDNER

T&P Tavern

🌙 **Best Bar Games:** With 24 beers on tap, a bank of HD and old-school video games and Skee-Ball, think of **Barcadia** as an adult Chuck E. Cheese (page 94).

🌙 **Best Grown-up Bar:** More than just a hotel bar, **The Library Bar**'s cozy leather chairs, upscale bar menu, and nightly jazz piano give it a comfy, but mature, air (page 98).

🌙 **Best Dive Bar: Ships** is tiny, cheap, and bedecked with an inexplicable nautical theme. In other words, it's the perfect dive (page 100).

🌙 **Best Atmosphere:** The **T&P Tavern**'s soaring two-story ceilings and spectacular art deco surroundings make it an impressive space to enjoy drinks (page 101).

🌙 **Best Gay Cowboy Bar:** Beautifully melding two of Dallas's storied demographics—cowboys and gay men—**The Round-Up Saloon**'s dance floor hosts a lotta same-sex line dancing (page 106).

🌙 **Best Jukebox:** After listening to the jukebox at **Adair's Saloon,** with its lonesome downhome country classics from the likes of Johnny, Waylon, and Patsy, you just might end up with more than a single tear in your beer (page 107).

NIGHTLIFE

Bars

THE AMSTERDAM BAR

831 Exposition Ave., 214/827-3433,
www.theamsterdambar.com
HOURS: Daily 2:30 P.M.-2 A.M.
COST: Free
Map 5

With its exposed brick walls, rustic wooden floors, and vintage pendant lamps, the Amsterdam glows with the amber-lit ambience of a much older city. A vaguely European atmosphere, cache of board games, copious variety of tasty craft beers on tap, and understated exterior on an eclectic, out-of-the-way street are usually reliable signposts of hipsterdom, but the Amsterdam pulls it off—along with a Monday jazz night—with an utter lack of pretension. The low-key staff is friendly and happy to help with the cultivated beer selection or drop cocktail knowledge if asked, but only in the least overbearing way imaginable. Clearly hooked into its transitioning, arty surroundings, the club hosts food trucks, sponsors gallery openings, and welcomes a small retinue of regulars who seem to like talking about beer and music for the most part. There is live music most nights, and a spacious patio in back, but a happy hour visit is rewarded with great beer specials and a subdued window seat at which to read, write, or muse on streetside goings-on.

ANVIL PUB

2637 Elm St., 214/741-1271
HOURS: Mon.-Fri. 4 P.M.-2 A.M., Sat.-Sun. 11 A.M.-2 A.M.
COST: Free
Map 5

Funny that a spot with such an English pub feel would kick it so Texan, but the Anvil Pub manages to cross the pond aesthetic-wise while keeping it local behind the bar. The proprietors of this Deep Ellum haunt stock plenty of local craft brews both on tap and in-bottle, and make sure to offer special deals on all sorts of Texas-concocted potables, from Fort Worth's Rahr beer to Austin's Tito's vodka. It's a clever balance to the exposed red bricks, dark lighting, high ceilings, and Brit-pop soundtrack that lilts out of the speakers. As with many Deep Ellum establishments, the food is better-than-average bar food, served to the tattooed, the well-coiffed, and the be-Conversed.

BAR BELMONT

901 Fort Worth Ave., 214/393-2300,
www.belmontdallas.com
HOURS: Sun.-Wed. 4-11 P.M.,
Thurs.-Sat. 4 P.M.-midnight
COST: Free
Map 6

Featuring one of the city's best views of downtown, Bar Belmont fancies itself a modern lounge. The mod furniture and low, pastel lighting might support that theory, but in reality, Bar Belmont is a laid-back, comfortable place. It's updated but not stuffy, and boasts a particularly good bar menu. If you're looking to escape loud joints filled with Golden Tee machines, but also want to skip the Uptown snoot, Bar Belmont is an excellent place.

◖ BARCADIA

1917 N. Henderson Ave., 214/821-7300,
www.barcadiadallas.com
HOURS: Mon.-Sat. 4 P.M.-2 A.M., Sun. 11 A.M.-2 A.M.
COST: Free
Map 4

With its bank of vintage video games and Skee-Ball, huge choice of beers, and 1950s motif, Barcadia consistently draws a crowd looking for a laid-back good time. The vibe here is casual, but definitely not dingy, with a constant stream of energy thanks to the young, hip crowd. Beware: At peak times, the line for Skee-Ball can be long; wait it out while people-watching on the always-packed porch.

BILLIARD BAR

1920 Greenville Ave., 214/826-7665
HOURS: Mon.-Sat. 5:30 P.M.-2 A.M.,
Sun. 5:30 P.M.-midnight
COST: Free
`Map 4`

Other Dallas pool halls may have a bit more room or better felt, but none compares to the Billiard Bar for atmosphere and location. True, this Greenville Avenue mainstay once cornered the market for retro-swank stick-and-cue environs, but now comes off as a bit faded. Still, the regulation-size tables are just fine, the sticks are straight, and the hip bar staff always plays good music.

BOOGER RED'S

105 E. Exchange Ave., 817/624-1246
HOURS: Mon.-Thurs. 11 A.M.-10 P.M., Fri. 11 A.M.-11 P.M.,
Sat. 9 A.M.-11 P.M., Sun. 9 A.M.-10 P.M.
COST: Free
`Map 11`

Named after a legendary Texas bronc buster, Booger Red's takes Fort Worth's Wild West aesthetic to kitschy extremes, from the saddle bar stools to the bordello-red walls to the large buffalo derriere that sticks out from the mirror behind the bar. Said derriere is the namesake of the Buffalo Butt Beer that is served here alongside a large variety of tequila and an excellent food menu.

BRYAN STREET TAVERN

4315 Bryan St., 214/821-4447,
www.bryanstreettavern.com
HOURS: Daily 11 A.M.-2 A.M.
COST: Free
`Map 5`

Half of Bryan Street Tavern's 20 tap beers are from Texas breweries, and many of the 60 bottled beers stocked here are craft brews—an embarrassment of riches that can make it difficult to decide what to order. It's a nice problem to have, and fortunately the bar's shuffleboard, comfy couches, and festive patio (replete with a great skyline view) also make it a place to sit a spell, so there's plenty of time to sample several.

Other draws: live music, good pizza, and hella hot buffalo wings.

THE CHAT ROOM PUB

1263 W. Magnolia Ave., 817/922-8319,
www.thechatroompub.com
HOURS: Mon.-Fri. 4 P.M.-2 A.M., Sat.-Sun. noon-2 A.M.
COST: Free
`Map 9`

It self-deprecatingly bills itself as "easily Fort Worth's eighth best bar," but as a laid-back neighborhood hangout, The Chat Room ranks far higher than that. It sits in a frankly ugly, square, squat building on cute little Magnolia Avenue, but inside you'll find a cozy, friendly pseudo-dive with wood paneling and Formica floors, friendly bartenders, and even Fort Worth microbrew Rahr beer on tap. The atmosphere is thick with hipster cachet—gimme caps and pearl snap shirts abound—but not in a particularly snooty way. Perhaps that's because patrons find themselves having too much fun playing Skee-Ball, pinball, or pool to bother with irony. Definitely check to see if there's a band playing; while the Chat isn't primarily a music venue, the choosy proprietors put their excellent taste to good use booking the occasional indie/local band, so the tunes are always top-notch.

COSMO'S RESTAURANT AND BAR

1212 Skillman Ave., 214/826-4200,
www.cosmosbar.com
HOURS: Daily 5 P.M.-2 A.M.
COST: Free
`Map 4`

Maybe the denizens of Lakewood are so comfortable at Cosmo's because with the thrift-store couches, dark lighting, and lava lamps, it feels like an extended version of their hipster living rooms. That's what makes Cosmo's such a popular destination—it's cozy and comfy, but still has an edge to it. Adding to the living room—writ-large sensation are the movie screens showing classics of all genres, the friendly familiarity of the patrons, and the free-flowing PBR. Cosmo's serves pizza that will do in a pinch, but don't consider it a dinner destination.

NIGHTLIFE

SOMETHING'S BREWING

Used to be, in DFW the only taps you'd find behind a bar consisted of the "holy trinity": Bud Light, Miller Lite, and Coors Light. Other choices: Lone Star, aka the "national beer of Texas," which has a certain Texas cool cachet, but if we are to be honest about it, basically is Pabst Blue Ribbon in a different can. Then there's Shiner Bock, for decades the only craft beer widely distributed here, often listed under the "import" section of menus, even though it's made in *Shiner, Texas*. Guess the brew's dark, European flavor threw everybody off.

In other words, the Texas palate has never been known for its sophistication when it comes to all things hoppy. It's not that North Texans don't like to drink beer, it's just that for a long time, North Texans didn't like to drink *good* beer.

At least until now. Recently, Dallas-Fort Worth has enjoyed a craft beer explosion, spearheaded by two local craft breweries: **Rahr & Sons** in Fort Worth (701 Galveston Ave., 817/810-9266, www.rahrbrewing.com), and **Deep Ellum Brewing Company** in Dallas (2823 St. Louis St., 214/888-3322, www.deepellumbrewing.com).

Fritz Rahr started Rahr & Sons with a tiny brewery and even tinier budget; within seven years, the company's brewing capacity had increased tenfold. The urge to brew runs through Fritz's veins: His great-great-grandfather, William Rahr, came from a long line of brewers. William emigrated to Wisconsin and opened the Eagle Brewery there in 1847. His operation soon grew and expanded, as he added a malt house that soon became a major national distributor of malted barley.

It's fitting, albeit rather sad, that William's career came to an end when he fell into a brewing vat while on an inspection tour of the brewery and suffered injuries from which he never recovered. In his honor, his sons renamed the operation William Rahr's Sons Co.

Today, Rahr & Sons brews up five year-round beers (the Ugly Pug Black lager is a must for beer-lovers) plus a handful of limited-edition seasonals, all of which can be found on tap and in bottles all around the Metroplex. Brewery tours are available Wednesday 5-7 P.M. and Saturday 1-3 P.M. Reservations are not required.

Where Rahr & Sons' story is steeped in tradition, Deep Ellum Brewing Company's tale bubbles with boisterous rebellion. John Reardon, Jim Piel, and Scott Frieling began their brewery—Dallas's first microbrewery—after deciding they were tired of bland, watery, mass-produced beer (dare we say, the holy trinity?).

The three met as competitors. Reardon submitted his application for the trademark to Deep Ellum Brewing Company to the State of Texas in 2010. Two days later, business partners Piel and Frieling did the same, unaware that Reardon had beaten them to the punch. Seems that the two parties had independently decided on the same name, for the same endeavor.

Reardon exchanged unpleasantries with Piel and Frieling until the three finally agreed to meet. After a few get-togethers, they realized they should work as a team, and the Deep Ellum Brewing Company was born. The company culture blends equal parts hard work and a goofy affability, as embodied in the DEBC's "beerfesto," which ends with a promise to "never serve a single glass of bad beer."

Now beer aficionados and casual drinkers tend to quaff DEBC Deep Ellum IPA, Double Brown Stout, or any of the company's other beers at bars and restaurants around the area—plus Austin and even Boston, Massachusetts—instead of defaulting to big-name pilsners. But one of the best ways to sip DEBC's wares is during their brewery tours (Thurs. 6-8:30 P.M., Sat. noon-3 P.M., $10 includes DEBC logo glass and beer tastings), after which patrons spill out into the beer garden to enjoy live music and pair the brews with nearby food trucks.

FLYING SAUCER
111 E. 3rd St., 817/336-7470, www.beerknurd.com
HOURS: Mon.-Wed. 11 A.M.-1 A.M., Thurs.-Sat.
11 A.M.-2 A.M., Sun. noon-midnight
COST: Free
`Map 8`

The Flying Saucer is part of a rapidly grow-ing chain, but given the charm and popularity of the downtown Fort Worth location, you'd never know it. The move from the original lo-cation in a freestanding historic building to less charismatic digs down the street saddened some, but it's tough to argue with a greatly ex-panded indoor and outdoor seating area and more than 100 beers on tap. The beer house stays constantly crowded, as brew enthusiasts ranging from hippies to defense contractors gather to quaff.

FRANKIE'S SPORTS BAR
3227 McKinney Ave., 214/999-8932,
www.frankiesbar.com
HOURS: Daily 11 A.M.-2 A.M.
COST: Free
`Map 2`

Have we mentioned DFW is a sports-obsessed part of the world? Sports bars are a dime a dozen, and large TVs tuned to the game can be found in almost every establishment in town, so a sports bar *really* has to give you a reason to patronize its particular establishment. With tons of beer on tap and a willingness to tune one of its dozens of screens to, as a friend of this author once noted, "your weirdo 2 P.M. hockey game," Frankie's makes a good argument. Get there early if the Cowboys are playing. There is also a location in Fort Worth (425 W. 3rd. St., 817/870-9090).

THE GOAT
7248 Gaston Ave., 214/327-8119,
www.thegoatdallas.com
HOURS: Mon.-Sat. 7 A.M.-2 P.M., Sun. noon-2 A.M.
COST: Free
`Map 7`

The Goat is dive bar heaven: We're talking

Frankie's Sports Bar provides private rooms for groups of fans.

cheap longnecks, a 7 A.M. opening time, and R&B dudes coaxing some good ol' Texas blues out of well-worn Stratocasters. The scratched up walls and duct-taped bar won't win any decor awards, to be sure, but what does it mat-ter when you're afforded people-watching as rich and varied as this? Plenty of regulars call this place home, but Wednesday and Sunday the place is populated more by hipsters who have succumbed to the siren's call of the best karaoke in town.

THE GOLD STANDARD
2700 W. 7th St., 817/810-9999,
www.thegoldstandardbar.com
HOURS: Mon.-Fri. 4 P.M.-2 A.M., Sat.-Sun. 6 P.M.-2 A.M.
COST: Free
`Map 8`

The standard bearer of Fort Worth's cocktail culture, Brad Hensarling has somehow man-aged to open three bars that belie the town's

© JONANNA WIDNER

NIGHTLIFE

traditionally beer-focused quaffing preferences—the Usual, the Chat Room, and most recently, the Gold Standard. The Standard, opened in the same West 7th standalone that once housed a beloved old bar called Seventh Haven, follows the dive bar aesthetic (albeit much more ironically than its dressed down brother the Chat Room), serving up old standards along with new twists on traditional standbys. This is an establishment unashamed to offer bison grass–infused vodka specialty cocktails right alongside the ol' Natty Light and a shot of rye.

THE IDLE RICH

2614 McKinney Ave., 214/965-9926, www.idlerichpub.com
HOURS: Mon.-Thurs. 3 P.M.-2 A.M., Fri. 11:30 A.M.-2 A.M., Sat.-Sun. 11 A.M.-2 A.M.
COST: Free
Map 1

It's hard to go wrong with an Irish pub whose owner is named Feargal McKinney, and the Idle Rich Pub doesn't disappoint when it comes to pubby staples like shepherd's pie, a Euro-heavy draught list, and dark, wood-paneled surroundings (Feargal imported much of the cabinetry from Ireland). Friendly, laid-back, and lively, the Idle is one of those places everyone can agree on, which is probably why it's often packed.

LAGRANGE

2704 Elm St., 214/741-2008, www.lagrange.com
HOURS: Mon. 10 A.M.-10 P.M., Tues. 10 A.M.-2 P.M. and 5 P.M.-2 A.M., Wed.-Fri. 11 A.M.-2 P.M. and 5 P.M.-2 A.M., Sat. 11 A.M.-2 A.M., Sun. 11 A.M.-midnight
COST: Free
Map 5

Yep, it's named after the town that's namechecked in a well-known song by Texas legends ZZ Top. Or, heck, maybe it's named after the song, which is named after the town . . . the semantics don't matter, because either way, this "swanky-tonk" spot is about all things Texas. Not spur 'n' saddle Texas, mind you, but rather that mix of traditional and underground that marks a goodly part of the culture here—think

everyone from outlaw C&W stars to serious weirdos like the Butthole Surfers (hence the live music, seven nights a week, that ranges from acoustic to punk). The prices and service can be a bit hinky, but the free booze-tinged snow cones (yep, it's legal!) and menu from neighbor Rock 'n' Roll Tacos make up for that.

LEE HARVEY'S

1807 Gould St., 214/428-1555
HOURS: Mon.-Fri. 11 A.M.-2 A.M., Sat. 3 P.M.-2 A.M., Sun. 1 P.M.-2 A.M.
COST: Free
Map 6

Yep, this semi-dive is named for Lee Harvey Oswald, whose taxi ride from the School Book Depository to his Oak Cliff home on November 22 passed near here. This name's irreverence extends to much of the attitude at this popular casual locale. While the jukebox swings wildly from obscure 1980s new wave to Prince to local alt-country, clientele of all types hang out at the picnic tables in the large outside yard or dance in the almost shack-like inner sanctum.

◖ THE LIBRARY BAR

3015 Oak Lawn Ave., 214/521-5151
HOURS: Mon.-Thurs. 2 P.M.-1 A.M., Fri.-Sat. 2 P.M.-2 A.M., Sun. 11 A.M.-midnight
COST: Free
Map 2

Elegant and stately, but not stuffy, the Library Bar is an oasis of good taste in flashy Uptown, and in that sense it's a microcosm of the Melrose Hotel in which it's found. On any given night, a piano might tinkle in the background, or perhaps an unobtrusive jazz singer might scat in the corner as patrons sit in overstuffed leather chairs and sip their sidecars or imported beers. Bookshelved walls hold hundreds of volumes of the classics, though one suspects the only thing anyone reads in here is the menu, which offers upscale bar food like five-spice calamari and venison chili. A nice way to enjoy the Library is to take advantage of Tuesday night's "classic cocktails and jazz," with $4 old-school drinks and a relaxed atmosphere.

THE MEDDLESOME MOTH

1621 Oak Lawn Ave., 214/628-7900,
www.mothinthe.net
HOURS: Sun.-Thurs. 11 A.M.-midnight,
Fri.-Sat. 11 A.M.-2 A.M.
COST: Free
Map 7

The well-coiffed and tasteful gather often at this little gem of a gastropub that acts as a central point for denizens of the rapidly rising Design District. As is evident from the neighborhood's name, aesthetics run the roost in this part of town, and the Moth does the area proud. An eye-catching row of some 40 beer taps runs behind the long, elegant bar, and the proprietors pay homage to the space's former incarnation as a tile showroom by retaining the original flooring. It's inviting yet chic, comfortable but not slovenly, as a well-designed space should be. The food's top-notch too.

THE MERIDIAN ROOM

3611 Parry Ave., 214/826-8383,
www.themeridianroom.com
HOURS: Mon.-Thurs. 4 P.M.-11 P.M.,
Fri.-Sat. 4 P.M.-midnight, Sun. noon-11 P.M.

COST: Free
Map 5

Some say the Meridian Room has gone downhill in recent years, and with its spotty service and uneven execution of the menu, there's an argument to be made for that. Still, something about this Expo Park hangout remains appealing. Maybe it's because its corner location, exposed brick walls, and understated hipsterdom feel local while simultaneously evoking a Brooklyn hole-in-the-wall. Maybe it's that it's nice and dark without falling into the dive category. It's most likely all of the above, although half-price food on Wednesday doesn't hurt either.

THE POUR HOUSE

2757 W. 7th St.
HOURS: Mon.-Sat. 11 A.M.-2 A.M., Sun. noon-2 A.M.
COST: Free
Map 10

A friendly favorite downtown regulars bar, the Pour House was forced out of its 13-year home abutting Sundance Square in 2008. Fortunately, owner Chris Matatall found new digs in the burgeoning 7th Street area, so this

NIGHTLIFE

© JONANNA WIDNER

The Pour House is a popular Fort Worth watering hole.

local-favorite sports bar should maintain its casual and upbeat vibe, complete with some of the best pub grub you can find.

SANDBAR CANTINA AND GRILL

317 S. Second Ave., 214/884-5528,
http://sandbarcantina.com
HOURS: Daily 11 A.M.-2 A.M.
COST: Varies depending on event
Map 5

Also known as "beach Ellum," Sandbar carves a sandy oasis out of the concrete desert of East Dallas. The feel here definitely aims for Margaritaville, with a rooftop deck, stage, palm trees, restaurant, and bar, all revolving around eight full volleyball courts filled with white, fine, powdery sand. The view from the "beach" is not the azure of the ocean but rather the multicolored lights of downtown Dallas, which, on a clear evening, more than suffice. Many nights of the week, the courts host league play, but pickup games occur before and after, and courts can be rented by the hour. Those less athletically inclined can kick it in the surf-themed bar, complete with pool tables, TVs, and video games.

█ SHIPS

1613 Greenville Ave., 214/823-0418
HOURS: Mon.-Sat. 10 A.M.-2 A.M., Sun. noon-2 P.M.
COST: Free
Map 4

Like any good dive bar, Ships has a story. The original owner was a sailor (hence the requisite nets 'n' anchors theme on the walls). His girlfriend helped manage the place, which, for its location and clientele, brought little trouble, perhaps thanks in part to the no-cussing rule. Somewhere along the way in the mid-1970s, sadly, trouble caught up to the place, and the girlfriend shot and killed the owner.

Not much has changed at Ships since then, not even the jukebox, which is stuck in some year that probably predates much of the clientele's births. The proportions haven't changed, either—the place is as cramped as a

submarine—and it looks as if the felt on the pool table hasn't been replaced since the Cold War. This is still a beer-and-wine-only, cash bar. Oh, and that no-cussing rule? It's still in effect. And they mean it.

SLIP INN

1806 McMillan Ave., 214/370-5571, www.theslipinn.com
HOURS: Mon.-Sat. 7 P.M.-2 A.M., Sun. noon-2 A.M.
COST: Free
Map 4

Don't let the cracked vinyl booths and location next to a dingy convenience store fool you—the Slip Inn isn't a true dive bar, because no true dive bar has Morrissey on the jukebox and a hip-hop DJ on weekends. Therein lies the brilliance of the Slip Inn: its ability to meld a come-as-you-are aesthetic with a hip, underground Brooklyn feel. Dance nights on weekends pack the joint.

THE STANDARD POUR

2900 McKinney Ave., 214/935-1370,
www.tspdallas.com
HOURS: Daily 4 P.M.-2 A.M.
COST: Free
Map 2

You will not find any of the following things at The Standard Pour: Red Bull. A Jägermeister tap. A Miller Lite poster. What you *will* find: a bar meant for grown-ups. Wood and brick accents highlight the design, while those two stalwarts of pre-Prohibition cocktails—gin and bourbon—highlight a cocktail list that emphasizes properly fashioned mules (served in proper copper mugs), fizzes, and punches (served in 440-ounce and 1,440-ounce bowls), plus a healthy smattering of absinthe choices. Unlike its liquid counterpart, the food menu tries too hard to be cute (appetizers are called "Breaking the Ice," desserts fall under the heading "Closure"), but the $9 fried chicken (found under "Centers of Attention," i.e., entrées) is worth ignoring such curlicues. Snoot alert: Folks wearing athletic clothing of any kind will be turned away, and collars are encouraged, although not required.

STRANGEWAYS
2429 Fitzhugh Ave., 214/823-7800
HOURS: 4 P.M.-2 A.M.
COST: Free
Map 2

Yes, it's named after the Smiths album; no surprise, then, that the bar music—think British pop circa, 1981–1991—at this unfussy spot remains a draw for the youthful and hip. Adding to the British feel are exposed brick walls and pints that slosh across the bar at a fast clip, thanks to a diverse and well-cultivated array of draught choices.

T&P TAVERN
221 W. Lancaster Ave., 817/885-8878,
www.tptavern.com
HOURS: Mon.-Fri. 4 P.M.-2 A.M., Sat. 3 P.M.-2 A.M.,
Sun. noon-2 A.M.
COST: Free
Map 8

Traversing the 5,000-square-foot patio leading into the T&P Tavern, you'd figure the outdoor area (complete with darts, cornhole, and a fan big enough to power a spacecraft) would be the most impressive space this downtown Fort Worth bar has to offer. Not even close. Housed in what was once the lobby for the T&P Railroad line, the tavern manages to remain casual, despite its two- (or is it three-?) story ceilings, bedecked with copper and tin molding, and original art deco ornamentation. Quite frankly, the place is shockingly impressive, so much so that its owners could merely, if they chose, stick a couple kegs behind the bar, toss together a half-decent staff, and call it a job well done. Fortunately, someone behind the scenes has done justice to the space. The staff is friendly, the beer choices heavily Texan, and the menu simple but thoughtfully constructed. The pièce de résistance: The T&P

building has been converted into loft apartments, and also serves as the terminal for the Trinity Railway Express, so the environs maintain a modern energy juxtaposed with a cool throwback feel.

TEN SPORTS GRILL
1302 Main St., 214/748-1010, www.tensportsgrill.com
HOURS: Daily 11 A.M.-2 A.M.
COST: Free
Map 1

Weirdly, downtown Dallas boasts very few sports bars (perhaps because, due to local obsessions with the Cowboys, Rangers, and Mavericks, TVs have replaced beer signs as the requisite wall decor in every bar around town). With that in mind, Ten deserves an endorsement neither for its decor nor its food, but rather just due to the fact that it is a spot for downtown visitors to catch a game, chomp some wings, and grab a beer.

THE USUAL
1408 W. Magnolia Ave., 817/810-0114,
www.theusualbar.com
HOURS: Mon.-Fri. 4 P.M.-2 A.M., Sat.-Sun. 6 P.M.-2 A.M.
COST: Free
Map 9

Don't worry if you slide onto one of The Usual's sleek bar stools, glance at the menu, and find yourself lost (Rum Agricole? Walnut Eau de Vie? What are these things?). The experts behind the bar know the ins and outs of all sorts of libations, and are happy to fill you in on the art of the cocktail, from the obscure to the old classics. Proprietor Brian Hensarling is positively obsessed with mixology, and his focus lends itself to a fun menu that proves creative but not frivolous. The same goes for the vibe here, with its clean lines, modern feel, and walls covered in gorgeous white oak.

NIGHTLIFE

Clubs and Lounges

BILLY BOB'S TEXAS

2520 Rodeo Plaza, 817/624-7117,
www.billybobstexas.com

HOURS: Mon.-Tues. 11 A.M.-10 P.M., Wed. 11 A.M.-
midnight, Thurs.-Sat. 11 A.M.-2 A.M., Sun. noon-10 P.M.,
Fri.-Sat. closed for sound check from 5-6 P.M.

COST: Varies depending on event

Map 11

It's billed as the world's biggest honky-tonk, and they ain't foolin'. At around 100,000 square feet, Billy Bob's feels more like an indoor amusement park than a club. Consider the concert hall, 32 drink stations, barn-size gift shops, full restaurants, and indoor rodeo with live bull riding if you need any convincing of the Texas-size proportions of this place.

Still, Billy Bob's is always about the music. Country music, to be exact. While the concert hall sees some of Nashville's best acts, as well as a few classic rock shows, it's the lariat-laced dance floor—complete with mirrored saddle in place of a disco ball—that sees the most action here. Billy Bob's is a place where line-dancing never died, where the Cotton-Eyed Joe and two-stepping set the pace, and where strangers still ask each other to dance.

THE WORLD'S LARGEST HONKY-TONK

Billy Bob's Texas doesn't have a mechanical bull. Let's just get that straight right off the bat.

If you're thinking mechanical bull, you're thinking Gilley's—the Pasadena, TX honky-tonk made famous by the John Travolta movie *Urban Cowboy*. But you're on the right path: Gilley's *used* to be the world's largest honky-tonk. Until Billy Bob's came along.

In April 1981, Billy Bob Barnett opened his namesake club in an old cattle barn. With 127,000 square feet of space (enough for 6,000 people), dozens of bar stations, and—forget some wannabe mechanical bull—an entire indoor rodeo arena, Billy Bob's soon made a name for itself as a Texas-size destination.

It's almost impossible to describe the scale of Billy Bob's—it's more like an amusement park than a nightclub. It helps to know a bit about the place's history. As a cattle barn, the Billy Bob's building held about 1,200 pens. During World War II, the building served as an airplane factory, and after that it served as a department store so large the stockers wore roller skates to get around faster.

With a place that big, and with so many entertainment options to offer, it's tough to navigate. So here's a handy guide to the World's Largest Honky-Tonk:

- **Hours:** Mon.-Tues. 11 A.M.-10 P.M., Wed. 11 A.M.-midnight, Thurs.-Sat. 11 A.M.-2 A.M., Sun. noon-10 P.M., Fri.-Sat. closed for sound check 5-6 P.M.

- **Cover Charge:** (Note: The following are for typical nights only. Cover charge can vary greatly depending on performer and entertainment.) Sun.-Tues. $2 before 7 P.M., $3 after 7 P.M., Wed.-Thurs. $2 before 8 P.M., $4 after 8 P.M., Fri.-Sat. $2 before 5 P.M.

- **Parking:** (Note: Prices are subject to change, depending on the event.) Billy Bob's own parking lot spans 20 acres—and it's advisable to use it, although there are other lots in the area, as the neighborhood can get a little rowdy after sundown. Parking is free Monday through Thursday. Weekend parking rates are as follows: Sun.-Thurs. self-parking is free; Fri.-Sat. self-parking is $5 after 11 A.M.; valet parking is available for $10 after 5 P.M.

- **Got Kids?:** Although it's a honky-tonk, Billy Bob's is quite family friendly and a popular destination for moms, pops, and their kids. Visitors 17 years old or younger must have a parent or guardian present. Guardians must be at least 30 years old and have a signed consent form, available on the Billy Bob's website. Visitors over 18 must present ID at the door (only 21 and up are allowed to drink alcohol, of course).

- **Dance Instruction:** Line dancing: Thurs. 7-8 P.M., free. Other beginner and

ESCAPADE 2009

10701 Finnell St., 214/654-9950,
www.escapadedallas.com
HOURS: Wed.-Sun. 8 P.M.-4 A.M.
COST: Varies depending on event
`Map 7`

Escapade 2009 is one of those mega-clubs with several separate clubs within, each featuring a different type of music. What makes Escapade unique is its six different dance areas catering solely to varieties of Latin music, from rancheros to reggaeton. The humming energy here is infectious, as the vast dance expanses are filed with both revelers and a super light show. Despite its size, Escapade is consistently packed on weekends, with hundreds of patrons happily shelling out cover charges that range from $12 to way beyond for a chance to boogie on the ample dance floors. If you want to get your cumbia on sans such expense, try getting there before 9 P.M., when entry is free.

LIVING ROOM BAR

2440 Victory Park Ln., 214/397-4100
HOURS: Daily 6 P.M.-2 A.M.
COST: Free
`Map 1`

Oh sure, there's a slightly pretentious, cougar-y vibe in the air here—after all it's the W—but the cool purple-hued furniture and expertly concocted cocktails provide a relaxing oasis in the middle of Victory Park.

---

intermediate lessons in different genres are available on a rotating schedule for around $5. Check the website for details.

- **Bull Riding:** You can't go to Billy Bob's without checking out the rodeo; after all, there's nothing better than dancing the Cotton-eyed Joe and then popping over to watch a 2,000-pound bull tossing around the 150-pound man on his back. Fri.-Sat. 9 P.M. and 10 P.M., $3.

- **Food:** Barbecue, Tex-Mex, and fried finger foods are available at the restaurant, although it's a touch overpriced and nothing to write home about.

- **Concerts:** Billy Bob's has two stages: The smaller one, for house bands and the like, is in the middle of the complex, between two dance floors. The larger stage, where huge country stars, classic rock bands, and even some pop bands play, sits at the end of the larger dance floor.

- **When music, dancing, and the rodeo aren't enough:** The video game arcade, Handprint Hall of Fame (with prints from everyone from George Strait to Ringo Starr), pool tables, and Dry Goods Store (aka the gift shop) round out the Billy Bob's experience.

BILLY BOB'S TRIVIA:

- Four movies have been filmed at Billy Bob's: *Baja Oklahoma*, *Necessary Roughness*, *Over the Top*, and *Pure Country*.

- The rhinestone-encrusted saddle that serves as a dance floor disco ball is from the Dolly Parton movie *Rhinestone*.

- Billy Bob's is about three times the size of the original Gilley's.

- Some parts of the floor at Billy Bob's are sloped, dating back to the days when the building served as a cattle barn—sloped floors were easier to clean.

- Country singer Merle Haggard set a world record at Billy Bob's by buying the entire house a beer.

- The Gatlin Brothers, Willie Nelson, and Waylon Jennings all played the opening week at Billy Bob's.

- Country greats George Strait and Rick Trevino both got their starts at Billy Bob's. Strait was an opening act and Trevino won a talent show there.

- After the *Urban Cowboy* craze died down, Barnett and his co-owner struggled to keep the club open. Billy Bob's closed in 1988, but fortunately reopened under new ownership and has been going strong ever since.

NIGHTLIFE

LIZARD LOUNGE
2424 Swiss Ave., 214/826-4786,
www.thelizardlounge.com
HOURS: Thurs.-Sun. 9 P.M.-4 A.M.
COST: Varies depending on event
Map 5

Okay, so it's the kind of place with a shot bar and bikini-clad go-go girls (not the retro kind, either), but if you want to dance to internationally and nationally known live DJs, slither down to the Lizard Lounge and stay after hours, because the pumping music makes up for the cheese factor. If house and hip-hop don't appeal, try the goth-themed "The Church" night on Thursday and Sunday.

ZUBAR
2012 Greenville Ave., 214/887-0071,
www.thezubar.com
HOURS: Sun.-Fri. 5 P.M.-2 A.M., Sat. 6 P.M.-2 A.M.
COST: Varies depending on event
Map 4

With its banquette tables and sponge-painted walls, Zubar would almost give off a restaurant feel if it weren't for the excellent DJs and dance space. With above-average hip-hop and house, two different rooms, and a classy vibe, Zubar is an energetic spot that's a perfect compromise between a cavernous dance club and a tiny bar. Honestly, the clientele here tend toward the young and the wasted, but if you're in the mood to boogie without making too big a night out of it, check this place out.

Gay and Lesbian

BJ'S NXS
3215 N. Fitzhugh Ave., 214/526-9510, www.bjnex.com
HOURS: Tues.-Sat. 6 P.M.-2 A.M., Sun.-Mon. 4 P.M.-2 A.M.
COST: Varies depending on event
Map 2

It's sort of an unwritten rule that any club whose name consists merely of initials is probably trouble, but BJs is the good kind of trouble. With its preponderance of waifish male dancers, chiseled bartenders, and special appearances by, er, certain types of film stars, this place is about as subtle as a disco ball, but continues to up the ante with big-name guest DJs and the occasional pop star. Former Pussycat Doll Kaya Jones gave a live performance in the fall of 2012, and of all the bars in Dallas, Adam Lambert made BJs his stop when his tour swung through in 2010.

THE BRICK/JOE'S
2525 Wycliff Ave., 214/521-3154, www.brickdallas.com
HOURS: Sun. 2-10 P.M., Mon. 4-10 P.M., Tues.-Thurs. 4 P.M.-2 A.M., Fri. 4 P.M.-4 A.M., Sat. 2 P.M.-4 A.M.
COST: Varies depending on event
Map 2

This former leather 'n' Levi's bar has reinvented itself as a dance club popular with the African American community, as well as a prime go-to spot for special event fundraisers. Hip-hop Fridays and Sensual Saturdays are big nights, as are nights when female DJ C Wade spins (Dallas is a bit behind the times when it comes to DJ diversity). Joe's is the smaller bar attached to the main club that features dancers and karaoke nights as well as a quieter place to drink.

CLUB REFLECTION
604 Jennings Ave., 817/870-8867
HOURS: Daily 2 P.M.-2 A.M.
COST: Varies depending on event
Map 9

It looks dark and dive-y from the outside, but inside, Club Reflection is a friendly, cute GLBT country-and-western establishment, replete with rustic decor and aw-shucks bartenders who smile sweetly under their Stetsons. While the Rainbow Lounge across the street pumps it up with beat-heavy dance music, here the dance floor is filled with two-steppers and line-dancers sashaying to the likes of George Strait and Randy Travis. Drinks are fairly priced and often on special, so it remains affordable to down a couple longnecks before embarking on a beginners line dance lesson (held weekly).

NIGHTLIFE

THE RAINBOW LOUNGE RAID

While the Rainbow Lounge is probably Fort Worth's favorite gay bar, it's well known for another reason. Some time after midnight on June 28, 2009, the club was raided by officers of the Texas Alcoholic Beverage Commission (TABC) and the Fort Worth Police Department. A number of patrons were arrested for public intoxication, and one man was seriously injured with brain and head trauma after being in custody.

The truth of what happened that night (which also happened to be the 40th anniversary of the Stonewall Riots triggered by a police raid on a gay bar in New York City, considered to be the beginning of the gay rights movement in the United States) will most likely be forever obscured. Witnesses say the TABC and police acted overly aggressively and seemed intent on roughing up innocent people. The TABC and police have long denied this.

The incident caused an uproar in the GLBT community in both Dallas and Fort Worth, as well as nationwide, including coverage by the *New York Times* and other major news outlets. An official investigation was launched, and although it was never proven that the bar was targeted specifically for its gay clientele, three officers were suspended, all charges against the arrestees were dropped, and the city of Fort Worth launched a comprehensive diversity program.

Although the incident ultimately triggered a shift for the better in Fort Worth's culture, it did little to dispel the perception that Texas is not a particularly GLBT-friendly state.

DALLAS EAGLE

2515 Inwood Rd., 214/357-4375, www.dallaseagle.com
HOURS: Sun.-Thurs. 4 P.M.-2 A.M., Fri.-Sat. 4 P.M.-4 A.M.
COST: Varies depending on event
Map 7

As Dallas's favorite bear club, Dallas Eagle isn't for everyone (hint: If you don't know what a "bear" is, you probably don't want to go). It's definitely a specific scene, catering to an older crowd and those who celebrate the old-school queer aesthetic. Perhaps the club's theme nights say it all: "Shirtless Tuesdays" lead to "Underwear Wednesdays" and beyond.

DALLAS WOODY'S SPORTS & VIDEO BAR

4011 Cedar Springs Rd., 214/520-6629,
www.dallaswoodys.com
HOURS: Mon.-Sun. 2 P.M.-2 A.M.
COST: Free
Map 2

This bar on the main drag of Cedar Springs is the chief supporter of Dallas's large contingent of queer athletes, lending its name and sponsorship to rugby, softball, and basketball teams in the community. Woody's has built a strong and consistent rep with the gay sports scene of Dallas, and the teams pay it back in full by calling Woody's home. But it has a lot more going on than just ball action. Non-sporties need love, too, and Woody's delivers it with live music on the back patio, show tunes every Tuesday, and karaoke with drag queens at various points during the week. Ample and clever patio space on both floors works for those who prefer the outdoors for their people-watching (read: cruising) while lighting up a ciggie or catching an autumnal breeze.

JR'S BAR AND GRILL

3923 Cedar Springs Rd., 214/528-1004,
www.jrsdallas.com
HOURS: Tues.-Sat. 11 A.M.-2 A.M., Sun.-Mon. noon-2 A.M.
COST: Varies depending on event
Map 2

Once one of the only gay bars on what's known as "The Strip," JR's is now the flagship in Caven Enterprise's fleet of queer-oriented nightspots. Even as a number of gay hangouts have cropped up around it, this lively, boy-friendly spot is still the place to go in the Cedar Springs neighborhood—a night out usually involves it in one way or another. The crowd is flirty, friendly, and mixed—folks of all stripes are welcome.

NIGHTLIFE

And, yes, it is named after the character from the TV show *Dallas.*

KALIENTE (DISCOTEC)

4350 Maple Ave., 214/520-6676, www.kaliente.cc

HOURS: Daily 9 P.M.-2 A.M.

COST: Varies depending on event

Map 7

You're likely to get frisked with an electric wand before paying cover and entering this Latino gay nightspot, but don't let that stop you from experiencing the energy of this place. Men and women mix well here while the DJ pumps out dance, reggaeton, rock *en español,* cumbia, and tejano jams. It's the rough edges that give this popular spot its character. Drag queens fill the calendar practically every night of the month when the DJ isn't filling the dance floor on the weekends. Kaliente also hosts the majority of the Latino-based pageants, as well as the occasional live music club act.

THE RAINBOW LOUNGE

651 S. Jennings Ave., 817/744-7723

HOURS: Mon. 3 P.M.-2 A.M., Tues.-Thurs. noon-2 A.M., Fri.-Sat. noon-3 A.M.

COST: Varies depending on event

Map 9

Stepping into the Rainbow Lounge is like taking a time portal to the 1990s—in a good way. On busy nights, scantily clad fellas glide by carrying trays of fluorescent Jell-O shots as DJ'ed house music thumps away, and while the bar caters mostly to men, plenty of lesbians and straight folks frequent the place. Expect plenty of sweaty dancing, go-go boys, and the more than occasional drag queen show.

(THE ROUND-UP SALOON

3912 Cedar Springs Rd., 214/522-9611, www.roundupsaloon.com

HOURS: Daily 3 P.M.-2 A.M.

COST: Varies depending on event

Map 2

Before there was *Brokeback Mountain,* there was the Round-Up, where that singular Dallas inhabitant, the gay cowboy, can go to two-step, shuffle, and waltz. Since 1980, the Round-Up has corralled thousands of patrons sporting checked shirts, tight jeans, and giant belt buckles, patrons who've spent many an evening dancing to the 24-7 C&W played by live DJs. The musical mix sashays from classic country to nouveau-Nashville, making a fine backdrop for chatty patrons at any of the six different themed bars. Even if you're not much of a country fan, don't worry—the crowd here is friendly and fun, and most folks will even teach you to dance if you ask.

STATION 4

3911 Cedar Springs Rd., 214/526-7171, www.station4dallas.com

HOURS: Daily 9 P.M.-4 A.M.

COST: Varies depending on event

Map 2

It's a good thing Station 4 is the size of a Wal-Mart, because it's the only real dance club in the middle of Dallas's gay district. This spot is exactly what a classic gay dance club should be—enormous, with different stations to keep the attention-deficit crowd pleased and an absolutely killer lighting system. The latter makes up for a lack of imagination in the music department—think bass-heavy oomph-oomph-oomph house—but the energy here flows as freely as the vodka and Red Bull.

SUE ELLEN'S

3014 Throckmorton St., 214/559-0707, www.sueellensdallas.com

HOURS: Daily 4 P.M.-2 A.M.

COST: Varies depending on event

Map 2

For years the girl bar Sue Ellen's played little sister to its always-hopping brother bar, JR's, up the street, but in 2007 Sue Ellen's moved to different digs and finally found her own identity. The new Sue Ellen's is a bi-level club straight out of *The L-Word.* The massive first floor opens to a glassed-in dance floor flanked by two bars, pool tables, and a car-size video monitor. Upstairs, the DJ lords over her kingdom from the second-story DJ booth. Up here, the glass soundproofing keeps the cacophony to a minimum, allowing for lower-key acoustic and rock acts to keep the crowd that buzzes around the two bars occupied.

Live Music

THE AARDVARK

2905 W. Berry St., 817/926-7814,
www.the-aardvark.com
HOURS: Tues.-Fri. 11 A.M.-2 A.M., Sat. 11:30 A.M.-2 A.M.,
Sun. 11:30 A.M.-midnight
COST: Varies depending on event
Map 9

The Aardvark sports a prime location just across the way from Texas Christian University, so it's no surprise that its spacious digs can fill up quickly, especially since it's a top booker of local bands.

ACROSS THE STREET BAR

5625 Yale Blvd., 214/363-0660,
www.acrossthestreetbar.com
HOURS: Tues.-Sat. 7 P.M.-2 A.M.
COST: Varies depending on event
Map 3

This SMU hot spot consistently draws the college crowd with five nights a week of music that, although varied, falls on the conservative side of things (you'll more likely catch a reggae band, say, than a punk band). It's a good size for a borderline dive, but when weekends come around, be ready to stand shoulder-to-shoulder, especially considering ATSB's famously cheap beer.

〔 ADAIR'S SALOON

2624 Commerce St., 214/939-9900,
www.adairssaloon.com
HOURS: Mon. 4 P.M.-2 A.M., Sat. noon-2 A.M.,
Sun. 2 P.M.-2 A.M.
COST: Free
Map 5

Adair's is what you might call a neighborhood honky-tonk. This family-owned hole-in-the-wall has Texas atmosphere to spare, with gimme caps stapled to the ceilings along with graffiti-scribbled walls, ceilings, and floors. The Adair family has a few rules posted, the most famous one being "You dance with the one who brung ya or you don't dance at all," and it's easy to

NIGHTLIFE

COURTESY OF ADAIR'S SALOON / MIKE RICHARD

Adair's Saloon

follow such advice with such a stellar jukebox. Filled with classics and hidden tracks from Patsy Cline, Bob Wills, and Ernest Tubb, among many other legends, the jukebox might just be the best in Texas. The bands that play here on weekends are cut from similar cloth.

BALCONY CLUB
1825 Abrams Rd., 214/826-8104
HOURS: Daily 5 P.M.-2 A.M.
COST: $5
Map 4

Pop up the wrought-iron stairs to the second story just above the much larger Lakewood theater, and you'll find the dark, quirky, and just slightly cramped Balcony. The club serves a popular brunch and strong cocktails, but is best known for its jazz, provided by the trios and quartets who crowd the tiny stage that abuts the front door. Music begins around 9:30.

CAPITAL BAR
3017 Morton St.
HOURS: Daily 11 A.M.-2 P.M.
COST: Varies depending on event
Map 10

Fans of classic rock, blues, and new country will like this joint, which boasts an impressive outdoor patio with downtown views, a great stage, and a state-of-the-art sound system. Folks who don't like crowds and the college demographic might be better off staying away, however, as the place tends to get packed with TCU students and a party-hearty crowd. The drinks lean toward pricey, but the happy hour specials (all day Sunday and Monday, 4–8 P.M. the rest of the week), including $2 domestic beers, make up for it. Wednesday nights are hosted by DFW new country station The Ranch, so bring your boots for scootin'.

THE CAVERN
1914 Greenville Ave., 214/828-1914,
http://thecaverndallas.com
HOURS: Mon.-Sun. 6 P.M.-2 A.M.
COST: Varies depending on event
Map 4

Patterned after the famous Liverpool club of the same name, this Greenville Avenue mainstay is indeed dark, insular, and often packed. While most venues on this street lean away from live music and more to the preppy side of things, the Cavern hosts an eclectic assortment of acts, from hip-hop nights to Southern rock quartets to lounge singers. Upstairs is a laid-back loft with comfy chairs, video games, and often a DJ.

CLUB DADA
2720 Elm St., 214/748-5105, www.dadadallas.com
HOURS: Tues.-Sun. 5 P.M.-2 A.M.
COST: Varies depending on event
Map 5

One of the few surviving clubs left over from Deep Ellum's most recent resurgence in the late 1980s/early '90s, Club Dada has seen its ups and downs, but remains a funky reminder of the neighborhood's roots and serves as an epicenter for eclectic music and art. Inside, the redbrick walls, ramshackle booths, and framed music posters lend Dada its atmosphere of downtown coolness. At the bar you'll find a friendly, efficient bar staff—sporting everything from Mohawks to nouveau-greaser pompadours—slinging free-flowing Shiner Bock and hard "root beer" shots. The club has a hipster vibe, but it's friendly and devoid of attitude; really, it's the music that matters most. The small stage has been home to local-heroes-made-good like Edie Brickell and New Bohemians, Reverend Horton Heat, and the Dixie Chicks, as well as countless popular national acts. Whether you're looking to chill on the lush, roomy back courtyard with a cool acoustic act and a cold beer or sweat inside with a high-powered punk trio and a potent cocktail, Dada is still the place to be.

THE CURTAIN CLUB
2800 Main St., 214/742-6207, www.curtainclub.com
HOURS: Thurs.-Sat. 9 P.M.-2 A.M.
COST: Varies depending on event
Map 5

The spacious but nondescript interior isn't really much to look at, but it has always been about the music at the Curtain Club anyway.

© JO-ANNA WIDNER

The Curtain Club

NIGHTLIFE

Back in the day, this space housed the cream of the Deep Ellum crop, the ample stage room hosting the biggest local acts and smaller national ones. Nowadays, the Curtain is the epicenter of the hard rock scene and battle of the bands competitions.

THE DOUBLE-WIDE

3510 Commerce St., 214/887-6510,
www.thedoublewidebar.com
HOURS: Mon.-Fri. 5 P.M.-2 A.M., Sat.-Sun. 7 P.M.-2 A.M.
COST: Varies depending on event
`Map 5`

Replete with revolving tornado atop the roof, the Double-Wide's half-ironic nod to Texas's trashy cachet lulls hipsters and music lovers from across the city. Surrounded on all sides by wood paneling and old-school beer signs, the main room always hops with tattooed scenesters, while across the patio, a second, sparsely fitted room features the stage, graced by local and smaller touring groups. Entering for the first time, you might feel like you've just crashed an intimate gathering of friends,

but don't worry—soon you'll feel right at home with the help of the alternative, alt-country, indie rock, and punk bands on the bill and an ice-cold PBR in your hand.

GILLEY'S DALLAS

1135 S. Lamar St., 214/421-2021, www.gilleysdallas.com
HOURS: Fri.-Sat. 6 P.M.-2 A.M.
COST: Varies depending on event
`Map 6`

The original Gilley's (made famous in the John Travolta classic *Urban Cowboy*) outside of Houston was cutting-edge in its day, but compared to its namesake in Dallas, it was just a run-down old honky-tonk. The new, updated version is a huge venue, tailor-made for C&W boot-scooting and swilling whiskey. If you want a genuine sawdust-floor dive, this ain't it, but with its swank space and modern cowpoke atmosphere, you won't find any other country joint that reflects Dallas better than this. The folks who patronize the place are friendly, but the prices definitely aren't, so take advantage of the free cover before 8 P.M. and the early free

© ANGEL FITZGERALD

Grab a cocktail at The Double-Wide.

dance lessons—besides, you'll need to learn a few two-step and line-dancing moves before you hit the floor. Oh, and yes, there is a mechanical bull.

THE GRANADA THEATER

3525 Greenville Ave., 214/824-9933,
www.granadatheater.com
COST: Varies depending on event
Map 4

For fans who eschew the homogeneity common to corporate-owned venues like the House of Blues and Palladium across town, the Granada is the best place in Dallas to see a show, hands down. The place oozes history, with dramatic murals, a spacious balcony, and detailed interior architecture, but still connects with current audiences, thanks to the lovingly painted psychedelic ceiling.

Unfortunately, despite its obvious character, the Granada struggles against its crosstown counterparts. With bigger resources and far-reaching contracts, the Palladium and the House of Blues snag most of the traveling shows that come through town. Still, the Granada manages to put together a consistently sizzling lineup of indie acts, roots music, and local biggies. Check the Granada's website—if you're in town and if they've booked a band you like, don't miss it.

LOLA'S

2736 W. 6th St., 817/877-0666,
www.lolasfortworth.com
HOURS: Daily noon–2 A.M.
COST: Varies depending on event
Map 8

When Lola's took over the spot formerly known as 6th Street Live in January 2008, Fort Worth didn't just gain a revamped venue—it also gained the services of one of the Metroplex's best concert promoters. Lance Yocom usually books top-name indie bands in Denton (north of Dallas-Fort Worth), with occasional forays into the big cities and Austin, but his Fort Worth presence increased dramatically as the spot's only booking agent. Yocom's indie taste is exquisite, and his contacts run deep—Lola's has already stolen several touring indie acts that usually go to Dallas and continues its string of strong local bands.

LONGHORN SALOON

121 W. Exchange Ave., 817/740-0078,
www.longhornsaloonfortworth.com
HOURS: Wed.-Thur. 4 P.M.-2 A.M., Fri.-Sat. noon-2 A.M.
COST: Varies depending on event
Map 11

As the oldest existing saloon in the Stockyards (built in 1919), the Longhorn has moseyed through a number of incarnations, and almost all of them have revolved around drink and dance of the boot-scootin' variety. The molded ceilings that still hover over the place have seen the likes of Hank Williams and Bob Wills get their twang on, and the 625-square-foot concert area and 1,000-square-foot dance floor have hosted many a great show in modern times (even Hank Williams III—the circle is complete). Shows alternate between better touring acts, top local groups, and DJs. If music's not your focus, the Longhorn still charms with rodeo and ranch paraphernalia, wood floors, and be-Stetsoned patrons.

THE PALLADIUM BALLROOM

1135 S. Lamar St., www.thepalladiumballrom.com
HOURS: Vary by showtime
COST: Varies depending on event
Map 6

The bad news is that the Palladium is a cavernous, sterile, corporate-owned venue with complicated, expensive parking and cruddy acoustics. The good news: The Palladium provides a much-needed venue for the middle- to upper-market touring shows, of which Dallas gets its fair share. The ballroom holds about 2,500 general admission patrons, who, despite the drawbacks, often sell the place out for newer acts such as Nas, M.I.A., and M83, and older faves like Tom Waits, Morrissey, and the Lemonheads. Even though the sight lines are favorable and the three bars ensure you won't wait in line for drinks, the place still sometimes feels like a warehouse gussied up for a prom. Not so for its smaller, more intimate upstairs club called the Palladium Loft, which houses smaller-draw national tours and tons of local groups. The Loft actually enjoys what its big-brother venue downstairs doesn't—character—and while the varnished wood and exposed ductwork may be a bit out of sync with some of the grittier bands who play there, the super-cool downtown view from the balcony brings everyone together.

POOR DAVID'S PUB

1313 S. Lamar St., 214/565-19295,
www.poordavidspub.com
HOURS: Wed.-Sat. 7 P.M.-2 A.M.
COST: Varies depending on event
Map 6

For more than 30 years, the stage at Poor David's has served as a launching pad—or sometimes, a home roost—for Texas's top roots music talent. The club began in 1977 on McKinney Avenue, relocated as a Greenville Avenue institution for 20 years, then nestled into the burgeoning entertainment district on South Lamar Street a few years ago. Owner David Card has an ear for the type of musicians so special that they transcend local scenes. The list of luminaries who have frequented Poor David's, then, is impressive but not surprising: Lyle Lovett, Jerry Jeff Walker, Robert Earl Keen Jr., The Dixie Chicks, Nanci Griffith, and so many others. Even today, no matter what night you pop in, the band performing will be special.

RENO'S CHOP SHOP

210 N. Crowdus St., 214/744-1200,
http://renoschopshop.com
HOURS: Mon.-Fri. 2 P.M.-2 A.M., Sat.-Sun. noon-2 A.M.
COST: Varies depending on event
Map 5

Don't let the rows of Harleys in front and the sound of chainsaw guitars emanating from inside scare you—Reno's is one of the friendliest biker/heavy metal bars you'll ever encounter.

NIGHTLIFE

Standing alone as a salt-of-the-earth kinda joint in the midst of hipster-heavy Deep Ellum, the place is dive-y but not depressing, with many patrons choosing the 2,000-square-foot deck out back where metal, industrial, and hard rock bands play. Those inhabiting the slightly crowded indoor area might be there for the karaoke, Tuesday's ladies nights, or any number of the surfeit of drink specials available every night of the week.

SANDAGA813
813 Exposition Ave. 214/616-0802,
http://sandaga813.com
HOURS: Tues. 8 P.M.-1 A.M., Thurs. 9 P.M.-1 A.M., Fri.-Sat. 10 P.M.-2 A.M.
COST: Varies depending on event
Map 5

Sandaga813 sits in a cool industrial building that once housed minc, a haunt of Erykah Badu, Questlove, and other hip-hop and soul

DEEP ELLUM'S MUSICAL LEGACY

Dallas loves music. We're not just talking that of the C&W variety—Dallas loves rock and blues, hip-hop and avant-garde, jazz and alt-country. Dallas loves to hear about music, talk about music, think about music, make music, and, most importantly, listen to live music. And no discussion of Dallas and music would be complete without including the history of the neighborhood just east of downtown, bordered to the north by Pacific Street, to the south by Canton Street, to the west by Exposition Avenue, and the east by I-75: Deep Ellum.

Deep Ellum's history goes back to the days when it was a stop on the "chitlin' circuit" and African American blues and jazz artists traveled the South, playing clubs in the black parts of segregated towns. In those days, the busy cobblestone streets full of grifters and preachers, the two-story brick pawnshops and juke joints, the readily available opiates, and the even more readily available audience lured many a blues performer: "Leadbelly" Ledbetter, Robert Johnson, Bessie Smith, and Blind Lemon Jefferson all lived and/or performed there.

Sadly, over the years Deep Ellum lost its panache as a hopping locale full of music and mystique. In the mid-20th century it fell into disrepair and transformed into an industrial neighborhood, home to warehouses and empty buildings. But in the late 1980s and early 1990s, a new generation rediscovered the gritty streets, and dozens of bars, art galleries, and music venues began popping up. Suddenly there was a scene.

New legends began: There was the rock club

Trees, where Nirvana performed just before hitting the mainstream jackpot, and where Kurt Cobain got in a fistfight onstage (recorded for posterity—you can find it on YouTube). There was the Good-Latimer traffic tunnel, coated in graffiti and street art. And there were the bands, whose energy and intensity lured thousands of people to Deep Ellum every night. Some of those bands hit it big: The Reverend Horton Heat, Edie Brickell and New Bohemians, the Old 97s, the Polyphonic Spree.

And then, as it did back during Deep Ellum's first musical era, the scene began to die. No one knows quite why. Some say it was an uptick in crime, others attribute it to oversaturation. Most likely, the scene ended because that's what scenes do, but for whatever reason, the buzz dwindled. One by one, clubs shuttered their storied doors, and even the Good-Latimer tunnel was destroyed to make room for a DART (Dallas Area Rapid Transit) station.

These days, while its vibrancy may have tarnished, the ghosts of Deep Ellum's history still make themselves known. The neighborhood is quieter now, but you can still feel a backbeat vibrating in the streets and once again cafés, fine-dining establishments, shops, large clubs, and tiny holes-in-the-wall have popped up. Several establishments—Murray Street Coffee Shop, Club Dada, the AllGood Café—remain as mainstays, and with its planned retail base, the very DART station responsible for the end of the tunnel might just kick-start a new chapter in Deep Ellum's history. If not, there's still plenty of old chapters to fall back on.

NIGHTLIFE

luminaries. The cool factor continues here but in the form of Tuesday and Thursday night jazz jams featuring local jazz luminaries, including top-notch musicians from the University of North Texas in Denton, known nationally for its music program. Hip-hop heads will still get their fill here on other nights, when the dark and airy digs host DJs and afterparties.

SCAT JAZZ LOUNGE

501 Houston St., 817/870-9100, www.scatjazzlounge.com
HOURS: Tues.-Thurs. 7 P.M.-2 A.M., Fri. 5 P.M.-2 A.M., Sun. 7 P.M.-2 A.M.
COST: Varies depending on event
Map 8

Local jazzman Ricki Derek may be best known for his smooth, suave, old-school lounge shows, which he performs at scattered Dallas venues. Anyone who's caught a Derek show knows he's a finely polished throwback who can croon Sinatra songs with the best of them. It's no surprise, then, that Derek's Scat Jazz Lounge is a tip of the fedora to the Rat Pack days. As in his own stage demeanor, Derek got the details right: a speakeasy-esque alleyway entrance under a retro sign; comfy booths; small, candle-lit tables. The effect is classy and of a certain time, but not in a hackneyed kind of way. The same goes for the music—top-notch local jazz, with an increasing presence of national acts.

SONS OF HERMANN HALL

3414 Elm St., 214/747-4422, www.sonsofhermann.com
HOURS: Tues.-Fri. 6 P.M.-midnight, Sat. 7 P.M.-2 A.M.
COST: Varies depending on event
Map 5

Proudly housed in a renovated building that dates back to 1911, Sons of Hermann Hall stands as a stalwart symbol of the evolution of Texas music. Inside, the decor is all genuine torch and twang, with a nice long bar, shuffleboard, and—most importantly—tons of room to scoot a boot. Folks like Marcia Ball, Jimmie Dale Gilmour, and Townes Van Zandt are but a few of the legends who have graced the stage here, but the hall is home to a large pack of young guns, too.

THE THIRSTY ARMADILLO

120 Exchange Ave., 817/624-2770, www.thethirstyarmadillo.com
HOURS: Mon.-Fri. 7 P.M.-2 A.M., Sat. 1 P.M.-2 A.M., Sun. 2 P.M.-midnight
COST: Varies depending on event
Map 11

Over the years the history of this place has meandered from locale to locale and aesthetic to aesthetic, but one thing has remained the same: If you're looking for true Texas music, the Armadillo is the place to go. Young guns slinging new country; storied singer-songwriters; and gee-tar slinging troubadours fill the Armadillo's music calendar seven days a week, while a crowd varying from TCU students to true cowboys surrounds the bar. You'll find the latter suitably stocked, but its real charm lies in its roadhouse utilitarian vibe.

TREES

2709 Elm St. 214/741-1122, http://treesdallas.com
HOURS: Varying
COST: Varies depending on event
Map 5

Mention Trees to any local over 35 years old, and they will insist they were at the storied rock club on a certain October night in 1991, when Nirvana's Kurt Cobain got into a dramatic fistfight, onstage in front of an overpacked club. Of course, 95 percent of the people who claim this were not there, but no matter—it's the stuff of legend in Dallas, and basically part of the city's collective memory anyway. Countless other fabled bands have held court here since the late 1980s—albeit most of them much less violently—and, while the place oozes history, it remains relevant today with a consistent spate of rock, punk, and hip-hop shows.

WHITE ELEPHANT SALOON

106 E. Exchange Ave., 817/624-8273, www.whiteelephantsaloon.com
HOURS: Sun.-Thurs. noon-midnight, Fri.-Sat. noon-2 A.M.
COST: Varies depending on event
Map 11

In its 100-year history, the White Elephant

NIGHTLIFE

NIGHTLIFE

© JONANNA WIDNER

The White Elephant Saloon is one of the most popular spots in the Stockyards.

has seen its share of a-fussin' and a-fightin'. In fact, the Elephant was the backdrop for the most famous shoot-out in Fort Worth history, between former city marshal Jim "Longhair" Courtright and gambler Luke Short. The two had long shared a rivalry that culminated on February 8, 1887, when their guns went to blazin', leaving Short dead.

Nowadays, the saloon sees its share of tourists and country music fans, both of whom flock to this Stockyard institution for its history, Texas music bands, and genuine Cowtown atmosphere—as the dozens of cowboy hats nailed to the walls attest. You probably won't see a bar fight (though it's not to be ruled out), but you'll definitely see guys in Wranglers and Stetsons boot-to-boot with those in suits and ties, which is about as Fort Worth as it gets. And, if you're lucky, you'll catch the reenactment of the Courtright-Short duel, staged every February 8.

ARTS AND LEISURE

World-class museums, art galleries, the performing arts, and almost every kind of recreation under the sun (and indoors, too)—such is the arts and leisure landscape of Dallas-Fort Worth. People of all stripes will find their to-do lists full every day, no matter what the season (although the summer heat puts a slight damper on things): Art lovers will discover famous works by the masters in museums and edgy works from up-and-comers in local galleries; sports fans can join 30,000 others at a Mavs game or 3,000 people to watch the Fort Worth Cats scrap it out. In between, there's history, beauty, and fun.

Any discussion of DFW arts must begin with Fort Worth's Cultural District. While Dallas's Arts District boasts a stunning new home—consisting of four Pritzker Prize architectural award winners in a row—for the Dallas Opera, symphony, several theater and dance companies, and many others, Cowtown's art museums have always enjoyed a quiet superiority to accompany their stellar reputations.

Outdoorsy types will love the jogging, hiking, and biking to be had in the Katy Trail greenbelts or the numerous recreation opportunities at places like Burger's Lake. And, of course, Dallas has always been sports crazy, from the inception of the Dallas Cowboys in 1960 to the newest local franchise, the major-league soccer team FC Dallas. On a smaller scale, the Metroplex is the proud home of a trio of minor-league baseball teams, whose

© KENNY BRAUN / TRAVELTEX.COM

intimate stadiums and family-friendly prices lure many a fan. And don't forget the rodeo: DFW provides ample choices for the "national sport of Texas," from the Mesquite Rodeo to the Black Rodeo. No matter which one you choose, no trip to the area is complete without catching a glimpse of the sport's masterful riders.

HIGHLIGHTS   LOOK FOR (TO FIND RECOMMENDED ARTS AND ACTIVITIES.

the Frontiers of Flight Museum

boasts several excellent companies, but for a taste of the unusual, try the **Hip Pocket Theatre** (page 124).

(**Best Movie Theater:** Forget sticky floors and uncomfortable seats—try beanbags, couches, and La-Z-Boys. The **Inwood Theater** shows art house films and special midnight classic screenings in the comfiest surroundings (page 125).

(**Best Cultural Event:** Draped in a dramatic history, the **Van Cliburn International Piano Competition** is one of the most respected competitions of its kind and a rare chance for experts and novices alike to enjoy the world's best classical pianists (page 127).

(**Best Annual Event:** Combining social tiers of all kinds, the resources of the Cultural District, and genuine Western traditions, the **Fort Worth Stock Show and Rodeo** just might be the Fort Worth-iest of all activities (page 129).

(**Best Heartbreakers:** Major-league baseball's **Texas Rangers**, with the legendary Nolan Ryan in charge, have made it to the World Series two times in a row—and lost both times (page 136).

(**Best Learning Experience:** The **Frontiers of Flight Museum** will blow your mind with its collection of planes and aviation paraphernalia (page 118).

(**Best Underappreciated Performing Arts Group:** Helmed by Jaap van Zweden, the **Dallas Symphony Orchestra** is edgy, cool, and right on target (page 122).

(**Best Surprise:** Who knew Fort Worth enjoyed such a vibrant theater scene? The town

(**Best Place to Explore:** Hiking the **Fort Worth Nature Center and Refuge** will take you through shady woods and critter-laden wetlands—a quick, convenient way to escape the city for a few hours (page 139).

(**Best Driving Range:** It's not really just a driving range—**Top Golf** is more like an interactive video game, spread out over several acres (page 144).

© JONANNA WIDNER

ARTS AND LEISURE

The Arts

MUSEUMS

ARLINGTON MUSEUM OF ART

201 W. Main St., Arlington, 817/274-4699,
www.arlingtonmuseum.org
HOURS: Wed.-Fri. and Sun. 1–5 P.M., Sat. 10 A.M.–5 P.M.
COST: $2 adult, $1 student and senior, free youth under 12
Map 11

Unaffected and unpretentious, the Arlington Museum of Art presents an opportunity to view the works of regional and up-and-coming artists that normally might escape the public eye. By no means does this translate to amateurism (well, OK, the "Walk with C.S. Lewis" show proved a *little* cheesy); the rotating exhibitions of contemporary Texas art culls from a large pool of talent. Tours and gallery talks often enhance the experience.

DALLAS FIREFIGHTERS MUSEUM

3801 Parry Ave., 214/821-1500,
www.dallasfiremuseum.com
HOURS: Wed.-Sat. 9 A.M.–4 P.M.

COST: $4 adult, $2 youth
Map 5

It's hard to imagine a time when Dallas only needed one firehouse, but the Firefighters Museum takes you back to those days. Filled with memorabilia like vintage equipment, helmets, and a pump truck dating back to 1911, the museum is housed in Dallas's first firehouse, a handsome brick building directly across the street from Fair Park.

FIRE STATION #1

Corner of 2nd and Commerce Sts., 972/262-4479,
www.fwmuseum.org
HOURS: Daily 9 A.M.–8 P.M.
COST: Admission varies by exhibit.
Map 8

Any exploration of Fort Worth should start at this site, which served as a working fire station from 1907 to 1980. Today, it holds the "150 Years of Fort Worth History" exhibit, which features artifacts, letters, and memorabilia chronicling the city.

© JONANNA WIDNER

The Arlington Museum of Art features a lot of work by regional artists.

ARTS AND LEISURE

◖ FRONTIERS OF FLIGHT MUSEUM

6911 Lemmon Ave., 214/350-3600,
www.flightmuseum.com
HOURS: Mon.-Sat. 10 A.M.-5 P.M., Sun. 1-5 P.M.
COST: $8 adult, $5 youth, $6 senior, free under 3
Map 7

Second only to the National Air and Space Museum in archival research and artifacts, the Frontiers of Flight Museum is a must-see. Its bright new space in a colossal former hangar has rightfully raised the museum's profile, as well as given its fine collection an appropriate home. The museum's displays provide an excellent overview of the history of aviation. The wide-ranging collection, from a restored World War I Sopwith "Pup" to items on loan from NASA's Apollo 7 mission to a series of deployed ejection seats, is a jaw-dropper.

INTERNATIONAL BOWLING MUSEUM AND HALL OF FAME

621 Six Flags Dr., Arlington, 817/385-8215,
www.bowlingmuseum.com
HOURS: Tues.-Sat. 9:30 A.M.-5 P.M.
COST: $9.50 adults, $7.50 senior and youth, free under 3
Map 11

A giant bowling pin greets visitors to this 100,000-square-foot campus dedicated to the art of the alley. Exhibits cover the game's beginnings 5,000 years ago in ancient Egypt (betcha didn't know that!) all the way through modern times. The kids' "Bowlopolis" zone features a tone of interactive fun, and adults will dig the interactive virtual bowling lane, while the Hall of Fame could keep true fans enthralled for days.

LEONARD'S MUSEUM

200 Carroll St.
HOURS: Mon.-Sat. 10 A.M.-6 P.M.
COST: Free
Map 10

Ironic that this little one-room museum houses memories of a store that, at its peak, covered eight downtown city blocks. From 1918 to the mid-1970s, Leonard's Department Store provided one-stop shopping for all of Fort Worth. We're talking *serious* one-stop shopping here, too—everything from farm equipment to toys to toothbrushes, along with services ranging from a beauty salon to car repair. Grown from modest beginnings, the celebrated store remained a beloved institution until it was sold, stamping the city with a lasting cultural imprint, right down to the private subway the Leonard's built to ferry customers to the establishment. Inside you'll find vintage advertisements, a menagerie of products once sold at the store, and memorabilia such as the old popcorn machine that fired up every day the place was open. Cap off your visit with one of the best burgers in town at the adjacent **M&O Station Grill** (200 Carroll St., #110, 817/882-8020), named after the Leonard's subway.

TOP O' HILL TERRACE

3001 W. Division, Arlington, 817/461-8741,
www.arlingtonbaptistcollege.edu
HOURS: Tours by appointment
COST: $5 donation
Map 11

What is now a conservative Baptist college used to be the site of one of the biggest, most successful, and most secret underground casinos ever to house a roulette table, called Top O' Hill Terrace. The college once downplayed this history, until Vickie Bryant (the wife of the school's president) chose to embrace the area's past. Bryant has dug up a wealth of details, which are now displayed at the school, and she gives tours of the site by appointment, pointing out highlights of the former gambling haunt.

TRAMMELL AND MARGARET CROW COLLECTION OF ASIAN ART

2010 Flora St., 214/979-6430 or 214/821-1500,
www.crowcollection.org
HOURS: Tues.-Thurs. 10 A.M.-9 P.M., Fri.-Sat. 10 A.M.-6 P.M., Sun. noon-6 P.M.
COST: Free, suggested donation $7 adults, $5 seniors
Map 1

This museum was always a family affair. For

years, Dallas's most well-known real estate magnate, Trammell Crow, and his wife, Margaret, had been collecting Asian art almost willy-nilly, simply because they liked it. With more than 7,000 pieces scattered among their homes, offices buildings, and hotels, they eventually decided to gather them in one place to share with the public. The family touch shows in the intimacy and warmth of the museum's design. Highlights include about 120 of the Trammells' beloved 1,200 jade pieces and a world-class grouping of 19th-century Chinese art.

ART GALLERIES

CENTRAL TRAK
800 Exposition Ave., 214/824-9302, www.centraltrak.net
HOURS: Wed.-Sat. noon-5 P.M. with appointment; hours for openings vary
Map 5

Named for the train tracks that once ran through what is now Deep Ellum and Expo Park, this gallery serves to house the University of Dallas's artist-in-residency program. The program attracts both national and international artists, who live and work in the attached loft space.

Under the helm of director Heyd Fontenot, the program has increased its reputation as a space for forward-thinking work, which sometimes proves a rarity in Dallas. If you're looking for edgy, intellectual, and challenging art, this is the place to be.

500X GALLERY
500 Exposition Ave., 214/828-1111, www.500x.org
HOURS: Sat.-Sun. noon-5 P.M.
Map 5

Existing since 1978 in the same spot—an Expo Park warehouse that dates back to 1916—hasn't made 500X complacent. As a matter of fact, if anything, this nonprofit art co-op has grown even more dynamic every year, providing a professional exhibition space for up-and-coming local and regional artists.

KETTLE ART
2714 Elm St., 214/573-7622, www.kettleart.com
HOURS: Thurs.-Sat. 7-10 P.M.
Map 5

Owned by one of the pioneers of the Deep Ellum renaissance, Frank Campagna, the not-for-profit Kettle Art is a scrappy neighborhood gallery that specializes in Texas artists and photographers. Not Texas *folk* art, mind you—Campagna's and gallery executive director Kirk Hopper's tastes run a little more intense and cutting-edge than that. Since it opened in 2005, the gallery has willed its way into the fabric of the underground Dallas community as an epicenter of music, film, and general artistic mayhem. But that mayhem has a purpose: Campagna and Hopper have brought Deep Ellum's rebellious spirit into the 21st century.

LUMINARTE FINE ART GALLERY
1727 E. Levee St., 214/914-4503, www.luminarte.com
HOURS: Mon.-Fri. 11 A.M.-5 P.M.
Map 7

LuminArte represents mid-career local, national, and international artists, and some of the work shown here is simply stellar. While painting and more traditional forms tend to dominate, there's definitely room for different media here, including video, audio, and found art. Owner Jamie Labar, who also runs the LuminArte Design room next door, and a stable of curators consistently put together solid shows, including a recent visit from the International Biennale Artists.

PHOTOGRAPHS DO NOT BEND
1202 Dragon St., 214/969-1852, www.pdnbgallery.com
HOURS: Tues.-Sat. 11 A.M.-6 P.M.
Map 7

Minimal and modern, as one might expect of a photo-based art gallery, Do Not Bend has proven one of the best and most reputable local galleries since 1995. Rotating exhibits (both solo and group shows) from local, national, and international photographers are the staple here, and the names keep getting bigger. The gallery also includes a wall of books for sale,

ARTS AND LEISURE

GRAMMY HIGH

Booker T. Washington School for the Performing and Visual Arts is kind of like the high school from the movie and TV show *Fame*, minus the '80s leotards and the spontaneous lunchroom dancing. Those who remember *Fame* most likely will recall a scene from the opening credits, when the steely dance instructor played by Debbie Allen warns her students, "You want fame, but fame costs. And here is where you start paying...in sweat."

Okay, that may be a little overdramatic, but drama is appropriate, as is dance, music, and art: Booker T. Washington is simply one of the best arts schools in the country. The kids *do* sweat, spending hundreds of hours rehearsing and building exceptional skills. And it pays off—many of Booker T.'s alumni are household names, well-known actors, and even Grammy winners.

But Booker T. began not as proud bastion of arts education but rather as an emblem of a less proud chapter in Dallas's history: segregation. In 1892 Booker T. began as the Dallas Colored High School, the only school that allowed African American students in the entire town. It remained the only one to do so for decades, in fact, even as the black population of Dallas grew.

In 1922, the school moved to a new building at 2501 Flora St., now the heart of Dallas's Arts District, where it still stands today. The school continued to take on every African American pupil in Dallas County, juggling schedules and enrollments to accommodate such a large number of students. Booker T. continued to expand and grow, morphing into a technical high school, until finally it became the Dallas school district's arts magnet school in 1976. From there, Booker T.'s destiny—and that of its talented students—blossomed.

Booker T.'s come a long way since 1892. Today, after a $55 million renovation and expansion, the school added 70,000 square feet to its original grounds. The original building, its classic schoolhouse brick still intact, now houses an art gallery, a theater, and a display area that shows off school history and student and alumni accomplishments. And while the school relies heavily on donations, it still part of the Dallas Independent School District, and as such stands as a public school success story.

NOTABLE BOOKER T. WASHINGTON SCHOOL ALUMNI

Erykah Badu: Badu, who still lives in Dallas, might be the school's most famous graduate. She went on to Grambling State for college and then basically started working her tail off on her music career.

It paid off. Many of Badu's neo-soul record-

---

including a number of signed copies of works from different artists.

THE PUBLIC TRUST

2919 Commerce St., 214/760-7170,
www.trustthepublic.com
HOURS: Wed.-Fri. 11 A.M.-6 P.M., Sat. noon-6 P.M.
Map 5

The Public Trust owner Brian Gibb has always shown a knack for pushing the artistic envelope with his *Art Prostitute* publication, but that doesn't mean said art is inaccessible. His Deep Ellum gallery (formerly also called Art Prostitute) provides a hodgepodge of edgy eclecticism, in an entirely inclusionary way. If you're lucky, you'll catch an opening here, and if so, be prepared to stay up late.

PERFORMING ARTS
THE BATH HOUSE CULTURAL CENTER

521 E. Lather Dr., 214/670-8749,
www.bathhousecultural.com
HOURS: Tues.-Sat. noon-6 P.M.
(10 P.M. on performance nights)
COST: Free (except for specific performances)
Map 7

The odd name comes from its proximity to White Rock Lake: One of the first structures in the Southwest to incorporate art deco architecture, the Bath House once held the changing

ings have gone gold, platinum, and even triple-platinum, and she's won several Grammys. She's probably best known for her 1998 masterpiece, *Baduizm*.

Badu's concerts are, quite frankly, mind-blowingly good, and she often makes surprise appearances with touring bands, including popular hip-hop/jazz/soul band the Roots, when they come through Dallas. She also performs in a free-form experimental collaboration called the Cannabinoids with local musicians

Edie Brickell: For years, Brickell was an integral part of Deep Ellum's second heyday–the late '80s to mid-'90s, when the streets there teemed with people and new bands popped up seemingly every five minutes. Reportedly, Brickell actually attended Booker T. to study visual art and had few musical aspirations until, on a bit of a whim, she jumped onstage one night to sing with a band called the New Bohemians. Coincidentally, a couple of the New Bohemians attended Booker T. as well, although they didn't know Brickell.

The rest is well-known history in Dallas. The band continued with Brickell taking the lead singing spot, was signed by Geffen Records, and released a hit record, *Shooting Rubberbands at the Stars*. The record's first single "What I Am" climbed to #4 on the Billboard chart.

While performing "What I Am" during an appearance on *Saturday Night Live*, Brickell caught the eye of guest host Paul Simon. The two were married in 1992 and live in Connecticut.

Roy Hargrove: One of the best American jazz trumpeters of our time, Hargrove graduated from Booker T. and then went on to Berklee music college in Boston for a year before landing in New York City, where he began recording with several established jazz performers. His first album, *Diamond in the Rough*, came out in 1989 on Novus Records, and he remained at the label until signing with legendary Verve Records. He's won two Grammy awards–one for his work on the album *Crisol* and one for *Habana*.

Norah Jones: The daughter of Ravi Shankar, Jones is another Booker T. Grammy-winner. Her 2002 debut album *Come Away With Me* won five Grammys, including Album of the Year.

Jones, who majored in jazz piano before dropping out of the University of North Texas's lauded music program to move to New York, transfixes audiences with an unlikely blend of throwback aesthetics and contemporary sounds. Her sultry, soulful vocals lilt over intricate but classic piano. It's a sound she didn't begin to explore until her time at Booker T.

area and lockers for folks looking to take a dip to escape the Texas heat. It has long since been converted to a unique 120-seat cultural center that hosts dance performances, plays, and music, like the White Rock Rhythms Jazz series, and also serves as White Rock Lake's humble museum.

DALLAS BLACK DANCE THEATRE

2700 Flora St., 214/871-2842,
www.dbdt.com
COST: $10-50
Map 1

The oldest continuously existing dance troupe in Dallas, the Dallas Black Dance Theatre

consists of 12 full-time dancers who perform a mixed repertory throughout the year.

DALLAS OPERA

2100 Ross Ave., 214/443-1000, www.dallasopera.org
COST: $129-1,020
Map 1

In 1958, the Dallas Opera kicked off its inaugural season with a recital by internationally renowned singer Maria Callas, and it has continued its tradition of combining rising stars with famous ones ever since. The company's prestige should increase even further now that it's moving into the stunning Winspear Opera House, in the Dallas Center for the Performing Arts.

ARTS AND LEISURE

◖ DALLAS SYMPHONY ORCHESTRA
2010 Flora St., 214/979-6430,
www.dallassymphony.com
COST: Varies depending on event.
`Map 1`

Under the direction of conductor Jaap van Zweden, the DSO has stepped it up a notch. The orchestra has always been generally well received, but van Zweden's bold leadership, along with new digs at the fabulous Dallas Center for the Performing Arts, has invigorated the institution. Each year, the DSO takes on a combination of traditional pieces along with more risky and commissioned works, which, in van Zweden's capable hands, appear less precarious than they actually are.

FORT WORTH SYMPHONY ORCHESTRA
Bass Hall, 525 Commerce St., 817/665-6100,
www.fwsymphony.org
COST: Varies depending on event.
`Map 8`

For 75 years, the Fort Worth Symphony Orchestra has exceeded expectations, delivering

GAMBLER'S HEAVEN, PREACHER'S HELL

Only in Texas would a former illegal gambling hotbed transform into a Baptist college. From the early 1920s until 1947, Fred and Mary Browning operated a secret and very elaborate underground gambling operation called **Top O' Hill Terrace,** smack in between Dallas and Fort Worth. The couple began their journey to infamy by purchasing a simple tearoom on a bluff overlooking the surrounding countryside. At 1,000 feet up, it was one of the highest points in the land, making it one of the most picturesque spots in the area. It also provided an excellent vantage point from which to espy approaching law enforcement.

The Brownings needed as much protection from the law as they could get. While the tearoom did a brisk business on its own, the real operation existed behind the scenes, in a series of concealed rooms housing a casino, brothel, and steakhouse. The steakhouse, of course, was legal, although it catered to diners who were there for more nefarious purposes than supping upon a T-bone (the beef, incidentally, enjoyed the reputation as some of the best around).

With guards, secret tunnels, and a series of hidden nooks and crannies—gamblers had to go through five different doors to even make it to the casino—Top O' Hill proved virtually raidproof, and that security, combined with the elegant surroundings, made it an extremely popular destination. Bonnie and Clyde, Clark Gable, Lana Turner, and John Wayne all tried their luck there. At its peak, the Brownings raked in between $50,000 and $100,000 a night, and double that on the weekends.

The operation wasn't quite so popular with a certain outspoken town preacher named J. Frank Norris, the flamboyant founder of the Fundamental Baptist Institute. The steely-eyed Norris was a master of the intense ovational style that marked fundamentalist Baptist oratory at the time, and in one speech he thundered, "Top O' Hill Terrace is a blight on Tarrant County! One of these days, we are going to own that place!"

He was right. Top O' Hill fended off raids over the years, until finally the Texas Rangers took 'er down in 1947. The property changed hands a few times, but six years later Norris's Institute, now called the Bible Baptist Seminary, purchased the land and buildings from the Lamar Life Insurance Company and transformed the area into what is now called Arlington Bible College. Norris never saw his prediction come true; he died in 1952.

For years the college, which remains quite conservative, downplayed the story, fascinating as it was. But when David Bryant took on the college presidency, his wife Vickie led the charge to take bushel off the light, so to speak. As the college's in-house historian and bookstore director, Vickie Bryant over the years has gathered a fascinating collection of artifacts, memorabilia, and stories about Top O' Hill, which she shows and recounts during the tours she gives there.

Bryant's dedication has paid off immeasurably, uncovering a story rich in detail and as many twists and turns as the casino's escape tunnels. Only a bit of that story is recounted here—it's highly recommended visitors take a tour to hear it all.

big-city quality to the 27th largest city in the nation. Unlike many orchestras around the country, the FWSO has shown a remarkable ability to adapt to the times, growing both its endowment and its attendance with creative programming. Especially popular, for instance, is the FWSO's Concerts in the Garden series, performed in the beautiful confines of the Botanic Gardens near the Cultural District. Other than similar off-site excursions, the orchestra makes its home at Bass Hall.

GRAPEVINE OPRY

300 S. Main St., Grapevine, 817/481-8733, www.gvopry.com

COST: $15 adult, $10 child

Map 11

Harkening back to the traditions of the Grand Ole Opry, this roots music hoedown has grown into one of the premier country music shows of its kind. Backed by a helluva house band, notable regional—and sometimes national—bluegrass and country performers get in on the act at the spontaneous shows, which are housed in the 1940 Palace Theater.

TEXAS BALLET THEATER

Bass Hall, 525 Commerce St., 817/763-0207, www.texasballettheatre.org

COST: Varies depending on event.

Map 8

With 38 professional dancers and two ballet academies under its domain, the TBT is the largest residential classical ballet company in North Texas. The company has settled into this role after the merging of the Fort Worth Ballet and Dallas Ballet, and mainly splits its performance time between Dallas's Winspear Opera House and Fort Worth's Bass Hall, although other venues dot the calendar.

And what a full calendar that is: The TBT performances, which stick to tried-and-true, traditional favorites, span almost the entire year. Highlights include the much-beloved Nutcracker and the TBT Festival, which takes place in May. Prior to select performances, members of the staff and/or visiting artists host free, 45-minute lectures to give patrons

the inside scoop (contact TBT for specifics, as these vary).

TURTLE CREEK CHORALE

2301 Flora St., 214/526-3214, www.turtlecreek.org

COST: Varies depending on event.

Map 1

This 225-member men's chorus has been blowing audiences away since 1980 with its dramatic and well-honed take on many different types of music. Each year since its inception, the chorale has grown increasingly popular, and in doing so has transcended mere regional recognition and grown into the most recorded men's chorus in the world. The chorale performs mainly at the Morton H. Meyerson Symphony Center on downtown's Flora Street, though special events are often scattered around town.

THEATERS AND THEATER COMPANIES

CASA MAÑANA

3101 W. Lancaster Ave.

COST: Varies depending on event.

Map 10

For decades, Casa Mañana's signature aluminum geodesic dome has housed some of the most popular theater in the city. The unique location introduced permanent theater-in-the-round to the country, and over the years the stage has seen countless productions of family-friendly fare, Broadway musicals, local productions, and top-name touring comics such as Jerry Seinfeld. By the late 20th century, the once-cutting-edge dome had grown dated; in 2003, a circular addition surrounding the dome updated the venue, but somewhat diminished its dramatic effect.

CIRCLE THEATRE

230 W. 4th St., 817/887-3040, www.circletheatre.com

COST: Varies depending on event.

Map 8

More adventurous than many of its local brethren, Circle Theatre specializes in producing contemporary plays, often local ones, out of its historic home in Sundance Square.

ARTS AND LEISURE

HIP POCKET THEATRE

1950 Silver Creek Rd., White Settlement,
214/246-9775, www.hippocket.org
COST: Varies depending on event.
Map 11

A primarily outdoor theater, Hip Pocket's unusual setting reflects its unusual mission: to produce cutting-edge plays, musicals, and other forms of stagecraft such as puppet shows. Hip Pocket has long been known for its eclectic lineup and penchant for experimentation, often with exquisite results.

JUBILEE THEATRE

506 Main St., 817/338-4411, www.jubileetheatre.org
COST: Varies depending on event.
Map 8

One of the best African American theater troupes in the country, the Jubilee stages consistently high-quality musicals and plays, many of them originals.

© JONANNA WIDNER

Jubilee Theatre

MAJESTIC THEATER

1925 Elm St., 214/670-3687,
www.liveatthemajestic.com
COST: Varies depending on event.
Map 1

The last working theater left in Dallas's old "Theater Row," the Majestic hosts an assortment of productions year-round. The Elm Street mainstay stands proudly restored, right down to the 23-karat gold-leafing and detailed molding, as host to local and national stage acts.

THE OCHRE HOUSE

825 Exposition Ave., 214/826-6273,
www.ochrehousetheater.com
HOURS: Vary by performance.
COST: Varies by performance.
Map 5

For thrill-seeking theater denizens, Ochre House's adventurous, original productions are a sure bet. The intimate, 45-seat playhouse and its production company, Balanced Almond, were founded by Matthew Posey, a native Texan, film and television actor (*No Country for Old Men, Temple Grandin, Lonesome Dove*), and idiosyncratic provocateur who takes a

disciplined approach to works that are imbued with a devotion to decadence. Posey writes, directs, acts, and sometimes plays music in Ochre House's plays and musicals, and while the close-knit company collaborates at many levels, its shows—which tend to feature fictionalized episodes from the lives of the famous and infamous (Charles Manson, Andy Warhol, Frida Kahlo), puppetry, live musicians, moments of true hilarity, and the occasional tighty-whitey man-dance—bear the unmistakable mark of his oddball vision. Within his deceptively tattered, homey playhouse are reliably top-notch productions offering the kinds of immersive, transformative experiences theatergoers crave.

STAGE WEST

821 W. Vickery Blvd., 817/784-9378,
www.stagewest.org
HOURS: Sun. and Tues.-Wed. noon-5 P.M.,
Thurs.-Sat. noon-9 P.M.
COST: Varies depending on event.
Map 8

Stage West isn't just extremely popular in Fort Worth—it has developed into a major regional

© DALLAS CVB

The Majestic Theater is the last working theater on Dallas's old "Theater Row."

theater. Since its inception in 1979, the company has bounced to several homes around town, producing about 200 plays ranging from Shakespeare to Edward Albee to P. G. Wodehouse, before finally settling down 25 years later in its original, funky old building near downtown. With a permanent home, Stage West also brought back its popular dinner service in the Ol' Vic Café.

MOVIE HOUSES AND FILM

ANGELIKA FILM CENTER
5321 E. Mockingbird Ln., 214/841-4715,
http://angelikafilmcenter.com
COST: $10 adult, $7.50 youth, $8.50 senior,
$8 matinee
Map 4

The Angelika combines the good parts of a mega-theater monolith with the chill aura of an art house. That is to say, there's plenty of comfy stadium seating, legroom, and amenities, but the lineup here lists toward indies and foreigns or, at the very worst, Oscar-nominated blockbusters. The lines at the lower-level bar

and coffee shop tend to get long just before showtime; one of the several cash bars upstairs might be a better option.

🎬 INWOOD THEATER
5458 W. Lovers Ln., 214/764-9106,
www.landmarktheatres.com
COST: $10 adult, $8.50 student, $8 senior,
$7.50 child, $8 matinee
Map 3

A DFW institution, the Inwood Theater once was the only place in Dallas to catch an art house flick. Things have changed—for one thing, the once independently owned theater is now owned by the large Landmark company— but the Inwood's distinctive history, its art deco panache, its dark bar that specializes in martinis, and its unique seating (couches, beanbags, recliners) make it a favorite.

MAGNOLIA THEATER
3699 McKinney Ave., Ste. 100, 214/764-9106
COST: $10 adult, $8.50 student, $8 senior,
$7.50 child, $8 matinee
Map 2

It's owned by the large theater conglomerate Landmark, but the Magnolia has the look and feel of an independent art house. Befitting its arty atmosphere, the warm, sophisticated lobby has a slow-paced, grown-up feel, with a cozy bar (and, yes, you're allowed to bring your cocktail with you to watch the movie). As you might expect, the theater sticks primarily to indie and foreign films and arty first-runs, and is a major destination for a number of film festivals.

THE TEXAS THEATRE
231 W. Jefferson Blvd., 214/948-1546,
www.thetexastheatre.com
COST: Varies depending on event.
Map 6

Aside perhaps from the Ford Theater, it would be impossible to find another theater with more history to it than the Texas Theatre, where Lee Harvey Oswald hid and was arrested after allegedly shooting President John F. Kennedy in 1963. It can be odd, knowing this, to saunter inside, buy some popcorn, and settle into your

ARTS AND LEISURE

seat, or plop down at the bar for a cocktail. But you get used to it, and besides, the local folks at Aviation cinema—who now own the lease on the building—balance out the gravitas with an arty mix of first-runs, cult classics, and local fare.

Festivals and Events

SPRING
DALLAS INTERNATIONAL GUITAR FESTIVAL
Dallas Market Hall, 2200 N. Stemmons Fwy., 972/240-2206, www.guitarshow.com
COST: $10-90 adult, $15 student
Map 7

Lovers of vintage gee-tars, banjos, mandolins, and just about every other string instrument you can pick flock to this yearly festival that has grown from humble, regional beginnings to the biggest and best festival of its ilk in the country. Hundreds of vendors, exhibitors, and fans mingle at the Dallas Market Hall in search of the perfect Tele or to catch one of the dozens of guitar-based bands who shred at the attendant MusicFest. Ticket packages include discounted multiday passes and pricier VIP selections.

DEEP ELLUM ARTS FESTIVAL
www.deepellumartsfestival.com
COST: Free
Map 5

For three days in the spring, the Deep Ellum Arts Festival shuts down the streets around Deep Ellum and lets the neighborhood do what it does best: rock. The fest features four music stages, all going simultaneously, with a parade of Dallas's favorite bands ranging from hip-hop to alt-country to indie rock. The tunes are often the center of attention, but they also provide a unique sound track for strolling the historic district and perusing the juried art shows, sipping a beer, or munching a treat from the many food vendors. Make sure to catch the pet parade.

HOOP IT UP
www.hoopitup.com
COST: Varies depending on event.
Map 7

Given Dallas's penchant for sports, it should come as no surprise that the most popular amateur 3-on-3 hoops tourney started here. The venue and exact dates vary from year to year, but the popularity of this event never wavers, as ballers of both genders vie for the championship in various age and skill categories in what amounts to the world's largest pickup game. Hoop It Up has turned into much more than just the competition—bands, celebrities, and food now vie for spectators' attention, though the basketball is always the top draw.

JUNETEENTH
www.juneteenth.com/5texas.htm
COST: Varies depending on event.

While Abraham Lincoln's Emancipation Proclamation freeing slaves nationwide went into effect on the first day of 1863, it took a while for the news to get to Texas. The proclamation had little effect on the lives of most African Americans in the state, until June 19, 1865, when federal troops arrived in Galveston to enforce it.

Since then, a huge celebration has evolved around the middle of June, and June 19 itself is a Texas state holiday. This is one of the largest and most anticipated African American celebrations of the year, with official cultural and artistic events around the city, as well as informal barbecues, parties, and get-togethers.

LOWER GREENVILLE ST. PATRICK'S DAY PARADE
Greenville Ave., www.greenvilleave.org
COST: Free
Map 4

Perhaps it's not the most authentic St. Patrick's Day parade as far as tradition goes, but when it comes to enthusiasm, Dallas's version ranks right up there. The parade began about 30 years ago as a loosey-goosey whim, but now

ARTS AND LEISURE

comprises one of Dallas's major civic events, with 100 floats (more than the Cotton Bowl parade), thousands of participants, and parade-watchers numbering somewhere in the six-digit range.

MAIN STREET ARTS FESTIVAL

Main St., 817/336-2787, www.mainstreetartsfest.org

COST: Free

Map 8

Perhaps no other event of the year shows off Fort Worth's escalating cultural cachet more than this four-day downtown festival. Named the number three fine arts festival in the country by the *Art Fair SourceBook,* this festival stretches all the way down Main, from the courthouse to the Fort Worth Convention Center—a full mile of juried fine art, crafts, music, and food.

MAYFEST

COST: $8 adult, $5 child ($1.50 if purchased online), seniors free on Thurs.

Map 10

Held every year for the past 40 years in a forested park nestled up to the Trinity River, Mayfest is intended as a celebration of the river as a civic resource. But really, it's just a hell of a lot of fun. For four days, a wide swath of shady land transforms into an enormous festival, with five different entertainment zones, including an excellent kids' area.

VAN CLIBURN INTERNATIONAL PIANO COMPETITION

Bass Hall, 525 Commerce St., 817/738-6536, www.cliburn.org

COST: Varies depending on event.

Map 8

In April 1958, smack in the middle of the Cold War, a Texas-raised, classically trained young pianist shocked the world—most notably, the Soviets—by soundly defeating the competition at the prestigious first Tchaikovsky International Piano Competition in Moscow. The event was meant to display Russia's cultural superiority, especially when it came to piano; instead, Van Cliburn's drubbing of the

competition was the concerto heard 'round the world. Inspired by his win, a group of Fort Worth schoolteachers established a competition in his honor, and the Van Cliburn International Piano Competition was born.

Today, the competition, held every four years (the year after each presidential election) is considered one of the most prestigious in the world—second only, perhaps, to the Tchaikovsky itself. Winners receive prize money, contracts, management, and touring opportunities. For Fort Worth, the competition is one of the highlights of the cultural calendar, as patrons fill Bass Hall by the thousands to witness the skill of familiar names as well as up-and-comers.

FALL

CEDAR SPRINGS HALLOWEEN PARADE

3900 block of Cedar Springs Rd.

COST: Free

Map 2

While the calendar for many gay communities revolves around Pride Week, in Dallas it centers on the Cedar Springs Halloween Parade. Each year, the festivities grow a little more outrageous (not exactly a kid-friendly event, this one), with floats, costumes, and drag queens galore entertaining thousands of spectators. Expect to go early and stay late—the traffic and parking get amazingly congested and stay that way. But given the wildness of the event and the good time abandon in the air, you'll probably want to linger anyway.

DALLAS PRIDE PARADE (ALAN ROSS FREEDOM PARADE)

Cedar Springs Rd. and Throckmorton St., www.dallasprideparade.com

COST: Free

Map 2

Some have argued that we live in a post-pride culture, that GLBT parades are unnecessary. Tell that to the roughly 40,000 people who crowd "the gayborhood," as the Oak Lawn area is known, every year to watch Dallas's version of the celebration. The parade is the highlight of Pride Week here (which mercifully

ARTS AND LEISURE

takes place in relatively cool September, while most across the country occur in the summer), which sees charity events, dance parties, shopping specials, variety shows, drag shows, and pretty much every gay thing under the sun, in one of the most gay-friendly cities in the nation.

FORT WORTH ALLIANCE AIR SHOW

Fort Worth Alliance Airport, 2221 Alliance Blvd.,
817/890-1000, www.allianceairshow.com
COST: Free
`Map 11`

Held at the Fort Worth Alliance Airport on the far northern border of town, this exciting yearly event is a mind-blower, as the famous Blue Angels thunder through the air and the U.S. Army's parachute show, the Golden Knights, deftly maneuver through the sky. Even without the main attractions, a day here is chock full of aerial treats, be they in the air or, like the static display, on the ground. The latter attraction, featuring restored military planes from all eras, is one of the biggest in the nation—tour guides are available, or visitors can meander around the old-school fighters and giant cargo planes. A kids' zone and other activities round out the experience. The best part? Admission is free—though coolers and outside food and drink aren't allowed, so expect to shell out some dough for refreshments. And don't forget to bring your earplugs.

GREEK FOOD FESTIVAL OF DALLAS

13555 Hillcrest Rd., 972/233-4880,
www.greekfestivalofdallas.com
COST: General admission: $5 adult, $3 youth, free under 5. Dinner plate: $15 adult, $11 youth. Lunch plate: $10 adult, $7 youth
`Map 7`

Somehow, over the course of more than 50 years, this little gathering has blossomed into a massive citywide affair, proving Greek food is so much more than just gyros and hummus. Each year, the asphalt corner of Hillcrest and Alpha Roads transforms into fertile ground, with Greek delicacies and traditional food as far as the eye can see. Besides the many food kiosks, you'll also find an *agora* (marketplace)

and a *groceria,* with loads of imported Greek foods, plus authentic dancing, singing, and other entertainment.

RED RIVER SHOOTOUT

Cowboys Stadium, 900 E. Randol Mill Rd., Arlington
COST: Varies annually.
`Map 11`

There's no worse blood in college sports than that between the University of Oklahoma and University of Texas football teams, as evidenced by the hype surrounding their annual matchup. The last time the game was played in the legendary Cotton Bowl was in 2008; the battlefield has moved to Jerry Jones's new state-of-the-art stadium in Arlington, but that hasn't lessened the intensity of the game, nor has it dampened the area-wide festivities that fill the week surrounding the event.

TEXAS STATE FAIR

Fair Park, 1121 1st Ave., 214/426-3400, www.bigtex.com
HOURS: Sept.-Oct. daily 10 A.M.-9 P. M.
COST: Varies annually.
`Map 5`

Every fall, Fair Park is home to the Texas State Fair, the largest of its kind in the country, attended by millions of visitors. Dramatically welcoming all State Fair visitors are two giant structures: a 52-foot-tall cowboy named Big Tex (which was rebuilt after the original Big Tex was destroyed in front of hundreds of startled fair-goers in an electrical fire during the 2012 fair), and North America's largest Ferris wheel, called the Texas Star, both of which lord over the fair's activities. Popular fair activities include auto shows, concerts, midway games, amusement park rides, animal shows, pig races, and pigging out on every type of food imaginable—fried.

WINTER

BIG D NYE

2500 Victory Ave., www.bigdnye.com
COST: Free
`Map 1`

The Dallas version of the Times Square ball drop, Big D NYE takes place in Victory Park

ARTS AND LEISURE

and features local bands, major sporting events, and a giant fireworks display at midnight.

🔘 FORT WORTH STOCK SHOW AND RODEO

3400 Burnett Tandy Rd.

COST: $10, $5 youth

`Map 10`

Once a year, even the most cosmopolitan of Fort Worth's citizens dust off their Ropers and starch their Wranglers in anticipation of one of the biggest events of the year: the Fort Worth Stock Show and Rodeo. It's a big enough deal in these parts that local schoolchildren receive an official day off to head down to the Will Rogers Memorial Center, where three weeks' worth of attendant events are held during the

end of January and beginning of February. During that time, every square inch of the Memorial Center—from the coliseum to the midway to the exposition centers—is filled with the bustle of commerce and competition.

The event is equal parts business and pleasure. For some, the stock show and exposition provide a venue for selling cattle and other hoof stock (in 2008, a record $4,322,000 was generated), for exhibiting different breeds, and for networking. But for many, the carnival, midway, and—especially—rodeo provide the best entertainment of the year. Hundreds of thousands of visitors descend upon the Will Rogers Coliseum to watch expert ropers and riders compete in what is truly a spectacle of the West.

Sports and Recreation

SPECTATOR SPORTS

COWTOWN SPEEDWAY

3925 New Hope Rd., Kennedale, 817/478-9952, www.cowtownspeedway.com

COST: Varies depending on event.

`Map 11`

Dubbed "the fastest lil dirt track in Texas," the Cowtown Speedway is an oval quarter-mile track that's been in operation since 1963. The Speedway hosts a variety of races for six classes of cars: Modified Class, Limited Modifieds, Street Stock, Sprints, Bombers, and Junior Mini Stock with go-kart nights and demolition derbies thrown in. It's a fast track indeed—some racers have been clocked up to 110 mph.

CROWNE PLAZA INVITATIONAL AT COLONIAL

Colonial Country Club, 3735 Country Club Circle, 817/927-4820, www.crowneplazainvitational.com

COST: Varies annually.

`Map 9`

One of only four invitationals on the PGA tour, this tourney has had many sponsors (and, hence, slight name changes) since its beginning in 1946, but it has always been steeped in history, and has always been held at Colonial

Country Club on the west side of Fort Worth. The Colonial began with a legendary bang: One of the game's greats, Fort Worth's own Ben Hogan, won the first two tournaments. You'd think it'd be all downhill from there, but the Colonial has a knack for big-name wins—other victors include Sam Snead, Tommy Bolt, Arnold Palmer, Ben Crenshaw, Jack Nicklaus, Tom Watson, and Phil Mickelson (though Hogan won it the most: five times). One big name is missing from that list: Tiger Woods hasn't played the tour stop since 1997, and it's unclear if he ever will again. Still, Colonial always provides fireworks, such as in 2003 when Annika Sorenstam became the first woman to participate in a PGA tourney since Babe Zaharias.

Tickets can be hard to come by, and they can be expensive, but the Colonial is a dream experience for golf fans (except for the fact that Tiger usually skips it). With the summer heat just beginning its annual boil, a large, sweaty, preppy crowd follows the stars of the links around like puppies. The cool green expanses and old-school country-club brick buildings provide an aura of history, and as the excitement swells on the final Sunday, so do the crowds—come early to stake out a favorite spot.

ARTS AND LEISURE

THE DALLAS COWBOYS

Where to begin? Five Super Bowl victories. Eleven NFL Hall of Famers. A value of well over $1.6 billion dollars. A crazy owner. Constant drama. These are the Dallas Cowboys, America's Team. To say they are beloved by their city is like saying a mother loves her son—you don't even *know*.

The Cowboys have a singular, storied, spectacular history, the type found only among a handful of teams in any type of sports. Though it has struggled of late, the franchise has racked up an impressive string of credentials: 10 conference championships, 19 division championships, and 29 playoff appearances to go along with those Super Bowls.

It also has provided a list of legends: Clint Murchison, the team's first owner (who, some believe, helped engineer John F. Kennedy's assassination); Tom Landry, the fedora-sporting coach for the team's first 28 years, under whom they won two Super Bowls; Don Meredith, the boozy gunslinging quarterback; fierce defenders like Bob Lilly, Lee Roy Jordon, and Thomas "Hollywood" Henderson; Tony Dorsett and NFL all-time rushing leader Emmitt Smith; and, of course Super Bowl winning quarterbacks Roger Staubach and Troy Aikman, now revered as Big D gods.

Despite such luminaries, the Cowboys have never been far from controversy, and that's never been more true than during the reign of current owner Jerry Jones. Upon purchasing the team in 1989, Jones infuriated fans with a series of PR missteps, the most egregious being his unceremonious firing of Landry. The first several years of the Jones era were pure misery, including a 1-11 season, but the franchise regrouped after trading superstar Herschel Walker to the Minnesota Vikings for tons of draft picks. Jones's blunders were forgotten when the 'Boys turned around a miserable team and won three Super Bowls during the 1990s.

In 2009, amid renewed fan anger against Jones for his indulgence of controversial players like Terrell Owens and an underachieving team, the owner unveiled the Cowboys' new stadium, located in Arlington. (The fate of Texas Stadium, home to the Cowboys since 1971, has yet to be determined.) The new stadium is a futuristic masterpiece, with a regular capacity of 80,000 (though that can be expanded to around 100,000), hybrid turf, and, as a continuation of the tradition of the "hole in the roof" at Texas Stadium, a retractable roof. Several big sporting events have already taken place during the new stadium's inaugural years, including the 2010 NBA All-Star game, some NCAA Final Four tournament games, and the 2011 Super Bowl. Cowboys fans, of course, hoped this last one proved to be home turf. They were disappointed, yet again.

DALLAS COWBOYS

Cowboys Stadium, 925 N. Collins, Arlington, 817/892-4200, www.dallascowboys.com
COST: Varies annually.
`Map 11`

One of the most storied franchises in sports, the Dallas Cowboys are not just a football team for Metroplex fans; they are a legendary collection of gods, worshipped in a brand-new cathedral—the $1.3 billion Cowboys Stadium—that rises dramatically out of the Arlington pavement and steals the show from nearby Rangers Ballpark.

This team has always been about spectacle, and Cowboys Stadium's ultra-modern glass and steel design, enormous HD television screens, and 63,000-square-foot retractable roof provide an appropriately dramatic backdrop for the battle taking place on the field below.

And that's way below. With an 80,000-person regular capacity and the ability to expand to 100,000, Cowboys Stadium may contain more nosebleed seats than fancy suites (though, to be sure, there are plenty of those too).

With an arena this size, hassles are to be expected. Cowboys officials claim the stadium is surrounded by 30,000 parking spaces—a big upgrade from the Cowboys' former home at Texas Stadium, but expect to pay, and to walk.

Oddly, although North Texas is obsessed with its 'Boys, and fans follow the team rabidly, crowds at the games can be subdued compared to other franchises. Once they get ratcheted up, however, expect cacophony. Similarly, even if fans are reserved, don't think that means you can sport the opposing team's colors without getting your fair share of razzing.

DALLAS MAVERICKS

American Airlines Center, 2500 Victory Ave.,
214/757-MAVS (6287), www.dallasmavericks.com
COST: Varies annually.
Map 1

The 2011 NBA Champion Mavericks began as an expansion team in 1980 under the leadership of their first owner, bowling alley "kingpin" Don Carter. For years, though they made the playoffs regularly with starters like Mark Aguirre, Rolando Blackmon, and Derek Harper, the Mavs were never much more than a blip on the NBA radar screen, save in their seven-game series against the L.A. Lakers in the 1988 Western Conference finals. In fact, for the entire duration of the 1990s, they downright sucked, flirting several times with the NBA record for most losses in a single season. Even new ownership led by former presidential candidate H. Ross Perot didn't help.

But when the young, brash Internet honcho Mark Cuban bought the franchise in 2000, suddenly the Mavs were on the map. A series of trade and draft acquisitions brought stars like perennial all-star forward Dirk Nowitzki to the team, and that, combined with Cuban's intense desire to win and his even more intense desire to spend money in order to do so, helped the Mavs surge further along in the playoffs. Things looked bright.

Until the big fiasco. The Mavericks as a franchise had never made it to the NBA Finals until 2006, when they arrived after a grueling playoff season, with home court advantage to take on the Miami Heat. The Mavs kicked off the series with a pair of convincing wins. The city of Dallas began drawing up parade plans. The team traveled to Miami with visions of

The American Airlines Center is home to the NBA's Dallas Mavericks and the NHL's Dallas Stars.

© CLAY COLEMAN/DALLAS CVB

ARTS AND LEISURE

bringing a championship back to Big D. Then the wheels came off: Miami won the next four games, snatching the title away. For Dallas, it was an epic failure.

It took years for Dallas—both the team and the city—to get over the heartbreak. The hangover lasted through five years of frustrating playoff losses. Until that magical summer in 2011, when the team achieved vengeance against the Heat, beating them in six games in the NBA Finals.

The championship launched Nowitzki into the upper echelon of Dallas sports worship, and probably had a similar effect on ticket prices.

Still, the Mavs remain a hot ticket, especially in the beautiful confines of the American Airlines Center. As long as the superstar continues to play, Mavs fans most likely will consistently post sellouts, so be prepared to shell out the bucks to ticket brokers or scalpers. Or try your luck close to game time: Ever popular with fans, Cuban has initiated several fan-friendly promotions, including a limited amount of "cheap seats" and other specials—check the website for details.

DALLAS STARS

American Airlines Center, 2500 Victory Ave., 214/467-8277, www.stars.nhl.com
COST: Varies annually.
Map 1

Sun-drenched Dallas may not be the most hockey-centric locale, but Dallasites certainly have adopted their Stars, who were imported in 1993 when the Minnesota North Stars relocated here, as native sons. And although there was much controversy when the NHL okayed the deal that sent a storied franchise into a heretofore hockey-ignorant town, the Stars have taken kindly to their Texas home. For those on either side who remained ambivalent, the team's 1999 Stanley Cup sealed the deal.

Although their popularity has waxed and waned, Stars games often sell out, and American Airlines Center always rocks to the rafters during home games (fans go so far as to yell "Stars!" during the part of the national anthem with the same word).

FC DALLAS

Pizza Hut Park, 9200 World Cup Way, Frisco, 214/705-6700, www.fcdallas.com
COST: Varies annually.
Map 7

A charter member of major-league soccer, FC Dallas began as the Dallas Burn, a successful franchise that played home games at the famous Cotton Bowl in Fair Park before moving to Pizza Hut Park—built specifically for soccer—in the Dallas suburb of Frisco in 2005. Pizza Hut Park seats 20,000, though the FC Dallas crowd averages about half that. Tickets for FC Dallas games are cheap compared to many other major sports and easy to come by.

The team is owned by Clark Hunt (son of National Football League legend Lamar Hunt), who also owns the Kansas City Chiefs, and has found great success since its inaugural 1996 season, having fought its way to the MLS championship three times and winning it once, in 1997.

Games at Pizza Hut Park are a fun, family-friendly affair, and the franchise churns out a constant stream of promotions and concerts to maintain interest. Be forewarned: The MLS season stretches from March to September, and in the summer months, the outdoor stadium can prove viciously hot.

FORT WORTH CATS

LaGrave Field, 301 NE 6th St., 817/226-2287, www.fwcats.com
COST: Varies annually.
Map 8

Even though they're part of a relatively small league, unaffiliated with major-league baseball, the Fort Worth Cats of the American Association of Independent Professional Baseball might be more popular among Fort Worthers than their big-league brethren up the road, the Texas Rangers.

One reason for their popularity is their history. Unlike the Rangers, who moved to North Texas in 1972 and have done little since, the Cats date back to 1888 (when they were called the Panthers). They began that year as members of the Texas League, where they stayed

ARTS AND LEISURE

COLLEGE SPORTS

While college sports are huge in Texas, the scene is dominated primarily by the tri-umvirate of big universities, **Texas Tech, Texas A&M,** and the **University of Texas.** DFW has smaller fare, but there's still plenty of excellent competition to check out—and tickets are much more readily available. Just now recovering from the NCAA's death penalty enacted in 1987, Southern Methodist University's football team continues to improve, thanks to big-name coach June Jones. The University of Texas at Dallas is small, but their soccer program is one of the best in the nation. Texas Christian University's Horned Frogs football and basketball teams are always in the running—and always entertaining. The University of Texas at Arlington's hoops squad is the area's other basketball Mav-ericks—and they too can often be found at the top of the standings.

until the mid-1950s. Along the way, the Cats played host to the likes of Ty Cobb, Babe Ruth, Lou Gehrig, and Rogers Hornsby, all of whom made their way to the Fort Worth home field to participate in exhibition games. Hornsby eventually ended up managing the club for a few years. For a while, the Cats were affiliated with the Brooklyn Dodgers and then the Chicago Cubs before branching off independently for good.

Besides their history, the Cats have another thing going for them: They've always been good. Back in the days when independent baseball was a hot ticket, the Cats consistently won Texas League championships. At one point, between 1919 and 1925, they rattled off seven straight championships in a row. During the 1930s, they won three more. The team also made a habit of winning the yearly Dixie Series, which pitted the Texas League cham-pion against the Southern League champion.

Yet even history couldn't save the Cats from the downslide in minor-league popularity, and

in 1964 the team folded. In 2001, however, the Cats came back, 36 years after the last out at LaGrave Field, which had since been torn down. The Cats' new owner, Carl Bell, decided to build a brand-new LaGrave Field on top of the site of the last one. Bell even made sure the new home plate stood exactly where the last one had.

Bell built it, and the fans came. The new Cats have been a big hit ever since, picking up where they left off, making the playoffs a mere two years after their resurgence, and winning the league championship in 2005, 2006, and 2007. A number of Cats have gone on to play in the big leagues, most notably pitcher Luke Hochevar, the number one pick in MLB's 2006 draft.

FRISCO ROUGHRIDERS

Dr. Pepper Ballpark, 7300 RoughRiders Trail, Frisco, 972/731-9200, www.ridersbaseball.com

COST: Varies annually.

Map 7

The RoughRiders haven't been around for too long, but they've certainly been burning it up since they got here. Formerly the Shreveport Captains, this AA squad, now a farm team for the Texas Rangers, arrived in 2003 and immediately made the playoffs as winners of the South Division of the Texas League. The 'Riders, led by a constant stream of sluggers, have in fact made the postseason almost every year since.

Frisco's home field is the awesome, $23 million Dr. Pepper Ballpark, a cool stadium built in 2003, which has consistently posted top attendance numbers for minor-league teams. The park has some fun touches—including a rentable swimming pool and seats built around both bullpens—and it seats more than 10,000 fans.

GRAND PRAIRIE AIRHOGS

QuikTrip Park, 1600 Lone Star Pkwy., Grand Prairie, 972/504-9383, www.airhogsbaseball.com

COST: Varies annually.

Map 7

For years, independent professional baseball

ARTS AND LEISURE

ARTS AND LEISURE

THE MIGHTY MITES: A DIFFERENT KIND OF TEXAS FOOTBALL LEGEND

This football story begins on a battlefield in France. In 1915, Rusty Russell was serving as medic at the battle of St. Mihiel during World War I. Led by General John Pershing, a combination of U.S. and French troops battled German forces in rain and wind. The U.S. troops dug into the mud and endured wave after wave of machine gun fire.

Then the Germans started dropping mustard gas. Russell couldn't escape. Yet, half-blinded by the gas, he crawled along the ground, continuing to help wounded soldiers, until he couldn't see at all.

He spent the next six months in a hospital, where he made a promise to God that, if he restored Russell's sight, he'd help kids any way he could.

A decade later he got his chance, when he left his position as head football coach at Temple High School, where he'd led the team to the state semifinals, to take the helm of the football squad at Fort Worth's Masonic Widows and Orphans Home.

It was like a movie, only it was real. In the midst of the Great Depression, the Masons home took in children who had lost their parents. One of Russell's players, Hardy Brown, had seen his bootlegger father killed right in front of him.

There's ragtag, and then there's literal rags. Called the Mighty Mites, the undermanned and undersize team had no matching uniforms, and what clothes they had were barely stitched together, threadbare and patched. Only six leather helmets were available for the 12 players. Their field was festooned with rocks, holes, and prickly pear cactus. They couldn't afford a ball, so they used two socks stuffed together to practice.

Russell drove them to their first game against powerhouse Mineral Wells with the team sitting the bed of his Dodge truck—after convincing the home's maintained crew to build a wooden railing on it so the players wouldn't go flying out. Before the game, the unassuming, bespectacled Russell asked the opposing coach if, in the unlikely event the Mighty Mites won, they could take home the game ball. The coach agreed.

The Mighty mites won, 34-14.

And so began the team's run of success, a run so wild, so unlikely, and so inspiring, it leapt beyond the Texas state lines, as national news-papers got ahold of the story. Fans all over the country found themselves enthralled by the box scores and games stories of this band of scrawny overachievers from Texas.

Constantly facing oversize opponents, Russell invented different schemes to take advantage of the Mites' seeming disadvantages, inventing the spread offense so that his players could, in the words of writer Jim Dent, "run through the competition like a bunch of field mice." The spread offense dominated the NFL in the 1980s and is the most popular system in the college ranks today. Russell also utilized timing patterns replicated later in the NFL's West Coast offense.

It worked. Over the years, the Mites faced teams twice their size, from schools ten times their size, but the team still blasted its way through the ranks of the highest level of Texas high school football with win after win. When they made it to the state championship game in Corsicana, Texas, 20,000 fans jammed into a stadium built for 5,000. Portions of the stands collapsed (no one was hurt); the police relented and allowed the crowd to stand on the field behind the offense.

Every year, the Mites faced the same obstacles. Every year, they kept on winning. They won over friends in victory—after losing to the Mites, the Highland Park High School fans took up a collection and bought them new uniforms—and in defeat—after narrowly losing a state semifinal, the Mites were met with a crowd of 12,000 chanting "Mighty Mites! Mighty Mites!"

The story ends with another war. As World War II loomed, most of the Mites were shipped off to fight in the Pacific, and Russell finally left to coach at Highland Park. The team never again reached quite so high, but many of the Mites went on to achieve great things. Among their ranks were several professional football players and a Texas Supreme Court Justice.

If you're curious to read more about the Mighty Mites, a good resource is Dent's *Twelve Mighty Orphans: The Inspiring True Story of the Mighty Mites Who Ruled Texas Football* (2007, Thomas Dunne Books).

in the Metroplex has been dominated by the legendary Fort Worth Cats, but a new squad on the scene, the Grand Prairie AirHogs, have already started to give the Cats a run for their money.

The Hogs (as well as the Cats) are part of the unaffiliated Southern League. In many ways, this is a last-ditch league, populated by young players who have gone unnoticed by big-league franchises and older players hoping for one last chance to be recognized by the majors. You'd think that would speak to poor-quality baseball, but quite the contrary: There's much at stake for all the players involved, and the spirit and intensity of the play make for excellent games. The Hogs made a fine choice in their first manager, former big-leaguer Pete Incaviglia (who once played for the Texas Rangers, among others), who guided the team to a Southern Division championship its inaugural year.

It helps, too, that the city of Grand Prairie spent $20 million on the AirHogs' home, QuikTrip Park. Seating only about 5,000, the intimate park features excellent views of the game from every seat. The park was built as part of a grander entertainment complex, complete with a bar and restaurant, cigar bar, playgrounds, and swimming pool. A day at the park is an exercise in attention-mongering. Inter-inning lulls are filled with giveaways, scoreboard games, and goofy on-field races. As is tradition in the smaller leagues, promotional nights are wild and silly, and the Hogs have garnered quite a bit of national attention with theirs.

HD BYRON NELSON CHAMPIONSHIP

Four Seasons Resort and Club, 4150 N. MacArthur Blvd., Irving, 972/717-0700, www.hpbnc.org/byronnelson
COST: Varies annually.
Map 7

This PGA tour stop began as the Dallas Open in 1944 and has shared its name with various corporate sponsors since, but to golf lovers everywhere, it will always be called the Byron

Nelson. Until his death in 2006, Nelson was a golden-boy legend around the world, and in Dallas he was a god. His name alone has lured the big boys from the PGA year after year—past winners include Tiger Woods, Phil Mickelson, and Sergio Garcia.

The tourney, held in late April/early May, is played at the TPC Four Seasons club and features an unusual setup: The first two rounds are played on both of the Four Seasons' courses—the TPC Las Colinas and the Cottonwood Valley Country Club—with TPC Las Colinas hosting the final two rounds.

LONE STAR PARK

1000 Lone Star Pkwy., Grand Prairie, 972/263-7223, www.lonestarpark.com
COST: $5-32, $3 children, free for Bar & Book
Map 7

Lone Star Park has only been around since 1994, but it has already built a name for itself as the premier Thoroughbred track in Texas (and much of the Southwest, for that matter). The world-class facility hosts a 65-date meet that lasts from spring to mid-summer. The stands for the seven-furlong turf course and one-mile oval track usually hold about 8,000 people, though they were greatly expanded in 2004 for the Breeder's Cup. The grounds also include a simulcast center, sports book, concessions, and seating ranging from box seats to terrace level to general admission.

MESQUITE CHAMPIONSHIP RODEO

1818 Rodeo Dr., Mesquite, 972/285-8777, www.mesquiterodeo.com
COST: $12-60
Map 7

If you only do one "Texas" thing during your time here, it should be the Mesquite Rodeo. An evening here vibrates with excitement: If you've never seen bronc bustin' or bull riding, the spectacle at the 5,000-seat Resistol Arena will leave you breathless. The rodeo sticks to the traditional—calf-roping, barrel races, steer wrestling—along with a few new events, like "cowboy poker" and chuck wagon races.

STOCKYARDS CHAMPIONSHIP RODEO

Cowtown Coliseum, 121 E. Exchange Ave.,
817/625-1025, www.stockyardsrodeo.com
COST: General Admission: $15 adult, $10 youth, $12.50
senior. VIP Club Seating: $20 adult, youth, and senior.
Reserved Box Seating: $20 adult, youth, and senior.
Map 11

This traditional, excellent indoor rodeo, held
every Friday and Saturday at the Cowtown
Coliseum in the Stockyards, is a thrilling way
to spend an evening. The price of admission
also includes Pawnee Bill's Wild West Show,
which alone is worth the excursion. The show
is a reenactment of a popular Old West troupe
that performed trick riding, trick roping, trick
shooting, and bullwhip acts. Keep in mind it's
cash only at the box office; credit and ATM
cards can be used online, for a $1-per-ticket
fee. Phone orders can be placed only Mon.–
Fri. 11 A.M.–9 P.M. and online orders no later
than Fri. 3 P.M.

TEXAS BLACK RODEO

Fair Park Coliseum, 1300 Robert B. Cullum Dr.
(main entrance) to 1438 Coliseum Dr., 214/565-9026,
ext. 304
COST: Varies annually.
Map 5

A celebration of the historically overlooked
African American cowboys, the Texas Black
Rodeo has been a mainstay since 1986. It also
just happens to feature some of the most skilled
bronc-busters, cattle-ropers, and horsemen—
and horsewomen—around. Proceeds benefit
the African-American Museum.

TEXAS BRAHMAS

NYTEX Sports Centre, 8851 Ice House Dr., North
Richland Hills, 817/336-4423, www.brahmas.com
COST: $13-30
Map 11

Texas may not be known for hockey of any
sort, much less the minor-league variety, but
the Brahmas have been a hot ticket ever since
moving from their downtown digs to North
Richland Hills, a suburb of Fort Worth. The
proud purple and black have tasted the postseason a couple of times in their short existence

since 1996, but the fans who sell out the
2,400-capacity NYTEX arena that serves as
the Brahmas' home base show up even in the
lean years. Tickets aren't as cheap as you'd expect, but the level of hockey is also better than
one would imagine, and with plenty of promos
and close-up action, the family-friendly atmosphere here is a definite draw.

TEXAS MOTOR SPEEDWAY (NASCAR)

3545 Lone Star Circle, 817/215-8500,
www.texasmotorspeedway.com
COST: Varies annually.
Map 11

Since it first opened in 1996, the 1.5-mile
oval track Texas Motor Speedway has shifted
from a sort of wannabe to a major player in
the NASCAR world. Track improvements
have played a major factor in the TMS's rise
in popularity: For the first few years of its existence, TMS officials struggled with constant
complaints about the track's safety, and also its
odd "double bank" configuration. Those problems were slowly resolved, the track was refitted
as a single bank, and the speedway is now one
of the fastest in the nation.

The second factor in its popularity is the
management. Upon taking over the reins at the
track, longtime racing promoter Eddie Gossage
introduced personal seat licenses and season
tickets to patrons, a first for NASCAR, and
he also allowed fans to bring their own coolers
into events, which endeared fans to the track.
Crowds at TMS can top 212,000, and usually
do, making TMS the second largest sports facility in the country.

Major events held at the speedway include
two NASCAR Sprint races—the Dickies 500
and the Samsung 500; NASCAR Nationwide
and Craftsman series events; and a single
IndyCar race, the Bombardier LearJet 550.

◖ TEXAS RANGERS

Rangers Ballpark, 1000 Ballpark Way, Arlington,
972/726-4377, www.texasrangers.com
COST: Varies annually.
Map 11

In 1972, major-league baseball's Washington

Texas Motor Speedway (NASCAR)

Senators packed their bags and moved south, beginning a new era as the Texas Rangers. Since the move, the team primarily has been known for three things: trading away a then-rookie Sammy Sosa in 1989; the fact that former president George W. Bush once owned them (in fact, it was he who okayed the Sosa decision); and—a bright spot—as the place where pitching great Nolan Ryan had some of his most memorable moments. Ryan boasted two of his record-setting seven no-hitters during his years with the team, and he also was wearing a Rangers uniform when he struck out his major-league record 5,714th batter. Ryan now co-owns the team and currently serves as the team's president of operations.

For decades, the team for the most part held mediocre—and sometimes downright awful—ground in the American League's Western division, but all that changed, finally, when the Rangers captured the American League pennant two years in a row: in 2010 and 2011, faltering both times in the World Series, but in the process generating a baseball thrill the likes of which the Metroplex has never seen.

Following the pennant years, the Rangers shattered their previous attendance records, and tickets became more and more scarce as folks decided to head out to the Ballpark (no, really, the Rangers' stadium is called the Ballpark). Gloriously rising from acres of Arlington asphalt, the stadium was built in 1991 with the cathedrals of the Great Game in mind. It's a fun place to watch a game, even more so because it's a home run hitter's dream.

PARKS AND RECREATION AREAS

BURGER'S LAKE

1200 Meandering Way, 817/737-3414,
www.burgerslake.com
HOURS: Daily 11 A.M.-7 P.M.
COST: $12, $5 child
Map 11

In a world full of expensive, high-tech, fancy water parks, many Fort Worth families prefer the chilled-out atmosphere of Burger's Lake,

ARTS AND LEISURE

© DALLAS CVB

Since the Texas Rangers' back-to-back World Series run, the Rangers Ballpark is always packed.

which essentially is a good old-fashioned swimming hole (accentuated solely by diving boards, a 20-foot slide, and a single trapeze). The lake—a one-acre, spring-fed pool—now serves as the centerpiece of a multi-acre park that has been privately owned since 1930. Sunbathers bask on the two sandy beaches that abut the lake, though most folks prefer the large swaths of shady picnic areas, and many people take advantage of the tennis and volleyball courts.

EAGLE MOUNTAIN LAKE

Lake maps available via the Tarrant County Regional Water District: 10201 North Shore Dr., 817/237-8585

Map 11

With almost 9,000 acres of surface, 60 miles of shoreline, and a depth of 47 feet at its deepest, Eagle Mountain Lake is very popular, partially because it's only about a 30-minute drive from downtown Fort Worth. Because of the relatively clear and smooth water, skiing and

sailboating are predominant activities here, as is fishing (species include largemouth, spotted, and white bass, along with catfish and white crappie). Surrounding accommodations include a number of resorts and cabins. Hiking and biking trails can be found at the 400-acre Eagle Mountain Park on the east side of the lake.

FOREST PARK

2700 Trinity Park Dr.
HOURS: 7 A.M.-11:30 P.M.
Map 10

Forest Park consists of a wide band of often thick packed greenery in the midst of the University area of Fort Worth, near many of the city's sights (occasionally, you'll hear a lion's roar from the nearby zoo). Highlights include a duck pond at the abutting Trinity Park, plus surrounding soccer fields and the ever-popular miniature train ride that runs through the park.

◖ FORT WORTH NATURE CENTER AND REFUGE

9601 Fossil Ridge Rd., 817/262-4479, www.fwnaturecenter.org
HOURS: Oct.–Apr. daily 8 A.M.–5 P.M., May–Sept. daily 8 A.M.–7 P.M.
COST: $5 adult, $2 child, $3 senior
Map 11

Just 10 miles from downtown Fort Worth, the Nature Center feels like what the DFW area must have been before it was settled. The 25 miles of trails on this 3,500-acre site meander through prairie, forest, and wetlands, all home to hundreds of species of flora and fauna, including a herd of buffalo (which, according to DNA testing, has no relation to domesticated cattle—a rarity for bison). The center offers programs, exhibits, tours, and canoeing for all ages.

THE LEGEND OF WHITE ROCK LAKE

The lake's choppy brown waters hold a good deal of history and folklore. From 1933 to 1941, a troop of the New Deal-commissioned Civilian Conservation Corps established a camp at Winfrey Point. Combined with workers from the Works Progress Administration, the crew epitomized the function of the New Deal by building bridges and piers in and roads around the lake. Several of the lake's signature sites date back to the CCC and WPA projects.

At the onset of World War II, the former CCC barracks at Winfrey Point were converted into an Army Air Corps boot camp, which functioned until 1944, when it became a prison camp for captured German troops. These weren't just any German troops, either, but elite soldiers from Erwin Rommel's Afrika Korps.

The history of the lake, however, takes a backseat to its primary legend, that of the Lady of the Lake. The legend takes many forms, but the one connected to another Dallas legend is perhaps most interesting. As author Frank X. Tolbert tells it in his book, *Neiman-Marcus, Texas: The Story of the Proud Dallas Store:*

One night about ten years ago a beautiful blonde girl ghost appeared on a road near Dallas' White Rock Lake. Mr. and Mrs. Guy Malloy, directors for display for the world-famous specialty store, Neiman-Marcus, saw the girl. Only they didn't recognize her, right off, for a ghost. She had walked up from the beach. And she stood there in the headlights of the slow-moving Malloy

car. Mrs. Malloy said, "Stop, Guy. That girl seems in trouble. She must have fallen in the lake. Her dress is wet. Yet you can tell that it is a very fine dress. She certainly got it at the Store."

By "the Store," Mrs. Malloy meant the Neiman-Marcus Company of Dallas. The girl spoke in a friendly, cultured contralto to the couple after the car had stopped. She said she'd like to be taken to an address on Gaston Avenue in the nearby Lakewood section. It was an emergency she said. She didn't explain what had happened to her, and the Malloys were too polite to ask. She had long hair, which was beginning to dry in the night breeze. And Mrs. Malloy was now sure that this girl was wearing a Neiman-Marcus dress. She was very gracious as she slipped by Mrs. Malloy and got in the back seat of the two-door sedan. When the car started, Mrs. Malloy turned to converse with the passenger in the Neiman-Marcus gown. The girl had vanished. There was a damp spot on the back seat. The Malloys went to the address on Gaston Avenue. A middle-aged man answered the door. Yes, he had a daughter with long blonde hair who wore nothing but Neiman-Marcus clothes. She had been drowned about two years before when she fell off a pier at White Rock Lake.

ARTS AND LEISURE

GATEWAY PARK

751 Beach St., 817/392-5700

HOURS: Daily 5 A.M.-11 P.M.

COST: Free

Map 11

Known primarily for its giant, friendly fenced-in dog park, Gateway actually is in the midst of a massive, multi-year renovation that has already reaped benefits, including 15 miles of new trails, improved soccer fields, and water-flow improvements. In the meantime, "Fort Woof," which was voted the #1 dog park in the country by *Dog Fancy* magazine, is a great place to relax with Fido.

GPX SKATE PARK

1002 Lone Star Pkwy., Grand Prairie, 972/262-4479, www.allianceskateparks.com

HOURS: Sun.-Thurs. 10 A.M.-10 P.M., Fri.-Sat. 10 A.M.-midnight

Map 7

It didn't take long for this $1.2 million state-of-the-art skate park to get some attention—in 2001, just one year after it was built, GPX hosted ESPN's X-Games and proceeded to do so the year after that as well. Every inch of this grand-scale facility is a skateboarder's dream, featuring courses for beginners, intermediates, and experts, including a 12-foot half pipe, bank ramps, handrails, inline hockey rink, and more.

KATY TRAIL

Trailhead at American Airlines Center, 2500 Victory Ave., www.katytraildallas.org

HOURS: Daily 7 A.M.-11:30 P.M.

Map 2

This 3.5-mile hiking/biking trail follows the original path of the now-abandoned Missouri-Kansas-Texas railway line. Originating at an elevated path near the American Airlines Center, the greenbelt winds around some of the most densely populated parts of Dallas, through lushly vegetated sections of Uptown.

Plans for the trail include construction of several new entry points and a soft-surface parallel trail made of recycled running shoes. Planners hope the Katy Trail eventually will be a leg of a comprehensive, countywide network of trails.

LAKE ARLINGTON

I-20 and Arkansas Ave., 817/459-5474

COST: $5 daily fee; permit required for all boating, including small craft like canoes and kayaks

HOURS: Daily 7 A.M.-11:30 P.M.

Map 11

Two parks—Richard Simpson Park to the north and Bowman Springs Park to the south—with boat launches and restrooms flank this 2,000-surface-acre lake. Kayakers and paddlers have taken to the Paddle Trail, which skims 10 miles' worth of the lake's bank. Fishing aficionados will find crappie, bass, and catfish at the end of their lines.

LAKE BENBROOK

7001 Lakeside Dr., 817/292-2400

Map 11

Although it's also known as a skiing and boating spot that's very convenient to most parts of Fort Worth, Lake Benbrook's strength is its laid-back vibe. You could happily while away a humid summer's day drift or bank fishing here, hooking channel catfish and carp. Locals recommend **Mustang Point, Rocky Creek Park,** and **Longhorn Park**—all near the east end of the dam that created the lake—as the best bank fishing spots.

LAKESIDE PARK

4601 Lakeside Dr.

HOURS: Daily 7 A.M.-11:30 P.M.

Map 3

Truly one of the most beautiful parks in Dallas, Lakeside's prominent features are a lily pad–covered pond and several oversize granite teddy bear sculptures, which are either exceedingly cute or exceedingly creepy, depending on your perspective. Either way, locals love to stroll the 14 green, relaxing acres here.

LEE PARK AND ARLINGTON HALL CONSERVANCY

3333 Turtle Creek Blvd.
HOURS: Daily 7 A.M.–11:30 P.M.
Map 2

Anchored by Arlington Hall (a two-thirds-scale replica of the Curtis-Lee Mansion in Arlington, Virginia, Lee Park oozes Southern heritage. This manifests in lovely ways, such as the brilliant and copious flowers and the stunning restoration of the hall, and more uncomfortable ways, such as with the statue of Confederate hero Robert E. Lee. There's no arguing the compact park provides a cooling respite, right next to the slowly flowing waters of Turtle Creek.

PANTHER ISLAND PAVILION/ TRINITY RIVER WATER SPORTS

395 Purcey St.
HOURS: Vary
Map 8

Frankly, Fort Worth's Trinity River revitalization project has gone more smoothly and with greater success than Dallas's (perhaps overly) ambitious Trinity River Corridor project. Perhaps it's because Fort Worth has a smaller area to deal with. Whatever the reason, folks have rediscovered the potential of the river and its surroundings.

Some of the best evidence of the revitalization is found at the tail end of the Trinity Trails on the northern fringe of downtown and the western edge of Trinity Park. Always a good spot for walking and biking, this area has upped the ante with the addition of **Panther Island Pavilion** (1098 W. Peach St.), an outdoor stage on the banks of the Trinity. During the summer, the pavilion plays host to a number of music events, including the weekly Rockin' the River series, during which patrons rent inner tubes and float about the stage as bands perform. Tubes and standup paddleboards are available for rent right at the pavilion from **Aloha Paddleboards** (817/403-5330, www.alohapaddlboards.com). Venerable Fort Worth outfitters **Backwoods** (817/403-6906, www.kayakfortworth.com) supplies kayak and canoe rentals. Both companies also offer lessons and rentals year-round for use on the entire revitalized stretch of the river.

RIVER LEGACY PARK

703 NW Green Oaks Blvd., 817/860-6752,
www.riverlegacy.org
HOURS: Daily 7 A.M.–11:30 P.M.
Map 11

A 1,300-acre oasis in the middle of the asphalt of Arlington, River Legacy Park is an unexpected little escape, offering miles of hike and bike trails winding along the Trinity River. The park is anchored by the River Legacy Living Science Center (Mon.–Sat. 9 a.m.–5 p.m.), a 12,000-square-foot facility filled with interactive exhibits. Designed to stand as a shining example of sustainability, the center is one of Arlington's signature sites.

TRINITY RIVER CORRIDOR

3700 Sylvan Ave.
214/671-9500, www.trinityrivercorridor.com
Map 6

At more than 10,000 acres and stretching 20 miles through the heart of Dallas, The Trinity River Corridor is the most ambitious park project the city has ever undertaken. For years the Trinity River, mainly abutting highways and industrial sites, sat stagnant and underappreciated, until the early 2000s brought a new plan to completely revitalize the river and its surrounding area.

The resulting urban park is one of the largest in the world, full of biking and hiking trails, still forested areas, bustling recreation areas, sports complexes, and water sports opportunities. One of the more popular trails is the Buckeye Trail (trailhead at 7000 Bexar St.), which ends at a massive stand of buckeye trees with a nice view of the river. A newer concrete trail takes visitors to an area shaded by a canopy of trees with boulders that serve as a great place sit while picnicking.

The signature feature of the Santa Fe Trestle Hike and Bike Trail (entrances at 2295 S. Riverfront Blvd. and 1837 E. 8th Ave.) is a historic railway trestle that has been restored

ARTS AND LEISURE

within modern safety specs, but as closely to its original 1879 aesthetic as possible. The bridge affords views of the river and downtown, while the trail meanders on through wetlands and forest. This is a good way to enter the Great Trinity Forest, an area of almost 8,000 acres of hardwood forest, wetlands, and ponds.

Water sports enthusiasts will love Dallas Wave, a man-made white-water area meant for kayakers and other adventurous boaters. The spot features a pair of boat launches, a spectator area, and a bypass should you prefer a more placid pace. (A word of caution here: The Dallas Wave is even more turbulent than its designers originally planned, so amateur kayakers might want to stay away.)

TRINITY TRAILS
600 Northside Dr., http://trinitytrails.org
HOURS: Daily 7 A.M.-11:30 P.M.
Map 8

Thirty miles of trails following the path of the Trinity River wind through some of the loveliest parts of the city. Although most sections of the trail are somewhat encumbered by reminders of the surrounding urban landscape, there are still plenty of river-cooled breezes, avian life (especially red-tailed hawks, egrets, and ducks), and the occasional cow pasture to provide bucolic enhancement. The trails have numerous access points and are a popular spot for joggers, walkers, and bikers. The city also periodically stocks the river with trout, bringing out bands of anglers, but the timing doesn't seem to follow any particular pattern or schedule; basically, if you see a bunch of anglers, run back home and grab your gear.

WHITE ROCK LAKE
8300 East Lawther Dr., www.dallasparks.org
HOURS: Daily 7 A.M.-11:30 P.M.
Map 7

Initially created in 1910 as a reservoir to help alleviate a citywide water shortage, White Rock Lake is a popular recreation area in the middle of the city. The lake, more than nine miles around, attracts tons of recreationists, especially bikers, and is the site of a myriad

cultural gatherings—although swimming and motor-operated boats are not allowed. It's also the site of the White Rock Marathon (www.runtherock.com), a unique event held in December, that combines the main race with music, a fitness festival, and attendant social events. As a Boston Marathon qualifier, the event attracts many of the top runners in the country, and it's considered one of the nation's top marathons.

BIKING
OAK CLIFF BICYCLE COMPANY
408 N. Bishop Ave., Ste. 103, 214/941-0010,
www.ocbicycleco.com
HOURS: Tues.-Fri. 11 A.M.-7 P.M., Sat. 10 A.M.-5 P.M.,
Sun. noon-5 P.M.
COST: $25-35 daily
Map 6

It's a smidge out of the way if you care to hit the Katy Trail or Trinity River Corridor, but this shop makes up for it with such reasonable prices (ask, and they'll usually work out discounts for those renting longer than a day or so) on a selection of cruiser and mountain bikes.

TRINITY BICYCLES
343 Throckmorton St., 817/484-6825,
www.trinitybicycles.com
HOURS: Mon.-Thurs. and Sat. 10 A.M.-8 P.M.,
Fri. 10 A.M.-10 P.M., Sun. 11 A.M.-5 P.M.
COST: $25-250
Map 8

The downtown Fort Worth location, convenient to the Trinity Trails, isn't the only good thing about Trinity Bicycles. The crew here is helpful and friendly, and the aesthetically inclined biker will love their cute rental rigs. The shop rents hybrid, road, and mountain bikes starting at $25 for two hours, and any of the three styles can be rented for up to a week.

FISHING
The fishing scene in and around DFW is as vibrant and varied as the species swimming in the area's lakes and rivers. Whether you're a casual cork-watcher or a hardcore angler, there are infinite resources to help you land your catch.

The **Texas Parks and Wildlife** website (www.tpwd.state.tx.us/fishboat/fish) provides an excellent starting point, with information on fishing licenses, species, best times and places to fish, bag limits, and much, much more. This is an Internet must-stop for any angler, especially if you plan on venturing out on your own.

BUG-A-BASS GUIDE SERVICE
817/874-9777, www.bugabass.net

Bug-A-Bass Guide Service is one of the most well-known guide services in the area, specializing in striper and catfish. Rates vary from $250 per person for a half day to $550 for a full for up to two people (each additional angler is $50).

REDNECK'S JUGLINES
214/736-2926, www.jugfishing.net

For a truly traditional experience, try Redneck's Juglines for a crew that specializes in the can't-fail method of jug fishing (they're best contacted via their website).

TEXAS CATFISH GUIDE SERVICE
817/522-3804, www.learntocatchcatfish.com

Should you prefer a guide, services abound. A foray with Texas Catfish Guide Service pretty much guarantees you'll catch some seriously huge bottom-feeders (call for rates and times, as they can vary). Guide Chad Ferguson has been helping folks catch catfish on rod and reel for more than 10 years on a number of local lakes. Bait and tackle is provided, as are cleaning and filleting.

UNFAIR ADVANTAGE CHARTERS
817/578-0028, www.unfairadvantagecharters.com

Unfair Advantage Charters runs half-day excursions on a 24-foot Ranger boat at $300 for up to three anglers, plus $75 for each extra person, and will tackle just about any North Texas lake.

GOLF

THE GOLF CLUB AT FOSSIL CREEK
3400 Western Center Blvd., 817/847-1900,
www.thegolfclubatfossilcreek.com

HOURS: Daily 6 A.M.-dark
COST: $29-65
Map 11

This gorgeous course stands as one of the last to be designed by Arnold Palmer, who messed with everyone's heads by bringing water into play on 13 of Fossil Creek's holes. Check online for specials or play discounted after 2 P.M. tee times, as the greens fees will cost you even more than all the balls you'll lose in the drink.

THE GOLF CLUB AT THE RESORT
5700 Resort Blvd., 817/750-2178,
www.thegolfclubattheresort.com

HOURS: Daily 6 A.M.-dark
COST: $25-52
Map 11

Thoughtfully placed bunkers and pins, deference to the terrain, and smaller, tough greens make this course a challenge, but not to the point that it discourages those closer to beginner on the golf scale. Not particularly long (6,626 yards), the course rewards shot-making rather than driving ability. Its location—close to Eagle Mountain Lake—provides a pretty, relaxing backdrop for a round, whether you're a duffer or a one-handicap. Need to practice before your round? Besides a driving range, the practice area provides putting, chipping, and pitching areas. Need to unwind after? The Resort's pool and dining options (which include fish fry, steak, and Italian nights) cap off a day on the links.

IRON HORSE GOLF COURSE
6200 Skylark Circle, Richland Hills, 817/485-6666,
www.ironhorsetx.com

HOURS: Daily 7 A.M.-dark
COST: $29-49
Map 11

Golf Digest digs this "thinkers" course a lot, having given it four stars in its "Places to Play" rankings. Even the lowest handicappers will find the variety of holes, pin placement, undulating fairways, and tricky greens provide constant challenges of both skill and brainpower. The course also has a slightly cutesy railroad theme, with copious rail ties and trestles flanking fairways and greens, and even railcar restrooms.

TENISON GOLF PARK

3501 Samuell Blvd., 214/670-1402,
www.tenisonpark.com
HOURS: Daily 6 A.M.-dark
COST: $20-60
Map 7

Tenison Golf Park consists of two different courses: Tenison Highlands and Tenison Glen. Don't play the Glen. Instead, brave the more crowded but infinitely higher quality Highlands course—the elevation changes, tougher greens, and 2001 renovation lure players of all skill levels and prove a challenge to all. The moderately priced park's amenities—putting green, driving range, on-site grill—rival those of pricier course.

TIERRA VERDE GOLF CLUB
AT THE RESERVE

7005 Golf Club Dr., Arlington, 817/478-8500,
www.arlingtongolf.com
HOURS: Daily 6 A.M.-dark
COST: $29-69
Map 11

This is a difficult, beautiful, and unique golf course. Designed and built in conjunction with Audubon International, Tierra Verde is the first municipal golf course in the world to be certified as an Audubon Signature Sanctuary. In addition to its commitment to environmental excellence (at least, as far as a 250-acre golf course can be committed to such), the course has been host to high-level events such as the Byron Nelson Qualifying Tournament for two years in a row. Each hole of this 7,000-yarder has five sets of tees, and the sculpted fairways are flanked by native grasses and trees. Amenities include a lighted driving range, a practice fairway bunker, and three practice holes.

TOP GOLF

8787 Park Ln., 214/341-9600, www.topgolf.com/dallas
HOURS: Sun.-Wed. 9 A.M.-11 P.M.,
Thurs. 9 A.M.-midnight, Fri.-Sat. 9 A.M.-1 A.M.

COST: $3.25-7 per game
Map 7

An excursion to Top Golf is guaranteed fun, even for those who don't particularly like the links. Why? Because there are no links at Top Golf. Rather, a double-decker row of weatherproof suites holds dozens of golfers who hit balls aimed at a number of pins on the driving range. The pins are surrounded by sensors in concentric circles around the target that pick up on a microchip in each ball. The microchips then report back to a computer—you get points for how close to the pin you get, and the computer screen at your station keeps track, so you can compete against your buddies. And trust us, with a chipper waitstaff delivering burgers and beer to your station, you'll need a computer to keep score for you. The facilities also include a fancy miniature golf course replete with a giant mountain and waterfalls, batting cages, and a pro shop. Plus, loaner clubs are available at no charge.

HORSEBACK RIDING
BENBROOK STABLES

10001 Benbrook Blvd., Benbrook, 817/249-1001,
www.benbrookstables.com
HOURS: Daily 9 A.M.-5 P.M.
COST: $15-30 per hour
Map 11

The Benbrook Stables make it easy for a beginner to get used to riding the range. The horses here are gentle; the trails, which wind a picturesque loop around Benbrook Lake, are navigable, even for the novice. In fact, fancy stuff—double riding, running, trotting—is prohibited, so your day in the saddle will be a leisurely one. Arena riding is also available.

STOCKYARDS STABLES

128 E. Exchange Ave., #300, 817/624-3446,
www.fortworthstockyardstables.com
HOURS: Daily 11 A.M.-5 P.M.
COST: $10-40
Map 11

Slap down your $40 and saddle up for a one-hour ride down the Trinity River, or, for the less adventurous, a mere $10 gets you 15 minutes in the corral. Either ride, surrounded by the history of the Stockyards, provides a glimpse into life in the Old West.

ICE SKATING

AMERICA'S ICE GARDEN

700 N. Pearl St., 214/720-8080

HOURS: Mon.-Fri. 10 A.M.-4:30 P.M., also Mon. 6:30-9 P.M., Tues. and Thurs. 6-9 P.M., Wed. and Fri., 5:30-9 P.M., Sat. 12:15-9 P.M., Sun. 1-5 P.M.

COST: $9 admission, $3 skate rental

`Map 1`

Tucked betwixt a pair of large downtown hotels, America's Ice Garden is as close as Dallas gets to Rockefeller Center.

GALLERIA ICE SKATING CENTER

13350 Dallas Pkwy., 972/392-3363, www.galleriaiceskatingcenter.com

HOURS: Mon.-Tues. 10 A.M.-5:30 P.M. and 8-10 P.M., Wed. 11 A.M.-5:30 P.M. and 8-10 P.M., Thurs. 10 A.M.-6 P.M. and 8-10 P.M., Fri. 10 A.M.-11 P.M., Sat. noon-11 P.M., Sun. noon-6 P.M.

COST: $9 admission, $3 skate rental

`Map 7`

It's kind of a rite of passage for youth around these parts to strap on the skates here, especially during the holiday season, when taking a few laps around the giant Christmas tree in the middle of the rink adds to the spirit of things. Since the rink sits in the midst of one of the best shopping malls in America, this is also a good place to drop off the kids while you put your credit card to use.

TOURS

COWTOWN SEGWAY TOURS

817/891-2346, www.fortworthsegwaytour.com

HOURS: Mon.-Fri. 9 A.M.-5 P.M., Sat. 11 A.M.-3 P.M.

COST: $49.99-59.99

If you can swallow the geek factor, the Segway tours are an excellent way to get to know large swaths of the city in a short amount of time.

The folks behind the Fort Worth Segway tours are friendly and down-home without making a big countrified scene about it, and they know their stuff, providing rolling tours through the Cultural District, Botanic Gardens, Trinity Trails, downtown, and the Stockyards.

DALLAS SEGWAY TOURS

972/821-9054, www.dallassegwaytours.com

HOURS: Daily 8:30 A.M.-5:30 P.M.

COST: $64.13-83.36

Three tours are offered: the West End, which covers much of downtown's historical and tourist stops; the Katy Trail, which is a more laid-back glide through tree-shaded concrete trails, in a parklike setting; and the American Airlines Center tour, which covers Victory Park.

SWISS AVENUE HOME TOURS

Runs southwest to northeast between Munger Blvd. and La Vista Dr.

COST: Typically around $20; varies from year to year

`Map 4`

There's no greater testament to the history of Dallas's grand opulence than historic Swiss Avenue. Gigantic historic mansions flank this wide boulevard, which runs for two-and-a-half miles smack through the middle of East Dallas. The street, with its more than 200 homes of varying architectural types, including Mediterranean, Prairie, Craftsman, Neoclassical, and others, is a must-see for lovers of 19th- and early 20th-century architecture.

The Swiss Avenue Historical District sponsors annual Mother's Day home tours of a several historic houses on the street, with all proceeds going to East Dallas nonprofits. The tours have become a favorite local event, with free mini-coaches and horse-drawn carriages, along with an alfresco brunch and art show. Although the tours only run officially once a year, it's still well worth your time to stroll up the wide avenue on your own.

ARTS AND LEISURE

WATER SPORTS

In the throes of both Dallas and Fort Worth's Trinity River revitalization, the Metroplex is just now getting its sea legs when it comes to water sports, so the pickin's are a bit slim when it comes to equipment rental.

ALOHA PADDLEBOARDS

480 N. Taylor St., 817/403-5330, www.alohapaddleboards.com

HOURS: Thurs.-Sun. 1-5 P.M.

COST: Paddleboard lessons for up to four people $75 per hour plus $25 per extra person; rentals $15 per hour

Map 8

In Fort Worth, Aloha Paddleboards is a great place to go to for gear up for floats on the Trinity River and other lakes in the area. Lessons, which cover safety, gear, and basics, last an hour and 15 minutes. Boards and paddles are provided during the lesson. Inner tubes and standup paddleboards are also available for rent.

BACKWOODS

2727 W. 7th St.

HOURS: Mon.-Fri. 10 A.M.-8 P.M., Sat. 10 A.M.-6 P.M., Sun. noon-6 P.M.

COST: $10-20 first hour, $5-10 each additional half hour

Map 10

Kayaks and canoes can be rented at Backwoods, which recently opened a concession kiosk for rentals at Panther Island Pavilion. Paddles and life vests are included. The concession has eight kayaks, four tandem kayaks, and six canoes. A second location is at 480 North Taylor Street.

TRINITY RIVER EXPEDITIONS

304 Lyman Circle, 214/941-1757, www.canoedallas.com

COST: Guided canoe trips $50, canoe and kayak trips $40-60

Map 6

Dallas's Trinity River Expeditions offers a number of options for guided canoe and kayak trips, shuttle service for those who have their own kayaks, and rentals.

SHOPS

Perhaps nowhere else in the country does a city have such an intimate, particular relationship with shopping. In Dallas, shopping is not just a pastime or a way of gathering consumer goods; rather, it's interwoven with the social, cultural—even historical—fabric of the city.

Evidence of Dallas's relationship with shopping is most easily seen in the abundance of shopping centers in town, including the world's first planned shopping center, Highland Park Village. Heavily influenced by Highland Park Village's model, Dallas's shopping geography consists mainly of areas built specifically for shopping and containing a high concentration of stores—basically outdoor malls.

Fort Worth shoppers might not quite achieve the bloodlust found in Dallas, but there's still plenty to be had here, mainly in the paradoxical form of large malls and small, intimate boutiques. You'll find neither town fears a chain store, especially a high-end one, but the shopping destinations expand to many locally owned furniture, home decor, and gift stores. And while there's no shortage of stores sporting the latest in couture and brand-new items, the city's resale, consignment, and vintage stores are also popular and continue to increase their presence.

To get your bearings, check out the *Dallas Morning News* website, which has an excellent shopping blog filled with the latest information on openings, closings, sales, and who

© JONANNA WIDNER

has what (the paper's weird *F!D luxe* shopping supplement, by contrast, proves pretty useless). Fort Worth's glossy magazine *Fort Worth, Texas* provides a good starting point in Cowtown. Finally, a frank word of warning: Amateur shoppers should pace themselves.

HIGHLIGHTS

LOOK FOR 🦶 TO FIND RECOMMENDED SHOPS.

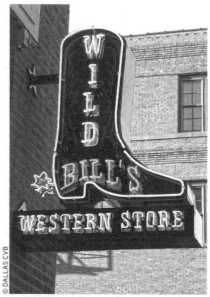

© DALLAS CVB

Wild Bill's Western Store is the best place to buy cowboy boots at cheap prices.

🦶 **Best Record Store: Good Records** is what a record store should be: filled with discerningly chosen vinyl and CDs, and chock-full of funky atmosphere. Bonus points for the best in-store selection, by far (page 152).

🦶 **Best Bookstore:** The Northwest location of **Half Price Books** is a grand palace of fiction, nonfiction, art books, kids books, poetry... well, you get the idea. And we mean "palace"—the place is the size of the Taj Mahal (page 153).

🦶 **Best Place to Find a Prom Dress:** Don't consider the **J. Saunders** boutique's selection small, consider it well chosen. Fort Worth ladies have been coming here to find the perfect dress for years (page 157).

🦶 **Best Outdoor Mall:** Is there any question? **Highland Park Village** is the world's first planned shopping center, and it's filled with couture (page 161).

🦶 **Best Shopping Center:** It's not really picturesque, but **La Gran Plaza,** which caters to Fort Worth's rapidly growing Latino population, features inexpensive Western shops and family wear, plus some fun treasures like *quinceñera* dresses (page 161).

🦶 **Best Indoor Mall:** Any mall that's made it on-screen as part of a Robert Altman movie has to be different. **NorthPark Center,** in whose fountain Farrah Fawcett frolicked in Altman's *Dr. T and the Women,* is indeed unusual, its upscale shops surrounded by world-renowned three-dimensional artwork and lushly sculpted gardens (page 162).

🦶 **Best Outlet:** The **Dickies Company Store** doesn't just have discounted work gear—it's got all the hipster gear, too, at low prices (page 167).

🦶 **Best Splurge:** If you need, say, an ornate, hand-stitched, custom-made saddle to give as a gift to some head of state or corporate bigwig, make your way to **M. L. Leddy's** (page 168).

🦶 **Best Hidden Secret:** Wild Bill's **Western Store** has a collection of new cowboy boots at used prices, around $100, which is unheard of in these parts (page 169).

Antiques and Vintage Clothing

CATTLE BARN FLEA MARKET

3401 W. Lancaster Ave., Barn 1, 817/473-0505

HOURS: Sat. 8 A.M.-5 P.M., Sun. 9 A.M.-4 P.M.

Map 10

Air-conditioned and jam-packed with antiques, collectibles, junk, and farm and ranch equipment, this is one of Fort Worth's most frequented flea markets. Besides the steals and deals, visitors enjoy the added benefit of the barn's genuine atmosphere—this is where real modern ranch folks do much of their buying, selling, wheeling, and dealing.

CLOTHES CIRCUIT

6105 Sherry Ln., 214/696-8634,
www.clothescircuit.com

HOURS: Mon.-Sat. 10 A.M.-7 P.M., Sun. noon-6 P.M.

Map 3

You know you're in Dallas when labels on even used clothes read "Chanel" and "Prada." That's exactly what you'll find at Clothes Circuit:

gently used couture and high-end ladies' wear, handbags, shoes, furs, and accessories. Don't go expecting bargain basement prices—you're not gonna find those Manolos at a thrift-store discount—but you'll find the inventory much more affordable than their brand-new counterparts. Be sure to check the racks of designer suits and seasonal furs.

CURIOSITIES

2025 Abrams Rd., 214/828-1886, www.curiosities.com

HOURS: Thurs.-Sat. 11 A.M.-8 P.M.,
Mon.-Wed. 11 A.M.-6 P.M., Sun. 11 A.M.-5 P.M.

Map 4

Curious, indeed—this Lakewood resale store is filled with wonderful gewgaws and awesome oddities that range from the kitschy to the glitzy. But don't figure on a granny's attic atmosphere: The goods are curated with an eagle eye for quality, and the store is crisply run and organized. Curiosities also features a

© JONANNA WIDNER

Fort Worth's Cattle Barn Flea Market is full of good finds.

gallery showcasing out-of-the-box artists, many of whom utilize folk art and found objects in their work.

DOLLY PYTHON

1916 North Haskell Ave., 214/887-3434, www.dollypythonvintage.com

HOURS: Tues.-Sat. 11 A.M.-6 P.M., Sun. and Mon. noon–5 P.M.

Map 5

Dolly Python, the ever-growing vintage goods emporium, has been kicking butt with a retro boot since 2005. This place stocks almost 4,000 square feet of carefully culled items that range from the practical (jewelry, clothing, furniture) to the kooky (taxidermied items, weird art, old baby dolls). With more than 25 vendors under its single roof, Dolly Python could end up a musty hodgepodge, but proprietor Gretchen Bell keeps things organized, right down to the rows of vintage cowboy boots.

JUNKER VAL

3458 Bluebonnet Cir., 817/266-6403, www.junkerval.com

HOURS: Fri.-Sat. 10 A.M.-7 P.M., Sun. 1-5 P.M.

Map 9

The name says "Junker," but that may be unnecessarily self-deprecating, as the dishes, clothes, knickknacks, and unique memorabilia (recent score: a beautifully designed, original program from a mid-1960s Van Cliburn competition) are culled from local estate sales with an eye for quality and uniqueness. Most of the stuff comes at a steal, too, and if you're purchasing vintage apparel, Val will give you a discount if you don it and let her take a photo for the shop's Facebook page.

© JONANNA WIDNER

For funky goods at cheap prices, try Junker Val.

TRADER'S VILLAGE

2602 Mayfield Rd., Grand Prairie, 972/647-2331, www.tradersvillage.com

HOURS: Sat.-Sun. 7 A.M.-dusk

Map 7

You'll literally find everything under the sun at this year-round, 106-acre outdoor flea market. Some of it's junk, some of it's secret finds—most of it's in between—but there's definitely something for everyone. Should you prefer other forms of entertainment besides browsing, Trader's Village is always hopping with kids' games, rides, festivals, and food.

Bath, Beauty, and Spa

MARIE ANTOINETTE'S PARFUMERIE
101 W. 2nd St., 817/332-3888,
www.marieantoinettespa.com
HOURS: Mon.-Wed. 10 A.M.-6 P.M., Thurs. 9 A.M.-7 P.M.,
Fri.-Sat. 10 A.M.-8 P.M.
Map 8

Worthy of the indulgent attachments of its namesake, Marie Antoinette's Parfumerie is a one-of-its-kind for Fort Worth. Here you can choose from delicate bath items like soaps, essential oils, and lotions, but the coolest part is the parfumerie, in which the staff will help you create your own personal scent.

SHAMBHALA BODY GALLERY
415 N. Bishop Ave., 214/943-7627,
www.shambalabodygallery.com
HOURS: Tues.-Thurs. 11 A.M.-6 P.M., Fri.-Sat. 11 A.M.-9 P.M.,
Sun. noon-4 P.M.
Map 6

Soothing and yummy-smelling, the soaps, scrubs, and lotions in this New Age–leaning

GET YOUR PINK ON

Alongside a busy highway in Addison, just north of Dallas, sits a large office building. Unlike many of the soulless glass-and-steel structures in this part of town, this one has character: It sprawls in a graceful half-moon arc around the entry grounds, the neatly trimmed grass cooling and welcome amid Addison's miles of corporate concrete. A huge, handsome fountain bubbles before the impressively heavy glass doors. Inside, the lobby's polished floors, fantastically high ceiling, and glossy wood make it feel more like a swank hotel than the usual hive for worker bees. Smartly dressed women, all in skirts—nary a pantsuit in sight—dart around, the click of their sharp high heels echoing off the... pink granite walls? Welcome to **Mary Kay's** world headquarters.

In 1963, Mary Kay Ash from Hot Wells, Texas quit her job. She was in direct sales and damn good at it, and the constant parade of men passing her by as they were promoted sickened her. So she quit, gathered up her $5,000 in savings, and started her own business.

Some would call it the business of selling makeup, but Mary Kay would call it the business of beauty. Her first headquarters on Exchange Park was as sparse as the current one is lavish: just one room, a shelf, and a few bits of furniture. The one in Addison? Thirteen stories. Thirty-four acres. Six hundred thousand square feet. She came a long way, baby.

Before her death in 2001, Mary Kay had built a multibillion-dollar company, famous for giving pink Cadillacs to its best salespeople, inspired an almost cultlike following, and became one of the most famous women in the world.

It's a feel-good story, but a controversial one. Many people consider Mary Kay's company to be a pyramid scheme that preys on the insecurities of American women. Others claim it's an empowering organization, one that boosts employee and sales staff confidence while helping others bring out their own beauty.

Whichever you believe, Mary Kay's hold on people is crystal clear the minute you eyeball the giant pink monolith that juts into the sky above Addison. There's no way to fully grasp the company's influence on American culture—and corporate culture—until you walk through those big glass doors.

Lest you feel odd about marching into a random office building, don't worry—Mary Kay aficionados flock to the **Mary Kay Headquarters and Museum** (16251 Dallas Pkwy., 972/687-5720, www.marykay.com, Tues.-Fri. 9 A.M.-4:30 P.M.), and it's encouraged (if you'd like a group tour, call three days in advance to book it). The museum is small, but impressive and fun, although the tributes to the "spirit of Mary Kay" can get a bit cloying. Definitely check out the displays about the much-coveted rewards given to salespeople, including the big mama of them all, the pink Caddy.

store make for perfect gifts for those who eschew mass-produced products. The "lotion sticks" are especially popular.

VESSELS
301 Main St., 817/882-8743, www.giftvessels.com
HOURS: Mon.-Thurs. 10 A.M.-8 P.M., Fri.-Sat. 10 A.M.-10 P.M., Sun. noon-6 P.M.
Map 8

The folks at Vessels proudly proclaim they will help you find exactly what you're looking for, even if you don't know what that is. Embracing that state of ambiguousness is the most fun way to approach this store and probably the best way to choose a gift. Browse around and sample the baskets of bath products and candles, or ask one of the friendly salespeople to pick out some chocolates and wine. Whatever you decide, the skilled hands here will wrap it beautifully, and to your specifications.

Books and Music

BILL'S RECORDS
1313 S. Lamar St., 214/421-1500, www.billsrecords.com
HOURS: Mon.-Sat. 11 A.M.-11 P.M., Sun. 1-11 P.M.
Map 6

You never know what you're gonna get from Bill's—selection-wise, service-wise, and price-wise. Back when it was called Bill's Records and Tapes, this place was a music lover's mecca, the only place to find obscure Texas vinyl and that rare Smiths import you'd been searching for since 1986. But it always came with a touch of oddness—owner Bill Wisener, for instance, decides on each item's price based on, well, his own whim. That hasn't changed, nor has the haphazard organization or the cloud from Wisener's cigarettes. All the quirks are a turnoff to some, but to many, Bill's stands as one of the few record stores left with any character.

CD SOURCE
5500 Greenville Ave., 214/890-7614
HOURS: Mon.-Thurs. 10 A.M.-10 P.M., Fri.-Sat. 10 A.M.-10:30 P.M., Sun. noon-10 P.M.
Map 3

With the constant stream of patrons both selling and buying used CDs at this strip-mall store on Upper Greenville, it's amazing the hinges on the front door don't break. Fortunately, the high volume here doesn't translate to a dilution in quality. Quite the opposite: CD Source has a knack for always stocking the good stuff, including a surprisingly large supply of box sets and lots of new releases.

FOREVER YOUNG RECORDS
2955 S. Hwy. 380, Grand Prairie, 972/352-6299, www.foreveryoungrecords.com
HOURS: Mon.-Sat. 10 A.M.-10 P.M., Sun. noon-6 P.M.
Map 7

Nowadays, any old place with three milk crates' worth of LPs is considered a record store; the family-owned and operated Forever Young reminds us what a real record store should be. Walking through the giant fake jukebox facade that makes up the store's entry, vinyl-heads are treated to an old-school sight: 250,000 pieces of vinyl, cassettes, eight-tracks, music DVDs, and yeah, even CDs. There's something here for everybody, be they casual collector or serious music scholar, and the inventory spans decades (and about 11,000 square feet).

◖ GOOD RECORDS
1808 Greenville Ave., 214/752-4663, www.goodrecords.com
HOURS: Mon.-Thurs. 10 A.M.-11 P.M., Fri.-Sat. 10 A.M.-midnight, Sun. 11 A.M.-9 P.M.
Map 4

It may be simply named, but Good Records has lots going on. This Greenville Avenue spot is a must-stop for Dallas lovers of independent and local music. The proprietors here know their stuff, as do all the staff; any choice from their rotating recommended selections is a guaranteed good listen. Here you'll find a

SUMTER BRUTON, A FORT WORTH INSTITUTION

You may or may not go to **Record Town** (3025 S. University Dr., 817/926-1331) to buy records. You *do* go to Record Town to *look* at records...to saunter through the dusty aisles, idly touching an old blues album here, a rockabilly 45 there. But the real reason you go to Record Town is to talk to the owner, Sumter Bruton.

Sumter Bruton is one of Fort Worth's semi-hidden gems. Those in the know are aware of his six-string prowess. Born and bred in Fort Worth, the son of a jazz drummer and brother of a multi-instrumentalist, Bruton started playing guitar in bands in college and soon made a name for himself as a master of the distinct blues style invented by fellow Texan T-Bone Walker.

Bruton played in a number of accomplished blues and boogie bands, but he established himself in the pantheon of Fort Worth culture in 1977 when he started the Juke Jumpers with his buddy Jim Colegrove.

The Juke Jumpers put out five albums, but their live shows were the stuff that really blew people away. Playing a combination of blues, jazz, swing, and rockabilly, the Jumpers were a hot ticket for 17 years, and they became the stuff of legend.

The Jumpers still get together for the occasional reunion gig, and Bruton still plays in bands, but by day you can find him running Record Town, the music store he's owned for decades.

Amiable, approachable, and *really* into music, Bruton is known as the fella to chat with if you're seeking out something obscure, rare, or ultra-specific. He's also a Fort Worth institution.

high-quality selection of new and used CDs, vinyl, T-shirts, and other cool stuff, plus periodic in-store visits from indie and up-and-coming artists.

well-stocked art/photography selection, tons of used records, and the clearance section, where many a fine book can be picked up for a dollar.

🄲 HALF PRICE BOOKS

5803 Northwest Hwy., 214/379-8000
HOURS: Daily 9 A.M.-11 P.M.
Map 7

Yes, it is a nationwide chain—heck, there are about six or seven Half Price outposts in the DFW area alone—but the sheer size of the Northwest Highway location makes it a must-visit for any reader. The sucker is as big and cavernous as several airplane hangars put together, housing an equally enormous selection of used books. Special treats are the

RECORD TOWN

3025 S. University Dr., 817/926-1331
HOURS: Mon.-Fri. 10 A.M.-6 P.M., Sat. 10 A.M.-8 P.M.
Map 9

Strangers to town might initially bypass the deceptively shabby facade of this record store. If they're music fans at all, they're well-advised to walk through the front door. Owner Sumter Bruton is a font of knowledge about all sorts of genres and is happy to chat about them, or to help you find the obscure disc you're seeking out.

Boutiques

A. HOOPER'S & CO.
4001 Camp Bowie Blvd., 817/348-9911
HOURS: Mon.-Fri. 10 A.M.-6 P.M., Sat. 11 A.M.-5 P.M.
Map 10

This popular, enduring, modern spot brings a touch of New York couture, including Vince, Michael Stars, and Chloe, to Cowtown. Beware: As with any true house of fashion, you'll need good luck finding anything larger than a size 6 or 8, and bring your platinum card.

ALLIE-COOSH
6726 Snider Plaza, 214/363-8616,
www.allie-coosh.com
HOURS: Mon.-Sat. 10 A.M.-6 P.M.
Map 3

Owner/designer Paulette Martsolf creates one-of-a-kind, practical apparel that suits almost every body type. Her boutique, in one of the most exclusive shopping areas in Dallas, features her collection of ladies' wear that is cut and stitched in her own workshop in town. All of Martsolf's works utilize luxurious materials, like high-quality wools and silks, with subdued colors and a classic touch—perfect for traveling or for upper-crust dinner parties at home.

ARMHOLE
1350 Manufacturing St., 214/760-7373,
www.armhole.com
HOURS: By appointment.
Map 7

Sigh. Back in the day, Armhole was housed in an Uptown storefront, and the coolest of the cool could saunter in and choose their iron-on art and a T-shirt, and the Armhole folks would press it right there on the spot at the "T-shirt bar." The company has since moved to the more industrial (and aptly named) Manufacturing Street in the Dallas Market District, making walk-ins pretty much an impossibility. A good business move, perhaps, but sad for folks who want to make one-of-a-kind riffs on "I'm With Stupid." The good news is the Armhole peeps

are still in the one-off business. Just give them a call and tell them what you're thinking, and they'll be happy to set up the T-shirt bar.

BENJI'S COLLEZIONI
1511 Main St., 469/547-0223
HOURS: Mon.-Sat. 10 A.M.-7 P.M.,
Sun. by appointment only
Map 1

Benji's provides Dallas with Italian couture for men and women, including high-end accessories, footwear, women's clothing, and men's suits. One of the few downtown boutiques still standing, the store offers traditional, quality service and modern Euro-chic offerings (think Prada, Dolce&Gabbana, and of course, Gucci).

BESS & EVIE'S
531 Foch St., 817/877-1300, www.bessandeveies.com
HOURS: Tues.-Sat. 10 A.M.-6 P.M.
Map 10

The prices may not please those in search of a true vintage bargain, but there are some gems to be found here, most notably on the "boot wall," where rows of one-of-a-kind footwear are displayed. Inventory changes almost daily.

CARLA MARTINENGO BOUTIQUE
4528 McKinney Ave., 214/522-9284
HOURS: Mon.-Sat. 9:30 A.M.-6 P.M.
Map 3

Who knew this tiny, exclusive little boutique would end up such a power player in the Dallas fashion world? With an elite collection of designer pieces (Chloe, Blumarine, Gaultier) that are tough to find in the United States, Martinengo's shop is like a bit of Milan transported to Dallas.

COWBOY COOL
3699 McKinney Ave., Ste. 407, 214/521-4500,
www.cowboycool.com
HOURS: Mon.-Sat. 10 A.M.-6 P.M.
Map 2

When Kid Rock needs some skull cowboy

NEIMAN MARCUS FLAGSHIP

It all began here.

Dallas's reputation as a place where shopping is considered a contact sport began at the corner of Main and Ervay Streets, where Herbert Marcus, his sister Carrie M. Neiman, and her husband Al Neiman founded Neiman Marcus stores.

Today, the square footage of all of Neiman Marcus Group's retail holdings totals about five million square feet. In 1914, when the store opened its second "original" location (the first, built in 1907, was destroyed in a fire), it was merely a few floors.

Those floors, however, held something unique. When Marcus and the Neimans planned the store, they insisted from the beginning it was not a department store but rather something new: a specialty store catering to women who desired items that were both high quality *and* ready to wear. For years since, the hallowed ground here has acted as the cornerstone not just of fashionable aesthetics but of good taste and customer service.

Even for those less inclined to splurge on the latest bit of couture revel in the elegant and storied surroundings of the original store. Walking in off the downtown street is like walking out of a time capsule and into an era when shopping was an experience, not just a chore. Elevators open up to reveal glorious displays on every floor. The Zodiac restaurant beckons with old-school lunches like lobster salad and strawberry butter popovers. Each floor is mod yet modern, with special decor and service with a personal touch.

All that would be nothing if the product lacked, but fashion-philes still consider the place a mecca. For all of Dallas's shopping destinations, none is as jam-packed with high quality names, goods from known designers and new phenoms, as Neiman Marcus is. It is the epicenter.

---

boots or Billy Bob Thornton needs some skull... anything, they head straight for Cowboy Cool, a hip little store that features rock 'n' roll–laced casual clothes for men and women. The place may be best known for its unique cowboy boots that riff on heavy metal and goth influences, and the shirts, jeans, and dresses follow suit. Check the cool collection of belt buckles if you're on a budget, and the small collection of rock memorabilia that's for sale if you're not.

CULLWELL & SON

6319 Hillcrest Ave., 214/522-7000
HOURS: Mon.-Sat. 9 A.M.-6 P.M.
Map 3

Housed in an enormous, beautiful store with dark gleaming wood and hardwood floors, Cullwell & Son has everything you need to smartly outfit several generations' worth of men: custom suits, shirts, tuxedos, shoes, and high-end casual wear for adults, adolescents, and boys, plus a tailoring department, "grooming room," and even a dry cleaners—all provided with excellent customer service.

DIRTY LAUNDRY

3007 S. University Dr., 817/924-0445,
www.shopdirtylaundryboutique.blogspot.com
HOURS: Mon.-Fri. 10 A.M.-6 P.M., Sat. 10 A.M.-5 P.M.
Map 9

Dirty Laundry is quite popular with TCU students, not because of its handy location across from campus, but rather because it serves as reliable supplier of trendy threads for the fashionable collegiate set. You'll find handbags, shoes, blouses, jackets, and other apparel aplenty at this bright little shop, which keeps the youth of its clientele in mind when it comes to pricing. Special highlights include unique TCU apparel and a consistently adorable selection of casual dresses.

EMERALDS TO COCONUTS

2730 Henderson Ave., 214/823-3620
HOURS: Mon.-Sat. 10 A.M.-7 P.M.
Map 2

Sure, Dallas has plenty of fancy-pants boutiques, but how about the loony lady stores? You know, with incense, big clunky jewelry, and

No store represents Dallas's hip Western look better than Cowboy Cool.

© KENNY BRAUN / TRAVELTEX.COM

flowing skirts? The kind of place where you can pick up a sweater for your aunt's birthday and a cute bracelet for yourself? That place is Emeralds to Coconuts. Hemp and linen clothes aren't for everyone, to be sure, but those who lean toward the more bohemian look will adore the flowy outfits here, along with the concha belts, flip-flops, and other kooky bits.

EPIPHANY BOUTIQUE
412 N. Bishop Ave., 214/946-4411,
www.epiphanyboutique.com
HOURS: Sun.-Mon. 11 A.M.-5 P.M.,
Tues.-Thurs. 11 A.M.-7 P.M., Fri.-Sat. 11 A.M.-10 P.M.
Map 6

Like the funky neighborhood that surrounds it, Epiphany is cool, laid-back, and eclectic. The collection of baby tees alone could easily provide a young Dallas woman with her summer wardrobe. Have one of the friendly staff help you match up one of those tees with some Chile Pepper jeans, and you're set for at least 85 percent of your social engagements. Epiphany also stocks spa and bath items.

EPIPHANY FOR MEN
413 N. Bishop Ave., 214/946-4413,
www.epiphanyboutique.com
HOURS: Sun.-Mon. 11 A.M.-5 P.M.,
Tues.-Thurs. 11 A.M.-7 P.M., Fri.-Sat. 11 A.M.-10 P.M.
Map 6

The foxy little brother to the Epiphany Boutique for women across the street, Epiphany for Men fills the oft-overlooked niche of men's casual wear. You won't find Dockers here, but you will find cool sports gear (beyond just the Cowboys, Mavs, and Rangers), Toms shoes, and a wide variety of hipster hats. The collection of pearl snap Western shirts is enviable, if a smidge overpriced (surprising, as almost everything at both Epiphany stores remains just this side of reasonable).

FLASH: THE UNIVERSITY STORE
3001 S. University Dr., 817/924-2626,
www.flashtheuniversitystore.com
HOURS: Mon.-Fri. 10 A.M.-5:30 P.M., Sat. 10 A.M.-5 P.M.
Map 9

Right across the street from campus, this is the

spot to pick up all things Horned Frogs, from frat boy baseball caps to pink Hello Kitty TCU baby tees. It's less about the atmosphere here and more about the rows after rows purple gear, much more in demand now that TCU's football team has picked up some steam.

FLIRT BOUTIQUE

2633 McKinney Ave., Ste. 150, 214/754-7001
HOURS: Mon.-Fri. 11 A.M.-7 P.M., Sat. 10 A.M.-6 P.M., Sun. 1-5 P.M.
`Map 2`

After a glass or two of chardonnay at Flirt's comfy wine bar, you may find you've loosened the strings on your pocketbook. Good thing the prices at this girly shop remain so reasonable; you can come home with an armload of big-name booty with much damage to the bottom line. "Flirt" is an apt name here, as the collection, which ranges from high-end denim to BCBG dresses to Ben Sherman pieces, is decidedly fun and feminine. There is also a location Fort Worth (2952 Crockett St., 817/744-7250; www.flirtboutique.com).

FORTY FIVE TEN

4510 McKinney Ave., 214/559 4510, www.fortyfiveten.com
HOURS: Mon.-Sat. 10 A.M. 6 P.M.
`Map 2`

The word "boutique" usually conjures up the idea of a small, intimate storefront. Forty Five Ten basks in a luxurious 8,000 square feet, complete with courtyard fountain, café, and celebrity clientele, but it's a boutique nonetheless; that is, despite its breadth, the aesthetic of this clothing/housewares/accessories/furniture store is governed by a unique sensibility.

HAUTE BABY

5350 W. Lovers Ln., 214/357-3068, www.hautebabydallas.com
HOURS: Mon.-Sat. 10 A.M.-5 P.M.
`Map 3`

The infant and toddler clothes at Haute Baby are precious in all senses of the word: Indeed, they are simply adorable, but also expensive. Still, if you're willing to spend as much on a onesie as you are on dinner, your rugrat will be the best dressed person in the room.

HD'S CLOTHING COMPANY

3014-3018 Greenville Ave., 214/821-8900 (women) or 214/821-5255 (men), www.hdsclothing.com
HOURS: Mon.-Fri. 11 A.M.-7 P.M., Sat. 11 A.M.-6 P.M., Sun. noon-5 P.M.
`Map 4`

In a town full of clothiers of all kinds, there is no other shop like HD's Clothing Company. Simply put, even though the shop has been around since 1981, proprietors Harry and Vicki DeMarco are always two steps ahead of the curve, filling their cool industrial space with the latest and most unique casual men's and women's clothing before anyone can say "Diesel." There's definitely a Euro-flair thing going on here, as the DeMarcos import their goods from all the continental hot spots: Milan, Rome, Paris. But don't let that scare you off—there's no attitude here, just Texas charm and personalized service.

JEAN GURU

2970 Park Hill Dr., 817/323-4878, www.store.jeanguru.com
HOURS: Mon.-Sat. 10 A.M.-7 P.M.
`Map 9`

It's jeans heaven at this hip little spot tucked away in a small strip near TCU. With an extensive list of brands, Jean Guru has everything a man or woman needs to wrap their legs in high-end denim. The friendly staff is happy to help you on your quest for the perfect fit, too.

◖ J. SAUNDERS

4303 Camp Bowie Blvd., 817/732-8155
HOURS: Mon.-Sat. 10 A.M.-6 P.M.
`Map 10`

For years, this Camp Bowie institution has been *the* source for Westsiders in search of well-priced, unique formalwear, especially prom dresses. It's a touch tiny, but the personalized service and unique selection are worth it.

KEN'S MAN'S SHOP

6025 Royal Ln., 214/369-5367,
www.kensmansshop.com
HOURS: Fri.-Wed. 10 A.M.-6 P.M., Thurs. 10 A.M.-8 P.M.
Map 7

No other men's clothing store in Dallas rivals Ken's for history and personality. Ken Helfman opened his store in 1964 and, through a bit of luck, found his natty threads had a following among many members of the (then-new and much more popular) Dallas Cowboys. In these parts, that's like God endorsing your wares, and since then, Helfman has successfully out-fitted generations of Dallas men and their sons. Fortunately, Helfman doesn't just have Tom Landry's legend on his side—he carries upscale labels as well as his own sophisticated designs and is known for the kind of stellar customer service you rarely encounter these days. If you buy a suit, take advantage of the on-site tailor and have it custom fitted or simply stroll around and eye the gifts and antiques that are for sale.

KRIMSON & KLOVER

3111 Cole Ave., Ste. 101, 214/871-2334,
www.krimsonandklover.com
HOURS: Mon.-Fri. 10 A.M.-7 P.M., Sat. 11 A.M.-6 P.M.
Map 2

Fashionable threads for the youthful set (read: SMU students) fill this cutesy little store that has made a name for itself as an Uptown shopping staple. Customers regard K&K's stock of affordable designer tees, dresses, and accessories as a reliable source for everything from casual, everyday wear to that hard-to-find wedding outfit. The bright collection here lists more to-ward fun, West Coast, L.A. style versus New York-y runway seriousness.

MINE

4423 Lovers Ln., 214/522-4700,
www.minedallas.com
HOURS: Mon.-Sat. 10 A.M.-6 P.M.
Map 3

This well-lit, high-ceilinged little shop (complete with exposed rafters and adorable chandeliers) houses a perfect collection for college women with credit cards or young professionals looking for an outfit for a casual night out on the town. Tom Ford, Yumi Kim, and Denim of Virtue are just some of the names you'll see sewn onto the labels of the high-end jeans, skirts, dresses, and accessories here.

RAGAN BURNS

5500 W. Lovers Ln., 214/369-1133
HOURS: Mon.-Sat. 10 A.M.-6 P.M.
Map 3

Simple and classy, the Ragan Burns clothing store stocks top names (like Robert Talbott, Burberry, and Ike Behar) in menswear and provides top service (like custom clothing and custom tailoring), to boot. In short, expect an old-school approach without the crustiness.

RICH HIPPIE

5350 W. Lovers Ln., Ste. 127, 214/358-1968,
www.richhippie.com
HOURS: Mon.-Sat. 10 A.M.-5:30 P.M.
Map 3

Rich Hippie owner Eric Kimmel recently created a line of clothing he calls "trashion," in which he takes name-brand items that are no longer usable to Sierra Leone, where Kimmel pays a collection of villagers to transform them with their own indigenous touches. There's no better name for the goods available at his boutique: funky, high-end, fashionable items that are utterly unique. From Park Cities society soccer moms to edgy fashionistas, everyone adores Kimmel's selection of jewelry, clothes, and groovy gewgaws.

SARTEL

4212 Oak Lawn Ave., 214/520-7176
HOURS: Mon.-Sat. 10 A.M.-6 P.M.
Map 2

Sartel owners Matthew Earnest and Lily Hanbury cultivate their inventory with a brand of particularity resembling that of a museum curator. All the intensity pays off, as very select pieces from various designers are interspersed with Eastman's own runway collection. There's

SHOPS

no filler at this boutique, just gorgeous, one-of-a-kind items.

SOBO FASHION LOUNGE

4109 Camp Bowie Blvd., 817/989-7626
HOURS: Tues.-Fri. 10:30 A.M.-6:30 P.M.,
Sat. 10:30 A.M.-5:30 P.M.
`Map 10`

Betsey Johnson dresses for $40? What? Yup, sometimes you get lucky here at this up-tempo little boutique. Other times, not so much, although the collection of adorable Yippee Ki Yay boots always makes Sobo worth a stop. The inventory consists of familiar names and stays fresh (sometimes the turnover is eyebrow-raisingly speedy), especially considering Sobo's commitment to staying on top of trends. Service can be spotty here, however.

SPOILED PINK

4824 Camp Bowie Blvd., 817/737-7465,
www.spoiledpink.com
HOURS: Mon.-Sat. 10 A.M.-6 P.M.
`Map 10`

Spoiled Pink keeps up with more youthful trends than a Tumblr site. The look here is designer denim, ironic T-shirts, and Betsey Johnson, but at prices even a teenager can afford.

TEESIE'S ATTIC

4000 Arlington Highlands Blvd., Ste. 169, Arlington, 817/465-7200, www.teesiesattic.com
HOURS: Mon.-Sat. 10 A.M.-6 P.M.
`Map 11`

Jeans, jeans, jeans—Texans love them, and there's no better place to get them than Teesie's. We're not talking Wranglers and Rocky Mountains (see Western and Work Wear for those); we're talking 7 for All Mankind, Joe's Jeans, Rock & Republic, and other premium brands, plus lots of shoes, handbags, and tops to match, all at this little piece of L.A. in the middle of Arlington.

V.O.D BOUTIQUE

2418 Victory Park Ln., 214/754-0644
HOURS: Mon.-Sat. 11 A.M.-6 P.M.
`Map 1`

Cool, breezy, and expensive, V.O.D Boutique doesn't fool around when it comes to high-end clothing. The one-of-a-kind inventory here covers a lot of the latest ground from designers such as Alexander Wang and Pauric Sweeny, but the real treats are the appointment-only shoe boutique-within-a-boutique and the collection of vintage wear curated by local store Archive Vintage. Oh, and you must check out Houston designer Diane Izzadin's line of jeans, available only at V.O.D.

Gift and Home

GRIFFIN TRADING COMPANY

159 Howell St., 214/747-9234, www.griffintrading.com
HOURS: Mon.-Sat. 10 A.M.-5:30 P.M.
`Map 7`

In the market for an antique hand-carved duck decoy? How about a Norwegian teak wastebasket? Perhaps a pair of mid-century chairs or a creepy antique circus sign? Nick Badovinus's showroom gives the impression he doesn't know what he has in mind when he sets off to procure his *objets,* merely that he knows one when he sees it. And his collection of art, antiques, and curiosities demonstrates that he has quite an eye, indeed. If you've ever wondered where cool people find those cool, oversize porcelain

letters they scatter about their lofts, you'll find them here, along with everything from art deco furniture to taxidermied barracudas.

NAMASTE

3418 W. 7th St., 817/989-0800, www.asia2africa.com
HOURS: Wed.-Sat. 10 A.M.-6 P.M.
`Map 10`

In the market for an African tribal headdress? How about a religious dance dress from Bhutan? A handwoven basket with boar tusk handles? Namaste has the market cornered on exotic wares from far-off lands like Africa and Asia. The store's far-flung variety sometimes resembles a museum, with rarities like Zulu spears and Tibetan

SHOPS

scripture tables, but smaller-scale objects like clothing, toys, and even ostrich handbags abound.

NEST
4524 McKinney Ave., 214/373-4444,
www.nestdallas.com
HOURS: Mon.-Sat. 10 A.M.-6 P.M.
Map 3

It's all about design at this home/stationery store. Nest is the kind of place you can find cute little items for the guest bathroom or tasteful new takes on mid-century furniture. If you're on a budget and can't afford a $2,000 chair, check out their collection of gorgeous imported stationery, teapots, or tableware.

PS THE LETTER
5136 Camp Bowie Blvd., 817/731-2032,
www.pstheletter.com
HOURS: Mon.-Sat. 10 A.M.-5 P.M.
Map 10

Owner Linda Motley manages to pack a surprisingly large inventory of famous-name china, classic tableware, and fine crystal into this modestly sized store in the middle of one of Camp Bowie's shopping strips. Of course, as the name indicates, there's plenty of stationery here, too, especially that of the wedding ilk—the store is a favorite resource for wedding needs and registries.

Shopping Districts and Centers

BISHOP ARTS
N. Bishop and W. Davis Sts.
Map 6

Bishop Arts, with its slower pace and tree-shaded redbrick storefronts, often feels like a small Southern town within Dallas's big-city limits. A leisurely walk around the area, which is only a few square blocks, reveals hidden gems, quirky shops, and neighborhood restaurants.

CAMP BOWIE
Camp Bowie Blvd. at University Dr.
Map 10

The long main drag that stretches through the West Side of Fort Worth, Camp Bowie's offerings range from eclectic and offbeat to stately and classic. Along the long strips of shops on both sides of the street, you'll find clothing boutiques, chain stores, houseware shops, tons of specialty shops, and jewelry stores. Sections of the boulevard are walkable, but keep in mind this is a long and busy street.

DEEP ELLUM
Between I-45 and Exposition Ave.
Map 5

Although Deep Ellum is better known nowadays as Dallas's music and art district, its neighborhood roots go back to a time when pawn shops

and other stores anchored the street life, so why wouldn't it make for fine shopping? A stroll along Main and Elm Streets doesn't tender as many options as it used to, but it reveals a number of boutiques, jewelry stores, tattoo parlors, and head shops, along with a few non-seedy sex shops.

DOWNTOWN DALLAS
Map 1

The granddaddy, the big poppa, the old faithful, Neiman Marcus, got its start downtown and continues to hold down the fort to this day. While a visit to Neiman's alone is worth a trip downtown—hell, a glance in Neiman's windows alone is worth it—small, upscale, hip boutiques are cropping up in the once-abandoned buildings that are benefiting from the city's revitalization projects. Meantime, on the outer edge of downtown, Victory Park provides glitz and glam with several cream-of-the-crop stores, while the West End draws in tourists with a smattering of souvenir and Western shops.

GALLERIA DALLAS
13350 Dallas Pkwy., 972/702-7100,
www.galleriadallas.com
HOURS: Mon.-Sat. 10 A.M.-9 P.M., Sun. 11 A.M.-7 P.M.
Map 7

This is the mother ship—four stories, 200

SHOPS

© DALLAS CVB

Galleria Dallas is home to several top-tier department stores.

stores. There's an ice-skating rink, restaurants, and so many parking garages and levels, navigating them is like driving up the Matterhorn. For shoppers, the mix of high end stores, popular chains, and more than a few surprises make the journey worth it.

GREENVILLE AVENUE
Greenville Ave., west of Lakewood
Map 4

Sometimes funky, sometimes ritzy, always busy, Lower Greenville Avenue is one of the best places in Dallas to stroll and not spend *too* much money. The strip from about Ross Avenue all the way up to Mockingbird features a mélange of thrift stores, antiques shops, and unique gift stores interspersed among the many bars and restaurants.

◖ HIGHLAND PARK VILLAGE
47 Highland Park Village, Dallas
Map 3

Leave it to Dallas to have a shopping center that's a designated historical landmark. Opened in 1931 in the town's toniest neighborhood, Highland Park Village proudly claims its heritage as the nation's first shopping center. Many of the boutiques, storefronts, and restaurants have changed since then, but the center's unique Spanish/Mediterranean visual motif and its focus on the swankiest products have not. This is where the cream of the social crop in Dallas goes to shop; the only place that compares in both heritage and stature is Neiman Marcus.

◖ LA GRAN PLAZA
4200 South Fwy., 817/922-8888,
www.lagranplazamall.com
HOURS: Sun.-Fri. 9 A.M.-9 P.M., Sat. 10 A.M.-9 P.M.
Map 11

This giant mall, based on the Latin tradition of a city square of shops, caters to the needs of Fort Worth's ever-growing Hispanic population. It's in a kind of depressing part of town, but La Gran Plaza's mix of shops is colorful and unique, including a supermarket, several Western wear shops, and retail stores of all types and sizes.

SHOPS

HIGHLAND PARK VILLAGE

It should be no surprise, in a part of the world where shopping is often termed a contact sport, that there's a shopping center designated as a National Historic Landmark: Highland Park Village.

To fully understand Highland Park Village, it helps to know a little about Highland Park. The neighborhood is, technically, its own city—complete with its own schools, police and fire departments, and parks. Originally intended as an elite enclave, Highland Park has lived up to its destiny. In 1906, developer John S. Armstrong purchased a large tract of land just north of Dallas. Armstrong and his two sons-in-law, Hugh Prather and Edward Flippen, hired the same design team that planned Beverly Hills to lay out their new town. The team designed and envisioned a tony burg full of fine homes and greenery—they immediately set aside 20 percent of the land for parks. After that came the country club—Prather and Flippen built it, and indeed the wealthy came. In 1913, when Highland Park applied for annexation, Dallas refused. No doubt that proved a mistake—Dallas certainly would have benefited from Highland Park tax dollars over the years.

Nowadays, the town-within-the-city remains an exclusive, preppy place. Mercedes and BMWs fly down the tree-lined streets of Highland Park's 2.2-square mile area. Multistory houses, many of them architecturally significant, nestle up to newly built McMansions, all homes to doctors, lawyers, oil tycoons, and football team owners (Dallas Cowboys owner Jerry Jones is a resident). Catering to many of Dallas's richest residents, Highland Park's charming bistros, full-service stores, and fancy shops definitely list toward the high-end.

An exclusive township needs an exclusive shopping center, and that's where Highland Park Village comes in. It was Prather and Flippen's idea, and they envisioned an open-air town square created from scratch. The two traveled the world for design inspiration, studying the architecture in Spain, Mexico, and California. They settled upon an unconventional open-air design, with stores facing away from the street (an idea which many people assumed would lead to the center's doom) and off-street parking. The fruits of Prather and Flippen's world travels show clearly in the tiled fountains, stucco-colored walls, and Latin architectural style. The addition of the Highland Park Theater in 1935 was the capstone, cementing the Village as a landmark. Just as its creators envisioned, the shopping center became quite a happening place.

And it still is. Over the years as it's changed hands, the center endured some downturns, but when Henry S. Miller purchased it in 1975, he restored it to its original glory, refurbishing facades, revitalizing the lush landscaping, and even restoring the theater at great expense. Today shoppers flock from all over the country to indulge in retail that rivals New York's Fifth Avenue, with names as familiar as those of family members: Chanel, Escada, Carolina Herrera, Harry Winston, Jimmy Choo, Ralph Lauren. And, as always, the valet parking is free. You won't find *that* in Beverly Hills.

MOCKINGBIRD STATION

5331 E. Mockingbird Ln., 214/421-5638, www.mockingbirdstation.com

Map 4

A fairly new development, Mockingbird Station's hip, modern outdoor design comprises the bottom floor of a loft apartment building popular among SMU students. The shops here—American Apparel, West Elm, Urban Outfitters—cater to such a demographic. One end of the area is anchored by the lovely, arty

Angelika theater and the hopping Irish pub Trinity Hall.

(NORTHPARK CENTER

8786 N. Central Expy., 214/361-6345, www.northparkcenter.com

HOURS: Mon.-Sat. 10 A.M.-9 P.M., Sun. noon-6 P.M.

Map 3

You won't find any dingy head shops or discount stores at NorthPark Center, located just on the north cusp of the ritzy Southern

Methodist University area, but you will find a colossal AMC movie theater, world-class art like sculpture by Mark di Suvero, a garden courtyard, and a library. Oh yeah—there are shops, too, dozens of high-enders like Neiman's, Michael Kors, Bulgari, and many others.

7TH STREET AND FOCH STREET

W. 7th between Main St. and University Dr.

Map 10

Just around the corner from the Cultural District in Fort Worth, the West 7th Street area used to enjoy a laid-back vibe. No more: The area has exploded with modern mixed-use development, full of bars, restaurants, and shops.

MALL MASTERPIECES

Most shopping malls have some kind of stucco tile fountain as a centerpiece. Or, if you're lucky, there might be an ice skating rink.

What does Dallas's **NorthPark Center** have for its interior decor? Oh, just some giant sculptures by some of the most famous artists in the world, plus some large-scale paintings thrown in for good measure. No biggie.

An explanation: The founder of NorthPark Mall is none other than real-estate developer Raymond Nasher, the same man who founded the Nasher Sculpture Center in downtown Dallas. Nasher's commitment to art and aesthetics has been well known for years, and when he conceived the mall in the early 1960s, he set a high standard for design, materials, and execution of the space, which sat on 97 acres.

Art was Nasher's passion, and he and his wife Patsy amassed one of the largest and most important sculpture collections in the world before his death in 2007. This was not a man who hoarded his priceless works. He wanted the world to experience them. Even without the art, his mall felt less like a place for the shopping hoards and more like a sleek, naturally lit museum, and so the high art, believe it or not, was and is a natural fit.

Throughout his life, Nasher rotated selections for display in the mall (in a particularly delicious piece of consumerist meta-irony, Andy Warhol's 1985 piece Ads can be found between Dillard's and Macy's on the first level). After he died, his daughter Nancy picked up the mantle and took over the operation of the mall. Under her guidance, NorthPark underwent an extraordinary renovation, which included the addition of a 1.4-acre CenterPark Garden, home to Claes Oldenburg and Coosje van Bruggen's witty 1999

sculpture, *Corridor Pin, Blue* (1999) and several other defining pieces. Some other select works and their locations:

• Frank Stella *Waves*, 1985-89: Near NorthCourt and Dillard's Court, Level One

• James Rosenquist *F 111*, 1974: Near Dillard's Court, Level One

• Mimmo Paladino *A Surrounded Figure (Assediato)*: Near NorthPark Center Concierge between Neiman Marcus and Nordstrom, Level One

• Alain Kirili *Rediscovered King*, 1987: Between Neiman Marcus and Dillard's, Level One

• *The Maeght Scarves*, 31 scarves by 27 artists including Valerio Adami (1971), Marc Chagall (1958), Raoul Ubac (1964), and Pierre Tal Cott (1962): Near NorthPark Center Management Office, Level One

• Barry Flanagan *Large Leaping Hare*, 1982: Between Nordstrom and Macy's, Level One

• Jim Dine *The Field of the Cloth of Gold*, 1987-88: Between Neiman Marcus and Dillard's, Level One

• Jonathan Borofsky *Five Hammering Men*, 1982: Between Neiman Marcus and Dillard's, Level One

• Beverly Pepper *Dallas Land Canal and Hillside*, 1971-72: At the south entrance to NorthPark Center from Northwest Highway (Loop 12) between Neiman Marcus and Dillard's

SNIDER PLAZA
Snider Plaza at Milton Ave.
Map 3

A slightly larger, slightly less stuffy version of Highland Park Village, Snider Plaza is a repository for some of the best boutique shopping in town. The walkable outdoor center is a perfect place to find unique items, especially stationery, gifts, housewares, children's wear, and even pet items. Snider Plaza also houses a wide variety of excellent eateries, ranging from hamburger joints to fine dining.

STOCKYARDS STATION
131 E. Exchange Ave.
Map 11

If you're looking for a giant belt buckle, checkered cowboy shirts, or a pair of custom-made boots, the Stockyards can't be beat for variety. There's no better way to shop for Western duds than by strolling down the creaky wooden sidewalks here and peering into the many stores. Beware, though, that with the touristy atmosphere often come touristy prices.

SUNDANCE SQUARE
333 Throckmorton St.
Map 8

The nostalgic buildings, unique civic additions (like shrubs cut in the shape of longhorn cattle), and fellow shoppers definitely get you in the mood to spend in this historic district downtown. Keep an eye peeled for hidden secrets like the gift shop of the Sid Richardson Museum, as well as large chain stores like Barnes & Noble books.

WEST VILLAGE
Intersection of Lemmon and McKinney Aves.
Map 2

Some people find this mixed residential/retail development to be a touch plastic; others find it to be a nexus of hipness. Either way, it's certainly got a lot of shops. The West Village is basically an inverted mall—branches of upper-echelon chains like Brooks Brothers and Ralph Lauren nestled elbow-to-elbow with a few locals, only they all are outside, facing sidewalks.

UNIVERSITY PARK VILLAGE
1612 S. University Dr., 817/654-0521,
www.universityparkvillage.com
Map 9

This outdoor mall has everything you need when it comes to the better franchise stores—Banana Republic, Ann Taylor, Talbots, etc.—plus a few locals thrown in.

Stockyards Station is a one-stop shop for souveniers.

© JONANNA WIDNER

Sports

BASS PRO SHOPS

2501 Bass Pro Dr., Grapevine, 972/724-2018,
www.basspro.com
HOURS: Mon.-Sat. 9 A.M.-10 P.M., Sun. 10 A.M.-9 P.M.
`Map 11`

Bass Pro Shops are, of course, an enormous nationwide chain, but their outposts are so massive and so well stocked with fishing, hunting, camping, and other outdoor goods that no sports enthusiast should bypass a visit. The word "store" doesn't do the DFW location justice: Here, thousands upon thousands of square feet of rods and reels, kayaks, guns, tents, boats, golf gear, taxidermy, clothing, and orienteering gear abound, surrounded by dramatic artifice like a fishpond and waterfall. The store also offers tons of outdoor skills workshops and classes.

COLLECTOR'S COVEY

5550 W. Lovers Ln., 800/521-2403
HOURS: Mon.-Sat. 10 A.M.-6 P.M.
`Map 3`

Think of Collector's Covey as the antithesis of Bass Pro Shops. Whereas the latter is buzzing, democratic, and overstuffed with outdoor gear, the former is quiet, restrained, and bedecked with the accoutrements of the sporting life. The Covey's clubby feel manifests in its inventory of manly goodies, like expensive knives, hand-carved duck decoys, stamp prints, and watercolor paintings of mallards. This is the place to buy something for the man who not only owns his own duck blind, but the 1,000 acres it sits on as well.

DALLAS COWBOYS PRO SHOP

310 Main St., 817/348-8252
HOURS: Mon.-Sat. 10 A.M.-8 P.M., Sun. noon-6 P.M.
`Map 8`

Sure, you could get your official gear at one of the many Cowboys Pro Shops in the Dallas-Fort Worth airport, but the Sundance Square location is a lot more fun, especially considering the crazy items that qualify as official

Dallas Cowboys Pro Shop

© JONANNA WIDNER

Dallas Cowboys merchandise—you know, things like sequined dresses—and cool collectibles that abound here.

LUKE'S LOCKER

Dallas: 3046 Mockingbird Ln., 214/528-1290;
Fort Worth: 2600 W. 7th St., 817/877-1448;
www.lukeslocker.com
HOURS: Mon.-Fri. 10 A.M.-7 P.M., Sat. 10 A.M.-6 P.M.,
Sun. noon-5 P.M.
`Map 3`

Those horrible souls in life we know as "people who exercise" will find themselves in heaven at Luke's Locker. Runners especially will swoon at the selection of Nike gear, tons of running shoes, and those little short shorts. Luke's has been around for years and is the go-to place when you need something in which to sweat. Best of all, the salespeople really know their stuff when it comes to running shoes.

ST. BERNARD SPORTS

5570 Lovers Ln., #388, 214/357-9700,
www.stbernardsports.com

HOURS: Mon.-Sat. 10 A.M.-8 P.M., Sun. noon-6 P.M.

Map 3

Originally a ski and surf apparel store, St. Bernard has expanded over the years to offering shoes and preppy sportswear. Although there's plenty of the latter, from Penguin sweaters to Patagonia vests, the place's heart clearly always has been attached to climes much colder than Dallas, and shoppers here reap the benefits in St. Bernard's collection of chic ski and après-ski apparel. If you're in the market for anything upscale, fur-lined, puffy, or boot-y, you'll want to stop here first.

TEXAS RANGERS TEAM SHOP

2222 McKinney Ave., 214/261-5200

HOURS: Mon.-Sat. 10 A.M.-6 P.M.

Map 1

New ownership and newfound success have injected life into the Rangers' fanbase; as result, Rangers T-shirts, caps, replica uniforms, and other accoutrements of fandom have become wardrobe staples in the DFW area. And, although the Rangers Ballpark might exist a 30-minute drive away in Arlington, the brick-laden downtown Fort Worth store (316 Main St., 817/273-5128, Mon.–Thurs.

Texas Rangers gear is a wardrobe must-have in the DFW area.

© JONANNA WIDNER

10 A.M.–8 P.M., Fri.–Sat. 10 A.M.–10 P.M., Sun. noon–6 P.M.) and the McKinney Avenue location in Dallas both make you feel like you're out at the ballpark, minus the parking hassles, when you're picking up some official gear.

Toys

FROGGIE'S 5&10

3211 Knox St., 214/522-5867, www.froggies5and10.com
HOURS: Mon.-Sat. 10 A.M.-9 P.M., Sun. noon-6 P.M.
Map 3

The parking sucks, the location is tough to get to, and it's a touch pricey. So why go to Froggie's? Two words: Sea Monkeys. Actually, that's not all they have. While Froggie's is one of those toy stores that secretly caters to adults, it's still a welcome respite from hyperactive video games and blingy Barbies. It's old-school here, and said Sea Monkeys have plenty of company amid the great kids' books, science games, and Rubik's cubes, which may be easier to solve than getting a parking spot.

MISS MOLLY'S TOY & CANDY SHOP

4802 Camp Bowie Blvd., 817/732-6711

HOURS: Mon.-Sat. 10 A.M.-5 P.M.
Map 10

While walking into any toy shop is a joy for kids (and most adults), passing through the front doors of Miss Molly's, with its row upon row of unique, stimulating toys, just might send them into overdrive. Would the giant displays of awesome gourmet candy have anything to do with it? Definitely. All of that is well and good, but what really makes the independently owned Miss Molly's the best toy store in Fort Worth is its inventiveness. The staff here constantly seeks out new was to engage children, be it via a visit from be-costumed ballet professionals to putting together kiddie gift baskets, this place is tops. Oh, and it *stocks* tops, too: both the toy variety and the children's clothes variety.

Western and Work Wear

🄲 DICKIES COMPANY STORE

521 W. Vickery Blvd., 817/877-0387, www.dickies.com
HOURS: Mon.-Sat. 9 A.M.-6:30 P.M., Sun. noon-5 P.M.
Map 8

Dickies's colorful sideways horseshoe logo should be familiar to anyone who has paid attention to hipster clothing trends in recent years, but the work clothes supplier was cool in Fort Worth well before fashion developed its blue-collar fetish. That's because Dickies, which began in Fort Worth in 1922 as the Williamson-Dickie company, has long provided the town—and eventually the nation—with high-quality, low-cost work gear. Building on the brand's recent upswing in popularity, Dickies has been expanding its line to cute, durable casual wear that only hints at its blue-collar legacy. The outlet is tucked away on an industrial street just south of I-30 where it meets downtown, and it's filled with cool attire for the whole family: men's cargo shorts, ladies' fitted logo tees, even kids' pajamas are available at a discount. Oh, and you can still

find that perfect pair of work boots or a good pair of chef's pants, too, all at prices a working guy or gal can afford.

JUSTIN BOOT COMPANY FACTORY OUTLET

717 W. Vickery Blvd., 817/885-80989,
www.justinboots.com
HOURS: Mon.-Sat. 9 A.M.-5 P.M., Sun. noon-5 P.M.
Map 8

It's a little hard to find, but once you open the door and the smell of leather hits you in the face, you know you've got the right place. Any cowboy worth his oats has at least one pair of Justins in his closet and another on his feet; the Fort Worth–based Western wear firm is a respected name in boot-making and a favorite brand among all types of cowpokes, because of the footwear's durability, style, and comfort. At the outlet store, you'll find a huge selection of "irregular" cowboy and work boots, most of which have slight defects that are hardly noticeable, at discounted prices.

LUSKEY'S/RYON'S WESTERN WEAR

2601 N. Main St., 817/625-2391, www.luskeys.com

HOURS: Mon.-Sat. 9 A.M.-6 P.M., Sun. 1-5 P.M.

Map 11

Since 1919, the Luskeys and the Ryons have outfitted Fort Worth with both off-the-rack and custom-made Western clothes, work clothes, and tack and saddle (the Luskey family takes care of the garments, while the Ryons do the leatherwork). Nowadays, the well-stocked store features all sorts of Western wear from big names like Wrangler, Justin, and Carhartt. It's a good place to one-stop shop, from hats to boots.

MAVERICK FINE WESTERN WEAR

100 E. Exchange Ave., 817/626-1129,

www.maverickwesternwear.com

HOURS: Mon.-Thurs. 10 A.M.-6 P.M.,

Fri.-Sat. 10 A.M.-10 P.M., Sun. 11 A.M.-6 P.M.

Map 11

Where else but Texas could you belly up to the bar, order a cold one, and then turn around and shop for Western gear? Yep, Maverick Fine Western Wear sells two things that Texans love—booze and boots—all in the middle of the ambience of the Stockyards. Weirdly, along with their fine supply of cowboy clothes, the folks at Maverick also carry biker-style jewelry and clothing.

◖ M. L. LEDDY'S

2455 N. Main St., 888/565-2668, www.leddys.com

HOURS: Mon.-Sat. 9 A.M.-6 P.M.

Map 11

This spacious store, appropriately situated on the same corner in the Stockyards since before World War II, offers an excellent variety of Western clothes and accessories for men and women. But Leddy's is really known for its leatherwork—detailed, hand-tooled boots; custom saddles hand-worked from start to finish; beautifully crafted stirrups. Whether it's a yellow rose etched on an ostrich boot or an intricate design on a $5,000 saddle, if it's from Leddy's, it has been made with four generations of care behind it.

PETER BROS. HATS

909 Houston St., 817/335-1715, www.pbhats.com

HOURS: Mon.-Sat. 9 A.M.-5 P.M.

Map 8

Any cowpoke worth his or her salt will tell you that when it comes to hats, there's more than just Stetsons. That's where Peter Brothers comes in. This store has been around for decades, and they've never made anything except hats—every form and model you can imagine. They also custom-make hats and can even re-create one from a photograph.

RETRO COWBOY

406 Houston St., 817/338-1194

HOURS: Mon.-Thurs. 10 A.M.-7 P.M.,

Fri.-Sat. 10 A.M.-10 P.M., Sun. noon-5 P.M.

Map 8

Tongue-in-cheek Texas goods are in abundance at Retro Cowboy. Make sure to order a Dublin Dr. Pepper when you step inside to check out all the Western-theme souvenirs (like the John Wayne lunch boxes) and sip on that sucker while you peruse the pearl snap shirts, cowgirl bags, and baby-size cowboy boots.

© JONANNA WIDNER

Looking for boots and hats? Try Maverick Fine Western Wear.

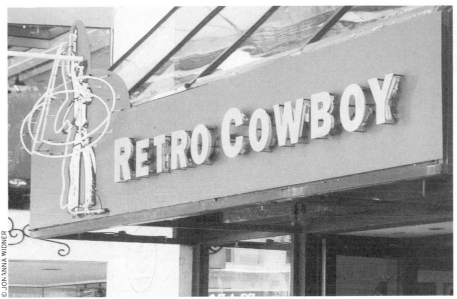

© JOANNA WIDNER

Retro Cowboy's eclectic goods make it a prime spot for gift shopping.

WESTERN WEAR EXCHANGE

2809 Alta Mere Dr., 817/738-4048,
www.westernwearexchange.com
HOURS: Mon.-Sat. 10 A.M.-6 P.M.
Map 10

Western Wear Exchange is a pearl snap–lover's dream. This consignment/resale store has racks and racks of vintage and used cowboy wear, including the hipster-favored pearl snap shirts, plus all sorts of famous brand-name jeans, boots, hats, and belts. The store takes 50 percent off the asking price, which gets cut by another 25 percent after 60 days. The proprietors are sticklers for both condition and quality—much of the stock borders on new.

€ WILD BILL'S WESTERN STORE

311 N. Market St., 214/954-1040,
www.wildbillswestern.com
HOURS: Mon.-Fri. 10 A.M.-9 P.M., Sat. 10 A.M.-10 P.M., Sun. noon-6 P.M.
Map 1

For such a touristy locale, Wild Bill's certainly maintains some decent prices, especially on oft-marked-up Western wear like boots and belt buckles. Wild Bill's has those for as little as $100 and $12, respectively, which is unheard of in these parts. Steer clear of the overpriced menswear and hats, though. And while the lower-priced boots are there for a steal, Bill's also provides custom boots for a much heftier fee.

HOTELS

The accommodations in Dallas, as in many large cities, lean heavily on chains, and there are plenty of those to choose from in any price range. For the most part, this section doesn't include those obvious choices, unless there's a particular quality—amenities, location, luxury—that makes it a notable choice.

As far as hotels in general, Dallas likes to go big, opulent, and amenity-laden, and "trendy" might be added to that list of late, as a number of nationwide name hotels have sprung up around town—the W Hotel and Hotel Zaza, to name but two. There's no lack of high-end accommodations, from the staid and stately (such as the Mansion on Turtle Creek and the Adolphus) to the sleek and mod (such as the Palomar and the Hotel Lumen).

Although many of Dallas's hotels sprawl in a grand scale, in recent years a number of boutique—or at least boutique-*ish*—hotels have cropped up, but these also list toward the high end.

You won't find too many low-key hostels or B&Bs around these parts. Like the rest of Dallas, the hotel world here keeps it big and boisterous.

For years, Fort Worth endured a dearth of hotel rooms that severely crippled its ability to lure large groups and conventions. Sure, the town could boast tourist attractions, a revamped convention center, and a lovely downtown, but even those features couldn't make up for a lack of lodging.

It's not that Cowtown's preexisting accommodations weren't top-notch; upscale places like the Ashton Hotel and the Worthington provided luxury, while numerous B&Bs and Stockyards

COURTESY OF NYLO HOTELS

HIGHLIGHTS

LOOK FOR ◖ TO FIND RECOMMENDED HOTELS.

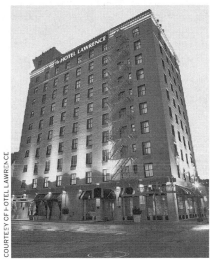

COURTESY OF HOTEL LAWRENCE

Hotel Lawrence

◖ **Best Hotel Bar:** Try either of the two bars at **The Hotel Adolphus.** If you can't afford to stay there, at least you're able to bask in the opulence and people-watch those who can (page 172).

◖ **Best Haunted Hotel:** Several ghosts supposedly haunt the 10th floor of the **Hotel Lawrence,** from which a woman reportedly jumped in the 1940s (page 173).

◖ **Best-Kept Secret:** Park Cities' **Hotel Lumen** is sleek and cool with an excellent location (page 178).

◖ **Best View:** The rooftop pool atop the **NYLO Dallas South Side** offers beautiful panoramas of downtown and Fair Park (page 179).

◖ **Best Redo: The Ashton Hotel** renovation involved refurbishing not one but two old buildings, and now the cozy lobby and restaurant host lovely teas within the historic confines (page 180).

◖ **Best Kitsch:** The themed rooms at **Etta's Place** B&B are fun but not cloying, and the location can't be beat (page 180).

◖ **Best B&B:** The friendly atmosphere at the **Texas White House Bed and Breakfast,** coupled with its easy-to-navigate location, make it a great place to stay (page 182).

◖ **Best Atmosphere:** For authentic Western digs, you can't beat **Stockyards Hotel,** where ranchers, cattle barons, and meatpacking industry kings often cut deals in the lobby (page 183).

HOTELS

spots provided more casual digs for the temporary guest. There simply weren't enough beds.

Until at last, in 2009, the final brick was laid on the Omni hotel downtown. The addition provided the extra bit of oomph the hospitality industry needed, and has cemented Fort Worth's place in the pantheon of tourist destinations.

CHOOSING A HOTEL

Dallas is such a spread-out city that it can be difficult to figure out where to stay in relation to your destinations. A great bet is downtown. While prices here can be a touch more expensive than other parts of town, the convenience of the central locale can be worth it. Moreover, many of Dallas's downtown hotels aren't as

pricey as their counterparts in other cities. Take care, though, to book rooms as far in advance as possible: The city attracts its fair share of conventions, and downtown rooms book up quickly—and more expensively—when large groups are in town.

If downtown doesn't appeal, try Uptown, where hipness prevails. You'll find yourself close to nightlife, shopping, and restaurants. Gay and lesbian travelers might try Melrose, which sits at the very epicenter of the gayborhood.

In all honesty, in Fort Worth, your hotel chooses you. Around TCU, the West Side, and most other residential areas, chain hotels are the most common—and often the only—choices. Downtown and the North Side's

HOTELS

PRICE KEY

💲 less than $150 per night
💲💲 $150-250 per night
💲💲💲 more than $250 per night

Stockyards areas provide a touch more variety. Although chain hotels show a presence downtown, some of the more unique lodging spots in that area cost about the same, so if you prefer a little character along with your turndown service, check for the best deals. For tourists, downtown and the North Side will be the most convenient locations.

Downtown Dallas   Map 1

ALOFT DALLAS 💲
1033 Young St., 214/761-0000, www.aloftdallas.com

A subdivision of the W Hotel group, the Aloft Dallas is even sleeker and cooler than its mother ship down the street. Everything here is all the exposed concrete, beams, and the giant columns that define the interior look. Expect W-like service and W-lite amenities, such as the 24-hour re:fuel food station. On the edge of downtown and within close proximity to Deep Ellum as well as the burgeoning South Side/Cedars district, the digs here allow for a hipper, cheaper alternative for the young business set.

THE FAIRMONT DALLAS HOTEL 💲💲
1717 N. Akard St., 866/540-4427, www.fairmont.com

Location plus luxury make the Dallas link in this high-end chain a good choice, especially for business travelers and those planning on visiting the Dallas Arts District. Amenities are all what you would expect from a luxury hotel, including Keurig coffeemakers, in-room business amenities, and a 24-hour business center. Although the hotel has been around since 1969, the powers-that-be continue to update it with increasingly modern and relevant touches, including and on-site art gallery called, fittingly enough, The Gallery at the Fairmount.

🄲 THE HOTEL ADOLPHUS 💲💲
1321 Commerce St., 214/742-8200,
www.hoteladolphus.com

Easily the grandest, most opulent hotel in downtown Dallas, this gorgeous old stalwart is a stately elm among saplings. While newer hotels often opt for sleek minimalism, the Adolphus, built in 1912 at the behest of beer baron Adolphus Busch, showers each guest in an atmosphere so unabashedly posh, even Marie Antoinette might blush. The outside of the multi-floor building is as ornate and lovingly detailed as a wedding cake, while the interior features antiques, grand staircases, and gilded frames. The crème de la crème here is the French Room restaurant. "Rococo," "baroque," and "Edwardian" are words often used to describe the atmosphere, and the exquisite bas-reliefs, polished marble floors, and lush murals on the 18-foot ceilings prove such words are not overstatements; the same goes for the meticulously crafted French cuisine. While such grandiosity easily could be overkill, with the Adolphus it works, mainly because of the gorgeous details that transform old-fashioned camp into old-school lavishness.

It's not just window dressing—the Adolphus sets a high bar for service and amenities. Each of the 400-plus rooms is fit for royalty; in fact, a number of international royals have stayed here. Besides the opulent French Room, the Adolphus has a less formal bar and grill as well as a charming, casual bistro and two other bars. Of course, there are the usual perks—an exercise room, meeting areas, a business center—but how many hotels also offer afternoon tea?

HOTEL CRESCENT COURT 💲💲💲
400 Crescent Ct., 214/871-3200,
www.crescentcourt.com

For a hotel with such a giant footprint, it's a wonder that the Crescent manages such

The Hotel Adolphus offers old-school luxury.

personal—and personable—service. At around $500–600 a night, one should expect nothing less, of course, but the Crescent always delivers, greeting guests across the elegant gymnasium-size, marble-floored lobby by name. The building itself takes up several Uptown blocks—all the more room to indulge in the Crescent's spa service, many shops, and glorious pool.

HOTEL INDIGO $$

1933 Main St., 800/972-2518

The Hotel Indigo can be had, if you're lucky, for closer to the $100 side of things, and if you've booked it at that price, the place is a good bargain for a downtown stay. Even though it's owned by a chain, it's a boutique chain, so expect some character—in this case, manifested in hardwood floors and pastel, beach-y color schemes (which, admittedly, are a bit out of place in downtown Dallas). While the Indigo's little corner of downtown isn't the most convenient if you don't have a car, you can rely heavily on the hotel shuttle, which will take

you almost anywhere. A friendly staff tops off the charm of the place. Free wireless Internet.

◖ HOTEL LAWRENCE $$

302 S. Houston St., 214/761-9090,
www.hotellawrence.com

The rooms are a touch small and the place hasn't reached the level of its clear ambition to transform into a European style boutique, but the Hotel Lawrence has little amenities such as bottled water, shuttle transport to downtown sights (including the Arts District and the Sixth Floor Museum), and wireless Internet in each room—all free—making it a desirable place to stay. The faint of heart, however, should stay away: The Lawrence is famously haunted, and even offers spooky Halloween stay-overs for ghost hunters.

HOTEL ST. GERMAIN $$$

2516 Maple Ave., 214/871-2516,
www.hotelstgermain.com

It's easy to surmise that there's no other hotel like this in the world, or at least definitely not

DALLAS GHOSTLY OVERNIGHTS

If you're one of that strange breed who loves a case of the paranormal shivers, look no further than the **Hotel Lawrence** for accommodations in Dallas. The hotel was built in 1925, and while it now serves as an affordable boutique hotel, it has a deliciously creepy pedigree.

For one thing, the basement once held a seedy underbelly of illegal gambling (many ghost hunters there today use poker chips to tempt the possible spirits to make themselves known). Hotel employees to this day report strange goings-on in the former casino–laundry baskets moving themselves, lights going on and off, electrical devices ceasing to work.

But the real spooky high jinks can be found on the 10th floor. Legend has it this is where a young woman fell–or jumped–to her death from the Presidential suite sometime during the 1940s. Alternate stories claim it was a man who fell–or jumped–and some even say that he was a congressman.

Well, no matter who fell or jumped, some odd stuff happens on the 10th floor now. This is where staff members have repeatedly report feeling "cold spots," and hotel patrons swear they've seen someone walking around who disappears into the night air. People also report hearing footsteps and a woman's voice at odd hours of the early morning. The most striking ghostly activity, however, has occurred when staff and guests have tried to open doors to no avail. Folks who have encountered this phenomenon swear it feels as if someone is holding the knob from the other side.

A stuck doorknob proves a subtle haunting, however, in comparison to the ghostly hubbub at the **Hotel Adolphus,** just a few blocks down the road from the Lawrence. The Adolphus is known as one of the most refined, fanciest hotels in the country, and this was true in the early 20th century, too, when the 19th floor ballroom hosted big band shows and parties. Descriptions of the ballroom sound similar to the one from the movie *The Shining:* It was glamorous, filled with champagne-swilling revelers in black-tie splendor dancing the night away.

To this day, graveyard shift desk attendants at the Adolphus receive calls from 19th-floor guests, complaining about hearing the music drifting in from the ballroom. The thing is, that ballroom has been abandoned for decades. Maybe the band plays to entertain the spirit of a longtime guest who still is sighted taking her usual seat at the hotel's Bistro. Or maybe it's the jilted bride who has spooked more than one hotel guest.

While the stately Adolphus keeps the ghostly fuss to a minimum, a nonprofit group called the DFW Ghost Hunters has been hot on the Hotel Lawrence case for some time now. The group even holds its annual Halloween conference at the Lawrence, and the public is welcome to join in for a $25 fee (check www.dfwghosthunters.com for details). The conference begins in the evening, with speakers and lecturers, followed by the midnight ghost hunt. The kindly hotel even offers half-off lodging specials for conference participants, in case you want to spend the night. Not that you'll be getting any sleep, mind you.

in Dallas. The St. Germain transports guests back to the sleepy elegance of old New Orleans. French antiques, gilded mirrors, and ever-present ivy transform this turn-of-the-20th-century house into a romantic inn. Canopied feather beds, 24-hour concierge service, and modern amenities transform it into pampering accommodations. The St. Germain is one of the best-kept secrets in Dallas.

HOTEL ZAZA $$$
2332 Leonard St., 800/597-8399, www.hotelzaza.com

When it comes to the melding of opulence and stylishness, Hotel Zaza has no equal. The decadence in this case is in the details: Thick carpets cover every square inch of the rooms and suites, dense feather pillows await you on the bed, and heavy drapes block out the Texas sun. The general theme and decor are of luxurious international exotica, with zebra stripes blending into Middle Eastern and Mediterranean patterns everywhere you turn. The hotel's signature motif, however, is its "concept" rooms and suites, which follow themes like "Rock

Star" and "The Last Czar." The service can be cloying (turndown service involves retro candy; the free shuttle is called the Magic Carpet), but you'll be so blissed out from the spa, cocktails at the Dragonfly bar, and stellar service, you won't notice. Of course, the hotel features all the usual amenities such as a fitness center, a pool, room service, and a business center.

HYATT REGENCY DALLAS ⑤⑤
300 W. Reunion Blvd., 214/651-1234, www.dallasregency.hyatt.com

Normally, another cog in the corporate hotel chain might not be worth a mention, but when that cog just happens to be attached to a 55-story tower with a giant, revolving ball on top—well, it makes for memorable accommodations. The downtown Hyatt's proximity to Reunion Tower affords guests access to the landmark's amenities, such as the top-level (literally) rotating restaurant helmed by Wolfgang Puck. The hotel's other amenities are to be expected: several restaurants, a coffee shop, a fitness center, etc.

THE JOULE HOTEL ⑤⑤⑤
1530 Main St., 214/261-4491

Much, much more than a place to rest your head, the Joule is a destination in and of itself. The downtown hotel, housed in a 10-story gothic building connected to the Neiman Marcus flagship store, has no equal when it comes to combining the warmth of a boutique hotel with the most modern aesthetics and amenities that luxury accommodations have to offer.

The building's remodel was custom designed by Adam Tiheny, and the results are astonishing. Tiheny incorporated two signature elements that make the Joule truly unique: The first is the cantilevered rooftop pool that juts out eight feet over the edge of the building; the second can be found in the lobby, where a pair of enormous gears loom over the exquisite combination of dark yet sleek ambience. Combined with the gothic architecture, the dramatic details feel like an industrial vision of the future, à la *Metropolis*.

The aura extends to the much-praised gourmet restaurant Charlie Palmer at the Joule, which sits under the aegis of two industrial wind turbines.

If the atmosphere is grand, the service is understated and friendly, and amenities are plentiful (the phones even have a direct line to a Neiman's personal shopper). Of course, expect to pay for it, as rooms vary from around $400 to $5,000 for the penthouse suite.

THE MAGNOLIA HOTEL ⑤⑤
1401 Commerce St., 214/915-6500, www.magnoliahoteldallas.com

The Magnolia is hard to miss: It's the building with the giant red neon winged horse on top. Even without the iconic rooftop sign (a leftover from the building's days as the headquarters for an early incarnation of the Mobil Oil Company), the building itself would turn heads. Built in 1921, the 29-story neoclassical edifice was once the tallest building west of the Mississippi (and the first skyscraper in the country to have air-conditioning). Today, the refined, modern interior doesn't exclude the building's original detailed touches; instead, it incorporates them into a quietly chic aura. Boutique and unique, the Magnolia may not have the dramatic amenities of large chain hotels, but it does have an excellent continental breakfast and evening milk and cookies. And a Starbucks.

OMNI DALLAS ⑤⑤
555. S. Lamar St., 214/744-6664, www.omnihotels.com

It's difficult not to be impressed by the futuristic glitz of this particular Omni hotel. Of course its location adjacent to the Dallas Convention Center is a plus, but the real hook here is the light show that turns the mid-rise into what looks like a gargantuan Lite Bright. And while the amazing display might at first appear gimmick-y, the hotel considers it an artistic medium. Case in point: Local Deep Ellum artist Frank Campagna, who owns Kettle Art Gallery, recently was asked to create a light piece for the building, and he came

HOTELS

COOL POOLS

Let's face it: In the Texas heat, a pool is essential, and they've come to be an expected amenity at most hotels worth their salt. But a handful of hotels have taken it to the next level, literally, with their rooftop and upper-floor pools So if a kiddie pool and high dive aren't quite enough for you, try these out:

- **The Joule** ups the ante on infinity edges with its ingenious and, if you're afraid of heights, scary rectangular "Joule Poule" that juts eight feet past the roof and over the sidewalk, many, many floors below. A café and cocktail attendants round out the luxurious feel. The pool is open to the public Sun.-Wed.

6-10 P.M. and Thurs.-Sat. 6 P.M.-midnight.

- The views from the supermodern **NYLO Dallas South Side**'s rooftop pool can't be beat. Set just a smidge outside downtown, the hotel's vantage point allows for dramatic skyline vistas. The poolside bar, Soda Lounge, is pretty sweet too.

- While it is somewhat annoyingly named "Wet," the 16th-floor pool at the **W Hotel** doesn't disappoint if you're looking for the perfect mix of views, decadence, and the beautiful people. With its smattering of support columns and lounge furniture, the combined deck and pool area gives the feel of a Roman bath—with cocktails.

up with a touching tribute to his son, who had passed away suddenly a few years before.

Inside the hotel you'll find the same commitment to local art, as the large-scale works on the lobby walls and smaller ones within the room are all special commissions from area artists. Fittingly, the spacious, well-edited gift shop here looks more like a museum gift shop than hotel lobby afterthought. The hotel also features an outpost of the excellent local steak house, Bob's, and the most dazzling sports bar you'll ever set foot in.

THE W HOTEL $$$
2440 Victory Park Ln., 214/397-4100,
www.starwoodhotels.com

Most people know the W's modern upscale reputation, and the Dallas version doesn't disappoint. At 33 stories, the W tower affords fantastic views, but the best one might be of the American Airlines Center, home of the NHL's Dallas Stars and the 2011 NBA champion Dallas Mavericks, and its *Blade Runner*-esque video screen and neon-drenched plaza. Besides the views, amenities include incredible service, a heated upper-floor infinity-edge pool, a Sweat fitness center, business center, and in-room wireless Internet for about $10 a day. Also a plus: Pets are not only welcome here, they're well-serviced. The hotel offers pet treats, dog-walking services, and a special W pet bed.

Uptown Dallas   Map 2

BAILEY'S UPTOWN INN $$
2505 Worthington St., 214/720-2258,
www.baileysupstowninn.com
Cute, comfortable, and convenient, this B&B sits in one of the best locales in Dallas for travelers. The area surrounding the inn provides plenty of food and entertainment options,

along with easy access to the McKinney Avenue trolley, which takes riders downtown. Rooms come with DirecTV, Internet access, and private baths. Many of the higher-end rooms come with fireplace, whirlpool bath, and/or private porch. Owner Andrea Friedheim offers up special rates on a regular basis, and discounted rates are available for those who prefer to skip breakfast.

DAISY POLK INN ❸❸

2917 Reagan St., 214/522-4692

GLBT travelers will feel right at home in this super-cute little Arts and Crafts home that evokes a cozy European abode. In the mid-1990s, proprietor Wayne Falcone purchased the 1906 home from the family of Daisy Polk, who was a local opera star with quite a story, and the inn is a quick walk away from "The Strip," home to most of Dallas's GLBT hangouts. The inn is divided into three suites (all of which have private baths): The Daisy suite and the Reagan suite both house queen-size beds, while the Dickason has a double bed.

ROSEWOOD MANSION ON TURTLE CREEK ❸❸❸

2821 Turtle Creek Blvd., 214/559-2100, www.mansiononturtlecreek.com

Once the magnificent estate of a cotton magnate and his family, the Mansion feels more like home than any other hotel in the city. Granted, 10,000 square feet of living space may not be the norm for most people, but the warmth and character of the Mansion, derived from the fact that a family once lived here, provides an extra touch of comfort. It's luxurious, too—the original opulence remains in the form of marble floors, exquisite staircases, stained glass windows, and intricately carved inlays. Although it's famous for its grandeur, favored by rock stars and heads of state alike (Pakistan's President Musharraf stays here on visits to Dallas), the Mansion is even better known for its restaurant, which was begun by star chef Dean Fearing and his famous tortilla soup, and after a 2007 renovation, has moved brilliantly into the era of modern fine dining.

THE STONELEIGH ❸❸❸

2927 Maple Ave., 972/262-4479, www.lemeridiendallasstoneleigh.com

Even though it recently underwent a multi-million-dollar renovation, the Stoneleigh still oozes history. The redo embraces the 1921 original's signature touches like marble columns, art deco details, and bold, glamorous lines, while adding some much-needed urbanity. Rooms start at well more than $200, but that's a bargain, considering the Stoneleigh's Uptown, centralized location close to the bars and shops of McKinney Avenue, the gayborhood, and downtown. While the price is right and many amenities such as wireless Internet, bathrobes, and shoeshines are free, keep an eye out for other cranked-up prices ($4 for a Coke; $14 for a coffeemaker). The hotel also takes pride in its signature spa, which is one of the best in town.

WARWICK MELROSE HOTEL ❸❸

3015 Oak Lawn Ave., 214/521-5151, www.warwickdallas.com

Even though it was recently purchased by the large Warwick corporation, the Melrose still retains its boutique feel. This 184-room hotel was built in 1924, and its classic aura shows in the charming redbrick exterior, detailed interior, and handsome wood-paneled Library Bar. The old-school intermingles with the modern, however, especially in the sleek lines of the exquisite Landmark Restaurant—one of Dallas's best. Located right at the very epicenter of the gayborhood—the nexus of Oak Lawn Avenue and Cedar Springs—the Melrose is popular among GLBT travelers, but is by no means exclusive to them, and caters ably to the business crowd with T1 lines, personalized voicemail, and large work desks.

HOTELS

HOTELS

Park Cities
Map 3

HILTON DALLAS PARK CITIES $$
5954 Luther Ln., 214/368-0400,
www1.hilton.com/en_us/hi/hotel/dalpchf/index.do

Like everything else in Park Cities, the Hilton here goes a step above the usual luxury treatment. Here you'll find the standard amenities of an upper-end chain hotel, but the location and excellent service let you know you're in one of the most exclusive parts of town. The Park Cities Hilton is also close to all the major shopping areas and in a tree-lined, character-filled section of the area. Extra bonus: If you stay here, you'll be surrounded by hundreds of restaurants, but if you prefer to eat in, the Hilton houses OPIO, helmed by well-known Dallas chef Billy Webb.

HOTEL LUMEN $$
6101 Hillcrest Ave., 214/219-2400,
www.hotellumen.com

Hotel Lumen is one of Dallas's little secrets. A four-story boutique hotel, the Lumen is situated just down the street from Southern Methodist University, making it a perfect place to rest your head during parents' weekend (if you plan on staying there during football season, make reservations well ahead of time). The accommodations here feel more like an L.A. hot spot than a stately hotel: Expect lots of mood lighting, mid-century decor, and luxury with a light touch.

Greenville
Map 4

HOTEL PALOMAR $$$
5300 E. Mockingbird Ln., 214/520-7969,
www.hotelpalomar-dallas.com

One of the newest modern luxury hotels in Dallas, the Palomar is housed in what was once a dodgy, drug-infested motel. It's completely renovated now, of course, in neons and pastels that evoke Hollywood cool. The Palomar is the first Texas foray of the high-end hotel brand from Klimpton and, as such, bears just about every amenity imaginable—including pampering for your pet. The chic downstairs restaurant, Central 214, and the old Polynesian stalwart Trader Vic's comprise the popular dining options, but the gorgeous bar is where the action really is.

East Dallas
Map 5

CORINTHIAN BED & BREAKFAST $$$
4125 Junius St., 214/818-0400,
www.corinthianbandb.com

Folks like to apply the term "transitioning" to the neighborhood surrounding the Corinthian, but really, the environs are just plain bad. But adventurous souls are rewarded once they arrive on the wide swath of columned porch that wraps around the B&B. There are five different suites, ranging from the Mayor's Suite to the Presidential Suite, all of which achieve a perfect balance between comfort and antique comeliness. The bright, airy rooms all feature king-size beds, TVs, and wireless Internet. The Corinthian sits on Junius Street, one of the most historic roadways in Dallas, just around the corner from magnificent Swiss Avenue.

South Dallas   Map 6

THE BELMONT HOTEL $

901 Ft. Worth Ave., 214/393-2300,
www.belmontdallas

Thank goodness for the parties responsible for rehabbing this classic 1940s hotel, because it has turned out to be one of the best boutique hotels in the region, if not the country. With 64 unique guest rooms—from bungalows to two-story lofts— the Belmont stays true to its Art Moderne design, and charms with its vintage feel. Perched on a cliff just outside of downtown, the property offers super views. Locals spend a lot of time here, lulled by the ever-popular Bar Belmont, the lauded restaurant SMOKE, and the weekly pool parties and free outdoor movies. A friendly, one-of-a-kind place, the Belmont is not particularly convenient to downtown (although it's not far), but does allow easy access to the Bishop Arts District and funky South Dallas.

(NYLO DALLAS SOUTH SIDE $

1325 S. Lamar St., 214/421-1080, www.nylohotels.com

A little sibling to the gargantuan and very cool South Side on Lamar apartment lofts next door, the NYLO South Side charms from the get-go with its vintage ocher-red bricks and funky feel. That's "funky" in a Soho kind of way, in that the hotel combines chic urbanity with a healthy love of the surrounding neighborhood's street-level grit. You'll remain far from the latter, however, lounging about the rooftop pool, which offers a dazzling downtown view. You'd never know the historic building, bright and cleverly refurbished, was once a coffin factory. Rooms and suites are large and loft-style, with 10-foot ceilings and locally sourced artwork, 42-inch HD televisions and wireless Internet. Other features of the smoke-free property include a bar, a bistro, a business center, and dry cleaning.

HOTELS

COURTESY OF NYLO HOTELS

a guest room at NYLO Dallas South Side

Greater Dallas

Map 7

HOTELS

DALLAS IRVING BACKPACKERS $
214 W. 6th St., Irving, 972/262-4479
Backpackers and low-budget travelers are hard-pressed to find hostel-type digs in the DFW area. The Dallas Irving Backpackers is the best of the bunch. The hostel isn't conveniently located per se, situated as it is in Irving, a Dallas suburb, but it's pretty much equidistant between Dallas and Fort Worth, and is close to the TRE train that will take you to either town. The hostel's friendly, if somewhat disorganized, staff will put you up in a bunk bed (four to a room). Wireless Internet, outdoor grills, and a large kitchen are also available.

WESTIN GALLERIA DALLAS $$$
13340 Dallas Pkwy., 866/716-8137
Those with business in North Dallas often find themselves at the Westin, which is a good place to be. This is a world-class business hotel, fresh off a recent renovation and flush with amenities. Excellent service, wireless Internet, a gym, a business center, and proximity to a number of highways are all well and good, of course, but really it's the fact that the Westin is literally connected to one of the largest (and swankiest) shopping malls in the world—the Dallas Galleria—that lifts these accommodations above the usual.

Downtown Fort Worth

Map 8

THE ASHTON HOTEL $$
610 Main St., 817/332-0100, www.theashtonhotel.com
Modern luxury in a historic setting defines this boutique hotel, perfectly located a few steps away from both Bass Hall and Sundance Square. The hotel actually comprises two buildings, one constructed in 1890 and the other in 1915. A 2001 renovation and restoration reestablished their charm. With only 39 rooms, the Ashton's intimacy translates to personalized hospitality—in the dusk of evening, the glow of the warmly lit lobby of the Ashton practically begs passersby to drop in for a drink and a steak from the hotel's much-lauded 610 Grille. Amenities include free wireless Internet in all rooms, babysitting service, and 24-hour room service.

AZALEA PLANTATION B&B $$$
1400 Robinwood Dr., 800/687-3529,
www.azaleaplantation.com
Decorated with more antiques than you'd find in your grandma's garage, this genteel B&B provides a relaxing haven for those who prefer books to 2 A.M. partying. Gardens and greenery buffer the Azalea's large spread from

the surrounding neighborhood, which is not particularly picturesque. The B&B is a bit off of the beaten path, but particularly convenient to the Stockyards and the Texas Motor Speedway.

ETTA'S PLACE $$
200 W. 3rd St., 817/255-5760, www.ettas-place.com
It's fitting that Etta's Place can be found on Sundance Square, since the B&B's namesake was the Sundance Kid's sweetheart, and indeed, history and location make up a good deal of the appeal here. While it's billed as a bed-and-breakfast, Etta's can feel more like a historic hotel, with spa, business amenities, and large, airy rooms—you won't find any of the musty Victorian frill that overtakes so many period-themed accommodations. What you will find are tasteful, fun nods to Cowtown's Western heritage.

HOLIDAY INN EXPRESS DOWNTOWN $
1111 W. Lancaster Ave., 877/863-4780
If the words "Holiday Inn" conjure up images of dingy rooms and mustard-colored carpet, you'll change your thinking after visiting this

inexpensively priced update on the old family-road-trip standby. This Holiday Inn is clean and sharp, with almost over-the-top mod furniture and appointments. The rooms, though perhaps a touch smaller than most, prove comfy and tidy. Since it cozies up to downtown, convenient to Sundance Square, the Cultural District, and TCU, the hotel might just have the best location in Fort Worth for the price. Ditto for the amenities, which include a shuttle bus, workout room, pool and hot tub, and breakfast buffet.

THE OMNI FORT WORTH ❸❸

1300 Houston St., 817/353-6664, www.omnihotels.com
While the rooms are pretty much standard for an upscale hotel chain, it's the grandeur of the common areas that make this brand-new, city-initiated, downtown centerpiece such a thrill. Built specifically to lure conventioneers and other large groups to the city (which suffers a dearth of hotel rooms), the Omni's thoughtful decor belies its scale (614 rooms, 25 suites, 29 meeting rooms, 777,000 square feet, four restaurants). Case in point: The striking $1

million limestone wall—a creative nod to Fort Worth's Western heritage with a 21st-century flair—that anchors the lobby. By the way, the luring strategy worked: Whichever AFC team is lucky enough to make it to the 2011 Super Bowl, which will be held at the nearby Dallas Cowboys stadium, will be staying here.

RENAISSANCE WORTHINGTON HOTEL ❸❸❸

200 Main St., 800/433-5677,
www.marriott.com/hotels/travel/dfwdt-renaissance-worthington-hotel-fort-worth
Once a favored spot for traveling oil execs and out-of-town businesspeople, the Worthington's luxurious rep was matched only by its footprint on downtown. With the opening of the over-the-top new Omni Hotel, however, the Worthington might find its reputation as the best downtown hotel in jeopardy. Still, the instantly recognizable, pyramid-shaped building strikes a nostalgic chord, as well as a more tangible one. The service here has always been top-notch, the luxurious treatment devoid of frills, and the location unbeatable.

TCU and Vicinity   Map 9

HATTIE MAY INN ❸❸

712 May St., 817/870-1931, www.hattiemayinn.com
The serenity of this stunningly restored 1904 Queen Anne beauty belies a notorious history—in 1917, the house's owner, local gentleman James Liston, was shot and killed on the back porch as he returned home with the profits from his Hell's Half-Acre Saloon. His wife continued to live there for years afterward, and one of the six bullets shot at Liston is still visible today. Other than that, the wraparound porch, antiques, and charm of Hattie May's place inspire nothing but comfort, along with modern conveniences like cable TV, hair dryers, and an ironing board. Guests can choose from a number of tempting accommodations, from the Oriental Oasis room with its claw-foot tub to the Americana Room's sleeping porch.

Inquire about special package pricing for adjoining rooms.

RESIDENCE INN UNIVERSITY ❸❸

1701 S. University Dr., 817/870-1011
Empty-nester moms and pops who make the trip to TCU for a parents'-weekend glimpse into their kids' college life might struggle to find suitable digs. That's where the Residence Inn University comes in. While much of what this place offers sticks to the mid-level, large-chain paradigm, the inn is clean, easy, and convenient to the school and other Fort Worth sights. This branch also manages a touch of character, considering it once was an actual residence—many rooms even have fireplaces—but you can still expect free Internet and rooms with microwaves, mini-fridges, and a stove top.

HOTELS

☕ TEXAS WHITE HOUSE BED AND BREAKFAST ❸❸❸
1417 8th Ave., 817/923-3597,
www.texaswhitehouse.com

You won't find Secret Service agents at this White House, but you will find the hospitable service of owners Grove and Jamie McMains, who are well versed in all things Fort Worth and happy to share their knowledge. Of course, considering the antiques, gardens, and gazebo, you might not want to leave the premises. If you do, however, the convenient location close to downtown Magnolia Street comes in handy.

Greater Fort Worth   Map 11

MISS MOLLY'S BED AND BREAKFAST ❸❸
109 W. Exchange Ave., 817/625-1522,
www.missmollyshotel.com

This former bordello embodies the history of the Stockyards perhaps more genuinely than any other establishment in the area. Eight different rooms—each decorated so devotedly to the Old West era, the place could be a museum—encircle a central parlor, where back in the 1800s certain types of ladies waited for their clients to come calling. All of the rooms share a bathroom down the hall (robes are supplied), except for Miss Josie's Room, which has a private bath and is a little bit bigger (naturally, since this was once the madam's chamber). While the quarters are snug, they make up for lack of room in charm, and the location can't be beat for those wishing to explore the Stockyards.

SANFORD HOUSE INN & SPA ❸❸❸
506 N. Center St., Arlington, 877/205-4914,
www.thesanfordhouse.com

Although the Sanford House's charming Southern architecture evokes a B&B ambience, it really serves more as a freestanding hotel. If you're expecting a quiet, singular

GOOD GOLLY, MISS MOLLY

If you're looking for a true Texas B&B experience, Miss Molly's is the perfect place to pull off your boots and rest a spell. Once a boardinghouse, then a brothel, and now a proper bed-and-breakfast, Miss Molly's bursts at the seams with history and character.

And what unique seams those are—the primary decor motif here adheres to the period of the building's heyday (it was constructed in 1910), with Victorian and Edwardian furnishings; heavy velvet drapery in some rooms, lace in others; oak furniture, metal beds, and busy floral patterns, as befits the early 1900s tastes.

Each of the seven rooms has its own theme—cowboy, rancher, gunslinger, and the like—which would be cloying if they weren't so much fun. The largest room, Miss Josie's, is named for a former madam, and a few of the other rooms are named for the brothel's working girls.

Some of those girls, it seems, never left. The hotel is considered one of the most active paranormal sites in the state, with repeated reports of mysterious goings-on. Guests report seeing a young girl wandering the rooms, even when children are not present on the property, along with toilets flushing on their own, weird noises, doors refusing to open, cold spots, and other oddities. One housekeeper quit, claiming that she would clean a room after guests had checked out, leave for a minute or two, and find coins in the same room where they were not before.

Considering its bawdy, rollicking past, it's no wonder some of its former inhabitants want to stick around. If you're looking for lodging full of history, you probably will, too.

experience, you might be disappointed, but the lovely decor, gourmet food, and beautiful gardens definitely provide a luscious experience, even amid the mid-city concrete and large-scale tourist spots like the Texas Rangers ballpark just up the road. Guests choose between intimate cottages that surround the pool and rooms in the main house. Amenities are plentiful, including plasma TVs, wireless Internet, breakfast, a bar, and a concierge.

STOCKYARDS HOTEL $$$
109 E. Exchange Ave., 817/625-6427,
www.stockyardshotel.com
You'll practically hear the spurs a-janglin' when you enter this century-old bastion of Western-style luxury. With leather furniture, bordello-red paint, and longhorn-laden walls, the Stockyards Hotel plays up its history to the hilt—and when your former guests include everyone from Bonnie and Clyde to Michael Martin Murphy, why not? (Bonnie Parker's pistol, by the way, adorns the wall in the suite named after her.) Despite the historic flair, the service and amenities here definitely fall under the modern category.

STOCKYARDS HYATT PLACE $$
132 E. Exchange Ave., 817/626-6018,
www.stockyards.place.hyatt.com
It's all about location here, as this Hyatt is plunked right in the thick of things down in the Stockyards. The usual large-chain hotel amenities abound, with the added plus of free wireless Internet, but the real benefit of staying here is its proximity to all things North Side and downtown.

STONEHOUSE BED AND BREAKFAST $
2401 Ellis Ave., 817/626-2589,
www.bedandbreakfastfortworth.com
Originally a boardinghouse for cowboys (you can't help but wonder if they ambled down the block to the former bordello that now serves as Miss Molly's B&B) fresh off the Chisholm Trail, the Stonehouse charms with 10 themed rooms featuring original solid wood floors and tons of cowpoke charm. Some rooms share a common restroom, and others have their own, so call or check the website for your preference.

HOTELS

EXCURSIONS FROM DALLAS AND FORT WORTH

The sights, sounds, foods, and attractions of Dallas-Fort Worth are more than enough to keep you occupied, but should you feel the need to stretch your wings, the surrounding areas offer plenty of activity for anything from a day trip to a weekend excursion.

While DFW doesn't lay claim to a particular countryside lifestyle like, say, Amish country or even the Hill Country down near Austin, the outlying areas do maintain a certain thematic consistency. For miles around the Metroplex, you'll find the stillness of low, quiet prairie land broken by farms and small ranches, some of which are nestled up to increasingly sprawled suburban development. Along the way are small Texas towns, many of them ratcheting up the charm factor with refurbished town squares surrounded by blocks of Craftsman and Victorian homes.

Five destinations in particular offer the perfect combination of fun sights, activities, and laid-back nostalgia. Southwest of DFW, the Glen Rose/Granbury area has a unique combination of old-fashioned Victorian charm and amazing natural history sites. Due south is the Hillsboro/West/Waco area, which offers a variety of historical attractions and activities. Just north of the Metroplex is "Texomaland," which borders Oklahoma and the Red River, where you'll find surprising roots of American political history abutting water recreation on Lake Texoma. Also to the north, Denton's combination of music, history, and outdoor life lull many a visitor. Finally, the city of

© LIANE HARROLD/123RF.COM

HIGHLIGHTS

LOOK FOR (TO FIND RECOMMENDED SIGHTS, ACTIVITIES, DINING, AND LODGING.

© GRAPEVINE CONVENTION & VISITORS BUREAU

the Grapevine Vintage Railroad

(**Best Learning Experience: Dinosaur Valley State Park** has some of the best-preserved dinosaur tracks in the world. Kids and adults alike will enjoy this adventure (page 192).

(**Best Antiques Stores:** Sherman's **Kelly Square** houses several antiques shops under one quaint roof (page 202).

(**Best Designated Driver:** The **Grapevine Vintage Railroad** will take you from the Stockyards all the way out to the Grapevine wine country and back. If you're staying in the Stockyards, you can just stumble to your hotel (page 205).

(**Best Place for Kids:** With its fantastically enormous indoor water park, online gaming lounge, and other kid-friendly attractions, the "lodge" part of Grapevine's **Great Wolf Lodge** is almost an afterthought (page 206).

EXCURSIONS

Grapevine (north as well) provides a down-home take on wine country as well as modern destinations.

Speaking of wine, a quick note about booze: Many of the counties surrounding DFW are dry counties, meaning if you'd like to order a beer or cocktail at a restaurant, you'll have to sign up for a "membership," which basically means filling out an information card. Occasionally, memberships come with a fee, but most places waive them. It's a rather silly piece of bureaucracy, but don't be surprised if your server brings it up.

PLANNING YOUR TIME

All of these spots are within an easy hour or two's drive of either city and can be done in a day, should you choose your sites carefully, although a weekend would best do justice to their rich heritage, pretty scenery, and friendly folk. As is the way in this part of the country, there's not much in terms of public transportation, so a car is pretty much a must. You might consider, however, bringing bikes or ATVs along, as there's plenty of wide-open country to enjoy.

About equidistant between Fort Worth and Dallas, Grapevine is the closest to both

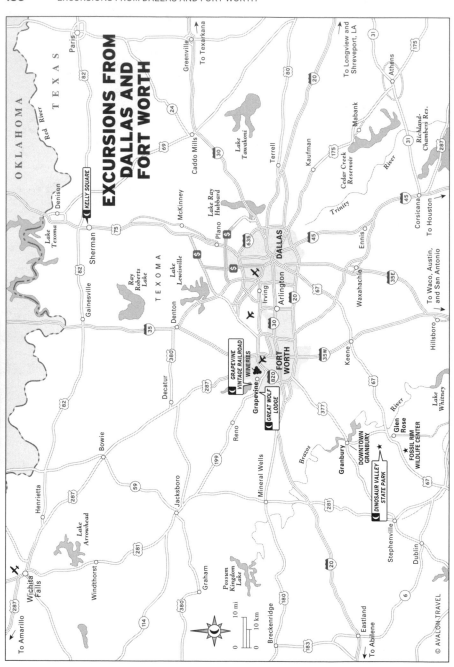

EXCURSIONS FROM DALLAS AND FORT WORTH

OKLAHOMA

TEXAS

Red River

Paris

82

Greenville

To Texarkana

To Longview and
Shreveport, LA

31

175

80

20

Athens

24

69

Caddo Mills

30

Lake
Tawakoni

Terrell

Kaufman

175

Cedar Creek
Reservoir

River

31

Mabank

Richland-
Chambers Res.

287

KELLY SQUARE

Denison

Lake
Texoma

Sherman

75

McKinney

Lake Ray
Hubbard

Plano

635

DALLAS

45

Ennis

Corsicana

45

To Houston

Gainesville

82

Ray
Roberts
Lake

Lake
Lewisville

TEXOMA

Denton

Irving

Arlington

20

67

Waxahachie

35E

To Waco, Austin,
and San Antonio

Trinity

35

380

GRAPEVINE
VINTAGE RAILROAD

WINERIES

Grapevine

820

FORT
WORTH

Keene

35W

Hillsboro

Decatur

287

GREAT WOLF
LODGE

377

River

Lake
Whitney

Reno

Bowie

82

199

Mineral Wells

Brazos

Granbury

DOWNTOWN
GRANBURY

Glen
Rose

FOSSIL RIM
WILDLIFE CENTER

67

Henrietta

287

Jacksboro

59

Graham

281

DINOSAUR VALLEY
STATE PARK

20

Lake
Arrowhead

281

Possum
Kingdom
Lake

Stephenville

Dublin

6

Windthorst

380

Breckenridge

180

Eastland

183

Wichita
Falls

287

To Amarillo

114

10 mi

10 km

0

0

To Abilene

© AVALON TRAVEL

cities, followed by Denton, which takes about an hour to get to from either city and Glen Rose/Granbury—about a half hour south of Fort Worth, and nearly an hour from Dallas. Hillsboro/West/Waco are a 45-minute to hour-and-a-half drive south. Texomaland can be found about an hour north of Dallas, two hours north of Fort Worth, though that increases if you end up spending time at Lake Texoma.

Of all these day trips, Glen Rose proves the only one that's a bit tricky to get to. Keep in mind that, if you're coming from the south, I-35 splits into West I-35 (to Fort Worth) and East I-35 (to Dallas) at Hillsboro, and remerges in Denton.

Denton

For several years in a row, *Money* magazine has listed Denton as one of the "Top 100 Places to Live In America." Of course, said periodical bases such judgments on a lot of monetary factors, but North Texans love this town of about 100,000 for a variety of reasons. Known primarily as the home of the University of North Texas and, to a lesser extent, Texas Women's University, Denton has much to offer music and art lovers, antiquers, and outdoors enthusiasts.

Like most large schools, UNT has an enormous influence on the culture of the town, in this case, especially when it comes to music. The university's jazz studies program is known world-wide as one of the best, and it has spawned the careers of scores of famous and not-so-famous musicians. As a result, the area enjoys a music scene that rivals that of any large city, not just for jazz but also Americana, folk, and indie rock. The venerable *Paste Magazine* named Denton the best music scene in the country in a 2008 article.

Perhaps due to the creative energy fostered by UNT, Denton remains a curious combination of bohemian mecca and quaint, historic prairie town. The population is a fascinating mixture of country folk, bearded hipsters, and burnt-out hippies. Heavy manufacturing companies exist side-by-side with underground music venues. Farm equipment stores sit across the street from record stores. Rugged ranchers dine under the same roof as baby-faced college students. And everyone seems to get along just fine.

While the Denton town square is the place to be for antiques shopping, sightseeing, and community activities, the surrounding area affords fantastic options for recreationists. Ten miles south of Denton you'll find the man-made Lewisville Lake, known as "The Urban Bass Fishing Capital of Texas," and Ray Roberts Lake sits even closer. The Denton area also is known as one of the largest concentrations of horse farms in the United States, providing numerous opportunities for riding and farm tours.

SIGHTS
The Denton County Museums

To explore multiple facets of the rich history of the area, visit **The Denton County Museums** (940/349-2850, Tues.–Fri. 10 A.M.–4 P.M., Sat. 11 A.M.–3 P.M., suggested donation of $1 covers all three museums).

Much of the **African American Museum** (317 W. Mulberry St.) is dedicated to the Dr. Edwin D. Moten Collection. Moten, who was the only African American doctor in the county, and his family were prominent members of the African American community in Denton from 1907 to 1920. The collection contains more than 600 of Dr. Moton's letters, along with accoutrements of his practice, including photographs, medical records and the shingle from his office. The museum is located in what was known as Quakertown, where most African Americans lived until the early 1920s.

Just next door sits the **Bayless-Selby House Museum** (317 W. Mulberry St.), a Queen Anne–style home built at the turn of the 19th century, which houses a number of exhibits detailing the life of Victorian Dentonites.

The three large rooms of exhibits at the **Courthouse-on-the-Square Museum** (110 W. Hickory St.) detail the history and culture of Denton via different media, including a large stock of historic photos donated by the *Denton Record-Chronicle*. Rebuilt twice after two different fires—the last time in 1896—the courthouse itself is one of the most architecturally interesting in the state.

Denton Fire Fighters Museum

The modern, high-tech gadgetry and equipment at the Denton Firefighters Museum (332 E. Hickory St., 940/349-8840, Mon.–Fri. 8 A.M.–5 P.M., free admission) are fascinating, but even more interesting is the collection of firefighting gear from the early 1800s. Highlights include a hose cart from the 1830s, equipment from a 1935 ladder truck, and a collection of rare "breathing equipment." You'll find this museum housed in the lobby of Denton's Fire Station No. 1.

Texas Women's University

Often overshadowed by UNT, Texas Women's University (1216 Oakland St., 940/898-2401, www.twu.edu) actually boasts several notable sights: An architectural marvel, the Little-Chapel-in-the-Woods features artwork, stained-glass window, flooring, lighting, and woodwork all designed by students. The building was dedicated by Eleanor Roosevelt in 1939 and has hosted hundreds of weddings. TWU's Administration Conference Tower is home to the Texas First Ladies Historic Costume Collection, displaying dozens of original and replicated dresses worn to the Texas Governor's Inaugural Ball. The Blagg-Huey Library boasts the Women's Collection, the highlights of which include a fascinating archive of the history of the Women's Airforce Service Pilots (WASPs) and other female aviators; a permanent exhibit covering Texas women's history; and a cookbook collection in the culinary arts section. Nearby Hubbard Hall houses the Texas Women's Hall of Fame.

The University of North Texas

With 36,000 students, The University of North Texas (1155 Union Circle, 940/565-2000, www.unt.edu) upholds a reputation as a good school across disciplines, but it is known best for its music program. Although the program offers study in eight different fields, from opera to chamber music to experimental music, its jazz program is the most well-known, and deservedly so, having produced a long line of some of the most accomplished musicians in the world. Not surprisingly, the campus's Murchison Performing Arts Center is a big draw, especially its architecturally and sonically superlative Winspear Auditorium. Unfortunately, the football team hasn't enjoyed as consistent a tradition of success, but the new Apogee Stadium, with its towers of wind turbines, still proves quite a sight.

RESTAURANTS

There's nothing terribly new to **El Guapo's** (419 S. Elm St., 940/566-5575, www.elguapos.com, Sun.–Thurs. 11 A.M.–4 P.M., Fri.–Sat. 11 A.M.–11 P.M., $10–20) Tex-Mex, but the food is tasty and inexpensive, although most likely much less nutritious than what you'll find at **Cupboard Natural Foods &Café** (200 W. Congress St., 940/387-5386, Mon.–Sat. 8 A.M.–9 P.M., Sun. 10 A.M.–8 P.M., under $10).). The live music at **Banter Bistro** (219 W. Oak St., 940/565-1638) might annoy you; if it doesn't, this friendly, eclectic café makes a great spot for lunch or a light dinner.

Coffeehouses abound here. Try **Art Six Coffee House** (424 Bryan St., 940/484-2786, Mon.–Thurs. 7:30 A.M.–11 P.M., Fri. 10 A.M.–11 P.M., Sat. noon–11 P.M., Sun. 2–10 P.M., under $10); **Big Mike's Coffee** (1306 W. Hickory St., 940/565-1860, daily 24 hours, under $10); or the funky little **Jupiter House Coffee Shop** (106 N. Locust St., 940/387-7100, daily 6 A.M.–midnight, under $10).

NIGHTLIFE

The nonsmoking bar (these are less common than you'd think in this college town) at the **Hickory St. Lounge** (212 Hickory St.,

940/387-2222, www.hickorystreetlounge.com, Wed.–Sat. 11 A.M.–2 A.M., Sun.–Tues. 11 A.M.–midnight) emphasizes the art of cocktail-making rather than the art of drinking in large quantities.

Although its steeped in Denton history, the character-laced **Paschall Bar** (122 N. Locust St., daily 4 P.M.–2 A.M.)—think wooden bookcases, a staircase, and low lighting—might be better known now as the bar owned by the members of the indie band Midlake.

Lots of bars on the Denton square cater to the common denominator of broke college students looking for a shot with a PBR back. But not **Wine Squared** (110 W. Oak, 940/984-9463, www.winetimeswine.com, Mon.–Wed. 4–10 P.M., Thurs.–Sat. 4 P.M.–midnight, Sun. 2–8 P.M.), with art on the walls courtesy of UNT students and a classy atmosphere where sipping, not chugging, is the M.O.

RECREATION

Fishing and Boating

Lake Lewisville's 30,000 surface acres of lake are home to bass, crappie, and catfish (the white bass and catfish prospects here are especially good). About the same size as Lake Lewisville, Ray Roberts Lake also offers some good bass and catfish fishing. If you're looking to hook a lug 'un, **North Texas Catfish Guide Services** (817/522-3804, www.txcatfishguide.com) can help you bag a 20- to 30-pounder. **Bob Grady**'s (www.bobgradyfishing.com) pricing may be a smidge more than others, but he also bears 20 years of experience and an up-to-date knowledge of the latest gear and trends. The folks at **David's Fishing Guide Service** (214/460-1502, www.goneslabbin.com) really know their way around both lakes.

Boat rentals are available at the **Lake Ray Roberts Marina Sanger Unit** (940/458-7343).

Horseback Riding/ Horse Country Driving Tour

The Denton area is home to a thriving equine community, not just of the ranch horse variety, but also racehorses, show horses, rodeo horses, and therapeutic horses. The **Denton County**

Visitors and Convention Bureau (110 W. Hickory St., 888/381-1818, www.discoverdenton.com) offers a number of behind-the-scenes tours, or visitors can follow their own route (www.horsecountrytours.com).

There are a number of trail riding options around Denton. Most of the stables in the area can be found in small communities just outside of town. Close to Ray Roberts Lake, **Black Mustang Ranch** (9375 Jack Gray Rd., Pilot Point, 817/915-8455) offers horse rental and guided tours, including half-day adventure excursions. **Four Fillies Farm** (11242 Friendship Rd., Pilot Point, 940/391-4293, www.fourfillies.com) also provides guided trail rides on the trails of Ray Roberts Lake. **Twin Star Farms** (214/929-0205, www.twinstarfarms.com) also uses Ray Roberts's trails, and offers special "brunch and rides." **RNR Stables** (3114 Parkridge Dr., Corinth, 940/321-8880, www.rnrstables.com) will set you up for both arena and trail rides at Ray Roberts Lake and Lewisville Lake.

Hiking and Biking

Outdoors enthusiasts will love the **Ray Roberts State Park and Lake Lewisville Greenbelt Corridor**, a 20-mile multiuse trail system (12 miles of equestrian trails, 10 miles for hike and bike) stretching from Ray Roberts Dam to Lake Lewisville. Trailheads can be found at FM 455, FM 428, and Hwy. 380.

The greenbelt hugs the banks of a heavily wooded section of the Trinity River, which feeds both lakes. It's an easy trail with few elevation changes, winding from woods to grassland, perfect for either a leisurely or a long excursion, and is popular among bird-watchers.

FESTIVALS AND EVENTS

The rapidly growing **Denton Air Show** (held in June at the Denton Airport) hosts a rotating lineup of civilian aerobatic and military performers along with static displays of all sorts of aircraft.

Expect big crowds at the free, three-day **Denton Arts and Jazz Festival** (525 Fort Worth Ave., 940/565-0931), held the last

THE BEST MUSIC SCENE IN THE COUNTRY

Music fans, take heed: A quick trip north from DFW, up I-35, through suburban sprawl and country prairie, lands you smack in the middle of the best-kept music scene in the country: Denton, Texas.

At first, Denton might strike visitors as a midsize, quiet college town, home to the University of North Texas and not much else. There's a charming town square, B&Bs, plenty of grassy plains and Texas sky. But stay a few hours, do some exploring, and it grows more noticeable. Young, skinny guys with hipster facial hair stroll the streets, sporting trucker caps and beer coozies. Casual collegiate-types hide behind sunglasses. By nightfall, young ladies don their thrift-store best and begin to file into one of the many DIY venues that can be found in unlikely places. Yep, the signs are there—there's music to be had.

Denton has always been fertile ground to creative types. The University of North Texas is one of the finest music schools in the country, a beacon for serious students (mainly of jazz) looking to take their craft to the next level. The school's output is prolific and a fine product, and even nonstudents from miles around are familiar with the Grammy Award–winning One O'Clock Lab Band, which consists of performers who must win a spot in the lineup, the most coveted on campus (the band is named for its place in UNT's class schedule). UNT has also produced other stars like Roy Orbison, Norah Jones, Don Henley, Meat Loaf, the members of Brave Combo, and even Pat Boone.

But there's an edgier side to Denton, one that extends way beyond the campus boundaries. It is in this scene you'll find synth-rock experimentalists and finely honed pop creations, hard punk and smart alternative country, singer-songwriters, DJs, and revamped California rock. This is the scene that has spawned names that are perhaps lesser known, but praised and worshipped by critics and indie fans. Artists like Doug Burr, Midlake, Shiny Around the Edges, Baboon, Slobberbone, and Centro-matic have all honed their chops in Denton.

You're sure to find a great band in one of the many laid-back venues that dot the Denton map. Although they all enjoy their own singular personalities, the clubs' independent spirit and communal philosophy reflect that of Denton itself, so a cross-genre aesthetic pervades.

weekend in April. The fest showcases music, dance, choral, drama, and visual arts on seven stages at Quakertown Park. Grammy-winning UNT grads and polka-punk juggernaut Brave Combo often headlines.

It may get eclipsed by the enormous, month-long Texas State Fair held in Dallas, but that's okay; the **North Texas State Fair and Rodeo** (2217 N. Carroll Blvd., 940/387-2632, www.ntfair.com) charms by hearkening back to simpler times. The NTSF attracts 100,000 people over its nine-day run and, frankly, the music offerings are far superior to the schlocky lineup at the larger counterpart to its south. It's a good option for folks with younger kids, too, considering the smaller crowds, the kids' fun zone, and the generally cheaper prices (these vary from year to year, so call for details).

Begun in 2005 to showcase Denton's wealth of musical talent, **35 Denton** has blown up into a huge four-day festival headlined by some of the biggest names in the indie and alternative musical world: The Flaming Lips, Jesus and Mary Chain, Built to Spill, and many more. The festival still books plenty of Denton, Dallas, and Fort Worth acts, to be sure, and manages to retain its local, homegrown feel, due to the army of volunteers who run the thing, plus its walkability and downtown Denton location. The festival is meant to run around the same time as the behemoth South by Southwest festival in Austin, which occurs every spring.

HOTELS

Yes, we mean "Inns," with an "s": **The Heritage Inns** (815 N. Locust St.,

Hailey's (122 Mulberry St., 940/323-1160, www.haileysclub.com), for instance, provides a haven for cutting-edge dance music. We're not talking the generic brand of thud-thud-thud house that pervades most dance clubs; Hailey's sets expand the genre into all sorts of hybrid and experimental realms. The club also houses some of the best local and indie touring bands.

Dan's Silverleaf (103 Industrial St., 940/320-2000, www.danssilverleaf.com) leans toward a more roots music feel, with many local and mid-level acts sharing the stage, but still makes room for every genre (like nutty, profane soul man Blowfly). Try to catch Denton stalwart and musical genius Paul Slavens at his weekly Monday night gig here.

If you are the type whose musical taste often requires earplugs, try **Andy's Basement Bar and Grill** (122 N. Locust St., 940/565-5400), right on the downtown square.

If there is an epicenter of Denton indie music, it's found in the former cement factory that is now **Rubber Gloves Rehearsal Studio** (411 E. Sycamore St., 940/387-7781, www.rubberglovesdentontx.com). A mecca for experimental and original bands, the stage at RGRS has held greats like Daniel Johnston, Jonathon Richman, and Modest Mouse.

The sheer number of high-quality Denton bands can be intimidating for a newcomer, and while your odds of discovering something you like—or at least something interesting—are good, a good rule of thumb for narrowing down your options is to explore the roster at two Denton production companies: **Spune** (www.spune.com) and **Gutterth** (www.gutterth.com). Both companies bring an almost obsessive drive and spirit to the scene, producing local showcases and festivals that feature the best Denton bands and a good deal of national acts. Look for a Spune- or Gutterth produced show—there's one almost every night—or check out their websites for just a taste of what Denton has to offer.

Of course, as any Dentonite will tell you, this is just the tip of the iceberg. The scene moves fast and is always spawning new bands, new movements, new ideas. The way to get to know Denton's music landscape is to live there. But if you're just visiting, the best option might just be to take a chance. You definitely won't be bored.

EXCURSIONS

940/565-6414, www.theheritageinns.com, $105–115 d) are a pair of restored Victorian houses conveniently located within walking distance of the downtown square. In addition to amazing breakfasts, the Inns sit next door to Guiseppe's Italian Restaurant, should your hunger preclude you from exploring more than a few steps away. The Inns are surrounded by lovely gardens, and the rooms (many of which have claw-foot tubs) are cute and very reasonably priced.

Other than infants under 18 months, it's adults only at kooky but cool **Old Irish B&B** (3030 N. Trinity Rd., 214/505-0754, www.patrickspastures.com, $179 d) set on an alpaca ranch. Yep, guests can pet and feed the alpacas and interact with other animals that call the place home. With a series of cabins set around a small lake, the Old Irish was designed with a specific retro feel in mind, and the nostalgic charm comes through, especially when sitting in a rocking chair on your private porch, listening to the cicadas in the 100-year-old trees that dominate here. There's an on-site spa and one cabin with a wheelchair ramp. Call for details since the proprietors note that it is not 100 percent ADA compatible.)

Located in the country near Lake Ray Roberts, the **Reality Ranch Horse Country Lodge** (1316 S. Hwy. 377, 940/686-9324, www.horsecountrylodge.net) is an excellent choice for folks visiting for recreational purposes (and, obviously, those interested in horse country). The two-story B&B offers six rooms and baths in a rustic, lodge-like atmosphere.

Exceptionally well-priced and set amidst four secluded acres, **The Wildwood Inn Denton** (2602 Lillian Miller Pkwy., 866/840-0713, www.denton-wildwoodinn.com, $149 d) is a sort of hybrid between a boutique hotel and a corporate chain; the former, due to its unique rooms (just 14 of them); the latter, because of amenities like a 24-hour concierge, pool, restaurant, room service, and free wireless.

GETTING THERE

To get to Denton from either Dallas or Fort Worth, simply take I-35 north until you hit the town. The distance from both Dallas and Fort Worth is around 45 miles, and the trip takes about an hour (do consider traffic when you decide a departure time, as rush hour can add delays). Typical of the area, there are no convenient public transportation routes between Denton and DFW.

Glen Rose and Granbury

Glen Rose and Granbury offer two very different types of tourist sites, but seeing how they sit just down the road from each other, they're best taken as a package. In its earliest days, Granbury, as the seat of Hood County, saw a good bit of action, but it never blossomed into a large town (today, the population hovers around 5,000–6,000). Two events helped the small burg escape oblivion: In 1969, Lake Granbury was formed by the damming of the Brazos River, and in the mid-1970s, the town engaged in a massive refurbishing and revitalization of the town square. Both now draw thousands of day visitors, weekenders, and tourists. With its numerous bed-and-breakfasts, Granbury is a good home base for exploring nearby Glen Rose. Just a few miles south of Granbury down Highway 144, Glen Rose itself isn't much to write home about, but it's home to Dinosaur Valley State Park and a number of other destinations.

SIGHTS
◖ Dinosaur Valley State Park

Highway 205 west of Glen Rose leads straight to Dinosaur Valley State Park (1629 Park Road 59, Glen Rose, 254/897-4588, www.tpwd.state.tx.us, 8 A.M.–10 P.M., $7, free children 12 and under), which has some of the finest specimens of dinosaur tracks in the world. Turns out the limestone and sandstone bed of the Paluxy River, which runs through the park, was perfect for petrifying the giant prints from about 100 million years ago. Today, several well-preserved

tracks of sauropods and theropods crisscross the western edge of the 1,524-acre park.

The park is also a beautiful place for hiking, biking, and camping. At this point in the local topography, some of the monotony of the plains begins to change to rockier, hillier, more picturesque ground, and here it serves as a home for many different types of wildlife. Check out the park's website for detailed information regarding camping permits, access, and hours.

Barking Rocks Winery

In 1977 Lawrence Tiberia took a train to Texas from California on a whim, and he's never lokked back. Thus began the history of Barking Rocks Winery (1919 Allen Ct., Granbury, 817/579-0007, www.barkingrockswine.com). The son of Italian immigrants, Tiberia and wife Sissy Andrews (a native Texan) began making wine in a converted barn in 2002. Tiberia specializes in reds, and prefers a small-batch, hands-on approach (he still uses a wooden basket press. The cute, low-key tasting room, now in the barn, is a great place to sip on Tiberia's signature cab, especially when he books a band or singer-songwriter. True to his charmingly laconic form, Tiberia notes that tastings occur "every Saturday afternoon, by appointment, or by chance," so call beforehand for times.

Downtown Granbury

Filled with refurbished Victorian buildings, antiques stores, and other points of interest,

NOT BURIED IN GRANBURY?

Not one, not two, but three of American history's most nefarious figures faked their own deaths, then ended up spending time in Granbury. At least, that's what the locals say.

To start, Granbury folks are convinced that the man known as J. Frank Dalton, who lived in their midst until 1951, was actually none other than the outlaw **Jesse James.** Although the official story is that James was killed by Robert Ford in 1882, people in these parts insist that story is a ruse, and that James hid out under the Dalton alias in Granbury until his death at the age of 104. His Granbury headstone (found at **Granbury Cemetery, at the corner of N.** Crockett and Moore Streets, about eight blocks north of the town square) reads, "CSA–Jesse Woodson James. Sept. 5, 1847–Aug. 15, 1951. Supposedly killed in 1882."

Another supposedly dead gangster, **Billy the Kid,** also lived out a long, quiet life after his fake demise. The official story is that Sheriff Pat Garrett shot and killed Billy the Kid in 1881 in Fort Sumner, New Mexico, not too far from the Texas border, where the gunslinger was then buried. The unofficial tale, however, insists that Garrett shot someone else and then covered it up, and Billy the Kid settled in Hico, Texas, but traveled to Jesse James 102nd birthday party—in Granbury, of course—in 1949. When the real Billy the Kid died of a mundane heart attack at age 90 in 1950, say the unofficial theorists, his gravestone in Fort Sumner went missing, only to turn up in Granbury.

Finally, none other than Abraham Lincoln's assassin, **John Wilkes Booth,** reportedly ended up in Granbury after his pretended demise. Based on the 1907 book *Escape and Suicide of John Wilkes Booth* by Finis L. Bates, Booth went by the alias John St. Helen and tended bar at a Granbury establishment that is now a bakery called the **Nutshell** (137. E. Pearl St. 817/279-8989, www.nutshelleateryandbakery.com, daily 7 A.M.–5 P.M., under $10). After St. Helen died, Bates had his body mummified and traveled the country displaying it as apart of a circus sideshows, until 1977. Attempts to exhume the body thought to be the "real" Booth have been rebuffed by the courts.

the entire charming "downtown" of Granbury is on the National Register of Historic Places. The fantastical stories of Jesse James and Billy the Kid's Granbury reappearance make more sense in the context of the back-in-time feeling of the town square. The old limestone **Hood County Courthouse** (1200 W. Pearl St.), with its original grand clock tower, was built in 1890 and still lords over the picturesque scene. Across the way you'll find the former **Hood County Jail** (208 N. Crockett St., 817/573-5135, Sat.–Sun. 1–4 P.M., $2), now home to the chamber of commerce, with its old cell blocks and creepy hanging tower still intact and open for visitors' perusal. Finally, a stroll down the road apiece lands visitors at the **Granbury Opera House** (116 E. Pearl St., 817/573-9191, granburyoperahouse.net). The opera house, run by a nonprofit group that stages Broadway-type musicals and Branson-like events, is a popular stop.

Fossil Rim Wildlife Center

Fossil Rim Wildlife Park (2155 County Rd. 2008, 254/897-2960, www.fossilrim.org, winter daily 8:30 A.M.–3:29 P.M., spring and summer daily 8:30 A.M.–5:29 P.M., fall daily 8:30 A.M.–4:29 P.M., cost varies per season) feels like a safari in the middle of Texas. The 1,700-acre facility is first and foremost a refuge that specializes in captive-breeding programs for endangered species—we're talking giraffes, rhinos, zebras, and other exotics. But it's also a drive-through park, wherein $8 will buy you a bag of feed and the animals will walk straight up to your car. In addition to the drive, several viewing and pen areas allow up close views of cheetah, ibex, and tons of other animals.

The park offers a variety of experiences. One cool option is to spend a night or two on-site, either at the lovely, comfortable lodge (around $200 a night, depending on season and occupancy) or at one of the more rustic cabins or

EXCURSIONS

bunkhouses (around $85, again depending on season and occupancy).

Entrance prices vary from season to season. Even if you're there for just an afternoon or a day, tours range from the self-guided drive (around $10 a person, depending on season and day) to the "behind-the-scenes" tour (around $50 a person, depending on season and day) to the adventure tour (about $300, depending on season and day). The pricing schedule is a bit confusing—best to check the website or, better yet, call to confirm prices.

The Promise

Performed in an impressive amphitheater specially built for the purpose, *The Promise* (Texas Amphitheatre, 5000 Texas Dr., 254/897-3926, www.thepromiseglenrose.com, $22–40, with $5 discount for seniors, students, and military) is a musical passion play of bewildering scale. It's quite popular among the Christian community.

RESTAURANTS

Besides the bakery **The Nutshell** (137. E. Pearl St. 817/279-8989, www.nutshelleateryandbakery.com, daily 7 A.M.–5 P.M., under $10), another popular lunch place is the **Pearl Street Station** (120 W. Pearl St., Granbury, 817/579-7233, www.pearlststationgranburytx.com, daily 11 A.M.–close, under $10), a Cajun/barbecue joint famous for its "granny" beans and turkey sandwiches on jalapeño cheese bread. For the full home-cookin' experience, try **Debbie's Restaurant** (1102 Hwy. 67, Glen Rose, 254/897-4399, Mon.–Fri. 5 A.M.–1:30 P.M., Sat.–Sun. 5 A.M.–noon, under $10)—it's short on atmosphere, but the buffet is tasty and a great deal at about $8 a person. Perhaps the most random (fortunately so) dining option is celebrity chef Grady Spears's **Line Camp Steakhouse** (4610 Shaw Rd., Tolar, 245/835-4459, www.gradyslinecamp.com, Thurs.–Sat. 5–10 P.M., $20 and up). Inspired by country cowboy cooking of old, Spears's menu offers an inventive take on old standards like chicken-fried steak, regular ol' steak, and chicken and waffles.

NIGHTLIFE

There's not a lot of nightlife to speak of here, as most places close shortly after the dinner hour, but the 1950s-throwback **Brazos River Drive-In** (1800 W. Pearl St., Granbury, 817/573-1311, www.thebrazos.com, Fri.–Sat. until dusk) will take you back. Twenty dollars a carload gets you two movies on weekend nights.

RECREATION
Lake Granbury

At 8,300 acres and with 103 miles of shoreline, this narrow lake may not dominate the landscape, but it certainly is popular. Surrounding shore environs feature five park areas, all of which provide restroom and parking, and most of which provide camping and picnic areas. One highlight is the Granbury City Beach, a length of fine, white sand imported from South Padre Island, dotted with tiki huts, children's water features, and palm trees.

Water sports of all kinds are popular here. Boat, Jet Ski, and other equipment rentals are available through **Lake Granbury Marina** (2323 S. Morgan St., Granbury, 817/279-1000, www.lakegranburymarinainc.com, hours vary by season). **The Dock** (1003 White Cliff Rd., Granbury, 817/579-8200, www.groggydawg.com) also rents Jet Skis and serves as a great little seafood joint (under $10), perfect after a day of sailing or skiing, and you can boat right up to their floating restaurant.

Other casual dining options include the Marina's **Stumpy's Lakeside Grill** (Tues.–Sat. 11 A.M.–9 P.M., Sun. 10 A.M.–8 P.M., under $10), and the burgers and catfish joint **Irby's** (804 E. Pearl St., Granbury, 817/573-7311, under $10).

As far as fishing goes, the lake is stocked annually with bass and occasionally catfish as well. A fishing license *is* required.

For information on campsites, RV camping, and fishing licenses, contact the **Granbury Chamber of Commerce** (3408 E. Hwy. 377, Granbury, 817/573-1622, www.granburychamber.com) or the **Brazos River Authority** (817/573-3212, www.brazos.org)

SHOPS

Granbury's **Historic Shopping District** around the downtown square is the place to go here. The square's storefronts are peppered liberally with ladies boutiques and plenty of antiques shops, along with unique stores like **Dakota's Kabin** (202 N. Houston St., 817/579-0275, www.dakotaskabin.com, Mon.–Thurs. 10 A.M.–5:30 P.M., Fri. 10 A.M.–6 P.M., Sat. 10 A.M.–6:30 P.M., Sun. noon–5 P.M.). The Kabin is stuffed with one-of-a-kind and well-cultivated Western-themed furnishings, accessories, clothing, and accoutrements. **Doug's Sports House** (120 N. Crockett St., 682/936-2729, www.dougssportshouse.com, Mon.–Thurs. 10 A.M.–5:30 P.M., Fri.–Sat. 10 A.M.–7 P.M., Sun. 11 A.M.–5:30 P.M.) stocks everything from koozies to jerseys.

Off the square, **Cowboy Marketplace** (4170 E. Hwy. 377, 817/570-1315, www.cowboymarketplace.com, daily 9 A.M.–6:30 P.M.) satisfies both the touristy and the local's need for true gear like tack and saddles. You'll find it near **Bella Rosa Consignment Gallery** (1440 E. Hwy. 377, 817/578-8588, Tues.–Sat. 10 A.M.–6 P.M.), a popular spot for gently used women's and teens' clothing.

HOTELS

It seems like every other house in this area serves as a B&B. Why not, since their gorgeous turn-of-the-20th-century refinement is tailor-made for that type of thing? A favorite is Granbury's **Iron Horse Inn** (616 Thorp Springs Rd., 817/579-5535, www.theironhorseinn.com, $245 d), which, at 7,000 square feet, is also one of the largest in town. Six rooms make up the accommodations in the century-old Craftsman-style house. Each room features wood floors, a double bed, and private bathroom. The full, hot breakfasts in the antique-laden dining room consist of gourmet-level vittles such as waffles, quiche, and fruit.

One of the better bargains of the Granbury B&B scene, **Alfonso's Loft** (137 E. Pearl St., 817/573-3308, www.alfonsosloft.com) is also one of the quirkier choices the town has to offer, as well as one of the most private: Unhosted, the B&B consists of one space, the top floor of one of the oldest buildings on the square.

The first floor, the bakery and lunch spot **The Nutshell,** is where you'll find your breakfast component, plus an odd bit of local lore. The former occupant of The Nutshell was the very bar where a certain John St. Helen slung drinks. Reportedly, on his deathbed, St. Helen confessed to his real identity—he claimed to be John Wilkes Booth, the assassin of Abraham Lincoln. Murals depicting Booth and the outlaw Jesse James (who it's said also faked his own death and settled in Granbury) adorn the walls of The Nutshell.

Glen Rose offers the B&Bs **Bussey's Something Special** (202 Hereford St., 254/897-4843, www.busseys.net, $125 d) and **Cedars on the Brazos** (2924 County Rd. #413, 254/898-1000, www.cedarsonthebrazos.com, $125 d), with a gorgeous location overlooking the river (the proprietors wear their Christian faith on their sleeve, so if that's not your cup of tea, you might want to look elsewhere).

GETTING THERE

To travel the 47-mile, one-hour trip from Fort Worth to Granbury and Glen Rose, take Hwy. 377 South. The highway can be accessed either via I-20 or Loop 820, which encircles Fort Worth. To get there from Dallas (72 miles, 1.5-hour drive), take either I-30 or I-20 West, then merge onto 377 South. Don't expect to find any public transportation that will get you back and forth between the Metroplex and Granbury/Glen Rose.

EXCURSIONS

Hillsboro, West, and Waco

When driving south down I-35, most North Texans wouldn't give a second thought to the towns of Hillsboro, West, and Waco.

Oh sure, they may stop to pick up some good deals at the Hillsboro Outlets, maybe pause to grab a box of kolaches in West, or pull off to grab some fast food in Waco, but pretty much, they blaze down the highway with the idea of getting to another place.

Frankly, such an attitude is understandable. At first blush, this trio of towns doesn't appear to offer much beyond the promise of interstate travel restroom options, divided by large swaths of flat country dotted with hay bales.

A closer inspection, however, reveals that the initial banality of the three lulls travelers into complacency. The truth is all are rich with history, activities, and surprises.

The closest of the three to the Dallas-Fort Worth area, Hillsboro is the county seat of Hill County (where legendary Texan Willie Nelson was born) and, while not particularly picturesque, is dotted with restored Victorian homes that date back to its founding in 1853. While the turn of the 20th century brought some success to the area as both a railroad hub and a cotton producer, the growing popularity of synthetic materials ultimately stymied its growth. Hillsboro has enjoyed intermittent rounds of prosperity, but population growth here has always remained glacial.

Hillsboro has no signature claim to fame, but rather rests on an amalgamation of attractions and notable moments. For instance, much of the 1996 Wes Anderson movie *Bottle Rocket,* starring James Caan and Luke and Owen Wilson, was shot here.

A teeny burg of about 3,000 people, West (named after its first postmaster, not the geographical information) possesses a fascinating history of Czech heritage. The town existed initially as a railroad stop, with a depot serving the Katy Railroad that ran through the area, and farming rapidly gained popularity as well.

In December of 1851, the first ship carrying Czech immigrants to the United States set sail from Liverpool, England. The vessel docked 63 days later in Galveston, Texas, with 74 Czechs aboard. Most of them settled in Austin County, but a few made their way farther north, where West sits today. After the Civil War, the immigration of Czechs continued. Many were single men recruited as laborers; others were families, attract by the call of large plots of available farmland. Almost all remained in Texas, mainly for the reason that the vastness of the area as well as the fact that Texas hadn't quite firmed up its own cultural identity allowed Czechs to maintain their own culture with little outside harassment.

There's no greater evidence of the strength of that culture than West, where many of its 3,000 or so citizens still speak Czech and a traditional Czech pastry called the kolache can be found everywhere.

The largest and farthest south of the three towns, Waco's known best as home to Baylor University, and, sadly, also as the site of the ill-fated 1993 confrontation between the Branch Davidian religious sect and the FBI.

The town is much more than that. The Brazos River, which has played a notable part in Texas history, runs picturesquely through Waco, provide scenery as well as recreation, and the surrounding area is dotted with sites and activities of interest.

Although it was named for the indigenous Huaco Indians, Waco's founding resulted from attempts by the Texas Rangers to build a fort intended to fend off local tribes. The project was ultimately abandoned, but Waco's proximity to the river gave its growth momentum that other towns did not have, and being a stop on the Chisholm Trail didn't hurt its prospects either. The city has grown to well over 125,000 people.

SIGHTS
Cameron Park Zoo
One suspects that that tigers and other big cats

at the 52-acre Cameron Park Zoo (1701 N. 4th St., Waco, 254/750-8400, www.cameronparkzoo.com, Mon.–Sat. 9 A.M.–5 P.M., Sun. 11 A.M.–5 P.M.) feel right at home in the steamy North Central Texas climate. Their companions include tortoises from the Galapagos Islands, African birds, and the crocodiles, spiders, and snakes who inhabit the herpetarium. Two unique exhibits mark the zoo: The Brazos River Country exhibit follows the footsteps of the Spanish explorers who traversed the Brazos River and features the flora and fauna they encountered along the way. The Asian Forest exhibit starts at ground level at the habitat of said tigers, and slowly elevates listeners through different levels of the tree canopy where, if they're lucky, they'll catch glimpse of a rare orangutan or two.

Hawaiian Falls Water Park

Hawaiian Falls Water Park (900 Lake Shore Dr., Waco, 254/892-0222, www.hfalls.com, Sat.–Sun., Wed.–Thurs. 10:30 A.M.–6 P.M., Tues. 10:30 A.M.–8:30 P.M., Fri. 10:30 A.M.–10 P.M., $25.99 adult, $19.99 for youth, seniors, and active military, children under 2 free) is part of a chain of Texas water parks, but that doesn't make Hawaiian Falls any less fun. Highlights include the 65-foot free-fall Monsoon and Typhoon rides and a twisting 65-footer called the Tsunami, plus plenty of splash-around fun for the younger set. Outside food is not allowed, so be prepared to spend some cash at the food court. Lockers and cabanas are available for rental.

Note: Hours tend to change often, and the park closes for the season around Labor Day. Your best bet would be to call before your visit to confirm hours and availability.

Historic Waco Foundation Historic Homes Tour

The Historic Waco Foundation provides docent-led tours of the four historic homes that date to the mid-1800s, recounting the history of each particular house's occupants, along with context from their lives, through the Historic Waco Foundation Historic Homes Tour (810

S. 4th St., Waco, 254/753-5166, www.historicwaco.org). Weekend tours take visitors to all four homes, while weekday tours vary greatly in scheduling and destination (as do fees), so call ahead for information.

Homestead Traditional Crafts Village

Run by the Ploughshare Institute for Sustainable Culture, the Homestead Traditional Crafts Village (608 Dry Creek Rd., Waco, 254/754-9600, www.sustainlife.org, Mon.–Sat. 10 A.M.–6 P.M.) shouldn't be confused with a living history village. Rather, it's a showcase for a community of craftspeople who have mastered certain homesteading skills such as beekeeping, pottery, cheesemaking, and other sustainable arts. Visitors will find a number of demonstrations of these skills against the backdrop of charming, rough-hewn buildings and an adorably rustic gift barn. It can be a smidge confusing to find your way out here unless you travel in a covered wagon, so best to call for very specific directions.

Improved Order of Red Men Museum and Library

According to the promotional material for the Improved Order of Red Men Museum and Library (4521 Speight Ave., Waco, 254/756-1221, www.redmen.org, Mon.–Fri. 9 A.M.–noon, 1–4:30 P.M., free), "The Order of Red Men traces its origin to certain secret patriotic societies founded before the American Revolution...the Improved Order of Red Men and Degree of Pocahontas are dedicated fraternal organizations that believe on [sic] Freedom, Friendship, Charity, and the American Way of Life." The small collection here is only slightly less perplexing than the explanation of its origins, but therein lies its charm. It all in some way pertains to the order's history, and what an eclectic array it is; Aaron Burr's writing desk, Cochise's moccasins, and Rudolph Valentino's ring are among the highlights. The 41,000-volume library proves equally varied and fascinating, including a complete set of *National Geographic* magazines dating back to 1888.

EXCURSIONS

Texas Ranger Hall of Fame & Museum

Consisting of the Homer J. Garrison museum gallery; the Texas Ranger Hall of Fame; and the Texas Ranger Research Center, the Texas Ranger Hall of Fame & Museum (100 Texas Ranger Trail, Waco, 254/750-8631, www.texasranger.org, daily 9 A.M.–5 P.M., $7 adults, $6 seniors and military, $3 youth 6–12) serves as a comprehensive repository for the artifacts, history, and celebration of this famed law enforcement agency. The museum holds more than 14,000 pieces of Ranger history, a huge collection of historic badges, revolvers, photographs, items confiscated from outlaws like Bonnie and Clyde, and much more. Rotating exhibits trade off with permanent ones such as Rangers in Popular Culture. Don't be surprised if you spot a real Ranger strolling about—the complex also houses the headquarters of the active Texas Rangers Company F.

Texas Sports Hall of Fame

Woo-wee, do Texans love their sports, a fact no better illustrated than upon entering the 35,000-square-foot monument to the greatness of the state's finest athletes, teams, and athletic programs known as the Texas Sports Hall of Fame (1108 S. University Parks Dr., Waco, 800/567-9561, www.tshof.com, Mon.–Sat. 9 A.M.–5 P.M., Sun. noon–5 P.M., $7 adults, $6 seniors, $4 students, active military and under 6 free). Football gets its due here, obviously, alongside basketball, baseball, track, golf, auto racing, and tennis (the latter garnering a strangely copious amount of coverage). While the interactive and multimedia elements provide some pizzazz, the most awe-inspiring exhibits are the ones with memorabilia from some of Texas's most illustrious sports figures: The sight of Emmitt Smith's jersey, Davey O'Brian's Heisman trophy, and Arnold Palmer's clubs just might send chills up your spine, if you're one of the ESPN-inclined. An entire gallery dedicated to the much beloved and bereaved Southwest Conference also impresses, while the High School Football section just might send you into *Friday Night Lights* overload.

The Texas Rangers Hall of Fame & Museum is home to thousands of pieces of memorabilia.

© WACO AND THE HEART OF TEXAS

EXCURSIONS

MAMMOTHS AND TIGERS AND CAMELS, OH MY

It wouldn't be that weird to find a bone lying around the environs of the Bosque River. The Waco area sits near a jutting elevation change called the Balcones Escarpment, a fault line caused by the slow erosive force of the Brazos and Bosque Rivers, and the subterranean strata it exposes reveal all sorts of curiosities, from fossils to an animal bone or two.

But in 1972, when Paul Barron and Eddie Bufkin were hiking around looking for arrowheads near the Bosque, they found themselves face-to-face with a giant bone jutting from the earth, and they knew it wasn't just from a cow. The two men removed the bone and took it to nearby Baylor University's Strecker Museum.

It didn't take long for the museum folks to identify the item as a mammoth bone—a Columbian Mammoth, the be exact, and before you could say "Pleistocene," they had organized an excavation crew and got to work.

What they found was a glorious mystery. From 1978 until 1997, using small brushes and bamboo scrapers, crews uncover the remains of 22 mammoths, a camel, a saber tooth tiger, and an unidentified animal.

To this day, scientists remain stumped as to how the animals died. The most popular theory holds that they died in separate incidents, starting with 68,000 years ago, when the first 19 mammoths, caught up in rapidly rising floodwaters, drowned, probably along with the camel. Subsequent floodwaters buried the herd and camel.

The sabertooth tiger and mystery animal most likely died together, although in what manner has not been determined, and were also ultimately buried by flood detritus, followed by the final incident, 15,000 years after the first, in which a bull, adult female, and juvenile died, also most likely trapped by rapidly rising water. (Sure seems like there were a lot of floods back then!)

A visit to the site does much to capture the drama of the discovery. Now open to the public, the dig area sits in a climate-controlled shelter with a suspended walkway from which visitors can peer directly into the excavation where the bull and camel remain.

Even without the archaeological drama, the park itself is worth a visit. Covering around 100 acres, dense with oak, mesquite, and cedar, the peaceful area contains winding trails and, of course, a gift shop.

The Waco Mammoth Site

Much of Texas is a hotbed of prehistoric discovery, full of fossils and the like, but the Waco Mammoth Site (6220 Steinbeck Bend Rd., 254/750-7946, www.wacomammoth.com, Tues.–Fri. 11 A.M.–5 P.M., Sat. 9 A.M.–5 P.M., $7 adults, $6 students, senior, and military, $5 children 4–12, free 3 and under), where the remains of a family of mammoths, a sabertooth tiger, and a camel were found, really takes the cake.

RESTAURANTS

The classic burgers-n-shakes joint known as **Health Camp on the Circle** (2601 Circle Rd., Waco, 254/752-2186, www.health-camp-waco.com, daily 11 A.M.–9 P.M., under $10) has absolutely no business putting the word "health" anywhere near its menu, but its superior drive-in fare makes any sacrifices to your waistline well worth it.

Texas Czechs know their meat. You can tell by the abundance of sausage shops in the area. And **Nors Sausage and Burger House** (126 N. Main St., West, 254/826-4427, Tues.–Fri. 11 A.M.–2 P.M., 6 P.M.–9 P.M., Sat.–Sun. 11 A.M.–10 P.M., under $10), a casual family-owned eatery housed in a 120-year-old building in dusty downtown West, sourced theirs locally before it was cool. It's easy to fall under the small-town charm here in the downstairs dining area, surrounded by exposed redbrick walls and manly, rough-hewn wood trim.

Tourists buy their kolaches from bakeries right off the highway; real North Texans know to take a slight detour to the **Village Bakery** (113 E. Oak St., West, 254/826-5151, Mon.–Fri. 6:30 A.M.–5:30 P.M., Sat. 6:30 A.M.–5 P.M.,

EXCURSIONS

under $10), where the warm, pillow-y treats taste just a little bit better than their roadside counterparts. Oh sure, the bakery may have been written up in *Guns & Garden* and *Gourmet* magazines, but folks from all around have known about it since it opened in 1952. The bakery serves up the best kolaches this side of the Atlantic and also functions as the kind of small-town community gathering place that is becoming increasingly rare. Owner Mimi Irwin also serves as West's town historian, and if you catch her in a chatty mood, you'll be treated to a fascinating tale of the town's Czech heritage.

NIGHTLIFE

The only Irish pub in Waco, **Barnett's Pub** (420 Franklin Ave., 254/714-1356, www.barnettspub.com, Tues.–Wed. 4–11 P.M., Thurs. 4 P.M.–midnight, Fri.–Sat. 4 P.M.–1 A.M.) is a cozy place to nestle up to a Jameson's or Guinness. The beer selection transcends the usual mid-Texas preference for watery pilsners.

A place for grown-ups, the charming little downtown **Legacy Café and Art Gallery** (725 Austin Ave., 257/752-5200, Waco, Mon.–Thurs. 10 A.M.–10 P.M., Fri.–Sat. 10 A.M.–11 P.M.) can list toward the quiet, but gets quite packed on the live jazz nights. A nice place to have a glass of wine and a nosh.

If the old joke that the students at the primarily Baptist Baylor University aren't allowed to dance were true, would the town really need a honky-tonk the size of **Wild West Waco** (115–119 Mary Ave., 254/759-1081, Thurs.–Sat. 8 P.M.–2 A.M.)? Ditto the similar joke about no drinking; otherwise, the four bars housed in this 12,000-square-foot joint would struggle for a raison d'être. The truth is, the bars get plenty of use, as do all 8,000 square feet of this solid oak dance floor.

RECREATION

You'd never know it by just looking out your car window on the highway, but this area boasts some impressively scenic locales and ample recreation opportunities, including camping, hiking, biking, fishing, water sports, and boating.

Bikes (mountain, road, hybrid, and tandem) and watercraft (paddleboards, kayaks, and canoes) can be rented at **Outdoor Waco** (215 S. University Parks Dr., 254/300-4448, www.outdoorwaco.com) for reasonable rates. Rental hours are Mon.–Sat. 9 A.M.–9 P.M. and Sun. noon–6 P.M. Outdoor Waco is a great resource for information about local recreation and also serves as a coffee shop (Mon.–Sat. 7 A.M.–9 P.M., Sun. noon–6 P.M.)

Waco Historic Suspension Bridge/Park System

Stretching 475 feet across the Brazos River and built by the same company that built the Brooklyn Bridge, the Waco Historic Suspension Bridge was the longest suspension bridge of its time when it was completed in 1870. The construction required almost 3,000,000 bricks and took two years to build from planning to completion (surprising, considering the sandy river banks shifted constantly, much to the engineers' consternation).

This was no bridge to nowhere. Back in the 1800s, the river presented quite a problem to Chisholm Trail cattle drivers and other commercial entities that needed to get to the other side. Before the bridge, the crossing was costly, time-consuming, and dangerous, usually requiring a ferry. Once it was built, the bridge became a metaphorical connection to Waco's future: The traffic it attracted ensured the town's survival.

Nowadays, the bridge also connects several different parks in the Waco area—Indian Springs Park on the west bank, Martin Luther King, Jr. Park on the east bank—with a landscaped riverwalk leading to the Waco Tourist Information Center, and beyond to Cameron Park 9 University Parks Dr. between Franklin Ave. and Washington Ave.).

Of all the history that surrounds the bridge, this bit is definitely the weirdest: Baylor University students often partake in a longheld tradition of climbing various parts of the bridge to engage in "tortilla tossing," which is, literally, the art of tossing tortillas like a Frisbee into the river. Whether or not this is connected to the fact that Waco is in a dry county is unknown.

Brazos Bluffs Ranch

It's a little tough to believe this relaxing retreat sits less than 10 miles from the Baylor University campus, and even fewer from the whoosh of I-35 traffic. The pastoral setting of the Brazos Bluffs Ranch (5 miles north of Waco, 5 miles west of Elm Mott, 254/722-9182, www.brazosbluffsranch.com) serves as a bucolic backdrop to the many activities Brazos Bluffs (which also serves as a working ranch) has to offer: fishing, canoeing, kayaking, hiking, and horseback riding. Lodging is available in the form of a single, adorable log cabin, built in 2011, that sleeps six.

SHOPS

The shabbiness of "downtown" West belies the quality of the wares sold inside **Olde Czech Corner Antiques** (130 N. Main St., West, 254/286-4094, daily 10:30 A.M.–5:30 P.M.), which has been here since the 1980s. Antiqueshunters will find nirvana in owner Lisa Muska's well-edited collection of dishes, furniture, jewelry, rugs, knickknacks, and art, both from consignment sellers and from Muska's own exploratory shopping forays deep into the crooks and crannies of Texas. Those looking for junk and kitsch should keep searching, however, as this is no ratty flea market. Consider, for instance, the corner rented by the Harris Creek Trading Company (800/732-7842, www.giftsofperfection.net), whose collection of motion clocks and music boxes alone is worth the drive down I-35. The charm of the stores 100+-year-old building, which was erected around a still-standing old water well, only adds to the experience.

At 14,000 square feet and with well over 60 vendors, **Antiquibles** (94300 I-35, Waco, 254/829-1921, www.antiquibles.com, daily 10 A.M.–6 P.M.) is a real whopper of an antiques

mall. Don't get too distracted, though, because the mall also houses the world's largest museum dedicated to dogs. Admission is free.

There's some junk at **Timeless Treasures** (1301 N. Loop 340, Waco, 254/799-2464, www.timelesstreasureswaco.com, Tues.–Sat. 10:30 A.M.–6 P.M., Sun. 1–5 P.M.), sure, but also tons of jewelry, purses and bags, and gewgaws galore.

HOTELS

Located in the middle of Waco's refurbished downtown, **The Camille House Bed & Breakfast** (1515 Columbus Ave., Waco, 254/235-0768, www.thecamillehousebandb. com, $115–175) provides a cute and relaxing alternative to the chain hotels and motels that flank I-35. The four queen-size rooms all come with television and free wireless Internet. Owners Ronnie and Michael Fanning offer a variety of discounts related to Baylor sports, so calling to inquire about rates is advised. More on the luxurious side, **The Cotton Palace** (1910 Austin Ave., Waco, 254/753-7294, www.thecottonpalace.com, starting at $120) offers five-star environs and a gourmet breakfast at central Texas prices.

Hillsboro's **Windmill B&B** (441 Hill County Rd., 254/582-7373, www.windmillnbb.com, starting at $90) is named for the quaint windmill that anchors the rose garden, which sits amid 21 acres of old-growth pecan and oak trees. The rooms here are a bargain.

GETTING THERE

Hillsboro, West, and Waco are all straight shots down I-35, pretty much equidistant from either Dallas or Fort Worth. Hillsboro (65 miles, approximately an hour and 15 minutes to drive) is farthest north and closest to the Metroplex, followed by West (80 miles, an approximately 1.5-hour drive), then Waco (100 miles, an approximately two-hour drive). Greyhound Bus services all three cities from Dallas-Fort Worth, but it is not recommended, as visitors will still most likely require cars to see the scattered sights.

Texoma

The area flanked by I-35 and I-75 north of DFW is known as Texoma—so named for its proximity to the Texas-Oklahoma border. Although dozens of small towns dot the Texoma map, activity centers around the region's twin towns, Sherman and Denison, which are about 10 minutes apart via Highway 89. The two towns are bitter rivals in some respects. The annual football game between the Denison and Sherman high schools, for instance, is called "The Battle of the Ax," and it's something straight out of *Friday Night Lights*. The Sherman natives also tease Denison citizens for living closer to Oklahoma.

For the most part, though, Texomaland is marked by "small-town values," bucolic expanses, and a "ya'll come back now" charm—it's a very Texas-y place. While its latest claim to fame is as the hometown of the Hudson Hero, Captain Chesley B. Sullenberger III (who was born and raised in Denison), the area also spawned famous former Speaker of the House Sam Rayburn and former president Dwight D. Eisenhower.

Other Texoma attractions include the small liberal arts Austin College and Kelly Square—both in Sherman—and the huge Lake Texoma, formed by the damming of the Red River (which also makes up the border between Texas and Oklahoma), to the north of Denison.

SIGHTS
Sherman
Sherman is a good introduction to the lay of the land. As the seat of Grayson County, this town of 37,000 proves a little more hopping than many of the smaller hamlets that surround it. Part of the energy is due to the presence of **Austin College** (900 N. Grand Ave., 903/813-2000), a small liberal arts school with about 1,200 students. The oldest college in the state still operating under its original charter, AC's campus is small and strollable. Make sure to check out the bookstore, where you can find plenty of paraphernalia featuring the school's mascot, the kangaroo.

◖ Kelly Square
Downtown Sherman's flagship is Kelly Square (115 W. Travis St.), a collection of cafés and antiques and knickknacks shops that take up a block of downtown. An adorable, turn-of-the-20th-century setting, Kelly Square is actually four old buildings refurbished and connected. Antiques lovers will really like the **American Victorian Furniture Museum** (201 E. Lamar St., 903/893-7509, Tues.–Sat. 10 A.M.–4 P.M., free), while history buffs will enjoy the **Red River Historical Museum** (301 S. Walnut St., 903/983-7623, Tues.–Sat. 10 A.M.–4 P.M., free), which displays everything from old farm equipment to antique china.

Dwight D. Eisenhower Birthplace State Historic Site
To find the Dwight D. Eisenhower Birthplace State Historic Site (609 S. Lamar Ave., Denison, 903/465-8908, Tues.–Sat. 9 A.M.–5 P.M., Sun. 1–5 P.M., $4 adults, $3 6–18, free 5 and under), head north up Business 75 toward Denison's Main Street. From there, head south on Crockett Street to Nelson Street, then west to Lamar Avenue. The main feature of the site is the two-story house in which Eisenhower was born, coupled with the visitor center's small museum. The site also includes six acres of hiking ground, some of which lead to the Denison Dam, where bald eagles often seek out fish during the winter.

Hagerman National Wildlife Refuge
This 11,000-acre refuge (6465 Refuge Rd., Sherman, 903/786-2826, free), open year-round from dawn to dusk, dominates the southern end of a jutting section of Lake Texoma. Here you'll find excellent birding, fishing, picnicking, and boating (even some limited hunting is allowed). The visitor center (Mon.–Fri. 7:30 A.M.–4 P.M., Sat. 9 A.M.–4 P.M., Sun. 1–4 P.M.) provides auto tour maps and other information.

Dwight D. Eisenhower was born in Denison, Texas.

© TRAVELTEX.COM

EXCURSIONS

Lake Texoma

You'll find Lake Texoma fairly accessible from just about any town in the area. One of the largest reservoirs in the country, Lake Texoma is an extremely popular place for recreation—in fact, on weekends it can be tough to find a secluded spot. Anglers, sailboaters, and other water recreationists count Texoma as one of their favorite destinations.

Fishing is almost a must at Lake Texoma, so guides abound. **Rex Bridges Fishing and Hunting** (800/211-7808) is one of the most popular, and down-home, services, offering six-hour trips, private charters, cleaning and bagging services for fishing, and a number of other options for duck hunters.

Because Lake Texoma boasts one of the most liberal striper fishing limits in the country, the services of licensed striper fishing guide **Steve Brewster** (111 Cambridge Shores Dr., Pottsboro, 903/818-2507, www.fishstriper.com) are called upon often. Brewster provides bait, rods, reels, and, sometimes, lodging. Two other good guide companies are **Stripers Inc.** (300 Little Mineral Rd., Pottsboro, 903/815-1609, www.stripersinc.com), and **Captain John Brett's Texoma Striper Fishing** (903/786-9279, www.texomastriperfishing.com).

Sam Rayburn Library and Museum

The other political figure from these parts was Sam Rayburn, perhaps the nation's most famous Speaker of the House, a title he held for 17 of the 49 years he spent as a representative from Texas. Although Rayburn wasn't born in Texas, as a youth his family moved to Bonham and settled into the 12-room home that now serves as the Sam Rayburn Library and Museum (800 W. Sam Rayburn Dr., Bonham, 903/583-5558, Mon.–Fri. 10 A.M.–5 P.M., Sat. 1–5 P.M., free). Rayburn established the library before his death as a gift to his beloved hometown. Besides its existence as a research library, the building houses a replica of the Speaker of the House's private Washington office, as well as memorabilia from his life.

RESTAURANTS

This area isn't exactly known for its cuisine, but a few decent spots can be mentioned.

THE BATTLE OF THE AX

Lest you think *Friday Night Lights* exaggerates the influence of high school football in Texas, behold the Battle of the Ax—the oldest football rivalry in the Lone Star State. Sherman versus Denison. A Texoma Armageddon.

These two towns, just a few miles apart, have so much in common. They hover around similar populations: Sherman's 38,000; Denison's 22,000. Both sit on the jagged border between Texas and Oklahoma. Both share a common core of small-town values.

Yet when it comes to football, these towns are all Hatfield and McCoy. The rivalry began innocently enough, with a game in 1901 between the Denison Yellow Jackets and Sherman Bearcats. Sherman won on that particular battle, and most of the subsequent ones (although both schools have had their time as state champs and powerhouses.)

As the years went by, the intensity grew, until it was so heated, the postgame traditions started taking a violent turn to vandalism. That's when a Denison businessman, Jack Barker, who owned an ice cream shop, offered up a symbol of sportsmanship, to be given to the winner: An ax. Why an ax? Who knows?

The violence ceased, but the intensity built: The battle is now previewed, reviewed, and live-blogged. Its every nuance is studied by coach and townsperson alike. Television coverage begins months beforehand. Young student-athletes are interviewed as if they were on ESPN. Prayers are lifted unto the heavens, begging the good Lord above to guide various players into the promised land of the end zone.

To the victor goes the symbolic ax, carved with the names of winning teams of the past. To the loser goes the head-hanging shame. Moms will hug their sons, dads will pat their backs, and the community will sit under a collective cloud of sadness.

Until, after a few weeks pass, and the crack of shoulder pads and helmets knocking rouses a familiar hope: There's always next year.

You'll find the cute diner **Fried Pie** (202 W. Main St., Gainesville, 940/665-7641) a little off your path, but close to Lake Texoma, and the fried namesakes are only $1.50 and worth a few extra miles. A good Lake Texoma choice, **Pelican's Landing** (500 Harbour View Rd., Gordonville, 903/523-4500, winter Wed.–Thurs. 11 A.M.–8 P.M. Fri. 11 A.M.–10 P.M., Sat.–Sun. 8 A.M.–8 P.M., summer Wed.–Thurs. 11 A.M.–9 P.M., Fri. 11 A.M.–10 P.M., Sat. 8 A.M.–8 P.M., Sun. 8 A.M.–9 P.M., $10–20) is popular among locals. **Huck's** (2811 Trail Dr., 903/337-0033) specializes in hand-breaded fried catfish. For barbecue, try **Cackle & Oink** (3210 Texoma Pkwy., Sherman, 903/981-3200) or **Hickory House** (630 W. Woodard St., Denison, 903/463-3600, Mon.–Fri. 11 A.M.–7 P.M., Sat. 11 A.M.–2 P.M., under $10). Coffee shops are hard to find, but **Country Java** (514 W. Main St., Denison, 903/327-8984) does the trick.

NIGHTLIFE

Ask any Austin College student about Texoma nightlife, and they'll likely give you and incredulous stare; after all, this place ain't Dallas. Still, a few spots are hoppin' on Friday and Saturday nights. **Loose Wheels** (4716 Pool Rd., Denison, 903/464-9119, www.loose-wheelstexas.com) welcomes bikers and honky-tonkers, especially during the weekend when live country bands play. The bar is built out of an old Air Force radar tower, and house rules include "Only positive attitudes allowed," "No drinks on the dance floor," and "No pissing contests." Fair enough.

The oldest bar in Grayson County, the **Good Time Lounge** (2520 TX 91 N., Denison, 903/463-6086, www.goodtimelounge.com) bills itself as "Texomaland's only real alternative nightclub." That it is, to be sure, attracting most of the GLBT community in the area. Don't expect the glitz and glamor of big-city discos here, however; the Good Time Lounge is a dive, out in the middle of the country. Still, it's a unique experience to visit there. Denison also is home to **Calhoun's** (4801 Texoma Pkwy., 903/463-3561), a honky-tonk that attracts a lot of students from Austin College.

SHOPS

You could spend all day at this three–story antique emporium, with its 150 booths of organized and, frankly, sometimes underpriced offerings. **A Touch of Class Antique Mall** (228 W. Lamar St., Sherman, 903/891-9379, www.antiquestexas.com, Mon.–Sat. 9:30 A.M.–5:30 P.M.) also serves as Sherman's visitor center, with plenty of pamphlets by the front door, although just asking a friendly local for recommendations might be the way to go.

Collectors will find themselves in heaven at the sight of the wild bounty of military gear dating back to the Civil War at vintage military collectibles store **Grandpa's Footlocker** (308 E. Houston St., Sherman, 903/870-0002, Mon.–Fri. 9 A.M.–5 P.M., Sat. 9 A.M.–1 P.M.). This is no surplus store; the inventory runs the gamut from coins and flags to historic military vehicle parts.

What the heck this hip kids' apparel boutique is doing in the quiet downtown of a tiny Texas town is anyone's guess, but why question a place that provides such natty threads for the younger set? **Posh Little Pig** (125 N. Travis St., Sherman, 903/870-4040, www.poshlittlepig.com, Mon.–Fri. 10:30 A.M.–5 P.M., Sat. 10 A.M.–2 P.M.) stocks adult-quality attire for babies and toddlers, including stunningly adorable holiday dresses, Petunia Pickle Bottom wallets and bags, and even duds for that oft-overlooked population, toddler boys.

HOTELS

Sprawled over 900 acres, **The Tanglewood Resort** (290 Tanglewood Cir., Pottsboro, 800/833-6569, www.tanglewoodresort.com, $100–450) doesn't exactly meld with its forested lakeside environment—the place rather resembles a huge Embassy Suites plopped next to a lake—but it can't be beat for amenities. The resort's swimming pools, golf course, large rooms, outside tennis and basketball courts, and business facilities please pretty much all crowds. The place is flexible, too: Rooms can accommodate parties of one to eight.

Moms and dads up for Austin College's Parents' Weekend might consider **Hart's Country Inn** (601 N. Grand Ave., Sherman, 903/892-2271, $125 d), a beautifully restored Victorian divided into five different rooms, directly across the street from the school. If you prefer Denison, try the **Inn of Many Faces** (412 W. Morton St., Denison, 903/465-4639, $110–140), a rambling, turreted Victorian with gorgeous rooms and fair prices.

GETTING THERE

The gateway to Texomaland, Sherman is accessible from Dallas via an hour-long drive north up I-75 (a distance of around 60 miles). There are a number of ways to get there from Fort Worth. The easiest is to take North I-35 West, then taking exit 498A to US 82 East, turning right on Farm to Market Rd. 131 North/Travis Street, then left on Lamar Street. The 90-mile drive from Fort Worth takes about an hour and 45 minutes to two hours. Greyhound Bus has stops in Texoma but, like many day destinations, it would be difficult to navigate locally without a car.

Grapevine

As you approach Grapevine from Highway 114 (coming from either Fort Worth or Dallas), don't be disheartened by the vast expanses of freeways, strip malls, and Chili's restaurants; when you get to the heart of it, Grapevine is a hidden Texas treasure. Strangely, even though Grapevine is home to such modern entities as the ginormous Dallas-Fort Worth International Airport, the town is deeply dedicated to preserving its heritage, at least that of its historic downtown section—it's here, amid many of Grapevine's well-known sights, where this town of about 45,000 shows its pride in restored buildings, quaint restaurants, and year-round festivals.

SIGHTS

◀ Grapevine Vintage Railroad

If you're beginning in Fort Worth, a good way to

EXCURSIONS

get to town is by hopping aboard the Grapevine Vintage Railroad (817/410-3123, www.grapevinesteamrailroad.com, $20) in the Stockyards. The train will drop you at the depot in downtown Grapevine, where you'll also find the **Grapevine Heritage Center** (701 South Main St., 817/424-0516, www.grapevinehistory.org). The center provides visitor information, maps, and itinerary suggestions, as well as housing a blacksmith, leather shop, and farmers market.

Grapevine is named after the mustang grapes that grow wild all across the region, and town denizens have finally started putting those grapes to use. Now Grapevine is known as an up-and-coming vintner's region, and it seems every few feet yields a new vineyard, wineshop, or tasting room. Try **Homestead** (211 E. Worth St., 817/251-9463, www.homesteadwinery.com, $5), a tasting room dedicated to regional wines only.

Great Wolf Lodge

Not all of Grapevine's highlights are quaint, however. Great Wolf Lodge (100 Great Wolf Lodge Rd., 817/722-3931, www.greatwolf. com), for instance, is a monstrous complex consisting of an indoor water park and other grand-scale diversions meant mainly for kids, to go along with hotel rooms. Kids love the place, though parents eye it warily with one hand on their wallet.

Grapevine Mills Mall

The Grapevine Mills Mall (3000 Grapevine Mills Pkwy., #214, 972/691-8559, www. grapevinemills.com) may not fall under the picturesque category, but it remains popular nonetheless as an outlet center. The *huge* (1.6 million square feet) mall has remained a consistent favorite, drawing shoppers from as far away as Oklahoma, mainly because of

EXCURSIONS

PUTTING THE "GRAPE" IN GRAPEVINE

The Mustang grapes that once grew wildly in the area gave Grapevine its name, but these days, Grapevine has become a hotbed for wine culture. On pleasant weekends, hundreds of DFW wine-lovers make their way to the small town, located almost equidistant between Dallas and Fort Worth, to sip new vintages and savor old favorites.

Note that vineyards and tasting rooms often host private parties and thus occasionally are closed during regular hours. In the case of public special events, they may offer extended regular hours. A good rule of thumb is to always call ahead.

CROSS TIMBER WINERY

Housed in one of the ten oldest structures remaining in Grapevine, this tasting room features wines from the town's sister city, Parras de la Fuente, Mexico. 805 N. Main St., 817/488-6789, www.crosstimerswinery.com.

DELANEY WINERY

While many of Grapevine's wineries are relatively small, Delaney is lush with roomy grounds and 10 acres of vines. The free half-hour tours that commence every hour cover everything from growing to bottling. Tastings begin every half-hour and cost $10 for a sampling of six different wines. Delaney Winery does things on a larger scale than most of the local tasting spots and is a popular locale for weddings, corporate events, and the popular harvest grape stomp. 2000 Champagne Blvd., 817/481-5668, www.delaneyvineyards.com.

D'VINE WINE

D'Vine has more than 32 different wines in production, including a chocolate/raspberry port and a blackberry merlot. 409 S. Main St., 817/329-1011, www.divinewineusa.com

HOMESTEAD WINERY AT GRAPEVINE

The winery's super-cute, single-story Victorian home provides a great atmosphere for chilling out and sipping any number of the handful of reds and wide variety of whites offered at Homestead. Try the strong, full-bodied merlot (but only if you have a designated driver—the sucker's alcohol content registers more than 14 percent). 211 E. Worth St., 817/251-9463, www.homesteadwinery.com, Mon.-Sat. 11 A.M.-5:30 P.M., Sun. noon-5:30 P.M.

its high-quality discount stores: Last Call by Neiman Marcus, Nike, and Saks 5th Avenue's Off 5th, to name a few.

RESTAURANTS

Mmm...a bowl of chili at **Tolbert's** (423 S. Main St., 817/421-4888, www.tolbertsrestaurant.com, Mon.–Thurs. 11 A.M.–9 P.M., Fri.–Sat. 11 A.M.–9:30 P.M., Sun. 11 A.M.–7 P.M., under $10) simply can't be beat, especially in such charming historic surroundings as this tin-roofed, brick-walled café. **Bread Haus** (700 W. Dallas Rd., 817/488-5223, www.breadhaus. com) bakes luscious loaves daily, and its bars, cookies, and scones are delightfully sinful. If you're looking for someplace to wear your fancy boots, a dramatic limestone staircase and beautiful views greet visitors to the "casual elegant" **Vineyard Steakhouse** (1000 Texan Trail, 817/328-6111, www.vineyardsteakhouse.com,

Mon.–Thurs. 4–10 P.M., Fri. 4–11 P.M., Sat. 5–11 P.M., Sun. 5–10 P.M., $20 and up), one of the most popular (and nicer) restaurants in Grapevine.

NIGHTLIFE

If you're seeking out a true Texas evening, top it off with some boot-scooting at this honky-tonk. **Back Porch Tavern and Grill** (210 N. Main St., 817/251–8434, www.backporchtavern, Mon.–Thurs. 11 A.M.–midnight, Fri.–Sat. 11 A.M.–2 A.M., Sun. noon–10 P.M.) is a place where the C&W flows as liberally as the beer.

The vibe is a little looser at **Skybar** (1000 Texan Trail, 817/328-6111, www.vineyard-steakhouse.com, Mon.–Thurs. 4–10 P.M., Fri. 4–11 P.M., Sat. 5–11 P.M., Sun. 5–10 P.M.) than the downstairs Vineyard Steakhouse to which it is attached. You'll find some sweet views here that serve as a dramatic backdrop to the mellow

---

LA BUENA VIDA VINEYARDS

The grapes for the wines offered at La Buena Vida actually are grown in nearby Springtown but served here by the taste, by the glass, by the bottle, and in bottles to go. Definitely stick around to sip yours among the cool fountains, lush greenery, and Spanish tile. The winery boasts three different labels: Buena Vida, Springtown, and Walnut Creek, all locally produced, and specializes in ports. Let's not forget the vineyard's sister winery, La Bodega, which is the world's only winery located in an airport (Terminal A, Gate A15, and Terminal D, Gate D15 in Dallas-Fort Worth International Airport, to be exact.)

True to its commitment to the good life, Buena Vida also provides low-key live musical entertainment (often jazz) on Thursday evenings and on Saturday afternoons. 416 E. College St., 817/481-9463, www.labuenavida.com, Sun.-Tues. noon-5 P.M., Thurs. noon-8 P.M., Fri. noon-7 P.M., Sat. 10 A.M.-7 P.M.

SU VINO WINERY

Laid-back and friendly, the Su Vino Winery and tasting room has all the usual reds and whites,

made from their own varietals, but the site also features an interactive aspect: Visitors have the opportunity to bottle and cork their own wines, complete with custom-made labels. Su Vino also stocks a number of epicurean items—such as condiments, cheeses, and chocolate sauces—made with their wine, along with gift baskets, cute kitchen items and Texas-themed gifts. 120 S. Main St., 817/424-0123, Tues.-Sat, noon-7 P.M., Sun. 1-5 P.M.

WINE TRAILS

Organized wine trails, which involve a prepaid charge and stops at several different wineries, are also popular and a good deal. Here are some of the most trafficked offerings (keep in mind prices and dates vary, so go to www.grapevinetexasusa.org for up-to-date details):

· **Valentine Wine Trail** (Feb. 14 and 15)
· **New Vintage Wine Trail** (mid-April)
· **July the Fourth Wine Trail** (July 4 and 5)
· **Halloween Wine Trail** (Oct. 30)
· **Holiday Wine Trail** (early December)

EXCURSIONS

acoustic bands that work the room, along with a heady selection of more than 200 wines.

Definitely embracing historic kitsch (right down to the indoor antique car that references the space's original existence as a gas station), **Willhoite's** (432 S. Main St., 817/481-7511, www.willhoites.com, daily 11 A.M.–2 A.M.) is the place to go for karaoke, live music, and the occasional friendly biker crowds.

SHOPS

This area centered around Main Street in downtown Grapevine couldn't possibly boast a more densely packed collection of shops and boutiques. Two favorites are **Ooh La La** (408 S. Main St., 817/329-8636, www.oohlalatx. com, Mon.–Wed. 10 A.M.–6 P.M., Thurs–Sat. 10 A.M.–8 P.M., Sun., noon–5 P.M.), with its adorable collection of fashionable women's apparel and accessories, and **Coyote Cowboy** (417 S. Main St., 817/481-1315, www.coyotecowboy.com, Mon.–Thurs. 10 A.M.–6 P.M., Fri.–Sat. 10 A.M.–7 P.M., Sun. 1–5 P.M.), a slightly tongue-in-cheek shop with men's and women's Western wear. But it's not just about clothes; downtown Grapevine's shopping array runs a delightful gamut from British goods at **British Emporium** (140 N. Main St., 817/421-2311, www.british-emporium.com, Mon.–Sat. 10 A.M.–6 P.M., Sun. noon–5 P.M.) to tons of antiques shops.

HOTELS

The **Garden Manor Bed and Breakfast** (205 E. College St., 817/424-9177, www.gardenmanorbandb.com, $199 d) is the only lodging within the historic downtown area of Grapevine, and with only four rooms, it's in hot demand. In addition to its charm—each room follows a specific garden theme—the B&B's location can't

be beat; it's mere steps from the best parts of Grapevine, yet only seven miles from Dallas-Fort Worth International Airport.

In contrast to Grapevine's small-town feel, the mega-behemoth of the **Gaylord Texan Resort and Convention Center** (1501 Gaylord Tr., 817/778-1000, www.gaylordhotels.com/gaylord-texan, $175 d) feels more like a Las Vegas casino than your usual hotel. Once you pass through the looking glass, you'll find 4.5 acres of *indoor* gardens and waterways, more than 1,500 rooms, the Glass Cactus nightclub, and more restaurants than some small towns.

GETTING THERE

From Fort Worth, Loop 820 will take you to Hwy. 121 North, which you should take north/east until you get to the Williams D. Tate exit for Hwy. 114. Take the exit, keeping left at the fork and following the signs for 114/William D. Tate Ave. Take a left on William D. Tate, a right on W. Dallas Rd., and then a left on Main Street. The 25-mile drive should run about half an hour.

From Dallas, take the Stemmons Freeway to Hwy. N. 183 W., then connect to Hwy. 114 W. (follow the signs to Grapevine/Airport North Entry). From here merge onto Hwy. 121 and then exit on Hwy. 114 Frontage Rd., then take a right onto Main St. The drive also spans about 25 miles and a half an hour.

A refurbished Victorian train, The Grapevine Vintage Railroad (aka the Tarantula Train), takes visitors from the Fort Worth Stockyards straight to downtown Grapevine on Saturday and Sunday, this includes a "train robbery" stop). Service is rather limited, however, and it's pricey: $2–28 for adults, $10–18 for kids, round-trip. Check www.gvrr.com for schedules and information.

BACKGROUND

The Land

GEOGRAPHY

The Dallas-Fort Worth Metroplex is located in what is known simply as "North Texas," an area in the state just south of the Red River that separates Texas from Oklahoma. The term "North Texas" is a touch misleading, since the Panhandle is technically farther north, but DFW is indeed in the upper central part of the state, in what is known as the Blackland Prairie area of the Great Plains.

The Blackland Prairie stretches from the Red River down to San Antonio, about 6.1 million hectares in all, marked by a variety of clay soils and diverse tallgrasses, dominated by Indian grass and little bluestem. For centuries, the vegetation here was "disturbance maintained"—that is, growth of the grass was kept in check by grazing bison herds and periodic fires (which are still common today). The consistent maintenance also prevented a dense buildup of trees, and to this day the highest concentration of trees can be found around rivers, streams, and other bodies of water

What all these dry facts add up to is this: While both cities camouflage their geographic attributes with loads of concrete and asphalt, a short drive away from either reveals the area's Great Plains beauty. Gentle hills covered in prairie grass roll on for miles, and the wide-open sky unfurls.

© KENNY BRAUN/TRAVELTEX/MUSEUM OF NATURAL HISTORY, DALLAS

In springtime, vibrant wildflowers like bluebonnets, Indian paintbrushes, and black-eyed Susans blanket meadows and highway dividers alike. And the vegetation attracts wildlife, both in rural and urban areas. It's not uncommon to see a hawk swooping amid downtown buildings or a possum in someone's backyard. Deer and bird hunting are popular in nearby locales.

Although Dallas and Fort Worth are almost identical in terms of vegetation, wildlife, geography, and climate, the two cites retain a few topographical differences. The edge of the Austin Chalk Formation escarpment runs north-south through Dallas, and its 200-foot rise is most noticeable in the Oak Cliff section of town, but does not affect Fort Worth. For the most part, however, the two cities are relatively flat, and low—elevation is well below 1,000 feet.

CLIMATE

DFW has four seasons—barely. Actually, maybe it's closer to three, with winter losing out.

Summertime is infernally hot, exacerbated by the intense humidity that couples the 90-plus-degree temperatures. The heat index (a gauge, based on temperature and humidity, of what the air feels like to the body) regularly climbs well into the 100s. Of course, so does the regular temperature. Don't be surprised at

heat waves with the mercury topping 100 several days in a row.

Fall, meantime, is pleasant, though not "fall-like" in the sense that, say, folks from the East Coast might relate to. While the summer heat drags well into September, the leaves and air begin to change in October and November. A cold front, or "blue norther," might come through bringing chilly temperatures, but for the most part fall is mild, with nice days and jacket-necessitating nights. Fall is a time when many DFW denizens engage in outdoor activities.

Winter is dry and quite mild, often difficult to discern from fall. The mercury during the season hangs between the 55 and 70 degree marks, occasionally punctuated by a winter storm, during which the temperature plummets to below freezing. When coupled with precipitation, usually in the form of freezing rain, these storms wreak havoc on North Texas drivers, who are unused to navigating slick roads. It rarely snows.

Spring is the area's most dynamic season. During this time of year, the warm, moist airflow from the Gulf of Mexico often collides with dry, cold air from the north, causing extraordinary volatility. Strong, often dangerous, storms are thus common during spring in North Texas, and tornados, high winds, lightning, and hail are facts of life during the season.

History

DALLAS

The history of Dallas is based very much on Dallas business. Considering the player Dallas has become in the world economy, it's no surprise the city was founded by a man looking to trade (and, considering Dallas's one-of-a-kind character, it's no surprise the guy was half crazy).

In 1841, John Neely Bryan, an Indian trader from Tennessee, parked himself on a bluff overlooking the Trinity River near where Dealey Plaza is today. He planned to establish

an outpost there to deal with the local Caddo Indians.

The problem was, after a treaty pushed the Native Americans out, Bryan didn't have much of a customer base. So, knowing an extension of the Preston trail was due to pass through the area, he decided to establish a permanent commercial settlement instead. Bryan staked his claim, scrabbling together a population with pioneers lured from nearby settlements. From the beginning, Bryan worked hard to ensure the survival of his outpost—he was the town ferry

WHO THE HECK IS "DALLAS," ANYWAY?

The only surviving bit of information we have today about how **John Neely Bryan** named his town is that he chose to do it "after my friend, Dallas."

Not super helpful there, Mr. Bryan—there are a lot of people that could be. To this day, nobody really knows the identity of the "Dallas" after whom the city is named.

The most popular candidate is George Mifflin Dallas, who was James Polk's vice president. Yet Bryan's town was known as Dallas well before Polk became president, and moreover, George Mifflin Dallas and Bryan probably never met, so chances are they were never friends. (To confuse matters, records state that Dallas *county*, established several years after the town, was officially named after the veep.)

A second candidate is George's brother, Commodore Alexander Dallas, who fought against piracy in the Gulf of Mexico. Then there's Walter Dallas, who fought against Mexico in the battle of San Jacinto, or possibly *his* brother, who was a Texas Ranger.

In all honesty, we'll probably never know. But that's okay—Dallasites tend to look forward, rather than back.

operator, postmaster, and primary landholder. At the time, Texas was a free republic, having recently won its independence from Mexico. The Texas frontier was rapidly pushing west, and it didn't take long for Bryan's little town to start taking shape.

By 1846, Texans had voted overwhelmingly to join the United States. By 1850, Dallas counted 430 citizens. Dallas County had been organized, and the town of Dallas was designated as county seat.

Around 1855, a unique, colossal failure helped shape Dallas's cultural future. A few years before, a French socialist by the name of Victor Prosper Considérant had established a utopian colony in North Texas, near the site where Bryan had established his commercial one. The French colony, which went by the name La Réunion, was meant to function as a direct democracy, by which profits were dispersed to individuals in proportion to their labor and monetary investments. While about 2,000 people signed up to join the colony, only about 200 actually made it from France.

The members of La Réunion may have been idealists, but they weren't very good farmers. After about 18 months, the colony went bust, and by 1860, most of its members had dispersed—a good amount of them moving to Dallas.

This mini-diaspora changed Dallas's future.

While the La Réunion members may not have known how to work the land, they were thinkers, artists, and idealists. Their existence laid the cornerstone of Dallas's creative life today, a life manifest by the fertile music scene, the consistently sizzling art scene, and even the rapidly expanding downtown Arts District. For years, before the construction of the American Airlines Center, the main coliseum in Dallas was Reunion Arena, where Dallasites flocked by the thousands to see bands, shows, and other artistic endeavors. The word "Reunion" is still attached to many Dallas entities to this day.

At the time, however, the La Réunion influx meant little compared to the other changes that were occurring. A steady stream of settlers in search of good land continued to make their way to town. By the mid-1850s, the town had its first cotton gin, slaves, newspaper, and a covered toll bridge over the Trinity. In 1856, the Sixth Texas Legislature granted Dallas a city charter, and the town of around 700 adopted its first mayor, Dr. Samuel Pryor, along with a group of aldermen. By 1860, 2,000 people lived in Dallas, and the railroad, sure to attract even more business, visitors, and new citizens, was rapidly approaching.

Then came the Civil War. The townsfolk had voted 741-237 in favor of secession, and when the war began in 1861, Dallas was, for the most part, all for it. Far from the horrors of battle, the city actually benefited from the war. While many locals joined the Confederate Army, Dallas's primary role was as a transportation hub and supplier—yet another precursor to the city's role as a center of commerce. Specifically, the town served as a quartermaster and commissary post for the Trans-Mississippi Army of the Confederacy; built a munitions factory; and acted as a storage and transportation hub.

Because Dallas suffered little, if any, damage due to the war, it boomed during Reconstruction. While the fate and economy of many Southern towns plunged due to destroyed infrastructure, Dallas's commercial strength and prairie soil held promise. Many Southerners—their plantations destroyed—flocked to the area to take advantage of the fine land, while others, including a good deal of freedmen, realized Dallas was one of the few places where jobs could be found.

The postwar boom coincided with another key factor: developments in transportation. For years, after it turned out the Trinity River was unnavigable, Dallas had been held back from becoming a major player by its isolation. Dallas needed rail lines. In the 1870s, it got them, first the Houston and Texas Central, then the Texas and Pacific, and then the Missouri-Kansas-Texas. Suddenly, Dallas enjoyed a huge regional presence as a transportation hub, specifically for cotton, grain, leather, and buffalo products. Businesspeople, merchants, and entrepreneurs set up shop along the rail lines. By 1880, the population had jumped to more than 10,000 people.

From there, Dallas's maturation as a business center—and thus as a full-blown city—began picking up steam. From the latter part of the 19th century through the early part of the 20th, Dallas grew into the world's biggest inland cotton market as well as the world's leading manufacturer of saddlery and cotton gin parts, in addition to leading the region in a myriad other markets—wholesale liquor, printing, and jewelry, to name a few. Banks and insurance companies led by men whose names now adorn city street signs (Gaston, Ross, Kessler) cropped up

around the new industries. The industrial gains spawned social and cultural ones. Dallas now had two major newspapers, several schools, ready-to-wear department stores, a hospital, telephones, a state fair, a board of trade, electricity, and its first steel skyscraper, the 15-story Praetorian Building, built in 1907.

For the next couple of decades, Dallas continued to grow—by 1920, the population was 159,000—in a less than dynamic way. The federal government helped it along by designating it as a site for a Federal Reserve Bank, and on the north side of town, Southern Methodist University broke ground. A Ford Motor Company plant moved in, and the city expanded through the annexation of Oak Lawn and Oak Cliff. Perhaps most significantly, aviation became a factor during World War I, when Love Field was established as a training ground, for which the already established Fair Park was also used.

But it was oil that knocked Dallas up a peg. In 1930, an enormous oil field was discovered in East Texas, not too far from Dallas, spawning a dramatic boom. Even as the Great Depression loomed, Dallas quickly became the business and financial center for the oil economy of the entire region, even Oklahoma, and continued its pace of rapid construction. The money flowed, the building cornerstones were laid, until finally the force of the worldwide downturn, coupled with overproduction (a habit Dallas finds hard to break) overcame the upward momentum. The Depression finally hit Dallas as hard as any place: 18,000 people had lost their jobs by mid-1931.

While the oil boom had helped slightly soften the blow, it took another bit of drama to not just pull Dallas out of the Depression's downward spiral, but also to lay the foundation for the 20th- and 21st-century powerhouse the city was to become. World War II yanked Dallas from its status as a mid-level manufacturing center and into a role as a global leader. It began with war-related industries, such as aviation, that pushed industrial employment to 75,000. New attendant industries sprang up, at the rate of five new businesses a day and 13 new manufacturing plants a month by 1949. The modern presence in Dallas of huge, international private aeronautic and defense companies is but one legacy of the war.

Industrial money spawned entrepreneurship, a trend nowhere more noticeable than in the case of Texas Instruments' Jack Kilby. One of the unsung heroes of technology pioneering, Kilby perfected a version of the integrated circuit in 1958. Although the Silicon Valley story overshadows his efforts, and those of other Dallas tech innovators, Kilby and his ilk helped kick-start Dallas's leadership in technology and, later, telecom industries.

In 1974, the Dallas-Fort Worth International Airport opened, and again the business climate surged forward. This time, lured by the airport's convenience, plus Dallas's low cost of living, relatively cheap land, and generous perks, corporations by the dozens began moving their headquarters to the area. Today, more than 10,000 corporations make their homes here, including several Fortune 500 companies.

Today, Dallas is the ninth largest city in the country, home to 1,250,000 people, two airports, billions of dollars in commerce, major sports teams, and many legends. It's probably everything the old Arkansas tradesman Bryan could ever have dreamt of. By the way, after shooting a man, years of battling the bottle, and a struggle with mental problems, Bryan died in the state insane asylum. His story is proof that, no matter how much business Dallas does, it will never lose its wild streak.

FORT WORTH

It never really was all that much of a fort.

In May 1849, Major Ripley S. Arnold arrived at the confluence of the Clear Fork and the West Fork of the Trinity River. He had been commissioned with establishing a fort at the far western edge of the boundary between the farthest settlements and Indian country. Sixty miles north of the closest fort, Arnold and his Company F of the U.S. Second Dragoons staked their claim.

Even though it nudged up against Indian country, the area Arnold had chosen had some

things going for it. The most important attribute was location: It was atop a high bluff (where the county courthouse stands today), affording a 360-degree view for miles, which allowed the soldiers ample advance knowledge of local Comanche and Wichita raiding parties.

The real threat at the time, however, wasn't from any raid—it was cholera, which was ravaging the tribes and settlers alike. The death rates from the disease had jumped considerably in 1849 as it raged across the West, regardless of age, sex, or status. Cholera, in fact, took the life of Mexican War hero General Jenkins Worth, and thus Arnold named his fort in Worth's honor.

The native tribes never amounted to much of a threat, and you can't battle cholera with guns, so the site proved more of an outpost than a fort. Arnold and his men built quarters, storage, and a few other structures, but as far as fanciful ramparts, turrets, or even fences were concerned, there were none. At the peak of its four-year run, the fort hosted a maximum of about 70 men, housed in neat, whitewashed log and wooden houses, with nothing but a single six-pound howitzer and a rope fence to guard them.

The entrepreneurial spirit of North Texas is legendary, and it didn't take long for it to kick in among the pioneers Arnold was sent to protect. Two months after the erection of the fort, George Press Farmer became the area's first sutler, licensed by the government to sell goods to the dragoons.

The Western frontier eventually passed Fort Worth by, rendering it obsolete after a mere four years, at which point the fort was simply abandoned. The growing crop of families that lived nearby, many of whom had subsisted by trading with and selling wares to the company of dragoons, moved into the empty buildings rather quickly.

Slowly but surely, Fort Worth began to grow. By 1854, John Peter Smith had opened a school with 12 students. Soon after, a flour mill, general store, and department stores cropped up. The town was a main stop for the Butterfield Overland Mail and Southern Pacific Stage

Line, both of which extended all the way to California. In 1860, Fort Worth wrested the county seat designation away from neighboring Birdville (through a little ingenuity and a lot of, well, cheating). With close to 6,000 residents (850 of which were slaves), Fort Worth was on its way to becoming a bona fide city.

But, while the Civil War and Reconstruction helped Dallas, they almost wiped out Fort Worth. The war was hard on the newly established burg; food, money, and supplies grew scarce. The population dropped to below 200.

It was cattle that saved the town. After the war, the price of cattle in other parts of the country neared $30 a head, while in Texas, it was a mere $5. That got folks to move cattle pretty quickly, and, as part of the Chisholm Trail, Fort Worth became the gateway from Texas to the rest of the world as far as livestock was concerned.

The cattle industry equaled a classic boom. Between 1866 and the mid-1880s, Fort Worth saw about 10 million head of cattle herded through its streets, and the town exploded into a bustling burg of barter and commerce. Cattle were bought and sold, cowhands hired, suppliers haggled with, and general stores perused. Cowboys hitting the trail considered Fort Worth their last hurrah before facing weeks of dust and cow butts. Cowboys returning considered it the place to blow their just-acquired pay after months on the trail. Either way, it wasn't just cattle barons, suppliers, and ranch hands who made money here—it was also saloon keepers, gamblers, and ladies of the night. Actually, it was everybody with a hand in the game.

And there was more to be made right around the corner, if only Fort Worth could lure the railroads. In the late 1870s, it did. The Texas and Pacific began using Fort Worth as its westbound terminus on July 19, 1876, and it could be argued there was no more important day in the history of the city. As other railroads followed—eight of them—they lifted Fort Worth's cattle and wholesale industries to the level of national distribution. Once a trailhead, Fort Worth was now a railhead.

The next few decades were a time of huge growth, and things were a-bustle. The town officially incorporated with a mayor and a city council. Weekly newspapers thrived, modern amenities arrived, and churches, schools, and hospitals were established. Fort Worthers lured two rivals—Swift and Company and Armor and Company—to anchor the burgeoning meatpacking industry. Combined with the stockyard and shipping facilities already in place on the north side of town, this cemented Fort Worth's place as the center of all aspects of the cattle industry.

Three things would change all that. First, technological and ranching innovations slowly eroded the need for the type of centralized cattle processing/shipping Fort Worth had always thrived on. Second, World Wars I and II foisted great changes on Fort Worth, changes that transformed the city forever. With the wars came the aviation and defense industries, which have never left. American Airlines makes its home here, as does Lockheed Martin (formerly General Dynamics)—two enormous entities that play a great role in the local and regional economy.

The third change was oil. The big oil find in the late 1920s just east of the Metroplex shifted the boom from cattle pens to oil rigs. Fort Worth was soaking in oil money.

Nowadays, cattle are still bought and sold in the old Stockyards Exchange Building—via satellite. True to form, Fort Worth has spawned new industries and brought new ones in, in addition to maintaining its deep roots in defense and aviation.

Government and Economy

GOVERNMENT
Dallas

Okay, okay, so former president George W. Bush lives in Dallas, but that doesn't make the entire town Republican, does it? Seriously, even though it exists in one of the reddest states in the Union, and sits at the nexus of the conservative Midwest and the conservative South, Dallas is not as politically right as one might think. In fact, as the city's demographics shift, Dallas proper is starting to head into downright blue.

The 2004 presidential election, 2006 midterm elections, and 2008 presidential election all signaled a potential sea change. In Dallas County in 2004, Democratic presidential candidate John Kerry lost to Republican George W. Bush by just 10,000 votes, or a little over one percentage point. Dallas as a city voted overwhelmingly for Kerry, with 57 percent of votes. The same year saw Hispanic and open lesbian Lupe Valdez elected sheriff.

The 2006 election, though reestablishing Republican holds on state and federal representation, saw huge Democratic gains in the city of Dallas, including the election of a Democrat district attorney and the ousting of scores of Republican judges—41 of 42 seats went to Democrats.

While Dallas mayoral races are officially nonpartisan, the political party leanings of the candidates are always well known, making the elections de facto partisan competitions. In 2006, Republican Tom Leppert defied the leftward trend by defeating openly gay Democrat Ed Oakley (had Oakley won, he would have been the first openly gay mayor of a major city in the U.S.). Leppert's victory was a bit of an anomaly: The past two mayors had been Dallas's first African American mayor, Democrat Ron Kirk, and the rather liberal Democrat Laura Miller, former editor of the left-leaning alt-weekly the *Dallas Observer*.

In 2008, 57 percent of city voters in Dallas voted for Democrat Barack Obama for president. The margin was much closer in Dallas County as a whole, as it was in 2004, but in both cases the entire county still went for the Democratic candidate. The Dallas city/county dichotomy speaks to the dispersal of political parties in the area as a whole, as areas closer to the city center vote more Democratic, while the suburbs lean much more toward Republican.

Fort Worth

Even though it's more laid-back and centered around arts and culture than Dallas, Fort Worth is way more conservative than the big city to the east. Folks here tend to vote to the right. In the past three presidential elections, Tarrant County voters have pulled the lever for the Republican candidate in overwhelming numbers. Fort Worth is also home to Congressman Pete Geren, a rare Fort Worth Democrat, who served as Secretary of the Army under George W. Bush and Barack Obama. Fort Worth's other famous Dem, Jim Wright, served as the 56th Speaker of the House during the 1980s.

ECONOMY

For decades (centuries, really) the raison d'être of the Dallas-Fort Worth area has been commerce. Any interest the region might take in other matters—history, say, or artistic culture—has received only secondary attention, and even then only as appendages to commercial enterprise.

Put more bluntly: Oil, real estate, and business churn the butter here. Almost all of DFW's great cultural achievements, from Dallas's shiny diamond of a cultural district to Fort Worth's revitalized downtown, are merely rarified cream taken from the top. Hell, even our malls have world-class art in them, providing the ultimate symbiosis of capitalism and culture, and one imagines that said mall's J Crew store probably gets a lot more attention than the priceless sculpture that guards it.

The result of this evolution is a strange paradoxical effect: For the sake of commerce and "progress," DFW (although Dallas more so than Fort Worth) has long been willing to tear down or ignore what physical bits of history and culture have managed to survive the years (even the School Book Depository almost shook hands with a wrecking ball a while back). But once the dust settles, we feel guilty about. And, worse, we feel a collective insecurity in the face of other, more "sophisticated" cities that preserve their own history and foster high culture. (And by "other," we mean, for all intents and purposes, New York.)

So we build anew. Boy, do we build. It's been said the official bird of Dallas is a construction crane, so thickly do they lord over the downtown sky. Our insecurity has fueled an almost frantic scramble to prove our worth, manifested in an ever-lengthening list of projects and cultural constructions to which the modifier "world-class" is applied, initiated, paid for, and sustained by civic forces to some extent, but in reality by a handful of philanthropists who are responsible for most of the sights you'll find in this book.

Those sights, by the way, make DFW an attractive place to visit and to live, the latter made even more alluring by the low cost of living, lack of state income tax, and generally high employment rate. The strength of the DFW economy may indeed lie in its lack of sentimentality; the area's full-bore, business-first attitude fosters a constant stream of growth and its economic hardiness often puts up a better fight than most against recession and other national woes. And while oil once wore the crown here, the area is now ruled by a wide variety of industries, many of which have hunkered down with DFW as home base. The defense industry (Lockheed Martin, Bell Helicopter, and Rayethon), huge names in the tech industry (AT&T, HP, and Dell, to list but a few), and American Airlines all maintain a huge presence among many, many other recognizable names.

That said, this doesn't mean the Metroplex doesn't endure its fair share of struggles. The 2010 census data showed poverty on the rise in Dallas-Fort Worth. East and Southern Dallas remain some of the poorest parts of the city, while in Fort Worth, many people on the North, East, and Southwest sides struggle. In 2011, the percentage of Fort Worth families below the poverty line rose from 11.10 percent to 13.20 percent, and the overall poverty rate jumped almost 5 percent.

People and Culture

Let's face it: Texans have a reputation as rednecks and Republicans. Popular culture representation in TV shows like *Dallas* (both incarnations) don't help the widely held notion that the typical Texan is either a squinty-eyed country jackass or a drawly, ruthless oil baron.

The truth? Yes, upon your visit to Dallas-Fort Worth you will see a lot of pickup trucks. You might spy a cowboy hat or two (especially if you're at the rodeo or the Fort Worth Stockyards). If you are really lucky, you'll notice a bolo tie or a set of spurs, but that's not very likely. The DFW area is less a wide-open ranchland than it is a concrete prairie, and most of the population here probably feels more comfortable behind the wheel of car than atop a horse.

The real DFW culture is a friendly, sometimes hodgepodge mix of high and low culture, a place where you can drop $75 on a steak while wearing blue jeans, or where you can ride a mechanical bull while wearing a tuxedo (did y'all know that Gilley's does weddings?). For the most part, save for their football allegiances and accents (which range from almost nonexistence to syrupy), Metroplex denizens are hard to suss out from any other Americans. We tend to don khakis and T-shirts, not chaps and pearl snaps.

While the stereotypes might not hold, don't be fooled: DFW still boasts plenty of Texas flavor, from the traditions of the Texas State

Fair to the alternative country that pours out of Deep Ellum jukeboxes, there's still a twang in the air. It just might not sound the way you thought it would.

DEMOGRAPHICS

Thanks to a generally robust economy, low cost of living, and a surging influx of immigrants from other countries, Texas is one of the fastest growing states in the union when it comes to population, and the growth occurring in both Dallas and Fort Worth follows that trend. The 2011 census estimated the DFW population at 6,526,548, which is up from 1,200,000 from the 2000 census. The population has maintained a steady upward pace. Between July 2008 and July 2009, for instance, 146,530 new residents settled in the area, a gain higher than any other metropolitan area in the country. The city contains 444,000 households, 37.2 percent of which are married couples. The median age of Dallasites is 32.1 years. The racial makeup of the city continues to diversify. While Caucasians are still predominant at 57 percent, the Latino population continues to skyrocket and, at 42 percent of the population, is expected to surpass Caucasians as the majority. Twenty-three percent of Dallas is African American, 2.7 percent Asian, with a smattering of other races filling out the numbers.

Even though it's the 16th most populous city in the nation, Fort Worth is only the fifth biggest city in Texas, with a population of around 741,000 (this is up from 535,000 in 2000). The city contains 135,000 households, 46 percent of which are married couples. Caucasians comprise 50 percent of the population, followed by almost 30 percent Latino and 20 percent African American. When viewing the numbers by age, 8.3 percent of the population is under 18, 11.3 percent from 18 to 24, 32.7 percent from 25 to 44, 18.2 percent from 45 to 64, and 9.6 percent 65 older. The median age is 31.

RACE RELATIONS

The area's history concerning race relations involves a legacy of prejudice, racism, and exclusion (both overt and subtle). In a 2012 editorial, the *Dallas Morning News* stated: "Dallas has a sordid history of racial tension that has never been fully addressed." The same could be said for Fort Worth, although the sordidness there is of a quieter kind.

North Texas was populated from the beginning by primarily white Southerners, who naturally held onto their traditional prejudices and viewpoints and brought them over from their places of origin. Because the area did not endure some of the more dramatic turmoil of the Civil War and consequent Reconstruction, many people think that North Texas race relations have always been more peaceful and tolerant than other parts of the country. This is a consequence of both a misreading of history and of the decades-long effort by many white leaders to perpetuate the myth that Dallas and Fort Worth have always been more interested in business and profits than in oppression and racial violence.

The beginnings of race relations in the Dallas-Fort Worth area mirror much of that of the South. During the Antebellum period, slavery was common practice, and just before the Civil War, violence against slaves ensued in a series of events known as "The Texas Troubles." In July 1860, Dallas endured a devastating fire that destroyed much of the city. Even though the fire occurred during a drought and there was evidence that it was accident, word spread that it had been the work of slaves who were preparing a rebellion against their masters.

Other fires popped up in the area, and paranoia spread as quickly as the flames across the scrubby prairie. In August 1860, a letter supposedly written by a church bishop to local abolitionist minister Reverend Anthony Bewley was "found." The "Bailey Letter," as it was called, purportedly laid out the master plans of an abolitionist plan to join forces with slaves to set fires across the state, murder slave-owners, seize ammunition, and eventually take over the state. Bewley was hanged by a mob in Fort Worth.

Although the authenticity of the Bailey Letter, which was lost and never recovered, is highly questionable, it left even more devastation in its wake. "Texas became a killing field," says historian Michael Phillips, "with historian Alwyn Barr estimating that mobs executed 80 slaves and 37 suspected white abolitionists. As historian Wendell G. Addington suggested, pro-slavery Texans believed it was better to "hang 99 innocent men than to let one guilty one pass."

Reconstruction may have ended slavery, but with the increased profile of the Ku Klux Klan, it brought no respite. Both Fort Worth and Dallas openly and enthusiastically embraced the Klan. Huge chunks of Dallas' power elite belonged to the group, including police, politicians, and a future mayor, R.L. Thornton, after whom a local freeway is named. The Klan similarly dominated actually much of Fort Worth's leading class as well, both civic and private.

The Klan doled out extreme violence with impunity. Dallas authorities turned a blind eye when Klansmen burned the initials KKK into the forehead of a black elevator operator whom they had abducted and whipped. In Fort Worth, a local black gambler was publically tarred and feathered by the Klansmen. The group finally lost its terrible hold on the city at the end of the 1960s when a series of internal financial and sex scandals caused the North Texas Klan to self-destruct.

While both Dallas and Fort Worth remained deeply (and officially) segregated for the majority of the 20th century, much of the Africa American population managed to thrive within their restricted presence in the city. African American citizens were shoved into areas that were cut off by railroad tracks or highways from the rest of the population, such as Deep Ellum in Dallas and the remnants of Hell's Half-Acre in Fort Worth. DFW's entrepreneurial spirit still simmered in these areas, despite the oppression, and it was here that many African American businesses began. Deep Ellum developed into a bustling—if sometimes sketchy—hotspot, full of both legitimate businesses as well as dens of vice. It was here that many legendary African American blues and jazz players made their stops. In Fort Worth, African American newspapers, schools, department stores, and even hospitals cropped up as African Americans began to move in to other parts of town, especially the Como area on the west side of Fort Worth.

Still, tensions remained. Twice in Dallas' history—in 1940–1941 and again in 1950–1951, the homes of African American families moving into primarily white neighborhoods were firebombed. When the Brown vs. Board of Education decisions ended segregation nationally, many businesses complied quickly (some had already desegregated previously), but both cities dragged their feet when it came to integrating schools.

To this day, both cities struggle with the race issue. Despite the election of its first African American mayor, Ron Kirk, in 1995, Dallas politics has occasionally degenerated into shouting matches laced with racial slurs, and the north sector of Dallas remains in a state of almost de facto segregation, with very few people of color. Meanwhile, in Fort Worth, the 1980s saw unrest and occasional violence as African American citizens of Como clashed with police.

Kirk was appointed the United States Trade Representative in 2009 by President Barak Obama. It had been speculated for a while that he would be given the office of Secretary of Commerce.

Those interested in the history of race relations in DFW should seek out *White Metropolis: Race, Ethnicity and Religion in Dallas, 1841-2001*, written by Michael Phillips and the hard-to-find *The Accommodation* by revered Dallas journalist Jim Schutze.

RELIGION

North Texas is often called the buckle of the Bible Belt, but the preponderance of religion is more noticeable in rural areas than the urban centers of Dallas and Fort Worth. For what it's worth, there's an apocryphal tale that goes around claiming that Dallas has the most number of churches per capita and also the most number of strip clubs.

Visitors may notice more churches in these parts, with the primary religion being

DFW DENIZENS OF NOTE

We all know the Dallas-Fort Worth area has boasted its fair share of famous and infamous citizens of whom the area is quite proud. But here are a few that maybe even North Texans didn't know they could claim as their own:

- Dallasite **Jerry Haynes** hosted the popular *Mr. Peppermint* television show.

- His son, **Gibby Haynes,** is the lead singer of the psycho-punk band The Butthole Surfers.

- Although he is a Yankees fan, the singer **Meat Loaf** was born and raised in Dallas.

- Rapper **Vanilla Ice,** of "Ice, Ice, Baby" fame, grew up on the mean streets of Carrollton, a suburb of Dallas.

- Actor **Larry Hagman** may have been a star of the TV show *Dallas,* but he was born in Fort Worth.

- Two infamous assassins, **Lee Harvey Oswald** and **Mark David Chapman** (who shot and killed John Lennon), are from Fort Worth.

Protestant Christianity, Catholicism, and Judaism. Many of North Texas' most prominent universities—Southern Methodist, Texas Christian University, and Dallas Baptist University—are religiously affiliated.

Many members of the gay and lesbian community worship at the Cathedral of Hope, one of the earliest congregations in the country to cater to the LGBT community. With over 4,000 members, the church is located in the Oak Lawn "gayborhood."

Dallas also has large Muslim and Buddhist communities.

THE ARTS

Although Dallas is much larger in both population and reputation, Fort Worth actually stands as one of the most significant cities in the country when it comes to the visual arts and outshines its neighbor the east (much to the delight of Fort Worthers and to the chagrin of Dallasites).

As home to the Kimbell Art Museum, Amon Carter Museum of American Art, and the Modern Art Museum of Fort Worth, Fort Worth is known worldwide as one of the best visual arts towns in the world. It doesn't hurt that each of these museums stands on its own as a highly respected architectural work. They form the core around which the city's Cultural District is based, and visitors are well advised to devote at least a day, but preferably more, to exploring the area, not just for the visual arts, but also for the number of other types of museums there, such as the National Cowgirl Hall of Fame, the Science and History Museum, and many others.

If Fort Worth's cultural scene stands as an understated institution, Dallas' foray into the upper echelons of the arts has proven brassy and aggressive, with generally good results. The most notable example of this is the Dallas Arts District, a wide swath of impressive buildings that holds down a chunk of real estate on the western side of downtown. The district spans 68 acres and 19 blocks and is home to the city's largest venues, including the Morton H. Meyerson Symphony Center (designed by I.M. Pei), the stunning Winspear Opera House, and the Nasher Sculpture Center (designed by Renzo Piano).

ESSENTIALS

Getting There and Around

BY AIR

As the name implies, Dallas-Fort Worth International Airport, one of the biggest airports in the world, is the main air hub for both towns. DFW Airport is pretty much equidistant between the two towns. Put shortly, this is a major airport, the third busiest in the world, with almost every major carrier in service.

The airport is colossal: If you've never been there, give yourself plenty of time to do what you need to do. There are five terminals, and while the walk from parking to terminal is minimal by design, getting from gate to gate, much less terminal to terminal, can be a trek. Most of the terminals are designed in semicircles, and there are no shortcuts in between, so walking from end to end is particularly time-consuming. The Skyline people mover, fortunately, links the terminals efficiently.

Public transportation options to and from the airport are few. The Trinity Railway Express train that runs between Dallas and Fort Worth provides service to and from both towns, but not late or on Sunday or holidays. Keep in mind that if you use the TRE, you will have to take the free shuttle bus from the TRE airport station into your terminal, and this can take awhile, so, again, it's best to give yourself extra time. You might also consider one of the

© DALLAS CVB

many private shuttle companies that provide door-to-door service.

Dallas's Love Field is the second major airport in the area. Much smaller than DFW and servicing mainly Southwest Airlines' regional flights, the airport is easily navigable and quite convenient to many parts of central Dallas. There is no public transportation in and out of the airport.

BY TRAIN

Amtrak's *Heartland Flyer* and *Texas Eagle* lines service both Dallas and Fort Worth. Dallas's Amtrak station is downtown's Union Station (the main station for DART and the TRE as well), at 400 S. Houston St. The Fort Worth station is at 1001 Jones St., downtown Fort Worth.

BY CAR

Dallas and Fort Worth share I-35 (north-south) and I-30 (east-west), which run perpendicular to each other. It can get a bit confusing: I-35 splits north of the Metroplex, in Denton, into East and West I-35. East I-35 goes through Dallas, West I-35 through Fort Worth, until the two rejoin south of town in Hillsboro, Texas. I-30, which runs up through the Midwest to Minnesota, connects Dallas and Fort Worth (the area of I-30 between the two towns is called the Tom Landry Highway). I-45 doesn't run through Fort Worth, but connects Dallas and Houston.

Dallas is surrounded by Loop 12, parts of which are also called Northwest Highway. I-20 skirts to the south of each town, looping around Fort Worth in a segment called Loop 820. North Dallas is looped by I-635, which

ends at Highway 121. All of these highways are key access points into and out of the Metroplex.

BY BUS

Dallas and Fort Worth both are serviced by the Greyhound bus system. Dallas's station is downtown (205 S. Lamar St., within walking distance of the public transportation/Amtrak hub Union Station). Fort Worth's station is at 1001 Jones St., downtown.

PUBLIC TRANSPORTATION

Though the light-rail continues to expand and things continue to improve, don't expect much when it comes to public transportation. One of the few helpful modes of transport is the Trinity Railway Express that takes commuters between Dallas and Fort Worth, following more or less the route of I-20. The trains are clean and quick, with free wireless Internet and room for bikes. Despite several mid-city stops, the train ride only takes an hour, about the same it would take to drive. The end of the line in both towns, unfortunately, is downtown, although the Dallas Union Station terminal connects you with the Dallas Area Rapid Transit light-rail and the final Fort Worth stop lands you at a city bus terminus.

Speaking of that light-rail: The Dallas version, known as DART (Dallas Area Rapid Transit), doesn't cover the most expansive area in the world, but many new lines are scheduled. In the meantime, the light-rail stops, both on the north-south line and the east-west line, are few and far between, meant more for commuters than as a means to transport riders a few blocks one way or the other in the central part of the city.

Conduct and Customs

ALCOHOL

DFW likes to drink, to be sure, but of course the same liquor laws apply to the area as to the rest of the United States. Bars must stop serving alcohol at 2 A.M., and most close at the same time, though some of the more refined establishments close earlier—call ahead and find out if you're not sure. A few dance clubs will stop serving booze at that time and stay open and play music until 4 A.M. for those still wanting to boogie.

While Dallas and Fort Worth are in counties that allow the sale of booze, some of the surrounding counties still are technically "dry," which means alcohol purchases are restricted. This means you can't buy beer, wine, or alcohol within county lines unless you're at a restaurant or "club" (a bar, usually), where you have to buy a membership. Buying a membership entails filling out a card with your name and address and paying a minimal fee, though most places simply waive the fee or pay it for you. It's less of a hassle than it sounds. Otherwise, if you need a six-pack of Lone Star or a bottle of whiskey, you have to cross the county line to find a liquor store, and there are often several just across the line.

SMOKING

Smoking isn't as frowned upon in DFW as in some other parts of the country, but both Dallas and Fort Worth—and many suburbs and mid-cities—have laws banning smoking in restaurants, clubs, bars, and pretty much every public establishment. Many places have patios or close-by outdoor areas where smoking is allowed.

MANNERS

Texans are a strange mix of friendly and reserved. Strangers and service people will readily call you "hon" or some other term of endearment, but this is not the kind of culture where, say, sharing a table at a café with a stranger is common. Communal tables at restaurants, for instance, often remain empty, even if the place is packed.

Tips for Travelers

BUSINESS TRAVELERS

Business travelers make up a large amount of the folks who visit the DFW area. Trade shows, meetings, and conventions are running pretty much every month of the year. For that reason, hotels are often booked well in advance, and when large conventions (such as the Mary Kay convention, held every summer) are in town, it can be difficult to find accommodations, especially downtown. The city is currently planning a new convention center and giant hotel to go along with it, which will help ease the congestion, but even then, make sure you get reservations as early as possible—especially if you want the best available rates. The good news is, most hotels cater to business travelers, so on-site business centers with fax machines, computers, and Internet access are common, and desk clerks and concierges are more familiar than usual with information about local outposts for FedEx Office and other common companies used by businesspeople.

INTERNATIONAL TRAVELERS

Backpackers and those on a budget should know beforehand that there is a definite dearth of hostels and cheap lodgings in the Metroplex. Word of mouth and Craigslist are perhaps the best way to locate a place to lay your head.

If that's not a concern, DFW is definitely a friendly place for international visitors, but perhaps not the most sophisticated in terms of other languages. Spanish is by far the most common second language spoken here (it's a pretty common first language as well), and the Latino population has filled the area with lots of culture that will feel like home to many Spanish-speaking visitors. In addition, Dallas is home to the consulates of Peru and Mexico, as well as Thailand and Canada. Currency exchange is available at Dallas-Fort Worth International Airport and at many places in the area—try the **American Express Center** (8317 Preston Center Plaza, 214/363-0214) or one of the many **Travelex Currency Services** (www.travelex.com). Fort Worth and the two cities' greater areas have sparser coverage, so if that's where you're headed, best to exchange money at the airport.

CRIME IN DFW

An honest assessment of Dallas-Fort Worth's crime situation suggests a little extra caution is advisable. Dallas, especially, has a crime problem. While violent crimes such as rape and assault are more common here than elsewhere, you're more likely to suffer a property crime. Take special care to remove any valuables from your car and lock it, even if you are only going to leave it for a few minutes.

WOMEN TRAVELING ALONE

While it's always advisable for a woman traveling by herself to keep an eye out for potentially dangerous situations, Dallas requires a little extra precaution. Dallas's rape statistics are higher than the national average, and it's not advisable to walk around most neighborhoods alone at night. While your chances of getting into a scrape are still low, it's best to stay on the safe side. Also, women who visit nightspots alone might find themselves consistently hit on, depending on the bar or club. Fort Worth is a little better, but rape averages here also exceed national rates. Erring on the side of caution is always recommended, especially in the area around the Stockyards.

SENIOR TRAVELERS

Day or night, the heat of North Texas summers (and even the months surrounding them) can be brutal, even dangerous—especially for seniors. If you are a senior visiting the area between May and September, make sure your accommodations have adequate air-conditioning and check that any tours or activities you undertake involve plenty of shade.

DART offers senior discounts, but the catch is it requires a DART photo ID, which of course is not very expedient for travelers. If you have a Medicare card, it is also good for a discount.

TRAVELERS WITH DISABILITIES

Most of the DFW area is relatively easy to navigate for those dealing with a special challenge. However, some of the older parts of both towns can be difficult. The crowds combined with the old wooden sidewalks in Fort Worth's Stockyards may present some difficulties, and similarly some of the sidewalk infrastructure is either narrow or crumbling (especially in Deep Ellum). You'll be hard-pressed in either town to find a hotel that is not ADA-compliant.

All DART buses and light-rail trains are required to comply with ADA standards, which they do. DART also offers a discount to non-paratransit riders with disabilities, and free fare for paratransit riders, but unfortunately, both require a DART reduced fare photo identification card—not very convenient for visitors. However, Medicare card holders also receive a discount, sans DART ID.

All wheelchairs must be secured on buses, as per ADA standards, and each DART bus has two securement locations. Service animals are allowed on all DART transportation.

TRAVELING WITH CHILDREN

With so many suburbs and families, you'll find the Metroplex beyond kid-friendly, and just about every attraction is kid-appropriate. Even usual adult fare like art museums and historical sites make children's outreach a priority (the Modern Art Museum in Fort Worth especially). Similarly, the sports teams here, both major- and minor-league, incorporate a number of family deals into their promotions (the all-you-can-eat seats and family pack seats at the Texas Rangers Ballpark in Arlington prove especially good deals). Still, the sprawl of the area can take its toll on the little ones— it's advisable to account for travel time and legwork when you make your plans.

GAY AND LESBIAN TRAVELERS

Despite its rep as a stronghold of conservative values, Dallas-Fort Worth actually is a pretty comfortable place for GLBT travelers. Fort Worth has no designated "gayborhood" and few gay bars, but its culture, climate, and charm have attracted many gay and lesbian couples. The scene here is quieter, more family-oriented, and more woven into the fabric of the city. While Fort Worth may be a touch more conservative than Dallas, the town's pioneer roots promote a sort of "live and let live" mentality.

Dallas GLBT scene is more rowdy and visible. For decades, the scene here revolved around a row of bars, shops, and coffeehouses at the crossroads of Cedar Springs and Oak Lawn Avenues, known as "the strip" or "the gayborhood." Many GLBT-oriented businesses still stand there and are going strong, and the strip is still considered the epicenter of queer life in

Dallas. This is where most folks head on out for happy hours, weekend revelry, the Pride parade (held in September here), and the (in)famous Halloween parade. For years, this also was the neighborhood with the highest concentration of GLBT home owners and renters.

However, as in many cities, the need for a physical community has waned, as GLBT Dallasites have landed in increasing numbers in every neighborhood. Bishop Arts, Uptown, and downtown are all popular destinations, for instance. Dallas has long been a destination for queer travelers, especially men, and the expansion of this already very visible community has only increased its cachet.

While all of North Texas continues to trend Democrat and more liberal, it is by no means a hotbed for the type of activism and radical (some would say) politics that abound in other places like San Francisco, Portland, New York, and Austin, so travelers who identify more on that side of things might be disappointed, although to be sure, the local community is friendly and welcoming.

It's also worth noting that you might find some of the smaller towns and rural areas surrounding DFW less welcoming toward queer travelers. In all honesty, a same-sex couple holding hands might get a stare or perhaps a muttered comment directed their way, though such behavior is the exception, not the rule.

Communications and Media

PHONES AND AREA CODES

Denizens of central Dallas use the city's original area code, 214. Farther north it switches to 972, and other areas have switched to 469, though with the common use of cell phones, the geographical designations mean less and less. Fort Worth's original area code is 817, but the city has been forced to adopt a second area code, 682.

INTERNET SERVICES

DFW and its environs, like any metropolitan locale, present multiple choices when it comes to Internet service providers. Neither city leads the pack when it comes to providing free public wireless access, though it's useful to know that all highway rest areas in Texas do. If you have a laptop, the Dallas Public Library also has free wireless connections that don't ask for a password, though use of the library's communal computers requires a library card. Fort Worth public libraries also provide computers with Internet access as well as wireless, but both require a library card.

MAIL SERVICES

There are around 40 USPS offices in Dallas, including a downtown office near City Hall. Most are open 8 or 8:30 A.M.–5 P.M. on weekdays, but the DFW turnpike location has extended hours, even on weekends. Fort Worth's downtown location is a gorgeous, imposing historic building on E. Lancaster Avenue. There are about 25 offices in the city.

NEWSPAPERS AND PERIODICALS

Dallas is a huge media market—the fifth largest in the country, to be exact. Surprisingly, the city is only served by one daily newspaper, the *Dallas Morning News,* owned by the A. H. Belo Corporation. A. H. Belo also owns the local Spanish-language daily, *Al Día.* The *Dallas Morning News* was once considered a top paper in the country, winning several Pulitzers, though the last one it received for reporting came in 1994 (the two most recent, in 2004 and 2006, were for photography). Though the entertainment section can be hit-or-miss, the sports section provides excellent coverage of the local professional, semipro, and even high school teams, as well as national sports news.

The alternative *Dallas Observer* weekly has been an institution since its inception, though it, like many weeklies across the country, has been brought into the fold of the Village Voice/ New Times Media chain. Though many locals revel in criticizing the *Observer,* especially now that a large corporation owns it, it's still the go-to for cheeky sports, entertainment, and political news; provides a lefty counterpunch to the *Morning News* conservative bent (rare is the liberal who skips the *Observer*'s Jim Schutze's feisty, smart city politics column);

and is still very much a player in local media. Former *Observer* editor Laura Miller, for instance, served as Dallas's mayor between 2002 and 2007.

The weekly *Dallas Voice* is Dallas's only GLBT paper, and it's a good one. The paper covers politics, culture, entertainment, and other issues with a queer slant, and it's been known to scoop both the *Morning News* and the *Observer,* despite fewer resources.

D Magazine's able writers deftly combine service-y type coverage with excellent investigative and culture pieces, all of which cover the city.

The weekday circulation of Fort Worth's only daily, the *Fort Worth Star Telegram,* tops 200,000. Founded by local legend Amon G. Carter and now owned by McClatchy, the "Startlegram," as some call it, caters mainly to the western half of the Metroplex, including Fort Worth, Arlington, and even a bit of western Grand Prairie. The paper, like most nowadays, continues to endure financial struggles and recently announced it would be sharing some aspects of sports coverage with the *Dallas Morning News.* The *Star Telegram* now takes the Texas Rangers coverage responsibilities, while the *DMN* keeps an eye on the Dallas Mavericks and Dallas Stars. Both papers cover the Dallas Cowboys individually.

RADIO AND TELEVISION

Two airwave media companies stand out in Dallas: The Belo Corporation is a spinoff of the A. H. Belo Corporation and owns the local ABC affiliate WFAA and the Texas-wide cable news channel TXCN and manages a local independently owned station, KFWD. The second is Univision Radio, a Spanish-language radio company—the eighth largest radio company in the country and the largest in the state—owned by the Univision television corporation. Though the Univision mother ship is in Los Angeles, the Univision Radio Company is headquartered in Dallas.

Most television and radio stations provide service for both Dallas and Fort Worth. The major television affiliates for DFW are WFAA KDFW (FOX), KXAS (NBC), KTVT (CBS), KERA (PBS), KUVN (UNI).

Shared stations include:

- KEOM 88.5 FM and KVRK 98.7 FM— oldies
- KZPS 92.5 FM Lone Star 92.5— classic rock
- KDBN 93.3 FM i93—Top 40
- KFWR 95.9 FM The Ranch—authentic country, Texas country, alt-country
- KSCS 96.3 FM—country
- KEGL 97.1 FM The Eagle—rock, Top 40
- KBFB 97.9 FM The Beat—hip-hop
- KLUV 98.7 FM K-Luv—oldies
- KPLX 99.5FM The Wolf—country
- KJKK 100.3 Jack FM—rock, classic rock, Top 40
- KWRD 100.7 FM The Word— Christian talk radio
- WRR 101.1 NOW FM—classical
- KDGE 102.1 The Edge—alternative rock
- KDMX 102.9 FM Mix 102.9—Top 40
- KESN 103.3 FM ESPN radio—sports talk

- KVIL 103.7 FM Lite FM—adult contemporary
- KRNB 105.7 FM—contemporary R&B
- KHKS 106.1 FM Kiss FM—Top 40
- CASA 106.7 FM La Casa—Latin pop
- KOAI 107.5 FM MEGA—Latin pop
- KESS 107.8 FM—Latin
- KMKI 620 AM Radio Disney—children's radio
- WBAP 820 AM Newstalk 820—news/ talk radio
- KRLD 1080 AM—news
- KFXR 1190 AM Fox Sports Radio—sports

Notable stations include:

- KNTU 88.1 FM—The University of North Texas's station delivers top-notch jazz.
- KNON 89.3 FM—Known as "the voice of the people," KNON is supported by listeners and sponsorships from small local business. The eclectic blend of talk and music programming is very popular.
- KERA 90.1—The local National Public Radio affiliate features a mix of local shows and favorites like *All Things Considered* and *This American Life.*
- KTCK 1310 AM The Ticket—This irreverent local sports talk radio station is full of personality.

RESOURCES

Suggested Reading

TEXAS

Friedman, Kinky. *Kinky Friedman's Guide to Texas Etiquette.* Cliff Street Books, 2001. Written by the man whose Texas gubernatorial campaign slogan was "Why Not?," this guide will tell you everything you need to know about Texans and their ways. Friedman's famous for his mystery novels, humorous essays, and randy songs (his band is known as Kinky Friedman and the Texas Jewboys), and his unique humor runs throughout chapters like "Prisoner of War Camps in Texas," "Texas is the Only State," and "Big Hair For Jesus."

Selcer, Richard. *Legendary Watering Holes: The Saloons that Made Texas Famous.* Texas A&M Press 2004. Richard Selcer's final chapter in this book covers the legendary Fort Worth drinking spot, the White Elephant, which is still open today in the Stockyards. The excellent chapter doesn't just touch upon the lore and legends surrounding the saloon; it also provides a colorful and fascinating context, up to and including the history of the name "White Elephant," and the social and racial implications of Fort Worth's drinking culture back in the town's early days. A fascinating read.

DALLAS AND FORT WORTH

Hill, Patricia Everidge. *Dallas: The Making of a Modern City.* University of Texas Press, 1996. Even though its title suggests yet another dry recounting that could have been written by the chamber of commerce, Everidge Hill's book is actually a fascinating alternative history of Dallas. Rejecting the common notion that Dallas has always been about commerce, Hill's well-researched thesis is that much of the city's history rests on more communal, progressive, and sometimes even radical grounds.

Roark, Carol. *Fort Worth: Then & Now.* TCU Press, 2001 (contemporary photographs by Rodger Mallison) and *Fort Worth's Legendary Landmarks.* TCU Press, 1995 (photographs by Byrd Williams). Both of these books benefit from the extraordinary knowledge and resources of local expert Carol Roark, who provides succinct and educational context for all the photos. *Then & Now* is especially edifying, as photographer Roger Mallison reproduces the angles, vantage points, and perspectives of preexisting old photographs of Fort Worth as best as possible, allowing the reader to study the details of their juxtaposition. *Fort Worth's Legendary Landmarks* is more text-heavy.

Internet Resources

Al Dia
www.aldiatx.com
The web version of *Al Dia,* DFW's main Spanish language newspaper, features the latest local news (along with national), as well as lots of sports stories—especially on Los Vaqueros de Dallas.

Art&Seek
www.artandseek.net
The local PBS affiliate's arts blog stays on top of all sorts of arts and culture events, from underground art to huge opera extravaganzas.

Dallas Food
www.dallasfood.org
Less a Twitter-paced news blog and more a thoughtful look at dining, Dallas Food tends to follow along themes (a series of entries on Jefferson Avenue taquerias and tortas spots being a particularly good one). The blog also features close-up, large photos of meals, so you can see what looks delectable to you.

Dallas Morning News
www.dallasnews.com
Several of the stories on the *Dallas Morning New*'s site are behind a paywall, but the free sections of the blog will provide visitors with plenty of local news, sports, and entertainment info. The GuideLive section is notably useful, especially the food section, which contains top 20 lists for tons of different types of cuisine, price ranges, and locales, along with detailed reviews. The site also runs several blogs covering everything from sports to shopping (check the latter often for updated info on sales and specials).

Dallas Observer
www.dallasobserver.com
The site for Dallas's weekly alternative newspaper is much improved and now offers a great resource for the latest entertainment news and listings, along with music, food, and news blogs.

Dallas Voice
www.dallasvoice.com
The Dallas Voice is Dallas's only GLBT newspaper, and the website provides plenty of updated info on local queer goings-on. Check the Instant Tea blog for the absolute latest.

D Magazine
www.dmagazine.com
Dallas's glossy mag lists toward the upscale/high society side of things, although some of the younger members of the staff still have a finger on Big D's more fast-paced pulse. D's website offers Best of Dallas lists out the yingyang. There are the usual helpful ones, such as Best Margaritas, Best Tacos, etc., but also the unexpected, such as Best Dentist and Best Contractor.

Downtown Fort Worth, Inc.
www.dfwi.org
Easy to use and well organized, the Downtown Fort Worth, Inc. website contains basic info about living, working, and playing downtown. The handy lists of hotels, restaurants, entertainment options, and other services include phone numbers, street addresses, web addresses, and other vitals.

Find Your Way in Fort Worth
www.fortworthparking.com
Parking is much less of a hassle in Cowtown than it is in other places, mainly because the city provides a passel of free parking in popular areas like downtown and the Stockyards. This site provides interactive maps and directions that are easy to use and indispensably helpful.

FW Weekly
www.fwweekly.com
The web version of Fort Worth's alternative

paper provides listings and weekly picks with info on Cowtown arts and culture. If you're looking for a good band or the best place to find drink specials, the site is a good place to start.

FortWorthStockyards.org
www.fortworthstockyards.org
This site is a perfect resource for all things Stockyards.

Pegasus News
www.pegasusnews.com
One of the most comprehensive and easiest to use blogs ever, Pegasus News is an excellent way to get to know Dallas. The site utilizes its own staff to generate original local news, culture, and sports reports as well as compiling reports from other local sites and posting user-generated content. The result: hyper-local, hyper-accurate info about just about everything in the Metroplex. Dallas newbies will especially benefit from the search mechanisms that allow users to pinpoint food, events, music, entertainment, and attractions according to location and genre. The entertainment listings might just be the most comprehensive and an absolutely vital tool for anyone in DFW, whether as a visitor or a local.

Visit Dallas
www.visitdallas.com
While it's a touch on the bland chamber of commerce-y side (you won't find tips about the latest underground dance club here), this site is super-helpful when it comes to providing tourist information about sites, hotels, neighborhoods, sports, recreation, and just about everything else. There's not much in the way of calendars or picks, but the general information is more than enough to get travelers—be they individuals or families—plenty of background and information.

West & Clear
http://westandclear.com
West and Clear is a discerning blog that covers everything Cowtown, from culture to politics. It's especially helpful for choosing arts and entertainment options.

Index

Restaurants Index

Nightlife Index

Shops Index

Hotels Index

www.moon.com

DESTINATIONS | ACTIVITIES | BLOGS | MAPS | BOOKS

MOON.COM is ready to help plan your next trip! Filled with fresh trip ideas and strategies, author interviews, informative travel blogs, a detailed map library, and descriptions of all the Moon guidebooks, Moon.com is all you need to get out and explore the world—or even places in your own backyard. While at Moon.com, sign up for our monthly e-newsletter for updates on new releases, travel tips, and expert advice from our on-the-go Moon authors. As always, when you travel with Moon, expect an experience that is uncommon and truly unique.

KEEP UP WITH MOON ON FACEBOOK AND TWITTER
JOIN THE MOON PHOTO GROUP ON FLICKR

MAP SYMBOLS

══════ Expressway	**⟨**	Highlight	✕.	Airfield	⚓	Golf Course
───── Primary Road	○	City/Town	✕	Airport	**P**	Parking Area
·········· Secondary Road	◉	State Capital	▲	Mountain	▲	Archaeological Site
▫ ▫ ▫ ▫ Unpaved Road	⊛	National Capital	✛	Unique Natural Feature	⚲	Church
─ ─ ─ ─ Trail	★	Point of Interest			⬛	Gas Station
············ Ferry	●	Accommodation	⌇	Waterfall	⬭	Glacier
▰▬▰▬ Railroad	▼	Restaurant/Bar	▲	Park	▨	Mangrove
═══ Pedestrian Walkway	■	Other Location	⬛	Trailhead	▨	Reef
⟐⟐⟐⟐ Stairs	Λ	Campground	⛷	Skiing Area	▱	Swamp

CONVERSION TABLES

°C = (°F - 32) / 1.8
°F = (°C x 1.8) + 32
1 inch = 2.54 centimeters (cm)
1 foot = 0.304 meters (m)
1 yard = 0.914 meters
1 mile = 1.6093 kilometers (km)
1 km = 0.6214 miles
1 fathom = 1.8288 m
1 chain = 20.1168 m
1 furlong = 201.168 m
1 acre = 0.4047 hectares
1 sq km = 100 hectares
1 sq mile = 2.59 square km
1 ounce = 28.35 grams
1 pound = 0.4536 kilograms
1 short ton = 0.90718 metric ton
1 short ton = 2,000 pounds
1 long ton = 1.016 metric tons
1 long ton = 2,240 pounds
1 metric ton = 1,000 kilograms
1 quart = 0.94635 liters
1 US gallon = 3.7854 liters
1 Imperial gallon = 4.5459 liters
1 nautical mile = 1.852 km

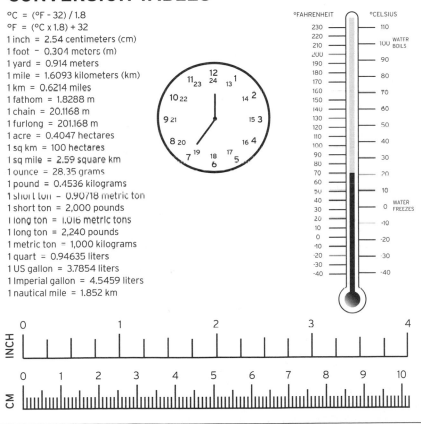

°FAHRENHEIT — °CELSIUS

°FAHRENHEIT	°CELSIUS	
230	110	
220		
210	100	WATER BOILS
200		
190	90	
180	80	
170		
160	70	
150		
140	60	
130	50	
120		
110	40	
100		
90	30	
80		
70	20	
60		
50	10	
40		
30	0	WATER FREEZES
20	-10	
10		
0	-20	
-10		
-20	-30	
-30		
-40	-40	

INCH   0 · · 1 · · 2 · · 3 · · 4

CM   0 1 2 3 4 5 6 7 8 9 10

MOON DALLAS & FORTH WORTH

Avalon Travel
a member of the Perseus Books Group
1700 Fourth Street
Berkeley, CA 94710, USA
www.moon.com

Editor and Series Manager: Erin Raber
Copy Editor: Ashley Benning
Graphics Coordinators: Kathryn Osgood, Elizabeth Jang
Production Coordinator: Elizabeth Jang
Cover Designer: Domini Dragoone
Map Editor: Albert Angulo
Cartographers: Heather Sparks, Kaitlin Jaffe,
   Andy Butkovic

ISBN-13: 978-1-61238-526-6
ISSN: 2150-8216

Printing History
1st Edition – 2009
2nd Edition – August 2013
5 4 3 2 1

Text © 2013 by Jonanna Widner.
Maps © 2013 by Avalon Travel.
All rights reserved.

Some photos and illustrations are used by permission and are the property of the original copyright owners.

Front cover photo: Dallas skyline from Reunion Tower © Jeremy Woodhouse/Getty Images

Title Page: Courtesy of Fort Worth CVB

Interior color photos: p. 2 Dallas skyline © gioadventures/istock.com; p. 24 (inset) Texas bluebonnets © Brandon Seidel/123rf.com, (bottom left) mj007/123rf.com; (bottom right) courtesy of Fort Worth CVB; p. 25 © Dallas CVB; p. 26 © Jonanna Widner; p. 27 © Kenny Braun/ Texas Tourism; p. 28 (top) Dallas CVB, (bottom) © Steve Zahn/123rf.com; p. 29 © Tim Hursley/ Nasher Sculpture Center; p. 30 © Galleria Dallas/ Dallas CVB; p. 31 © Kenny Braun/Texas Tourism; p. 32 courtesy of Dave Hensley

Printed in Canada by Friesens

Moon Handbooks and the Moon logo are the property of Avalon Travel. All other marks and logos depicted are the property of the original owners. All rights reserved. No part of this book may be translated or reproduced in any form, except brief extracts by a reviewer for the purpose of a review, without written permission of the copyright owner.

All recommendations, including those for sights, activities, hotels, restaurants, and shops, are based on each author's individual judgment. We do not accept payment for inclusion in our travel guides, and our authors don't accept free goods or services in exchange for positive coverage.

Although every effort was made to ensure that the information was correct at the time of going to press, the author and publisher do not assume and hereby disclaim any liability to any party for any loss or damage caused by errors, omissions, or any potential travel disruption due to labor or financial difficulty, whether such errors or omissions result from negligence, accident, or any other cause.

KEEPING CURRENT

If you have a favorite gem you'd like to see included in the next edition, or see anything that needs updating, clarification, or correction, please drop us a line. Send your comments via email to feedback@moon.com, or use the address above.